INTERROGATING THE ORACLE

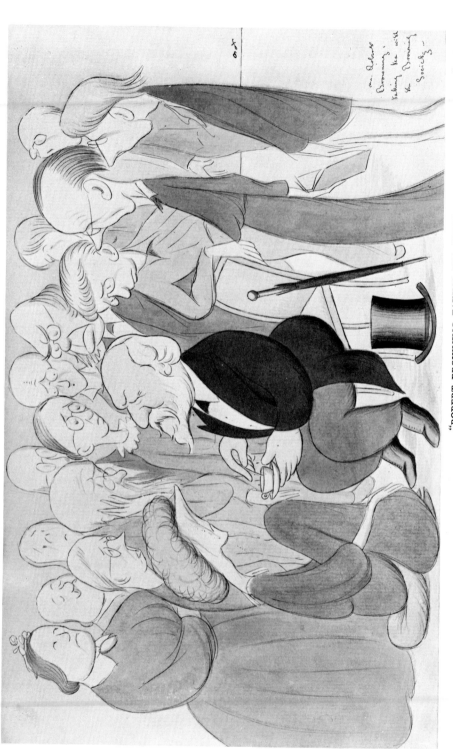

"ROBERT BROWNING TAKING TEA WITH THE BROWNING SOCIETY" Several leading figures of the Browning Society are recognizable in Max Beerbohm's famous cartoon: Emily Hickey (seated), F. J. Furnivall (with the beard), and Arthur Symons (far right).

INTERROGATING
THE ORACLE

A HISTORY OF THE LONDON BROWNING SOCIETY

BY

William S. Peterson

OHIO UNIVERSITY PRESS

ATHENS   OHIO

PREFACE

ONE OF THE CHIEF JOYS of completing a book is to be able to record one's indebtedness to so many individuals and institutions. My major expressions of gratitude must be reserved for Northwestern University, which has twice provided funds that allowed me to visit England during the spring of 1966 and the summer of 1967, and for Andrews University, which has paid my travelling expenses to several American libraries and granted a leave of absence from my teaching duties. Drafts of this book have been read and criticized, at various stages, by Professor F. E. Faverty (Northwestern University), Professor Lawrence G. Evans (Northwestern University), Professor Donald Torchiana (Northwestern University), Professor John O. Waller (Andrews University), and Professor Park Honan (Brown University); and I trust that I have profited from their advice, though of course they should not be held accountable for any errors in the book. Professor Faverty, I must add, has been of much assistance in other ways, and Professor Honan's enthusiastic encouragement has also been invaluable to me.

The bulk of my research was done at the Newberry Library in Chicago, the staff of which has been very helpful. The following libraries, all but two of which I have visited in person, have granted me permission to quote unpublished correspondence which they own: the Balliol College Library, Oxford University; the Armstrong Browning Library, Baylor University; the Bodleian Library, Oxford University; the Boston Public Library; the British Museum; the Cambridge University Library; the University of Chicago Library; the John M. Olin Research Library, Cornell University; the Harvard College Library; the Huntington Library, San Marino, California; the King's College (London) Library; the Rutgers University Library; and the Miriam Lutcher Stark Library, University of Texas (Austin). In addition, Sir Maurice

v

P. Pariser, a private collector whose interests center around T. J. Wise, has most graciously allowed me to use certain materials in his collection. Quotations from Browning's correspondence are made with the permission of Sir John Murray, K.C.V.O.

Portions of this book have already been published in the *Bulletin of the New York Public Library* and *Review of English Studies*. They are reprinted here, in slightly revised form, with the permission of these journals.

These individuals have rendered assistance in various ways: Professor Kingsbury Badger, Mr. John Carter, Miss Mabel Purefoy Fitz-Gerald, Mr. Kenneth Garside, Mr. C. Michael Hancher, Mrs. Aurelia B. Harlan, Mr. Jack Herring, Mr. Philip Kelley, Mr. Peter W. Kingsland, Professor William B. Todd, and Mr. Mark K. Whitlock. The final draft of the book was typed by Mrs. William Hessel.

To my wife, who sustained me through many difficulties, I cannot adequately express my debt, but she knows that without her encouragement I could not have written this book.

W.S.P.

Berrien Springs, Michigan

CONTENTS

ILLUSTRATIONS

ABBREVIATIONS

The following abbreviations, in addition to those listed in the *PMLA*
Annual Bibliography, are used in this book. A key to abbreviations of
manuscript locations is provided in my bibliography.

Acad.	*Academy.*
Alumni Cantabrigienses	Venn, John, and J. A. Venn, comp. *Alumni Cantabrigienses: A Biographical List of All Known Students, Graduates and Holders of Office at the University of Cambridge, from the Earliest Times to 1900.* 10 vols. Cambridge: Cambridge University Press, 1922–54.
Alumni Oxonienses	Foster, Joseph, ed. *Alumni Oxonienses: The Members of the University of London, 1715–1886.* 4 vols. London: J. Foster, 1888.
Broughton, *Bibliography*	Broughton, Leslie N., Clark S. Northup, and Robert Pearsall, comp. *Robert Browning: A Bibliography, 1830–1950.* Ithaca: Cornell University Press, 1953.
BSP	*The Browning Society's Papers.* 3 vols. London: Trübner, 1881–91.
DAB	*Dictionary of American Biography.*
DNB	*Dictionary of National Biography.*
Domett, *Diary*	Domett, Alfred. *The Diary of Alfred Domett, 1872–1885,* ed. E. A. Horsman. London: Oxford University Press, 1953.
FitzGerald	*Learned Lady: Letters from Robert Browning to Mrs. Thomas FitzGerald, 1876–1889,* ed. Edward C. McAleer. Cambridge: Harvard University Press, 1966.
FJF	Frederick J. Furnivall.

Intimate Glimpses	Armstrong, A. J., ed. *Intimate Glimpses from Browning's Letter File.* Baylor University's Browning Interests, 8th Ser. Waco: Baylor University Press, 1934.
LRB	*Letters of Robert Browning,* ed. Thurman L. Hood. New Haven: Yale University Press, 1933.
Munro, *Furnivall*	[Munro, John, ed.]. *Frederick James Furnivall: A Volume of Personal Record.* London: Frowde, 1911.
NL	*New Letters of Robert Browning,* ed. William C. DeVane and Kenneth L. Knickerbocker. New Haven: Yale University Press, 1950.
Partington, *Wise*	Partington, Wilfred. *Thomas J. Wise in the Original Cloth.* Rev. ed. London: Robert Hale, 1946.
PMG	*Pall Mall Gazette.*
RB	Robert Browning.
Times	London *Times.*
Who Was Who	*Who Was Who: A Companion to "Who's Who" Containing the Biographies of Those Who Died During the Period 1897–1916* [etc.]. London: A. & C. Black, 1919–.

INTERROGATING THE ORACLE

INTRODUCTION

Those who do not like to "crack the nuts" and "grind the kernels" of [Browning's *Jocoseria*] have Theocritus and Virgil, Ariosto and Spenser, to fall back upon. Those who enjoy this exercise are already forming themselves into societies in both hemispheres for a combined interrogation of the oracle.

—John Addington Symonds[1]

WHEN ALFRED DOMETT called upon his friend Robert Browning one March morning in 1873, the poet showed him a letter he had just received from a distinguished physician, who sought his help in curing a "lady patient" of a delusion—that Browning's voice was the voice of God. The lady, furthermore, desired an interview with Browning, whose advice, she was convinced, was "necessary to the future conduct of her life." Would he see her? Browning, though he thought the case "a great bore," felt he could hardly refuse such an urgent request: "of course he would advise her to follow strictly the injunctions of her physician when he had learnt them." [2]

This revealing little anecdote would have appealed to Lytton Strachey who, at the close of the first World War, set a new fashion by scrutinizing Victorian culture and religion with delicate, urbane mockery. What the physician failed to observe, Strachey might have added in his incomparably ironic manner, was that the deluded lady was not alone in suffering this affliction. Indeed, to an entire generation of our Victorian forebears, Browning spoke with the accent of divine authority. As the most striking manifestation of the "Browning craze" that swept England near the end of the nineteenth century, Strachey would doubtless have instanced the London Browning Society, founded in 1881 by Frederick J. Furnivall and Miss Emily Hickey.

And, to be sure, a writer of anti-Victorian bias would find it not at all difficult, in rowing over the "great ocean of material" which the Browning Society has left behind, to pull out of its depths in a little bucket "some characteristic specimen . . . to be examined with careful curiosity." (The metaphor is Strachey's.) There is ample evidence that many, if not most, members of the Browning Society thought of Browning not primarily as a poet but as a prophet, one who bore a message from heaven to an unbelieving and materialistic age. Paper after paper was read before the society on such topics as "The Religious Teaching of Browning" and "Browning as a Teacher of the Nineteenth Century." It is true that Furnivall once insisted that "the Browning Society is not made up of idolaters," [3] but the assertion is contradicted by the idolatrous expressions which his members habitually used. The Reverend Joshua Kirkman, in the first address to the Browning Society, explained that Browning was identical with religion itself.[4] Miss Catherine Whitehead observed that "Browning carried you through and over your worst crises. . . . Browning more than anyone else made life worth living." [5] Miss Dorothea Beale found Browning "ever cheerful and consoling, so that we turn to him in our trouble." [6] Perhaps the most immoderate praise of all was heaped upon Browning by Dr. Edward Berdoe, who described him as a "Buddha" rather than a "mere man." [7]

The examples might be multiplied. Yet a Stracheyan view of the Browning Society, delightful as it would surely be, must inevitably prove inadequate, because the heterogeneous membership of the society was not—as many have supposed—forever united in a hymn of praise. It would be closer to the truth to say that the Browning Society harbored all manner of dissenters, and that if today we hear most clearly the sweet harmonies of the loyal Browningites in the front row, we must not neglect the dissonant notes that came from the society's rear pews, where men like Bernard Shaw, Edward C. K. Gonner, and Augustine Birrell sat. The Browning Society was, in reality, a microcosm of the London literary world, in which every variety of attitude toward Browning's poetry was expressed; and we surely distort the facts if we ignore the complexity and diversity of the views held by Dr. Furnivall's Browningites.

Once we put aside the old stereotypes—which are epitomized in Max Beerbohm's amusing caricature of Browning taking tea with his admiring disciples from the society—it will become clear that the founding of the Browning Society was a significant event both in English literary history and in Browning's own career. Because it was the first society founded to study the works of a living poet,[8] the Browning Society was widely ridiculed and scorned during its eleven-year history (1881–92); but unquestionably it helped to establish Browning's reputation as a thinker and philosopher, and, according to Browning himself, it called widespread attention to his poetry at a time when his popularity was not otherwise great. The society, furthermore, had a hand in publishing nearly every book written about Browning in the nineteenth century. And from yet another point of view, the society's history represents an illuminating episode that tells us much about the curiously intimate relationship between the Victorian poet and his audience.

One possible way of regarding the Browning Society is to see it as the ultimate legacy of the Romantic poets, who had first exalted the spiritual authority of the poet and simultaneously created public curiosity about his private life. Throughout the nineteenth century, writers were treated as either divine oracles or celebrities—or perhaps as both at once. The cult of the literary personality soared to a grotesque climax during the middle and late Victorian era; it was an age when Carlyle numbered Shakespeare among his heroes who communed with the divine spirit of the universe, when hysterical women wept and fainted at Dickens' public readings, when Tennyson had to flush the curious tourists from the hedges at Farringford.

On the crudest level, then, the Browning Society can be viewed as a group of admirers who longed to see the Great Man and seek his advice on "the future conduct" of their lives. If one wished to press the analogy of the deluded "lady patient" a bit further, one might even regard Dr. Furnivall as the benevolent physician who tried in vain to cure his patients through interviews with Browning. Nearly every Sunday, we learn from contemporary records, he took some palpitating disciple to Browning's home, there to talk, for a few overwhelming moments, to the Master (Browningites always capitalized that word when referring to Browning) himself. Anne Thackeray, the novelist's daughter, has left an amusing record of a visit in 1887 to De Vere Gardens, where, as a family friend, she was invited inside immediately. "Come in," said Browning's sister Sarianna. "Not into the dining-room; there are some ladies waiting there; and there are some members of the Browning Society in the drawing-room. Robert is in the study, with some Americans who have come by appointment." [9]

The Browningites in the drawing room, however, were more than fluttery enthusiasts; for the most part, they were intelligent adults engaged in a serious search for spiritual authority. It is a commonplace of intellectual history that the nineteenth century witnessed the decline of old faiths and the rise of skepticism and secularism, yet we are in danger of ignoring the deep private anguish experienced by the men and women who were, like Matthew Arnold, caught between two worlds, one dead and the other powerless to be born. As dogmas crumbled, Victorians turned for spiritual solace to new sources of authority—to Carlylean heroes, to the doctrine of progress, to "culture" (in the Arnoldian sense), to de-mythologized religions, or, as in the case of the Browningites, to a great poet who seemed to straddle successfully the two worlds. It is significant that Browning's theological position was sufficiently broad—vague, if you please—so that his religious poetry could appeal to the entire spectrum of believers and unbelievers. Within the Browning Society, both the pious spinsters like Miss Whitehead and the militant agnostics like Furnivall could claim Browning as their own. In either case, he was seen as a teacher, a prophet, a seer, one who could remind men of spiritual realities in a world of doubt and anxiety.

It would be a mistake, however, to ascribe the formation of the Browning Society wholly to religious motives, for it also represented a conscious literary effort to redress the injustices done to Browning's poetry in the past. Unlike Tennyson, Browning was not able to live on the income from his verse, which had never been especially well received by either the critics or the reading public. Until the very end of his life, Browning's letters betray an impatience with the fickleness of popular judgment, or, as he phrased it himself in *The Ring and the Book*, with the "British Public, ye who like me not." To most Victorian readers, Browning's name suggested only the word "obscurity"; it called to mind *Sordello*, with the threadbare anecdote of Douglas Jerrold's fear that he had lost his mind when he could not understand the poem. Dr. Furnivall was not greatly exaggerating, therefore, when he wrote in the Browning Society's first prospectus that the charge of obscurity resulted largely from "want of faithful study." [10] He further observed at the first meeting that he had founded the Browning Society because "all my other Societies had been founded on behalf of poets not sufficiently studied, or who had not had their due meed of honour from their generation." [11] Clearly Browning was the one living English poet of stature whose reputation most needed the kind of rehabilitation in which Furnivall specialized.

Behind the founding of the Browning Society lay also the history of "all my other Societies" which Dr. Furnivall had established. Furnivall was a straightforward man who saw clearly while he was still young that English literary and linguistic scholars were handicapped by a lack of adequately edited texts and by the unavailability of much manuscript material. How could anyone study Chaucer with real seriousness, for example, unless he had before him all the variant texts of the *Canterbury Tales*? To a man of Furnivall's energetic temperament, to ask that question was to imply its answer: learned societies must be established to edit and publish materials, from manuscripts and rare editions, which would be of value to literary students. With astonishing rapidity, Furnivall founded a whole series of such societies, which, for all their shortcomings, put English literary scholarship on a new footing in the nineteenth century.

Needless to say, Furnivall had not invented the concept of the learned society, though he did create them prolifically. The earliest ancestor of all such groups was no doubt the Assembly of Antiquaries, established in 1572; but it was not until the nineteenth century, when antiquarian interests grew stronger and book-collecting became more widespread, that societies like the Roxburghe Club (1812), the Shakespeare Society (1840), and the Philological Society (1842) were able to flourish.[12] Furnivall's unique contribution, aside from his sheer industriousness, was his almost total emphasis on English literature, which prior to this century had not received the painstaking textual and critical study accorded the classics. Today English literature occupies a central position in the curriculum of schools in every English-speaking nation, but in Furnivall's time it was held in much lower esteem, and the very fact that we now recognize it to be one of the great literatures of the world can be attributed directly to the efforts of Furnivall and his contemporaries.

Furnivall's societies were not identical in structure and purpose. The Early English Text Society and the Ballad Society, for example, were solely publishing societies; the New Shakspere Society, on the other hand, also held monthly meetings at which papers were read and discussed. The Browning Society was patterned after the latter organization, even to the extent of publishing its transactions and having branch societies affiliated with the parent society. Nevertheless, the New Shakspere Society proved to be a specious model, for its elaborate trappings of scholarship were inappropriate to the study of a living poet. The Browningites had no manuscripts to edit, no historical problems that could be solved in the Public Records Office; so they turned instead to all that was really left for them to do—writing critical papers on Browning's poetry, most of them rather impressionistic and fuzzy. But the pretense of exact scholarship was kept up until the end in the society's published transactions, which included a Notes and Queries column, bibliographic "Scraps," and careful records of discussions.

These transactions, entitled *The Browning Society's Papers*, furnish us with a lively record of the delightful confusion which seemed always to prevail at the meetings of the society. The first half of each of the three volumes of the *Papers* is made up of the papers themselves, most of them formal, lengthy, and quite unreadable today. But the second half of each volume records the discussions at the meetings, and in these sections, it seems to me, we catch an intimate glimpse of the activities and prevailing attitudes of the late Victorian literary world—or at least of one large and important segment of it. The records of the meetings are replete with dramatic disagreements, humor (both intentional and otherwise), interplay of colorful personalities, and curious displays of ignorance and erudition. It is these transactions, so abundantly full of both literary and human interest, which form the basic source of this account of the London Browning Society's erratic history. I have of course supplemented the transactions with material from other published and unpublished sources (as my notes will indicate); but what I have tried to do above all is to discover the significance, motives, and consequences of the behavior of the men and women who crowd the pages of *The Browning Society's Papers*.

CHAPTER I

THE LEADERS

> Mr. Furnivall is a *Demiurge* who sits in the centre of his roll-
> ing worlds, and he says, "Let there be a Society,"—and there
> is a Society, and he beholds that it is all very good!
> —Edward Dowden[1]

"I OUGHT NOT to have so delayed an answer to your letter," Robert Browning wrote to Frederick J. Furnivall on June 7, 1881—"but in truth you ought to need no fresh assurance that I am always happy to see you whenever you incline to give me that pleasure,—and Miss Hickey will be welcomed as befits: I hope I value her sympathy as it deserves—it is not for me to find fault with its kind exaggeration." [2] The phrase "kind exaggeration" strikes a prophetic note in this letter, for when Furnivall and Miss Emily Hickey did at last call upon Browning a month later, the two had just decided to create an institution which was to epitomize for later generations the Victorian cult of poet-worship: the London Browning Society. As they walked across Regent's Park toward Warwick Crescent on Sunday morning, July 3, Furnivall said to her, "What do you think of a Browning Society? Would you help in one?" Miss Hickey, somewhat startled, confessed that she herself had made just such a proposal in a letter to Furnivall not yet posted. But, she continued, suppose Mr. Browning should disapprove of it? Then what would they do?

"Go on all the same and not mind him," replied her companion. "We want the society for ourselves, not only for him." Still, Miss Hickey hesitated. Was it really proper to form a Browning Society without Mr. Browning's approval? When they reached the poet's home, therefore, Furnivall bluntly asked Browning whether he had any objections. Browning, doubtless rather embarrassed, merely

9

changed the subject, a response which his visitors interpreted as consent.[3]

Although Furnivall did not organize the society overnight, as one account has it,[4] he did act swiftly. On July 9 the first public announcement of the Browning Society's formation appeared in the *Academy*, which was thereafter to serve as the chief outlet for news of the society's activities:

> It is proposed to start a Browning Society for the study and discussion of the works of the poet Browning, and the publication of essays on them, and extracts from works illustrating them. Students and admirers of Mr. Browning who are disposed to join such a society are asked to write to Mr. Furnivall, 3 St. George's Square, Primrose Hill, N.W., or to Miss Hickey, Clifton House, South End Green, Hampstead, N.W., Honorary Secretary. The opening meeting will probably be at the end of October.[5]

Shortly afterwards Furnivall spent an evening at the Inns of Court Hotel with Professor Hiram Corson of Cornell University, America's leading Browningite, who described his experiences in forming a small Browning Club at Cornell five years before; Corson also agreed to read a paper before Furnivall's society the following June.[6]

By the end of July, Furnivall had written the society's prospectus, organized a committee, persuaded three socially prominent figures to serve as vice-presidents, and told the Reverend Joshua Kirkman that he *must* deliver the inaugural address on October 28.[7] The prospectus, dated July 27, confessed that Browning's thought was frequently difficult to follow, but then were not even Aeschylus and Shakespeare sometimes obscure? "At any rate," wrote Furnivall, "the Browning student will seek the shortcoming in himself rather than in his master. He will wish, by conference with other students, by recourse to older scholars, to learn more of the meaning of the poet's utterances; and then, having gladly learnt, 'gladly wol he teche,' and bring others under the same influence that has benefited himself. To this end *The Browning Society* has been founded." [8] Furnivall, in other words, saw the society's chief function as the explication of Browning's poetry, especially the difficult passages. In a letter to the Boston *Literary World* the following March, he provided a fuller description of his aims:

> Our main reasons for starting the Society were, that the manliest, strongest, deepest, and thoughtfullest Poet of our time had had nothing like due study and honour given him; that he needed in-

terpreting and bringing home to folk, including ourselves; that this interpretation must be done during his life-time, or the key to it might be lost; and that we could not get together the workers we wanted, except by forming a "Browning Society." [9]

This was an eminently sensible view, eschewing the more obvious varieties of poet-worship, though it also displays a certain naïveté: it reminds one of the epigram quoted by Arthur Symons, in which the Browning Society members were compared to mice nibbling at the bonds of an imprisoned lion. "The epigram is scarcely as polite as might be wished," Symons remarked. "The notion that Browning himself is fettered or impeded by inability to turn his thoughts into form, by natural awkwardness, natural unmusicalness, or I know not what . . . is of course . . . ludicrous in the extreme." [10] Yet this was precisely Furnivall's view: he saw Browning as a poet possessing a great message yet so inarticulate that his ideas had to be interpreted to the world by the Browning Society.

The vice-presidents listed in the prospectus were chiefly ornaments, though they occasionally participated indirectly in the society's activities. Anna Swanwick (1813–99), for example, was a "cheerful elderly maiden lady," according to Alfred Domett,[11] whose chief literary effort had been a translation in 1873 of all of Aeschylus' plays and whose home was an important literary and artistic center: Browning himself was often a guest at her famous dinner parties, as were other Victorian notables like Tennyson, Gladstone, James Martineau, and Holman Hunt.[12] "She moved about among her guests with bright twinkling eyes," Domett wrote in his diary after attending one of the gatherings, "saying something agreeable to each—the twinkle looking a little as if forced, though always there; with a sort of consciousness in her expression, of her intellectuality." [13] (Another guest, displaying less hostility perhaps, spoke also of "her smiling wrinkles." [14]) As a vice-president of the Browning Society, Miss Swanwick arranged a series of Browning readings and discussions in her drawing room, but she declined to read any papers before the society.[15] Her "extreme liability to Bronchitis" made her reluctant to attend the evening meetings, she explained, and, furthermore, "Browning's poetry, under its various aspects, has already been so fully discussed, that I should feel at a loss to find anything new to bring before the Society." [16] Because she was neither attending the meetings nor reading the transactions, she wrote to the honorary secretary in June, 1888, asking that her membership be cancelled;[17] but her name continued to be listed among the officers through the society's last session.

The relationship of most of the other vice-presidents to the Browning Society was equally nominal. The Reverend Hugh R. Haweis (1838–1901), the energetic pastor of fashionable St. James, Marylebone—"little, limping, queer, genial, good," one of his contemporaries called him[18]—often preached on social and literary subjects and maintained a salon in Chelsea (the former tenant had been Dante Gabriel Rossetti) notable for its collections of "lions." [19] Haweis, like Miss Swanwick, had known Browning personally since 1866;[20] but, again, his duties in the society were extremely limited: his name appears in the transactions only as chairman of one meeting (May 26, 1882). Similarly, Alfred Domett (1811–87), one of Browning's oldest and closest friends, at first declined to serve as vice-president, but later agreed to do so on the condition that he never be asked to preside at a meeting.[21] And so it went with the other vice-presidents (not all of whom held office simultaneously): the Reverend John Llewelyn Davies, Henry Irving, Sir Frederic Leighton, the Viscountess Mount-Temple, J. Milsand, Walter Bache, and the Reverend Alfred Lyttelton.

The real executive power lay with the twenty-member committee, chaired by Dr. Furnivall, and the honorary secretaries, the first of whom was Miss Hickey. Before we turn, however, to the two cofounders, whose personalities so largely determined the Browning Society's course, it may be useful to sketch briefly the contributions of the three honorary secretaries who succeeded Miss Hickey. The honorary secretary was the chief officer of the society, primarily responsible for arranging papers at the meetings and handling other business; and in the choice of successively weaker secretaries, we may trace debilitating effects upon the Browning Society itself.

When Miss Hickey resigned the honorary secretaryship because of poor health in the spring of 1884, her immediate successor was James Dykes Campbell (1838–95), a tall, vigorous, likeable businessman who had retired in 1881 in order to devote his full time to literary matters.[22] Though he had worked for a pottery manufacturer as a young man and later became a partner in a Mauritius mercantile firm, Dykes Campbell had always been strongly attracted to literature and scholarship. In 1862 he privately printed some of Tennyson's early suppressed poems, and in 1864 he published three manuscripts of Addison's *Spectator* essays; it was during this decade also that he met Furnivall and volunteered to do work for the *Oxford English Dictionary*.

Campbell, as might be expected, became acquainted with Browning during the early eighties through an introduction by Furnivall. Having purchased a volume of Elizabeth Barrett Browning's verse,

Campbell wondered whether the small, neat handwriting in its margins could possibly be that of the authoress. Furnivall asked Browning, who requested to see the book, and thus began a friendship which lasted until Browning's death in 1889. Shortly after the Campbells moved into their flat in Albert Hall Mansions, Kensington Gore, Browning dropped in upon them quite unexpectedly one Sunday afternoon, and Mrs. Campbell, without any servants, was unable to serve even tea to the poet.[23] Despite this embarrassing beginning, Browning was a frequent visitor thereafter. Thomas J. Wise has left a vivid account of one of these occasions. After dinner, Wise and his host sat smoking in the bow window of his study, watching a band playing below, while Browning strolled about the room and looked at the two walls of books. "I see you have everything of mine, Campbell," Browning said at last. "No," he replied, "I still lack *Pauline*." "Oh, that gap can be filled," said Browning; "the other morning I happened upon two copies of it; one of them shall be sent to you tomorrow." [24] It was a considerable gift, as Wise jealously noted, for *Pauline* was even then one of the rarest of rare books. Campbell responded to this generosity by developing an intense affection for Browning. Following the poet's funeral in Westminster Abbey, which he had attended, he wrote to a friend:

> We miss him more and more as the weeks go on. He had such an abundance, such an overflowing of *life*, that if one were in the dumps at any time, one had only to go over and see him, and in ten minutes one had absorbed enough vitality to put one in spirits again. His vitality was simply tremendous, and so was his kindness and *bonhomie*. I think he was undoubtedly the most remarkable man of his century. His very last work before he left London was to write into my copy of his collected works all the corrections he wished made for the next edition—upwards of 250 in the first ten volumes. . . . I did not ask him to do this; he asked me to let him do it.[25]

By this time Campbell's interests were turning to the Romantic poets, especially Coleridge, of whom he completed an excellent biography in 1893.[26] His scholarly writings, in fact, illustrate the qualities that made him an admirable honorary secretary. Modest and unassuming, Campbell was nevertheless a meticulous scholar whose passion for exactness always astonished others. Moreover he was, as Bernard Shaw wrote many years later, "a very likeable gentleman. I must have had some correspondence with him," added Shaw, himself a member of the Browning Society; "for he complained that he could not decipher my handwriting without a magnifying glass, and was

surprised—when he did use one—to find that my letters were so perfectly formed that I must have a conscience. This was for him an
unexpected discovery." [27] After his retirement from the honorary secretaryship in 1886, Campbell remained a member of the committee
and occasionally attended the society's meetings; but the last years of
his life were spent chiefly in his study at St. Leonard's, where friends
found him always surrounded with heaps of letters, memoranda, papers, and books about Coleridge.[28]

If the Browning Society enjoyed distinguished leadership under
Dykes Campbell, the same cannot be said for his successor, Walter
Brindley Slater (1862?–1944), who was asked to fill the position only
after it had been declined by at least two other members.[29] Slater, a
manufacturing silversmith, had doubtless joined the society because
there he found others who shared his passion for book collecting.
With the help of his intimate friend, Thomas J. Wise, Slater was
building up an excellent private library that included rare books and
manuscripts by Browning, Dante Gabriel Rossetti, William Morris, Al-
gernon Swinburne, and particularly Walter Savage Landor.[30] In fact,
Slater was perhaps a much more enthusiastic bibliophile than he
should have been, for his firm (which he owned jointly with his
brother) was liquidated long before his death.[31] One detects something of his dissatisfaction with nonliterary concerns in an observation he made at the Browning Society meeting of March 26, 1888:
". . . A man's daily bread-earning work need not be his work at all,
properly speaking—merely a necessary means to enable him to do it,"
said Slater. "For himself, he fancied he could find his real work in life
only when he escaped from the work he had to do to earn money." [32]
Slater therefore sought the pleasures denied him by his occupation in
the secondhand bookshops and in literary societies like the Omar
Khayyám Club, the Whitefriars Club, the Society of Archivists and
Autograph Collectors, and the Browning Society.

Slater's first recorded appearance in the Browning Society was at
the annual business meeting of July 7, 1882, when he seconded a
motion by Wise;[33] after 1885 he attended the meetings quite regularly,
though his contributions to the discussion were invariably unimagina-
tive, naive, and indecisive. When two papers were read which sharply
disagreed with each other, Slater said that "he did not care to commit
himself to either side, but thought he could follow both, as both were
partly right." [34] He insisted that Browning's alleged obscurity could
actually be attributed to slow-witted readers, though he also confessed
that "whenever he could he avoided puzzling over difficult works." [35]
Browning, he said, "was entirely misunderstood as a poet, but it was

generally found that those who most disparaged his works were those who had never read them." [36] "As one of the orthodox school," he objected strenuously but not very intelligently to the agnostic viewpoint of Dr. Furnivall, William Revell, and above all Edward Gonner, whom he thought "sarcastic." [37] Slater was, in short, a fairly typical Browningite, which is another way of saying that he often possessed more zeal than knowledge.

Slater was far from successful as honorary secretary. "Your taking the Hon. Sec.ship of the Browning Soc. is a great relief & a real gain to us all," Furnivall wrote to him on May 3, 1886. "I told Browning of it yesterday." [38] But even the exuberant Dr. Furnivall must have been having second thoughts by the following autumn, when Slater was compelled to apologize for all the errors which were creeping into the *Papers*. "I hope you dont think I am an utter fool," Slater added plaintively.[39] It is not recorded what Furnivall thought, but we do know that shortly after Slater married in 1888, Furnivall wrote the following note to his bride: "I also hope that in your wifely duties you mean to include the Assistant Secretaryship of the Browning Soc., & get our two Parts of *Papers* of '86–7 & '87–8 out this month. If ever I want anything attended to, I shall send it to you & not to Slater." [40] This was probably a reference to Slater's increasingly frequent illnesses, since in February of 1890 Furnivall found it necessary to announce at a Browning Society meeting that Slater "was still very ill, and was not allowed by his doctor to transact any business." [41]

For the rest of the 1889–90 session, the society's affairs were handled by E. E. Davies, though Furnivall hoped to secure the services of E. H. Blakeney, leader of the Cambridge Browning Society.[42] However, Blakeney did not appear in London that summer, and so Davies was made the new (and last) honorary secretary. About Edward Ernest Underwood Davies (d. 1944) one can learn very little; doubtless his very obscurity is symptomatic of the fact that the Browning Society's leadership was no longer being drawn from the first rank. Davies, a clerk in the War Office and evidently a bachelor,[43] was neither a writer nor a scholar and in general seems to have been the least conspicuous of the society's secretaries. Whatever administrative abilities he may have possessed, Davies faced almost insurmountable problems: subscriptions had dropped so sharply by 1890 that the society was in the midst of a financial crisis, and, to make matters worse, Slater's hasty resignation had left the bookkeeping in a shambles. Writing in 1891 to encourage American members to pay their back subscriptions, Davies had to admit to Jenkin Lloyd Jones, leader of the Chicago Browning Society, that he had no financial records for the sessions prior to

1890–91, "as Mr. Slater, who was then Secretary, is still travelling abroad for the benefit of his health, & did not hand over his accounts to me before leaving England." [44]

Such was the muddled state of the society in its final years; probably there is some justice in William G. Kingsland's observation that the Browning Society would have ended on a stronger note had its original leaders stayed in office.[45] Certainly there is no denying that Miss Hickey (1845–1924), a woman of considerable business acumen, would have kept a tighter rein on the society's finances than did Slater and Davies. In the few scraps of her correspondence that have survived, Miss Hickey emerges as a patient, methodical worker, a perfect complement to the ebullient Furnivall. When Jenkin Lloyd Jones wrote her in July, 1883, that he wished to secure some of the society's publications for his Chicago Browningites, both Miss Hickey and Furnivall sent replies, and the contrast between their letters provides a striking revelation of their differing temperaments. "I'm very glad to see your letter to Miss Hickey," wrote Furnivall, "and am much obliged by your kind offer of help, which I gladly accept. I at once put you down as our Local Hon. Sec. for Chicago, and tell Miss H. to send you 5 or 7 copies of our books on sale, besides the three you will pay for." Furnivall then launched into a lengthy discussion of his favorite topic: the need for a Shilling Selection of Browning's poems. In contrast with this breezy, impulsive letter, Miss Hickey's is a study in restraint and precision: she merely enumerates each of the society's publications, providing in every instance the exact price for both members and nonmembers.[46] Even after her resignation from the secretaryship, she continued to fret over any sign of inefficiency. On December 13, 1888, she wrote to Slater:

> Will you think me very worrying if I ask you whether you cannot manage to arouse Messrs Clay & Taylor [the society's printers] to a sense of their iniquities? We have hitherto always had the tickets three or four weeks before the entertainment, I think. And it is almost a French compliment to send invitations with such a very short notice as we must now have.[47]

Miss Hickey's face presented "a calm exterior which might easily have been mistaken for coldness," according to her biographer,[48] but behind the air of efficiency was a strong sense of humor—an attribute not every Browningite possessed. Though Dr. Furnivall and the other leaders devoted at least part of each annual business meeting to a denunciation of the Browning Society's critics, especially the facetious ones, Miss Hickey stood up on one such occasion and observed, "If the proverb 'Laugh and grow fat' were true, the Society must rejoice in having contributed to the store of adipose tissue in England." [49] Years later she also recalled with obvious delight that two members of the Browning Society had once jokingly planned a book entitled *Browning Without Tears*. They even began, she added, "to render the story of *Iván Ivánovitch* in words of one and two syllables!" [50] Her appearance, too, was sometimes gay and mildly "aesthetic": a friend reported that one day in the eighties she "looked her poetry in a leaf-green Liberty silk and a wide velvet hat." But this same friend, describing the scene some years afterward, felt constrained to add, "She dresses more soberly now-a-days," [51] for shortly after the turn of the century Miss Hickey became an ardent convert to Catholicism and devoted the rest of her life to religious writing.

Though Emily Hickey was of Irish birth, her upbringing had been most emphatically Protestant. The daughter of a parson and ultimately—according to family tradition—a descendant of royalty, she was a bookish child who delighted in verse and as an adult could remember reading a novel at the age of ten while perched in a tree near the avenue gate. Later, at boarding school, a teacher introduced her to the traditional ballads, and a friend showed her Tennyson's *Maud*, which she copied verbatim "from the precious green-bound seven-shilling volume which he lent me." [52] Mrs. Browning's poetry also impressed her, though Browning himself she did not read until later. But Shakespeare was forbidden: "My father discouraged the reading of him, repelled as he was by his occasional Elizabethan coarseness." [53]

Her own first poem to appear in print, "Told in the Firelight," was published in *Cornhill Magazine* in 1866, and heartened by this small success, she sent the manuscript of a book-length collection of her verse to Alexander Macmillan. Though he declined to publish the volume, he did agree to use her poems occasionally in *Macmillan's Magazine* and encouraged her to complete a novel she had begun. But instead the indomitable Miss Hickey left her rural home in Ireland, came to see Macmillan himself, and decided to build a career as a poet in London. For many difficult years she supported herself by secretarial work, private teaching, governessing, and journalistic writing for the *Academy* and other periodicals. Eventually she became Lecturer on the English Language and Literature at the North London Collegiate School for Girls, a position she held for eighteen years, and became acquainted with Furnivall by reading a paper to his New Shakspere Society on *Measure for Measure*. Under his direction, she began to lecture on Shakespeare before other literary groups. Another important influence during the eighties was Roden Noel, a minor poet whose socialistic views lent a new note to her own poetry and encouraged her to begin volunteer work in the London slums.

In the meantime, Miss Hickey continued to write verse; during her lifetime she published more than a dozen volumes of poetry, as well as critical studies, translations, a novel, and numerous tracts for the Catholic Truth Society. The publication of her first book—*A Sculptor and Other Poems*—provided, in fact, the pretext that Furnivall needed to introduce her to Browning in 1881. Her verse, it must be said, is largely derivative—one hears in it strong echoes of Tennyson, Swinburne, and Shakespeare—and to modern readers would seem very dated. She did publish one book, however, that is still read with interest (though admittedly for its introduction by another writer), and this was also her sole contribution to Browning scholarship: a textbook edition of Browning's play *Strafford* (1884). During the Easter term of 1883 she taught the play at the Collegiate School for Girls and prepared a set of examination questions to accompany the text.[54] Having secured Browning's permission to reprint the play, she then wrote a brief preface, based chiefly on information supplied by the poet himself, and provided some elementary annotation, which Browning read and approved in proof.[55] Most of the questions at the end involved the inevitable comparisons with Shakespeare, as for example: "What makes the *tragedy* in 'Strafford'? Compare with what makes it in 'Macbeth' and 'King Lear.'" The chief merit of the book, from the viewpoint of literary scholars, is a learned introduction by Samuel R. Gardiner, Professor of History at King's College, London, in which he treats the discrepancies between the play and the career of the historical Strafford. Despite this accusation of factual error, Browning expressed his "complete satisfaction" with the book.[56]

Miss Hickey's contributions to the Browning Society's discussions seem to have been rare, though when she once read a paper for an absent speaker, as she would occasionally do, her fine reading voice was praised by the chairman, Hugh Haweis.[57] She also gave frequent Browning readings in London and elsewhere, always attempting at the same time to recruit new members for the society.[58] But in 1884 her health broke down, probably from the strain of living for so long on a meager income, and she resigned the honorary secretaryship in order to travel on the Continent. Soon after her return to England she became an Anglo-Catholic, and on July 22, 1901, she was received into the Catholic Church. Thereafter she dropped out of the literary circles in which she had once moved and devoted all her energies to Catholic Truth Society writings, for which she received the cross *pro ecclesia et pontifice* from Pope Pius X.[59] Browning was not forgotten in these years: she continued to write articles on "Glorious Robert Browning" [60] and his "Saul," in which, she said, the poet appeared "to lay his hand as it were, on the great verities of Christianity." [61] More than ever, she saw Browning as a religious poet whose ethical teachings were of supreme value. In 1921, only three years before her death, she was present for a July 4 celebration at the Browning Hall in London.[62] But, with her eyesight failing, she spent her last years mainly in seclusion. Miss Hickey was, in fact, a fitting symbol of the Victorian Browningites who lived beyond their time. Until the very end she seemed to move in the world she had known as a young woman; her final utterances on Browning suggest that she was totally unaware that the literary idol of London in the eighties had been toppled from his pedestal. In 1924 there were new poetic voices in the land, voices which would have sounded discordant to one accustomed to Tennyson and Browning, but Emily Hickey failed to hear them.

Yet if Miss Hickey's final years seem almost an anticlimax to the excitement of her earlier career, the same generalization would certainly not apply to the other founder of the Browning Society, Dr. Furnivall (1825–1910), whose entire life was characterized by vigor and movement. Even a few months before his death, Furnivall could be seen working at his desk in the British Museum Reading Room; on his eighty-fourth birthday he was still taking his usual fourteen-mile Sunday sculling trip on the Thames. People who met him during the final decades of his life remembered him as a merry old scholar with bright eyes and flaming red neckties who seemed always to be arguing energetically with younger men or bounding up the stairs of his favorite A.B.C. tea shop two steps at a time. Furnivall's vitality, in fact, tended to overshadow the less spectacular achievements of his cofounder, so that in 1889 Roden Noel found it necessary to remind the *Pall Mall Gazette* that Emily Hickey had also had a hand in establishing the Browning Society.[63]

Something of the man's energy can be seen in the blunt, sometimes rude language he habitually used. Furnivall's most striking trait was an instinctive honesty that compelled him to speak always with absolute frankness; it was a dangerous habit, and the wonder is that a person who spoke such unvarnished truths was tolerated in the Browning Society. Here, for example, is Furnivall's frontal attack upon the kind of rationalizing so often practiced by Browningites:

However popular it was among devotees to take a man's weak point—in Browning, want of music—and say, "Weak point! Nonsense! It's one of his strongest," yet Dr. Furnivall would not give in to this, but would protest that it was for other qualities than melody that Browning's poetry had a claim to greatness, and a right to ask that its readers should be content with strength, depth, thought, rather than any full allowance of music.[64]

After hearing a paper on "Childe Roland," Furnivall announced that "he must begin the discussion by applying a charge of dynamite to Mr. Kirkman's theory"; at another meeting, when several members insisted that Browning's verse was never obscure, Furnivall retorted that "he should like to cross-examine Miss Stoddart and Mr. Kingsland regarding certain passages, and he expected that he could speedily 'floor them.' " [65] Browning's poems he liked because they were full of "go" and "bounding life," though he did not admire all the personalities in them uniformly: Constance of "In a Balcony" he wanted "to shake well and smack." [66] The extravagant statements of Dr. Edward Berdoe, one of the most fanatical of Browning's disciples, often came under special attack from Furnivall's uncompromising sarcasm. Hearing Berdoe describe Browning's Andrea del Sarto as a repulsive weakling, Furnivall responded that "he hoped to be excused if he said it was the most truly Philistine view that was ever taken." [67] When, on another occasion, Berdoe said that Aprile in *Sordello* was representative of the Renaissance spirit, Furnivall exploded again: the analogy, he said, was "like taking a smart young man you meet in Hyde Park as a representative of the best sculler or the best football player in England." [68]

Furnivall became particularly annoyed at any praise of weakness or submissiveness. He was an agnostic, according to Shaw, because he "could not forgive Jesus for not putting up a fight in Gethsemane." [69] Arthur Symons had written in his *Introduction to the Study of Browning* (1886) that "Oedipus suffers . . . because he is wilful, and rushes upon his own fate" (p. 63), and Furnivall added in the margin of his own copy: "Rot!—is he not to be congratulated for defying fate instead of tamely submitting to it?" [70] Likewise, he vigorously rejected Joshua Kirkman's theory that the ultimate goal of Browning's Childe Roland was death, adding that he "decidedly preferred fighting to dying, in which he faild to see any use until all a man's work was done." [71] It is no surprise to learn that Furnivall's favorite Browning poem was "Prospice," in which the joys of being "ever a fighter" and a "strong man" are celebrated.[72] Indeed, at times he seemed ready to take on the entire human race at once: "There were a number of people yet in the world who were not lovers of Browning," Furnivall said in October, 1886, "and these the Society [has] got to tackle." [73]

Nor could Furnivall tolerate the notion that the nineteenth century was spiritually and intellectually crippled; it seemed to him to be rather a period of remarkable opportunities:

> . . . He was in no sympathy with that mere twaddle of feeble animals who were too shortsighted to see the glory and the power of this age. . . . Let a man set himself to any serious work, and he would soon find himself surrounded by a lot of splendid fellow-workers. In almost every part of real work we stood at a higher level, and did better things than had ever been done before.[74]

As an evaluation of the achievements of the Victorian era, this statement is vague and misleading, but as an autobiographical summary of his own life it is completely accurate. Furnivall's entire career had been devoted to the "real work" of literary and linguistic scholarship, for which he received no reward but his own pleasure in doing something worthwhile. He was indeed, as one acquaintance put it, "an agnostic who went about doing good." [75] Furnivall had long rejected the hope of a life after death; a man's business, he was fond of saying, was to do his "good stroke of work" while he lived, "never minding what came after." [76] Unlike Walter Slater (or most men, for that matter), he did not support himself with uncongenial labor in order to pursue his real interests in spare moments. Instead, he chose to remain poor and to devote all his time to work he loved. As a result, Furnivall appears to have been that rarest of all creatures—a completely happy man. The satisfactions that some men found in religion he found in unselfish, unpaid work. When one of his Browningites insisted that the loss of the Christian faith produced despair, Furnivall disagreed: "His experience was . . . that non-Christians were not so very sad. On the contrary many were decidedly chirpy." [77] Furnivall himself was among the chirpy ones.

He had at first seemed destined to an ordinary career as a solicitor, but his unconventional views, even while he was still a young man, changed all that.[78] Born in 1825 as the second of nine children to a physician in Egham, Surrey, he attended private schools at Englefield Green, Turnham Green, and Hanwell. After spending a year at London's University College, Furnivall matriculated in 1842 at Trinity Hall, Cambridge, where he displayed considerable intelligence but only moderate interest in his studies. He became absorbed in athletic activities, particularly boating, which was to be a passion for the rest of his life. (He was active in many rowing and sculling clubs, and in 1896 founded one of his own for the benefit of London shopgirls.) Though history and literature strongly attracted Furnivall, he seems to have preferred the informal aspects of his education, especially the conversations with friends on the river and with men like Daniel Macmillan, then the owner of a Cambridge bookshop. Whereas his tutors did nothing but give Furnivall "a little mathematical and classical cram," Macmillan taught him "to think, to read the books that made us think," and opened his "boating mind." "The impression he made on me was so strong that, when I took my degree in 1846, I wrote to my father, begging for a few thousand pounds to go into partnership with the Macmillans instead of to the Bar," he wrote later; "and grievously was I disappointed when the money was refused, and I was sent up to London to grind at conveyancing precedents. Yet I'm sure I should have done the firm much good," Furnivall added whimsically, "and prevented its getting so rich as it has become." [79]

The elder Furnivall, in fact, began to display concern that his son was more preoccupied with literature and social work in the slums than with his profession. Furnivall read law at Lincoln's Inn and Gray's Inn, was called to the bar in 1849, and set himself up as a conveyancer; but in the meantime he had met John Malcolm Ludlow, who converted him to Christian Socialism. The years of 1849–50 were a time of great social ferment in England and throughout Europe, and to a man of Furnivall's volatile temperament, establishing schools for children of the poor and supporting legislation to protect ballast heavers were infinitely more attractive than studying the dry technicalities of the law. Unfortunately, these extracurricular activities had to be financed by his father, who sent a strong letter of protest in August, 1851. "Your business is Law; mine is Physic," wrote Dr. George Furnivall. "Neither you nor I have any Business with Teachers or Ragged Schools. . . . Lawism, not Socialism, Schoolism, or any other ism, ought to be your End and Aim, your Duty, your Pleasure, and Pursuit. Don't play at Law and work at School teaching." [80]

It was a fruitless appeal, for his son was incapable of separating work and play. Furnivall believed that one's employment ought to be a source of pleasure as well as of income, and if law was dull, there was only one thing to do: he stopped practicing it, and instead introduced himself to the literary world by meeting Carlyle, Ruskin, Harriet Martineau, Charles Kingsley, Mrs. Gaskell, and Frederick Denison Maurice, the latter of whom he assisted in founding the London Working Men's College in 1854. At the college's first meeting Furnivall arranged to distribute reprints of Ruskin's essay "On the Nature of Gothic" to the men; in the evenings he also taught classes in English grammar and literature, and on weekends he supervised parties, forty-mile hikes, and excursions up the Thames for the students.[81] These very activities led in 1858 to a public quarrel between him and Maurice, who objected to such secular activities on Sunday. Though raised an orthodox Christian, Furnivall was by now an outspoken agnostic who saw Sunday as a day of recreation rather than worship. Eventually the disagreement subsided, and Furnivall continued to teach at the Working Men's College for several more decades.

In 1847 Furnivall had also joined the Philological Society, becoming in 1853 one of its honorary secretaries. As an officer, he played a large role in laying the initial plans for what was to be known later as the *Oxford English Dictionary*, one of the most monumental scholarly undertakings in modern times. The work was at first conceived as a supplement to the earlier dictionaries of Johnson and Richardson, but Furnivall recommended a completely new dictionary, an idea that was eventually adopted. From 1861 to 1876 Furnivall was in charge of the project, and even after James Murray succeeded him he continued to work for several years on a *Concise Dictionary*, which was not, in the end, published. This experience, however, started him on his career as a founder of learned societies, because his own research for the dictionary revealed the inaccessibility of much early English literature. "It was a sense of community, a socialist impulse to make all the treasures of learning available for all comers, that set him on his way as a student," according to W. P. Ker.[82] Furnivall's first published pamphlet had been entitled "Association a Necessary Part of Christianity," and he now saw that if these literary materials were to be made available to all in democratic fashion, it would be necessary for students of literature to apply the principle of association by banding together into societies so that the manuscripts and rare books could be edited and published.

It was as simple as that. With dizzying speed, therefore, Furnivall founded one society after another: the Early English Text Society (1864), the Chaucer Society (1868), the Ballad Society (1868), the New Shakspere Society (1873), the Browning Society (1881), the Wyclif Society (1882), and the Shelley Society (1885). The achievements of the societies varied, but it would be reasonable to say of them all, as Furnivall did of the Early English Text Society, that they

produced, with whatever shortcomings, an amount of good solid work for which all students of our Language, and some of our

Literature, must be grateful, and . . . rendered possible the be-
ginnings (at least) of proper Histories and Dictionaries of that Language, and Literature, and . . . illustrated the thoughts, the life,
the manners and customs of our forefathers and foremothers.[83]

The Early English Text Society, for example, published some 250 volumes; the Chaucer Society issued an important six-text edition of the
Canterbury Tales, edited by Furnivall himself; the New Shakspere Society printed papers by the most eminent Shakespearian scholars of
the nineteenth century. Taken together, his societies were the most
powerful force in the fostering of English literary and linguistic scholarship in Victorian England.

Behind all these diverse activities was the guiding hand of Furnivall, who organized committees, raised funds, planned meetings,
edited texts, and in general controlled each of the societies. For these
amazing efforts he received no salary, depending instead upon a modest inheritance from his father. However, he had invested it in
Overend and Guerney's bank, which collapsed in 1867, and despite
the occasional assistance of friends, he remained a relatively poor
man the rest of his life. In 1884 the financial burden was eased somewhat by a Civil List Pension from the Government of Gladstone, who
wrote to Furnivall that "with much personal satisfaction, I beg to
place at your disposal a pension of one hundred and fifty pounds per
ann. on the Civil List, for your life, in acknowledgment of your valuable services to the literature of your country." [84] Telling W. C. Hazlitt
of the news the next day, Furnivall confessed, "No man in England
has done so much work for nothing, so perseveringly, as I've done."
Whatever happened thereafter, he wryly observed, he hoped to be safe
from the workhouse.[85] In this same letter, Furnivall estimated that he
had personally donated more than £500 to his societies. The London
Times, after his death, reported that "in the course of his life he had
raised and expended upon printing more than £40,000." [86]

Furnivall's generosity extended to persons as well as societies. The
memorial volume issued in 1911 by his friends and edited by John
Munro, his literary executor, records scores of instances in which he
recommended young authors to publishers, provided work for unem-
ployed scholars, lent encouragement to aspiring poets, and gave un-
stintingly of his advice to other researchers at the British Museum.
Whenever someone wrote to him of an interest in one of his societies,
Furnivall would at once assign him some editing or ask him to prepare a paper; whenever a society member needed a book, Furnivall
would offer his own. "My experience in lending books is a sad one," he

complained in 1893. *"All* my sets of books have been ruind by loans: Ruskin, Browning, E[arly] E[nglish] Text, &c." [87] Unlike some scholars and collectors, who jealously guard their treasures against any encroachments by rivals, Furnivall seemed almost indifferent to the value of the letters he owned from Browning, Arnold, Tennyson, and other eminent writers of the age. Always pressed for funds, he would occasionally during the nineties sell Browning letters to collectors like Slater, though even these transactions were carried out with supreme indifference by Furnivall, whose impersonal attitude toward money prevented him from driving a hard bargain. Witness this letter to Slater in 1895:

> As to Brs. Letters: I put the 3 & 4 page ones at £1 each; the shorter ones at 10/–. On this scale the enclosed 11 are £10; but if you think this is too much, send me what you think the letters worth. Lately, [T. J.] Wise chose 20 to copy & print: some of these enclosed he has had: perhaps all: I took no note of them. If you like uncopied ones— or an additional lot—you can have em. I've given up the idea of printing them, as I shall never have money for it.[88]

Despite the somewhat careless handling of his personal affairs, Furnivall's many societies succeeded because his astounding energy was coupled with an impulsiveness which made difficult decisions easy to reach. Often he took the wrong course of action, but Furnivall never had time to regret an error; snap decisions were simply his mode of operation. If a young man wrote to him of his admiration for Browning, he invariably replied by assigning a paper to be read on a specific date before the Browning Society. The societies themselves were established in this same spontaneous, offhand way: when an acquaintance suggested that he found a Shelley society, Furnivall replied, "By Jove! I will. He was my father's friend." [89]

It was another friendship—his own acquaintance with Browning —that prompted him to set up a Browning society. Like Miss Hickey, Furnivall had been introduced to Browning's poetry through that of Mrs. Browning. Furnivall described his debt to her as "enormous," for the reading of her verse had been to him, as a student at Cambridge, "an entirely new revelation of the possibilities and capabilities of woman's nature." [90] If such a woman had been willing to marry Browning, Furnivall decided, her husband's poetry must also have some merit. He never met Mrs. Browning (he said he would have given his little finger to have done so[91]), though in July, 1855, he narrowly missed an encounter with both Brownings at John Ruskin's home on Denmark Hill. Ruskin had invited him to lunch at half past two, adding that Mrs. Browning would be coming to tea at six. However, the Brownings came early, and when Furnivall learned at the door that Ruskin had visitors, he declined to stay for lunch. The next day Ruskin complained: "Both you and I suffered for your politeness, for I wanted you to stay, and was truly vexed when it suddenly came into my head that you were gone! . . . you must come the next time Mrs. Browning comes, which I hope will be soon." [92] But the opportunity did not arise. The Brownings returned to Florence early in 1856, and in 1861 Mrs. Browning died.

Furnivall, however, did at last meet Browning in May, 1874, at Tennyson's drawing room in London,[93] and the two evidently liked each other from the beginning. Furnivall at once confessed his love for Mrs. Browning's poetry, and "there was no quicker way to Browning's heart," he admitted. For his part, Furnivall undoubtedly admired the poet's vigor, masculinity, and very unpoetic deportment. Thomas Hardy may have been distressed by Browning's resemblance to a "dissenting grocer," [94] but to Furnivall it was a recommendation: a poet, in his opinion, should be strong, manly, unpretentious, and Browning was all of these. He was, in short, Furnivall's kind of poet. Thereafter the two men corresponded and saw each other frequently. Browning's letters to Furnivall, nearly all of which have survived, display a pleasantly amiable tone, with only occasional annoyance or amusement at Furnivall's eccentricities. Browning was fond, for example, of joking about his friend's excessive enthusiasm for all sports. "When I read in a newspaper some adventurous somebody had chosen to skate down a steep incline and break his neck," Browning wrote him in 1887, "I thought of Dr. Furnivall literally riding his hobby [cycling] to death, and ruining the Browning Society." [95] It was a warm friendship, characterized on both sides by ample good will, though it is probably also a tribute to Browning's tact and patience that they never quarreled; Furnivall, who was quick to wrath, at one time or another disputed heatedly with nearly every other acquaintance.

Furnivall's first published remarks on the poetry of Browning appeared in *Notes and Queries* on March 25, 1876.[96] After the Browning Society was created in 1881, however, he began to send a spate of letters to the *Academy* about his favorite poet,[97] most of them in connection with a Browning bibliography he was preparing for the members of his newest society. The bibliography was not as complete as might be wished, he explained at the Browning Society's first meeting, because he was able to work on it only three weeks at the British Museum before taking a two-month holiday in Wales.[98] But in that short time he put nearly a dozen friends to work on the project,[99] plied Browning with countless questions, and brought together most of the materials he needed in order to produce the lists of Browning's publications and of their chief reviews. Excerpts from the reviews were interspersed with typically pungent observations by Furnivall (one writer, for example, he called a "feeble and pretentious religionist" [100]), but his original plan of printing the best reviews in their entirety was abandoned. Furnivall decided that "the money wanted for these old criticisms may perhaps be better spent in printing new ones from our Members' point of view," and Browning quite agreed: though he praised Furnivall and his fellow-workers as "the best suffumigators after this old smell," he urged them to "bid goodbye to it all," for the reviews served only to remind Browning, as he read and corrected the proofs of the bibliography, of the old hostility of the English public toward his poetry.[101]

In the last week of September, Furnivall assembled the bibliography and wrote the "Forewords" (an Anglo-Saxon word which he preferred to the Latinate "preface"), and a few days before the society's first meeting on October 28 it was distributed to all members. Despite the hastiness of its production, the bibliography was an enormous success; in fact, it was the only publication of the Browning Society which was received with unanimous approval by reviewers, since not even the journals of anti-Browning bias could find fault with a work which sorted out such intricate problems of textual variants and publication dates. A supplement, which included an index, was published as Part II of the society's *Papers*, and in 1882 a second edition of the bibliography, incorporating a few corrections, was issued. Another supplement, as well as a second edition of the whole, was also planned several years later but was never completed.

Though Furnivall occasionally spoke on Browning to other groups,[102] he delivered only two papers before the Browning Society, both of them appallingly dull. (Some impromptu remarks on "In a Balcony" which he made at the meeting of June 27, 1890, cannot really be regarded as a "paper.") Furnivall disliked subjective criticism; like Mr. Gradgrind, he saw himself as belonging to the school of hard facts, placing higher value on factual information than on critical opinions. Browning recognized this deficiency, for when J. T. Nettleship complained to him about the society's wildly allegorical interpretations of his poetry, Browning replied, "As for wishing to get behind any plain sense that might be discoverable, Furnivall, the founder, strikes me as going to the other extreme; disparaging anything but plain facts." [103] Unfortunately, the techniques of historical and textual scholarship, which were appropriate for the study of writers of past centuries, could not easily be employed in evaluating a contemporary poet. But Furnivall tried nevertheless. On February 25, 1887, he read to the society a paper entitled "A Grammatical Analysis of 'O Lyric Love'" [Browning's lines addressed to his dead wife in Book I of *The Ring and the Book*]. The paper was written, Furnivall explained, to supply an answer to the question many members were asking him: "What *can* be done to get away from the perpetually recurring discussions of Browning's theology?" His contribution scarcely suggested a reasonable alternative, since its dryasdust parsing of Browning's familiar lines served no apparent purpose; indeed, it bordered on self-parody. "An irreverent friend of Dr. Berdoe's has cald it 'Furnivall's Jubilee Conundrum,'" commented a note by Furnivall, who never lost his sense of humor in his footnotes, even when he was sounding like Mr. Casaubon in his text. "To some minds, nothing is sacred." [104]

On February 28, 1890, he presented his second paper, "Robert Browning's Ancestors," [105] a product of the kind of genealogical research which has served Chaucerian and Shakespearian scholarship so well. After consulting all available wills, court records, and lists of births, deaths, and marriages, Furnivall reached two startling conclusions (or at least they seemed startling in 1890): (1) Browning's father was "half-Creole"; and (2) the earliest known member of the family was a footman. Furnivall was pleased with his findings:

> As a radical and democrat, I of course rejoice that the descendant of a Dorsetshire footman has been buried with solemn pomp in Westminster Abbey (31 Dec., 1889), and that I preside over the Society which I helpt to found in his honour (July 1881). I hope too that the poet's American admirers, in their dealings with the negroes, will not forget the possibility—to me the certainty—that Browning's grandmother had dark blood in her.[106]

Others were less impressed. Edmund Gosse ignored Furnivall's research when he discussed Browning's ancestry in the *Dictionary of National Biography*, and Furnivall retaliated by sending an angry letter on the subject to the *Academy* in 1902[107] and placing an inscription upon the grave of Browning's "footman ancestor" at Pentridge. Browning's son, who lived on a pretentious scale at the Palazzo Rezonico in Venice, was infuriated. "Young Browning is *very* savage with me for proving that he is descended from a footman, & has no right to the Arms that he flaunts on his gondoliers' blouses," Furnivall told

Slater in 1895.[108] Even as late as 1938 Sir Vincent Baddeley, whose grandfather was a second cousin of Browning's father, wrote a violent diatribe in the *Genealogists' Magazine* against Furnivall's paper; Baddeley had stumbled upon the old controversy in 1931 when he discovered Furnivall's inscription at the grave of the "footman ancestor," which he promptly altered by obliterating any reference to the first Mr. Browning's occupation.[109]

Some of Furnivall's other activities pleased the Browning family even less. In 1890 he decided that John Forster's brief biography (1836) of Strafford, the hero of Browning's first play, had been written almost entirely by Browning rather than Forster, and Furnivall announced his latest discovery by dashing off a letter to the *Pall Mall Gazette*[110] and later (1892) reprinting the Strafford biography under the title *Robert Browning's Prose Life of Strafford*. Robert Barrett ("Pen") Browning was again indignant and attempted to prevent its publication. When that failed, he wrote to the Forster family: "Let me say at once that I have long ceased to have anything to do with Dr. Furnivall nor have I seen his book . . ." [111] This same year Pen was also distressed to discover that a picture of his father taken a few hours after death was used as a frontispiece to *Browning's Criticism of Life* by William Revell. The angry son, who had earlier refused to let the photograph be published by the Browning Society, then wrote this letter of complaint to the *Athenaeum*:

> My attention having been attracted by an advertisement to the frontispiece of a book by Mr. Revell, I wrote asking him how he had come by the original photograph. His answer contains a frank apology for having "sinned ignorantly," which I accept, and the explanation that the photograph had been "kindly lent by a friend."
>
> The "friend" can only be one of a very few to whose honour I had entrusted copies of this photograph—a person thoroughly unworthy of the trust, as he subsequently proved to be, but in whom I, so far, had seen nothing more objectionable than a singular lack of tact.[112]

The tactless friend was of course Furnivall, who had circulated the same photograph among those present at the first Browning Society meeting held after the poet's funeral.[113]

Even Browning's mild and somewhat colorless sister Sarianna found cause to condemn Furnivall, who, with some other Browningites, listened to a recording of the poet's voice on the first anniversary of his death. Among those present was Hugh Haweis, who sent an enthusiastic account of the experience to the *Times*.[114] Sarianna, upon hearing of this "indecent seance," wrote to a friend: "Poor Robert's dead voice to be made interesting amusement! God forgive them all. I find it difficult." [115] Edmund Gosse was probably not exaggerating when he claimed several years later that Furnivall was "perfectly loathed by the family of Mr. Browning." [116] Relatives of Victorian writers were notoriously zealous in protecting the supposed interests and reputations of the dead, and an outspoken iconoclast like Furnivall would have inspired distrust, if not terror, in the families of any of Browning's distinguished contemporaries. That such a person had created the Browning Society must have made him doubly obnoxious to the Brownings; but to us today, the incongruity of an idol-smasher leading the idolaters of the Browning Society can only be a source of amusement. It created a situation of subtle irony to which Browning alone could have done justice through his psychological probings in verse.

CHAPTER II

FURNIVALLOS FURIOSO

[Furnivall] was a good sort; but his quarrels were outrageous.
. . . He could not behave himself in a controversy, always
making such a fool of himself that it was impossible to feel
angry with him.

—Bernard Shaw[1]

FORTUNATELY for the Browning Society, Furnivall seldom read his
own papers to it; instead, his influence made itself felt in less conspicuous ways. Although all his societies had formal hierarchies
consisting of presidents, vice-presidents, honorary secretaries, and
committees, it is clear that in every instance he possessed ultimate authority: he raised funds, assigned papers, wrote the annual reports,
did much of the textual editing, and dominated discussions at the
meetings. Yet he lacked the instincts of a dictator. He did all these
things because they had to be done, and few other members were as
willing as he to take on so many thankless tasks. Evidently the limits of
his authority in each society were determined not so much by the
group's rules as by the amount of time Furnivall was able to devote to
its affairs. In the Browning Society, for example, he held the chairmanship of the committee, which met approximately once a month to
make all decisions of policy and to plan future meetings, and in this
position Furnivall wielded considerably more power than he would
have as the president, since the presidency of his societies was usually
occupied by a figurehead whose name would lend prestige and dignity
to the organization, while the real work was handled by the honorary
secretary and the chairman of the committee. In the case of the
Browning Society, Furnivall tried unsuccessfully to persuade Tennyson and the son of Edward Bulwer-Lytton ("Owen Meredith") to ac-

cept the presidency, and since they both declined, the office was not filled until the society's business meeting of June 24, 1887, at which time Furnivall himself was elected.[2] ". . . Indeed you have all along really 'presided,' " Browning commented a few days later, "and any interloper would cut a poor figure in your visionary stead." [3]

Actually, Furnivall presided at only about a fourth of the meetings, but at every meeting he talked incessantly.[4] His contributions to the discussion periods were so lengthy that they constituted, in effect, a second paper, or, more often, an exhaustive rebuttal of the paper that had just been read. Furnivall's observations were always provocative, racy, and commonsensical; without him, the Browning Society would have been as dull as some of its detractors claimed it was. Here, in an example taken at random, were some of the topics discussed by Furnivall at *one* meeting of the society (November 25, 1881): (1) the need for more papers on individual poems; (2) Browning's approval of the paper by John Sharpe; (3) Browning's explanation of an allusion in *Pietro of Abano*; (4) the historical background of the poem; (5) an anecdote about Lord Clive; (6) an application of the phrase "cleverness uncurbed by conscience" to the career of "a late political leader of England" (i.e., Disraeli); (7) a central idea that exists in a poem even if the poet is not aware of it; and (8) this principle applied to Shakespearean criticism. It was a typical performance, except that Furnivall said less at this meeting than he usually did.

A complaint frequently levelled against Furnivall was that he dragged into these discussions all his private prejudices (Disraeli) and preoccupations (Shakespeare), and indeed the charge is quite true. Impersonal objectivity seemed unworthy to him as a scholarly goal; though he seemed obsessed with "plain facts," as Browning put it, Furnivall was in reality much more concerned with the autobiographical element of literature. He valued poems and novels exactly in proportion to their revelation of the living personality that created them. Hence his high praise of Browning's essay on Shelley:

> The interest lay in the fact, that Browning's "utterances" here are *his*, and not those of any one of the "so many imaginary persons," behind whom he insists on so often hiding himself, and whose necks I, for one, should continually like to wring, whose bodies I would fain kick out of the way, in order to get face to face with the poet himself, and hear his own voice speaking his own thoughts, man to man, soul to soul. Straight speaking, straight hitting, suit me best.[5]

When Edith Rickert, the American Chaucerian scholar, published a novel in 1902, Furnivall sent her a note of congratulation which concluded: "When shall you try a book closer to your own life, with more of your own experience in it? That is what I want out of every writer." [6] Scholarship, like literature, ought to have as its subject matter persons and personal relationships, and therefore, from Furnivall's point of view, there was nothing irrelevant or improper about discussing what was closest to one's heart at a Browning Society meeting.

A most striking instance of the strongly personal element in Furnivall's speeches was his curious manner of commemorating the death of Miss Teena Rochfort-Smith, an attractive and intelligent young woman who had done work for the Early English Text Society, the *Oxford English Dictionary*, and the New Shakspere Society, her most notable achievement being a four-text edition of *Hamlet*. In April, 1883, Furnivall took her to Browning's home, where, after luncheon, the poet read to them eight new poems from the manuscript of *Jocoseria*. Miss Rochfort-Smith listened with rapt attention, understanding (according to Furnivall) even those gnarly passages which left the Browning Society's founder "quite in the lurch." The following September, several days after her dress had accidentally caught fire, she died of severe burns. At the November meeting of the Browning Society, therefore, Furnivall began his remarks by saying that "to him *Jocoseria* had an especial interest in connection with his dear young friend, Miss Teena Rochfort-Smith," and then he launched into a lengthy, circumstantial account of her visit with Browning and of her death. A footnote in the *Papers* added: "Mr. Furnivall proposes to issue to members a Woodbury-type of his dead friend, so that those who think fit, may put it to face this page." [7] That Miss Rochfort-Smith had no real connection with the Browning Society seems not to have mattered to Furnivall.[8] He even asked Browning to write a tribute to her, and when the poet refused, Furnivall issued a *Memoir* of his own in which photographs of both Browning and himself appeared.[9] Shortly after its publication, Alfred Domett met Browning at an exhibition and recorded in his diary that his friend "did not seem to approve much of Furnivall's having inserted his (B's) photograph into his memoir of 'Tina' (Miss Mary Lilian Rochford [sic] Smith), an enthusiastic admirer of his poetry, as he did not know much of the young lady." [10] To Furnivall, such an objection would have been incomprehensible; had not Teena recited Browning on her deathbed?

Given this strange combination, then, of unlimited personal authority, of long, subjective speeches at the meetings, and of pugnacity on the part of the founder, it is not surprising that nearly all of Furnivall's societies were torn by quarrels and feuds. One is even tempted to compose an epigram to the effect that the history of these societies could be recounted entirely in terms of the hostilities they provoked, though that would be neither fair nor accurate. The most notorious quarrel of this kind developed within the New Shakspere Society. Furnivall took the position that one of the society's chief aims ought to be the establishment of the chronology of the plays, and he proposed to achieve this primarily through the application of metrical tests, which would reveal, he said, a consistent pattern of growth in Shakespeare's developing poetic skill. Other scholars, both within and without the New Shakspere Society, preferred the more impressionistic criticism advocated and practiced by Swinburne, who objected to the "mechanical" procedure of counting feminine and masculine line-endings. The disagreement between the two factions became so heated that a satirical poem entitled "Furnivallos Furioso! and 'The Newest Shakespeare Society'" was published about it; but when Swinburne personally entered the lists against Furnivall in the late seventies, the invectives began to fly back and forth in earnest. Both parties displayed deplorable manners. Swinburne and Furnivall heaped abuse and ridicule upon each other in prefaces, letters to periodicals, and pamphlets, and even some relatively innocent bystanders like J. O. Halliwell-Phillipps were caught in the middle as blows rained down upon them from either direction.[11] It was, as John Munro says,

> the most unhappy public incident in Furnivall's career; and one would wish it had never been. But there it is, significant and revealing; speaking of the man as he was; not, therefore, to be ignored. One must set against it the noble and patient enthusiasm of Furnivall, exhibited in his Chaucer and Shakspere work proper.[12]

In the end, many of the eminent members and vice-presidents withdrew in embarrassment or anger from the New Shakspere Society, which never thereafter recovered its earlier vitality.[13]

The Browning Society was also wracked with quarrels, though none so serious as the Swinburne-Furnivall affair. With a single exception, they tended to be minor skirmishes rather than full-fledged battles; they produced occasional feelings of acrimony but no massive exodus of members. Yet, in their ultimate effect, these feuds were decidedly harmful, for they created a contentious atmosphere which must have hastened the Browning Society's demise. For the sake of brevity, only two of these skirmishes will be described here in detail (though others will appear incidentally elsewhere in this book): (1) Furnivall's attempt to produce a Shilling Selection of Browning's poems; and (2) a lawsuit brought against Furnivall by Leonard Outram.

A Cheap Edition of Browning

Long before the Browning Society was founded, Furnivall had come to the conclusion that Browning's poetry was not reaching a sufficiently large audience. The solution, Furnivall believed, was for George Smith, Browning's publisher, to issue an inexpensive selection of the poems, an idea which he suggested to Browning in 1876. "I am deeply obliged to you for the interest you take in my poems, and the wish you have for their increased circulation," Browning replied; "but depend on it, there is no help for what you consider my ill case, and what I am used to acquiesce in as my natural portion." [14] Not satisfied with this answer, Furnivall insisted that he would like to write the preface for such a cheap selection himself. Browning said he had no objections if Smith did not, but, as he later told his publisher, "What else could I say? Unless things are very much changed, I suppose you will *not* agree." [15]

There the matter rested until March, 1881, when Furnivall again raised the subject and Browning again pointed out that Smith had "objections." [16] In July of that year Furnivall was writing the prospectus for the Browning Society and evidently intended to mention in it the need for a Shilling Selection; he also corresponded directly with Smith, who sent his letters on to Browning. "I return the unwise letters of Furnivall," Browning wrote to Smith. "He has written to me— engages to 'never to write to you again, nor allude to the subject in his Prospectus'—whatever that may mean." [17] The Browning Society prospectus did not in fact mention the subject, though a footnote in Furnivall's Browning bibliography, issued that autumn, observed that "both a cheap Selection from Browning's Works and a cheap double-column Edition of them are sadly wanted in England." [18] Browning, by now resigned to Furnivall's persistent badgering, promised once more in October to discuss the question with Smith. [19]

It was probably also during 1881 that Furnivall himself called upon George Smith in order to argue his case. Furnivall was astonished, he wrote later, to discover that Browning's verse brought him an annual income only one-fiftieth that of Tennyson. If Browning would not change publishers—as Furnivall at first hoped he might— then perhaps Smith could at least be persuaded to print a Shilling Selection that would simultaneously spread abroad the gospel of

Browning and bring in new income for the poet. But Smith's position (as Furnivall later reported) was unyielding:

> It's all very well for you, Mr. Furnivall, to talk about a cheap edition of Mr. Browning's works, and fifty thousand of a shilling selection. But I know the facts. Our books show that we print 750 copies of a new poem: the first year we sell from 380 to 400 copies; the second year thirty to forty; the third year, a dozen; and afterwards only odd copies. And as to your shilling selection, we should print 10,000, we should sell 2,000, and be the laughing stock of the trade. Moreover, the shilling selection would stop the sale of the two six-shilling ones and render their plates useless. I will not recommend anything of the kind to Mr. Browning.[20]

Both logic and experience, it should be observed, were on Smith's side, for he had been publishing moderately inexpensive selections of Browning's poems since 1869.

Nevertheless, in the first annual report of the Browning Society, written by Furnivall and read at the meeting of July 7, 1882, mention was again made of a shilling edition. "But, as that issue has been hitherto refused," the report added wrathfully, "the limit fixt to Browning's influence by his publisher has been accepted as the boundary of the Society's operations." [21] In oral remarks at the same meeting, Furnivall also emphasized the importance of the matter.[22] In August, probably replying to these published complaints, Browning wrote to Furnivall: "I wish with all my heart I could content you about the 'Selections': those in use at present *sell*, and a second selection from them would, I suppose, act as a sucker from the main trunk and flourish at its expense. . . ." [23] Yet Browning was gradually yielding to Furnivall's blandishments, for a week later he wrote: "I think there is no great objection to the bringing out a small 'Shilling Selection' such as you speak of—'Hervé Riel & some Idylls': at all events I engage to speak about it to Smith when I return to London." [24] In his next letter, however, Browning had to urge caution:

> "Wisely but slow—they stumble who run fast." What I said was simply that I saw nothing objectionable in proposing such a Shilling Edition to Smith as would suit your purpose so kindly intended: but you have only to take it as a thing concluded on, and talk about it being a work of the Society's, to get it knocked on the head at once. If Smith allows it, you may be sure I will gladly relegate to you the business of picking and choosing the poems,—but if we begin by that natural ending—there will be objection enough:

I really want to do something in accordance with the views of one who has done so much for me—and for that very reason, I would take the right way to get it done. Pray believe in my experience in this matter—as I believe in your zeal and kind intentions.[25]

But once again the edition did not materialize, probably because of Smith's repeated disapproval.

A full-scale clash between Furnivall and Smith came finally in December of 1883. A few days before Christmas, Browning privately told Furnivall that Smith soon would publish two volumes of selections from both Browning's poetry and that of his wife, with perhaps a Shilling Selection to follow them in the future. Furnivall promptly inserted the following note in the *Academy* of December 22:

> We hear that Mr. Browning's publisher has at last resolved to yield in some degree to the appeals that have been made to him so persistently by the press and in private for the last few years for a cheaper edition of some of the poet's works. A new edition of the two volumes of the Selections is to be published, at 3s. 6d. a volume; and the volumes will be sold separately. Let us hope that a shilling edition of them will follow next year. That is what is needed.[26]

George Smith, in the meantime, had written to Browning suggesting that he might issue a Shilling Selection instead of the two-volume set, but Furnivall's unauthorized and premature announcement in the *Academy* made it impossible for the publisher to carry out his plans. "I have no idea how the 'Academy' got their information—but from the tone of the paragraph I conjecture that it was written by Mr. Furnivall," the irritated Smith wrote to Browning. "It would be difficult to say exactly how much that Gentleman's impertinent interference with your works has cost you, but it is no inconsiderable sum." [27] Browning replied on January 1 by explaining apologetically that he had been the "unwitting prompter" of Furnivall's action through confiding in him:

> I could not dream he would at once print the news with the offensive comment,—which could answer no possible good end. Of course, I am all the more hampered and embarrassed by the circumstance that, in spite of his blundering, Mr Furnivall means beyond a doubt to do me all the service he is able: it is the old story of the friendly bear who broke the teeth of the man with the stone he meant should brush away a fly that had settled on his mouth.

In a postscript Browning added: "I may tell you, I took occasion only last week, to write to our impulsive F. and beg him to confine his criticism to my writings and leave my doings altogether alone: may he only attend to a very earnest prayer!" [28]

When the *Academy* the following May published yet another note on the desirability of a Shilling Selection, Furnivall reprinted it in *The Browning Society's Papers* with the careful explanation that it was "Not by F.J.F." [29] However, in the society's annual report for 1883–84, he bragged that the new *Selections* were to be had at less than half their former price "mainly through the Society's action." [30] The truth, needless to say, was quite different: because of Furnivall's ineptitude and haste, the Browning Society was still deprived of the Shilling Selection it had so long desired.

William G. Kingsland, a member of the society and a friend of Browning's, revived the issue in March, 1885, by writing directly to the poet about a Shilling Selection. Browning's answer betrays some impatience and lack of candor: "I have no sort of influence with my publisher, and no knowledge whether, much less when, he will bring out a cheap edition of my works." [31] Kingsland also wrote to Furnivall in January of the following year to inquire "whether the Browning Society (through its publisher) could not get Mr. Browning's consent to issue a 'cheap selection' (say 6d or 1s.) from his short poems. . . ." Such a selection, he explained, would reach "the working people" and would not interfere with the sale of the present 3s 6d volume.[32] Furnivall, to Kingsland's subsequent embarrassment, passed the letter on to Browning,[33] who pointedly observed to Furnivall that Smith "has just brought out a cheap collection of my poems, and would not unreasonably object to the wind being taken out of his sails immediately by a still cheaper edition than his own[,] which goes off very well." And in a rare outburst of sarcasm, Browning, who must have been very tired of the whole matter, added: "K. 'believes the new venture would not interfere at all with the disposal of the present one': if he can convince Smith of *that*, the arrangement will be easy, of course." [34]

Furnivall complained no further about Smith's policies until 1889, when he ordered for the Browning Society two hundred copies of Professor William J. Alexander's *Introduction to Browning*, just published in the United States; but Smith was able to prevent the books from being brought into England, because, in violation of British copyright law, the *Introduction* printed several of Browning's poems in their entirety.[35] Enraged, Furnivall reprinted much of the book's editorial matter in *The Browning Society's Papers*[36] and sent a letter to Browning cursing George Smith. Browning once again patiently pointed out to Furnivall that George Smith had to make a profit on his books, and that naturally "he is disinclined to allow the payers-of-nothing there [i.e., pirating American publishers] to compete with his publications here, and pay nothing into the bargain." [37]

After Browning's death on December 12, 1889, Furnivall pressed the fight for a Shilling Selection with renewed vigor. In a letter printed in the *Daily News* on December 19 under the title "The Best Memorial to Robert Browning," Furnivall urged his readers to "tell Mr. Browning's son the pleasure that his erecting this much-needed memorial to his father's memory in their hearts [a Shilling Selection] would give them." He further explained in some detail that "the great hindrance and enemy of our work in popularizing Browning has been his publisher." [38] At the next meeting of the Browning Society, on January 31, 1890, Furnivall also presented the same request to Browning's son in a series of formal resolutions occasioned by the poet's death.[39]

The relationship between Pen Browning and Furnivall, as we have already seen, deteriorated badly in the months following the decease of Pen's father, and Furnivall became gloomily convinced that young Browning was on George Smith's side. "I fear we shan't get the Shilling Selection out of Browning's son," he wrote to E. H. Blakeney on February 25. "He seems to think that money for his pocket is more important than the increase of his Father's fame & power of doing good." [40] At the Browning Society meeting three days later Furnivall made the same dismal forecast.[41] Nevertheless, he circulated a memorial, which was then presented to Pen Browning, "asking for the issue of one or two shilling volumes." Finally, on March 7, the *Daily News* announced that "Mr. Robert Barrett Browning has informed the memorialists that he is in no way opposed to their wishes, and that a shilling selection of his father's poems may be looked for within a reasonable time." [42]

Ironically, when the Shilling Selection did appear later that year, Furnivall was dissatisfied with it. "The selection in the shilling volume is badly made," he complained, "inasmuch as the careless chooser of the poems has (1) put in several third-rate and uninteresting poems of Browning's, and left out some of his best . . . and (2) has confused the time-order of the pieces. . . ." [43]

The quarrel over the Shilling Selection had been long, tedious, and probably unnecessary, yet the story is worth retelling for the light it sheds upon the characters of Browning and Furnivall. The episode shows Browning, in the first place, to be a long-suffering, gracious person who never fully lost his temper, despite his uncomfortable role as mediator between the belligerent leader of the Browning Society and a resentful publisher; Furnivall, on the other hand, though his intentions were (as usual) good, made rather a fool of himself. Had he not sent the rash announcement to the *Academy* in 1883, the Browning Society would have had its Shilling Selection seven years earlier than it did.

However, we are guilty of misjudging the deepest motives of both Furnivall and his society if we assume that this fifteen-year crusade for a book was nothing more than a whim. Furnivall's passionate desire for a cheap edition of Browning's poetry reflects his belief that this poetry was an indispensable source of solace and moral inspiration which should be made easily available to the poor. Poets and writers had become the secular prophets of an age which was turning its back upon traditional Christianity, and Furnivall, in common with many other Victorian agnostics, saw in Browning's undogmatic faith an excellent compromise between rigid orthodoxy and destructive rationalism. Though no longer a Christian Socialist, Furnivall remained in sympathy with many of the ideals of that movement, in particular its wish to spread a spirit of religious idealism among the working men of England. And in Browning's poetry he found the perfect instrument for this task, a large body of poems that captured the flavor of Christianity without insisting upon its dogmas. The Shilling Selection was the product, then, of a primarily religious impulse, of a strongly felt concern for the poor. Browning for the moral uplift of the working class: that was the true rationale of Furnivall's protracted and unpleasant feud with George Smith.

Outram v. Furnivall

The Smith affair was settled more or less amicably in the end, but another of Furnivall's Browning Society quarrels had to be arbitrated in court. Once more his hot temper held sway over good judgment, though this time he was given a costly lesson in the hazards of public controversies. (To be specific, the lesson cost him and his friends more than £300.) The incident grew out of a Browning Society performance of one of Browning's plays, several of which the society produced during the decade.

On November 19, 1885, the society staged *Colombe's Birthday*, in which Alma Murray took the role of Constance, and Leonard Outram, an impecunious actor, that of Valence. The very next day Outram wrote to Furnivall offering to read a paper before the society "upon the great scene between Colombe & Valence in 4th Act of Colombe's Birthday showing the view taken by Miss Murray and myself of the poet's intention." Furnivall, with characteristic dispatch, immediately scheduled the paper for the Browning Society meeting of January 29, 1886.[44]

Three days later Outram offered his services for the society's next dramatic production,[45] an offer also promptly accepted, and by December 5 Outram was enthusiastically promising James Dykes Campbell, then the honorary secretary, that he would both play the title role of *Strafford* and direct it the following November. He felt confident, he wrote, of "a high achievement for the poet and the Society, with a little aspiration on my own behalf, since *the* cause is *my* cause." [46] When Furnivall sent him a circular advertising his newly founded Shelley Society, Outram volunteered to act in its forthcoming performance of *The Cenci* as well; and again his services were accepted.[47] His roles in the two plays, he told Furnivall on December 11, would give him stature as "an intellectual actor." "I shall count the labor I shall give to these tasks," he added, "as more than recompensed by the tasks themselves." [48]

But such high-minded idealism had disappeared by the following autumn. On September 28, 1886, he reported to Furnivall that he was "compelled to resign the privilege of doing *Strafford* for the Society." A broken arm had left him even more impoverished than usual; he was, he said, "now living in penury, in a house destitute of furniture, until the day arrives for me to leave town with the Drury Lane horseshow [*A Run of Luck*], in which I play a subordinate part, at a salary that will be just sufficient for the living expenses of my wife and self." [49] On October 2, however, Outram wrote to Furnivall that he was "sorry to hear that you are in trouble about Strafford" and regretted leaving "the Society in the lurch." [50] He visited Furnivall the next evening to discuss the matter, but what took place at the meeting is not clear, except that Outram left Furnivall's home as director and chief actor of *Strafford* once more. One thing is certain: that neither man understood the agreement they had just reached. Outram was under the impression that he was free to raise subscriptions by appealing to the entire membership of the Browning Society; Furnivall was equally convinced that he had told Outram to call personally upon only a few of the wealthier members of the society for financial assistance.[51]

For the moment, Outram was given £10 for expenses, and he again set to work on the play, though as a director he was disappointing. When Furnivall asked for a list of the seats in the Strand Theatre, where *Strafford* was to be performed, Outram sent a description of its "full accom[modation]"—but omitted the 500 seats in the pit.[52] George Foss, who was shortly to replace Outram as both director and actor, went to a rehearsal at his house and reported to Alma Murray "that O. did not the least seem to know what he wanted them to do with the play." [53]

But the final exasperating episode began on October 19 when Furnivall received in the mail from Dr. John H. Clarke, a member of the Browning Society committee, a guinea mysteriously described as "for the Testimonial to Mr. Outram." [54] Though Furnivall later insisted that he was "very angry" upon receiving this letter,[55] his immediate reaction was rather one of bewilderment. He confessed to Miss Murray:

> I never heard of it [the Testimonial] till now, but send the cheque to O. as if for his benefit.
>
> [Thomas J.] Wise [member of the Browning Society committee] says that O. writes to [Walter B.] Slater [the new honorary secretary] saying that he's living in deepest penury, &c. And W[ise] suggests advancing him £10 10s. more. But I do not at all incline to this course. If we take it, another £10 'll be wanted before November 5, I fear; and after all we may not get our *Strafford*.
>
> I hope all will go right; but I feel very uncomfortable.[56]

Well he might, for within a few hours after expressing his apprehension, Furnivall saw the circular which had prompted Dr. Clarke's gift.[57] Printed by Outram and sent to every member of the Browning Society,[58] the circular expressed the hope that "those who love Browning's poetry and appreciate the advantage of having it adequately rendered upon the stage will acknowledge Mr. Outram's services by a supplementary subscription for his benefit";[59] and, to compound the astonishment and rage of Furnivall, the circular appeared to be signed by himself. This, of course, was only an illusion. The last lines of the circular read:

> . . . such subscription to be remitted to
> Dr. Furnivall
>   3, St. George's Square
>   Primrose Hill, N.W.

Furnivall's name, then, was intended to be part of an address to which subscriptions would be sent; but the typographical arrangement made it appear to be a signature as well.

With explosive vigor, Furnivall at once struck back. Alma Murray, only a day later, wrote to Outram that she had "just heard from Dr. Furnivall in great indignation" about the circular and that she would

be therefore unwilling to perform in a forthcoming benefit for Outram.[60] Outram received an angry postcard from Furnivall the same
day at the Strand Theatre. And, most significantly—for this brought
the differences between the two men into the press for the first time—
Furnivall also published in the *Pall Mall Gazette* on that day a letter
emphatically denying that he had ever authorized Outram's circular.[61]
A reply from Outram appeared in the *Pall Mall Gazette* five days later.
Calling Furnivall's letter a "cowardly stab in the dark," he insisted
that his circular had been printed with Furnivall's "general authority
and by the special advice of Mr. J. Dykes Campbell, the ex-secretary
of the society, to whom he had referred me for ways and means of
raising money. . . ."[62]

Campbell, however, had already denied this allegation privately to
Furnivall on October 22:

> I so rarely see the *P.M.G.* now that it was by pure accident I bought
> one of Wednesday [October 20], and saw your disclaimer. Of course
> I "authorized" O. to do nothing—not even to send to Members notifi-
> cation of his own Benefit, without first consulting you and Slater.
> Such an idea as begging for *Strafford* for his profit, he naturally had
> not the audacity to name to me. I quite agree with you—cut clear
> of O. at all risks and all costs.[63]

He also answered the charge publicly in the *Pall Mall Gazette* of October 26, though here his denial was phrased more politely: "Mr. Outram," he wrote, "must be labouring under some misapprehen-
sion. . . ."[64] The editor in the same issue also announced that he had
received a "long and indignant letter—far too indignant for publication—from Dr. Furnivall." In the excerpt that the *Pall Mall Gazette*
did publish, Furnivall responded to Outram's "audacious misstate-
ment" by quoting from a circular of his own which he had just mailed
to the members of the Browning Society. Entitled "Mr. L. S. Outram's
Appeal . . . Warning from Dr. Furnivall," and dated October 23, the
circular condemned the action of Outram and summarized Furnivall's
position in these words:

> Had I seen it [Outram's circular] before its issue, I would never
> have allowed my name to appear in connection with it; and I look
> on its issue, without my sanction, as a scandalous attempt to get
> money from our Members under cover of my name. . . .
> You will not wonder that after such an attempt, I have given no-
> tice to Mr. Outram that I can have nothing more to do with him; that
> I have, with Miss Alma Murray's approval, accepted his withdrawal

from our production of *Strafford;* and that I have demanded the return of the £10 advanst to him for preliminary expenses (save £1 for postages, &c.).

I feel strongly that we must get quit of him. The performance of *Strafford* will probably have to be put off for a time until another actor of the principal part can be found.[65]

At this point the dispute, which was becoming rather stale, disappeared from the pages of the *Pall Mall Gazette*: these letters from Campbell and Furnivall had, in fact, been introduced by the editor with the wry comment that "we regret it is not within our power to issue from time to time 'Browning Society Supplements,' in which the general aspirations and mutual aspersions of that worthy body might receive adequate expression." In private, however, the letters continued to fly back and forth. Furnivall was still trying to recover the £10, and Outram had hired a solicitor, who wrote to Furnivall on October 30 that he must cease all activities calculated to damage his client's professional reputation. But Furnivall had just warmed up to the fight. "My instructions," the solicitor warned, "are to give you notice that unless these proceedings on your part be at once discontinued ['They won't be,' reads a note by Furnivall in the margin of the letter] I am to take steps against you for their prevention [Furnivall's comment: 'Go ahead!']."[66]

In the meantime, Furnivall and his society tried to struggle on with the production of their play. "We are looking forward with pleasure to our performance of *Strafford* on Dec. 21," Furnivall informed Professor Corson in the United States. "Had not Outram behaved so scandalously, we should already have seen the play."[67] Yet this was an oversimplification, for it neglected to mention a whole series of difficulties that beset George Foss, the new director.[68] The final blow came on December 12, when Alma Murray wrote to Furnivall:

It is with real sorrow that I am compelled to give up [the role of] Lady Carlisle. . . . For the last week or two one of my nervous troubles has been a swelling of the lips and eyes. . . . I cannot tell you how grieved I am, especially as Mr. Browning is to be present. . . .[69]

Despite Browning's suggestion that it be postponed,[70] *Strafford* was finally performed on December 21 after all, but Furnivall never received the £10, and Outram made good his threat by bringing a libel suit against Furnivall. The particular libels cited at the trial, which was held on February 2, 1888, were Furnivall's angry letter to Outram's solicitor and his "Warning" circular, in which he had described Outram's behavior as "scandalous." Though serious issues were involved, the trial at times acquired the richly comic atmosphere of the more famous case of *Bardell* v. *Pickwick.* Furnivall was forced to explain, for example, why he had communicated with Outram by postcards—a sinister detail which doubtless not even Sam Weller could have laughed out of court.[71] Walter Slater, Dr. Clarke, and Dykes Campbell testified on Furnivall's behalf, and the chances of an acquittal were probably good until Furnivall himself was cross-examined in the witness box. Once again intemperate language damaged his cause: "I did intend to make it hot for the plaintiff among my own set," he told the court. "I cannot say that I feel any regret for what I did in this matter." Mr. Justice Stephen observed in his instructions to the jury that "the defendant by his conduct in the box had turned a mere friction into a serious matter." The jury at once found Furnivall guilty and awarded Outram £100; the defendant was also made liable for costs.[72]

It was a stunning blow to Furnivall, who was far from a wealthy man. When Slater immediately offered financial assistance, Furnivall answered:

> I shall be only too glad of help. My Sister lends me £100 to keep the Sheriff out of the house tomorrow, & will also advance the costs. I shall give her a Bill of Sale of my Furniture & Books.
>
> She makes the advance out of her Quarter's income; & if you can enable me to give back any of it by March 1, I shall be greatly obliged to you, as then she won't have to sell one of her securities. It is most kind of you & Wise to come forward thus.[73]

He added in a postscript that his counsel had, along with Alfred Forman (the husband of Alma Murray) and Campbell, proposed to start a fund to defray the fine and costs. On February 6 Campbell invited Slater and other members of the Browning Society executive committee to discuss the matter at his home, at which time it was decided to send yet another circular to the society members and "a few outsiders," this time appealing for subscriptions to a Furnivall Fund.[74] The circular, dated February 8, announced that Furnivall had been "mulcted in damages and costs amounting in the aggregate to upwards of £200" and urged his friends to send subscriptions to either Campbell or Slater.[75]

At about the same time, the *Pall Mall Gazette* was becoming involved in the case again. Though on February 3 it had professed amusement at an argument advanced by Furnivall's counsel ("if the adjectives were taken out, there was nothing in what the defendant wrote which the plaintiff's circular did not justify"), the publisher visited Furnivall's home on February 5 and saw that he was very close indeed to financial disaster.[76] As a result, the *Pall Mall Gazette* of February 8 carried a long, eloquent defense of Furnivall. The writer found intense irony in a statement by Mr. Justice Stephen to the jury: "I would not believe a man on his oath who said he cared nothing for himself or his own advancement. It is contrary to nature and common sense." [77] (This was in response to Furnivall's insistence that members of the Browning Society were expected to give unselfish service, with no "sordid motives.") Yet, in point of fact, Furnivall was just such a person. Though the *Pall Mall* editorial did not explicitly say so, it implied what only a few knew: that Furnivall's labors for his many societies were entirely unpaid. Unfortunately, the judge, Fitzjames Stephen, was better known for his Johnsonian common sense than for a subtle understanding of human nature,[78] and he had been unimpressed by Furnivall's altruistic outlook.

Because of this article and the circular which had been distributed earlier, subscriptions were soon flowing in. The *Pall Mall Gazette* announced tongue-in-cheek on February 13 that "clearly Dr. Furnivall gave vent to his righteous anger against Mr. Outram in order that his friends might afterwards pay the costs, and so himself be richer by their expression of sympathy." [79] Furnivall, too, admitted that the kindness of his friends had been "the compensating part of the business." [80] Among the notable contributors was Arthur Symons, who told of his pleasure in sending a subscription and of his personal indebtedness to Furnivall.[81] William Poel, the Shakespearean director, agreed that "the 'Browning Society' was certainly never founded for people to make money out of it, and no one should have offered to do work for it with that view." [82] William Michael Rossetti, brother of Dante Gabriel, sent a check, with the hope that Furnivall would find "he himself has little, or even nothing, to disburse." [83] Holman Hunt, the painter, contributed a guinea, though he asked to remain anonymous.[84] Some of the other contributors were Alma Murray, Frederick Wedmore, Edward Gonner, and Richard Garnett.[85] All, it should be noted, already had some connection with the Browning Society.

One of the last to send a subscription was James Russell Lowell, who had returned to the United States in 1885 from his ambassadorship in England. He wrote to Dykes Campbell:

> I have seen your letter *in re* Furnivall & am much moved by it. I do not know the facts of the case (of which I had not heard before),

but I do know that our friend can ill afford to pay £250 & that chiefly because he has devoted himself unselfishly & unflinchingly to the interests of scholarship & of other people. No living man has done so much as he to promote the intelligent study of our language by supplying us with the necessary material. . . .[86]

Lowell's check for £10 was passed on anonymously, as he had requested. On March 20 Furnivall wrote to Campbell: "Thanks for the cheque [Lowell's], & your gratifying extract [from his letter]. Very kind of the anonymous Donor. Please tell him that I feel his kindness & delicacy." [87]

Even Browning took an interest in the case. As early as February 6, Campbell told of discussing the Furnivall Fund with him: "Of course he is very sympathetic and he & Miss [Sarianna] Browning desire to be associated in any scheme which may be planned." [88] Browning later wrote to Furnivall that the trial had confirmed his own "supreme contempt" for lawyers and added that Outram was "just the fellow to make money out of a kick, the beggar!" [89] But he was more candid about Furnivall's faults in a letter to another friend:

Do you see what a scrape poor Furnivall's incontinence of tongue (in the witness-box!) has brought him? So can a man be really in the right, as to feeling, and the wrong, as to the expression of it. . . . He was naturally angry, but played into the fellow's hands by folly enough.[90]

And in a letter to his son, February 4, 1888, he wrote:

By the papers, we see that Furnivall has got into a scrape, and been condemned to pay damages and costs—as usual, all through his unruliness of tongue,—the judge saying that it was his own evidence, or way of giving it in the witness-box, which made the case, originally a trifling one, serious. He was in the right, and put himself in the wrong by post-cards and strong language.[91]

Again, on February 25, Browning described the case to Pen and his wife Fannie:

You may have observed poor Furnivall's misfortune, in the action brought against him for libel. He was morally in the right, legally in the wrong, and socially—as to prudent behavior [—] altogether foolish. His friends are coming forward to help him. He had only to say, in the witness-box, "I was indignant, as who could help being? but I used hasty language which I now find was improper."—instead of which he repeated it more offensively than at first. His friends understand this, and are coming generously forward—as he unluckily needs.[92]

By the end of February Furnivall was able to repay his sister[93] and F. S. Ellis, who had also lent him £100. He was, furthermore, "richer by [his friends'] expression of sympathy," as the *Pall Mall Gazette* had predicted he would be. The final comment on the whole episode, however, surely belongs to the essayist Augustine Birrell, who made this perceptive observation:

> I am very glad to have an opportunity of sending as I do herewith a small sum for the good Doctor's benefit. None the less I quite agree with [the] Jury & with the observation of the plaintiff's Counsel that life would be intolerable if people were left free to denounce one another as Liars because they happen to be of that opinion. It doesn't matter how well founded the opinion may be. Therefore if the doctor is only taught to hold his tongue & withhold his pen the Trial will not have been in vain.[94]

But, he added, could a man like Furnivall be taught anything? The answer is obviously no: one of his last statements about the libel suit was phrased—to quote Halliwell-Phillipps, one of Furnivall's earlier antagonists—in language as "coarse and impertinent" as ever. "I only hope that my Solicitor'll be able to cut the 100 off O's sol[icit]or's costs of £156," Furnivall declared in a letter to Slater. "The Bill is a regular Swindle." [95]

*   *   *

That Frederick Furnivall, more than most men, had the capacity for forming warm friendships cannot be doubted; the testimony of his contemporaries, almost without exception, creates a picture of a man who was generous, lovable, and childlike in his simplicity. Yet in his public controversies he became a fierce, implacable polemicist. How does one resolve the paradox? Sir John R. Seeley, a member of the New Shakspere Society, addressed himself to the puzzle and offered (to Furnivall himself) this solution:

> You know very well you are an eccentric fellow. Now the difficulty with eccentricity always is that people who only read you without knowing you personally cannot understand it. *I* can enjoy your oddities of language because I know how characteristic they are, but it is very different with many members of the [New Shakspere] Society who perhaps never spoke to you.[96]

But "eccentricity" alone cannot explain the slashing attacks Furnivall made upon his opponents in public. One must also take into account his exuberance and zest for conflict, traits exaggerated by his glorification of "manliness." "Straight speaking, straight hitting" suited him best because they represented an open, frank manner of expression becoming to a man. That others should take offense at his plain speech perpetually amazed him. He did not realize that, in the minds of many, outspokenness and bad manners are synonymous.

Finally, it may be observed that in both the Shilling Selection affair and the Outram case, Furnivall lost his temper because he thought he detected self-seeking in others. In each instance, he was the victim of his own limited viewpoint. Being quixotically unselfish himself, he was incapable of seeing that the behavior of others could not, under the circumstances, be always selfless; he was astonished and annoyed, in other words, to discover that most people were quite different from himself.

Whatever the motives, Furnivall's quarrels were unseemly and did the Browning Society no good. Both of these that we have just examined, of course, lay only on the periphery of the society's activities, but his combative instincts in time touched and influenced everything: the papers and discussions at the meetings, the entertainments, the books written by members, particularly the public pronouncements of the society. Above all, his aggressive championing of agnosticism must bear a large share of the blame for introducing into the Browning Society meetings the theological questions upon which it eventually foundered. But that, as Kipling says, is another story, and it will be told in a later chapter.

CHAPTER III

SOME REPRESENTATIVE BROWNINGITES—I

> The "study" of Browning takes strong hold upon theorists,
> analysts, didacticians, who care little for poetry in itself, and
> who, like Chinese artists, pay more respect to the facial dimen-
> sions of his Muse than to her essential beauty and the divine
> light of her eyes.
>
> —E. C. Stedman[1]

FROM THE MOMENT of its inception, the activities and membership of
the Browning Society were evaluated by the press with elaborate sarcasm, and during those years certain misconceptions about the
Browningites took root which have survived to the present day. The
Saturday Review, for instance, charged that Browning's "most appreciative admirers" were not to be found in the society, and several decades later Edmund Gosse, who nursed a passionate hatred of Furnivall, claimed that Browning had asked Gosse and his other friends not
to join the society.[2] It is a fact that a few of Browning's intimates,
such as Gosse and Dowden, declined to become members, but many
others who knew Browning well (better, indeed, than Gosse) did belong: Alfred Domett, Milsand, Mrs. FitzGerald, Mrs. Orr, Mrs. Bronson. In the case of Mrs. Bronson, Browning even acted as an intermediary by forwarding her subscription and address to Furnivall.[3]
Nevertheless the legend persists, for in our century it is still fashionable to describe the Browningites as "ineffective eccentrics." [4] That
eccentricity abounded in the Browning Society one can scarcely deny;
but many talented, intelligent individuals were included among its
members as well.

Another rumor widely circulated during the eighties was that the
members of the Browning Society were slightly dreamy aesthetes—

"Hampstead professors, and long haired and lanky legged and long eared young men and women," as one journalist phrased it.[5] Actually, this description misses the mark so badly that it can only be understood by recalling that Oscar Wilde was the talk of London in this decade, and the almost simultaneous appearance in 1881 of the Browning Society and Gilbert and Sullivan's *Patience*, which most took to be a satirical portrait of Wilde, led some observers to confuse the two phenomena. The Browning Society, according to Bernard Shaw, was "reputedly an assembly of longhaired esthetes, but really [it was] a conventicle where evangelistic elderly ladies discussed their religion with Furnivall." [6] Though Shaw's statement exaggerates for comic effect, it is essentially true. The Browning Society members were, for the most part, devout, earnest, middle-class people, often with evangelical leanings. There were no working men, at least not among the leadership (William G. Kingsland was perhaps as close to the working class as any), and the few members of the aristocracy who belonged merely lent prestige by allowing their names to appear as "vice-presidents."

But one despairs of formulating an adequate generalized description of the members, for no one kind of personality completely dominated the society; indeed, much of the unconscious humor of its proceedings arose out of confrontations between such opposite types as Shaw and Miss Whitehead, one of the maiden ladies whom he described so vividly in his later remarks about the society. In the Browning Society clergymen jostled against agnostics, pious spinsters against famous scholars. Is it possible, given this heterogeneous group, even to categorize the Browningites? It is, of course, but the categories must be loose, overlapping, and tentative. The following list may nonetheless serve to provide us with a cross-section view, admittedly incomplete, of the major varieties of Browningites:

(1) Browning's intimate acquaintances, especially of his middle years. With the obvious exception of Mrs. Orr, these people tended to be unobtrusive members who joined the society only as an affirmation of their personal respect and regard for Browning.

(2) Writers, mostly young men yet to achieve success, such as Shaw and Arthur Symons. James Thomson also belongs in this category, though he was at the end rather than the beginning of his career. As a group, they were probably the most intelligent members of the society, but they never were in the majority and seldom participated in the decisions of the twenty-member committee.

(3) Scholars and teachers, including Hiram Corson, Edwin Johnson, J. B. Bury, R. G. Moulton, and Hall Griffin. Able men, they made public appearances without really becoming an effective part of the society's executive machinery.

(4) Bibliophiles, who exercised an influence out of all proportion to their numbers, since they became involved in the society's publishing ventures. The two most notable examples are T. J. Wise and Walter Slater.

(5) Women. As Shaw said, it was the "pious old ladies" whose subscriptions kept the society going.[7] James Thomson recorded the following notes in his diary about the audience at the first meeting of the Browning Society (October 28, 1881): "Miss [Frances] Buss & scholars; four lady nurses from Univ[ersit]y Col[lege] Hosp[ita]l, Miss [Eleanor] Marx. . . ."[8] Joshua Kirkman, in his address that evening, also remarked upon "the great proportion of *clergymen* and *ladies*! About 2 to 1 on the whole."[9] It was the era of the New Woman, who demanded to be treated as an intellectual equal, and the Browning Society represented one of the very few outlets for her restless energies. Hence the female Browningite was often an unusual woman—"remarkable," as her contemporaries would say—aggressively committed to the ideal of female education and culture.

(6) Clergymen, mostly Anglican, with a sprinkling of Dissenters. The overtly religious subject matter of many of Browning's poems accounts for their presence in the society. The Reverend Mr. Kirkman was undoubtedly justified in linking them with the ladies, for the two groups not only comprised, together, a majority of the membership but also had in common an unrelenting passion for discovering moral lessons in Browning's poetry. Like Robert Frost in this century, Browning had the misfortune—at least it seems a misfortune in retrospect—of attracting a large number of readers who prized his poetry for nonliterary reasons. In Frost's case, he has been too zealously praised by readers who see his work as embodying what they suppose to be the traditional American values of optimism and good sense; Frost enthusiasts have used this attitude, in its crudest form, as a platform from which to denounce poetry of other Americans like Pound and Eliot, who presumably have been "corrupted" by European values. Similarly, the Browningites, especially the clergymen and the more devout females, chose to regard Browning as a defender of religious orthodoxy and ignored all other elements in his poetry just as single-mindedly as Frost's chauvinistic readers gloss over his darker, more tragic moods. In the end, the ladies and their clerical counterparts produced an atmosphere of such cloying religiosity that many writers and scholars abandoned the Browning Society, which then

strangled on its own theological preoccupations. But in the early years the orthodox were not so oppressively powerful, and the members of a literary or academic bent had their say as well.

(7) Finally, the hundreds of members in England and America who never attended the London meetings but provided essential financial support. This book will not often speak of these people, since we can know nothing about them except their names, but in distant cities and villages they carefully read the transactions of the Browning Society, and when, after 1888, they were not pleased with what they read there—or perhaps merely lost interest in it—the society was immediately in trouble. The imagination of Browning was captivated by this picture of a vast company of silent, anonymous readers scattered throughout the land. "Exactly what has touched me," he wrote Miss Elizabeth West, "is the sudden assemblage of men and women to whose names, for the most part, I am a stranger." [10]

The list, of course, is not comprehensive. It fails to include such conspicuous members as George Barnett Smith (journalist), William G. Kingsland (proofreader), Dr. Edward Berdoe (physician), and J. T. Nettleship (painter). It omits, in addition, another large and important class of Browningites—those who declined to join the Browning Society but who sometimes supported its activities. Edward Dowden, for example, decided to run the risk of Furnivall's disapproval by staying outside the society, though he did take the chair at one meeting.[11] The Reverend F. W. Farrar also had to explain to Furnivall in 1881 that he was not "snubbing" the proposal to join but that he was already a member of far too many societies; besides, he doubted whether a Browning Society was the best means of making Browning more widely read.[12] Later, however, he presided at one meeting and spoke at another. Henry W. Longfellow, replying to a long, eloquent appeal from Furnivall, refused to become a member on the grounds that he was reluctant to join any society whose meetings he could not attend.[13] Sir Frederic Leighton, the well-known painter, offered perhaps the most cogent objections to membership:

. . . I fear that I cannot—to speak quite candidly—wholly sympathize with the idea of a 'Browning Society'—or any society that has for its objects the pressing on the public the merits of a poet of great Genius who is alive to speak for himself, now as forty or more years ago, and who is read in every country where English is spoken —indeed I very much doubt whether such action is quite respectful.[14]

But lest he be accused of not admiring Browning's intellectual qualities, Leighton agreed to serve as a vice-president of the society any-
way.

Like all stereotypes, the "representative Browningite" becomes
more elusive under close scrutiny. Members came into the society for
an amazing variety of motives and saw Browning and his poetry from
many points of view; but, in the end, a certain shadowy likeness of
the Victorian Browning enthusiast does emerge, though it must be a
composite portrait rather than a description of any single member of
the society. In this chapter and the next we shall scrutinize the careers of seven notable Browningites. They will include an alcoholic
poet, a devout physician, an allegorizing artist, a brilliant critic, an
ambitious young book-collector, an adoring Sunday school teacher,
and a spirit-haunted professor. A strange and incongruous group indeed—but all were members of the Browning Society.

James Thomson (*1834–82*)

Robert Browning was thought by his contemporaries to be the most
optimistic of all the English poets; James Thomson ("B.V."), the author of *The City of Dreadful Night*, was described by his friend and
biographer, Bertram Dobell, as "the laureate of pessimism." [15] The two
men had apparently little in common. Browning was vigorous and
healthy until his death at the age of seventy-seven; Frank Harris,
meeting Thomson—then forty-six years old—for the first time in
1881, noted that he was "shrunken together, prematurely aged; the
face was shrivelled, small, the skin lined and wrinkled, the expression
querulous; his clothes were shabby and illfitting; taken all in all he
looked an old wastrel." [16] Browning was already at this time regarded
as one of the two major poets of the age; in his home at 19 Warwick
Crescent he received countless admirers, and almost every evening he
dined with the most wealthy and distinguished members of London
society. Thomson, an impoverished alcoholic, was rarely seen in public and moved wearily from one rented lodging to another. Not surprisingly, Browning and Thomson never met.

Yet for all this disparity of temperament and circumstance, James
Thomson was deeply attracted to Browning, both as a man and a poet.
What he wrote about Browning, in fact, provides a curious revelation
of Thomson's uneasy atheism and his personal and poetic despair.
Browning was, in effect, a mirror into which he looked and saw his
own deficiencies; Browning symbolized to Thomson a serenity and
fullness of experience which he himself had never achieved. But if
there is a poignancy running through all of Thomson's statements on

Browning, the circumstances under which the last of these statements was written—for the Browning Society in 1882—afford a certain comic relief.

Disregarding for the moment Thomson's private motives for praising his fellow poet, one must observe his critical perceptiveness in recognizing Browning's genius so early. Unlike most of the English reading public, Thomson saw immediately the greatness of *Men and Women* (1855), though he was only twenty-one years old when it appeared. Several years later he passed his copy on to a young friend with these words: "I take the liberty of sending you by this post two volumes of verse which fell into my hands some time back. The author, Robert Browning, is about the strongest and manliest of our living poets." He added, in language that marked him as already a zealous Browningite, "Should you care enough for Browning to wish thoroughly to comprehend him, I shall of course be happy to render you what little assistance may be in my power toward the clearing up of obscurities." [17]

That Thomson's later poetry occasionally reflects the matter and manner of Browning has often been asserted,[18] and it is scarcely necessary here to cite particular lines to support the claim. It is well known that his work bore traces of Shelley, Leopardi, and Blake, among others; doubtless his very inability to assimilate these influences smoothly into the texture of his verse is the identifying mark of a second-rate poet. It would hardly be surprising, therefore, if the distant voice of Browning, whom he read so enthusiastically, should sometimes be heard in the cadences of his poetry. What is perhaps more relevant is that Thomson's periodical criticism displayed a persistent admiration for Browning. In 1865, for example, he described Browning as the one living poet who was "exerting sublime energies for us" and "exercising influence and commanding homage of which a lofty-minded and strong-minded man may justly be proud." [19] In 1876 he compared Browning with George Meredith: both, he wrote, were "quite unappreciated by the general public" yet were "ranked with the very highest by a select few." [20] It was a point on which Thomson, who was virtually unknown to Victorian readers, was uniquely qualified to sympathize with Browning.

Even as he wrote thus of Browning's small reputation, however, Thomson was forced to qualify his observation; such had been the state of affairs, he explained, "until of late years." Beginning in the early 1860's, the poetry of Browning at last received the recognition that had been so long denied it.[21] As if to redress the neglect of the past, many readers now developed a partisan devotion to his works that bordered on fanaticism. By the eighties there were complaints of the "Browning cult" and "Browning madness." Perhaps the most colorful manifestation of this belated interest in Browning was the Browning Society itself, which, in a highly amusing fashion, was to draw from Thomson his fullest and final observations on Browning's art and thought.

In March of 1881 Thomson, his health seriously deteriorating, met J. W. Barrs and his sister Harriet, who invited him to visit their country home near Leicester in the early summer. This he did, but when Thomson returned to London in August, one piece of mail that awaited him contained rather startling news. It was a proof of the first prospectus of the Browning Society, sent to Thomson for his approval, since his name appeared in it in three places: Furnivall had listed him as a member, had appointed him to the society's executive committee, and had scheduled a paper by him for January 27, 1882. The proof was Furnivall's characteristically blunt method of securing assent, but it unfortunately had not been forwarded to Leicester, and now Thomson, quite against his will, was saddled with new responsibilities.[22] He took it in good humor, as a letter to Barrs on August 28 shows:

> The enclosed [prospectus] will show you what that headlong and masterful young cuss of fifty, Furnivall, has committed me to utterly without my consent or knowledge. I am not only a member of his Browning Soc[iet]y, it seems, but on the Committee, & moreover I have to read a paper on a specified evening. This last imposition is atrocious. With work to do at my ease I may get thro' it some time or other; but fix me to a precise date, & my impulse to bolt or jib is almost irresistible. Besides how am I to prepare a paper for the 27th Janry., when Dick has threatened to have a Xmas pudding that shall lay me by the heels for a month? She ought in fairness to compose my paper as well as that stupendous indigestibility.[23]

The joking prophecy of his indisposition in January, it should be noted, was to be quite literally and grimly fulfilled.

He also wrote immediately to Furnivall, telling him that he could promise only a half-hour paper; Furnivall, to Thomson's astonishment, replied that he was counting on a paper about an hour and a quarter long, followed by a half hour of discussion. Thomson, recording this latest information in his diary, punctuated it with multiple exclamation points.[24]

Prompted perhaps by Furnivall's "imposition" and by a journalist's habit of exploiting his copy for more than one purpose, Thomson set to work on an essay about Browning's *The Ring and The Book*, which he submitted to the *Gentleman's Magazine* on September 21. It was a hymn of praise for Browning's poem, which he called "stupendous," "gigantic," "charged and surcharged with learning, knowledge, ever-active subtle intellect, ever-vital passion." The essay was published in December.[25]

In the meantime, Thomson received on October 14 an invitation to dine with Furnivall the following Sunday afternoon. He accepted, and after dinner the pair walked to the home of Miss Hickey, who told Thomson that the Browning Society already had fifty-nine members— "all doubtless highly respectable people barring myself," he explained wryly in a letter to his sister-in-law, "so I shall be in good company." [26] The next day he finished the first draft of his paper for the society. The following week he bought the society's first publication, a reprint of Browning's essay on Shelley, and on the evening of October 28 he attended its first meeting, held in the Botanic Theatre of University College. Furnivall, in his introductory remarks, alluded to Thomson as "a poet of high mark himself" who would soon tell the members much about Browning's art.[27] Thomson wrote a careful account of the meeting in his diary, indicating that he listened attentively to the Reverend Mr. Kirkman and others that evening, but whether he met with the committee just before the meeting is uncertain.

Thomson in November returned to the Barrs home, where pleasant holiday distractions prevented him from producing a fair copy of his Browning Society paper until after the New Year. This was the last fully happy and productive period in his life; by January Thomson was back in London and drinking more heavily than ever. Several days before January 27, he sent his paper to Furnivall with the explanation that illness would prevent his reading it in person to the society. The paper which he submitted, "Notes on the Genius of Robert Browning," was, as might be expected, highly appreciative. Browning's poetry, Thomson wrote, should be compared with the work of Chaucer, Rabelais, Shakespeare, Ben Jonson, Goethe, Scott, and Balzac; like them, "Browning drinks in the living world at every pore." Even his alleged obscurity results from an "overplus," not an "insufficiency," of intellect and energy.

The section of the paper expressing the deepest feeling, however, was that which dealt with Browning's religion. One of the characteristics of Browning's genius, he felt, was "his profound, passionate, living, triumphant faith in Christ, and in the immortality and ultimate redemption of every human soul in and through Christ." [28] Though an atheist himself, Thomson thought highly of the practical consequences of Browning's Christian faith:

> I look up to Browning as one of the very few men known to me by their works who, with most cordial energy and invincible resolution, have lived thoroughly throughout the whole of their being, to the uttermost verge of all their capacities, in his case truly colossal; lived and wrought thoroughly in sense and soul and intellect; lived at home in all realms of nature and human nature, art and literature: whereas nearly all of us are really alive in but a small portion of our so much smaller beings, and drag wearily toward the grave our for-the-most-part dead selves, dead from the suicidal poison of misuse and atrophy of disuse. Confident and rejoicing in the storm and stress of the struggle, he has conquered life instead of being conquered by it; a victory so rare as to be almost unique, especially among poets in these latter days.[29]

One of the faithless, defeated poets to whom Thomson referred was of course himself. Unlike Browning, he had never conquered life; poverty and a deep despondency had conspired to crush his vitality and health. His years of work for Charles Bradlaugh's *National Reformer* had served only to increase his disillusionment with militant secularism and atheism. Yet the skepticism that was a source of despair to Thomson merely provided a sense of release from religious burdens for other unbelievers like Furnivall, who was quite dismayed by Thomson's paper. Furnivall had, in fact, been advertising Thomson as an atheistic Browningite, for the Browning Society was already acquiring a reputation of Christian piety in its membership and papers, and Furnivall was eager to demonstrate that "tho men like Mr. James Thomson and myself don't care for the special Christian or doctrinal side of Browning's work, we can yet feel the worth of his teaching as a man or thinker, and admire his imaginative power, his strength and subtlety." [30] He was deeply disappointed, therefore, by Thomson's unexpected sympathy for Browning's religious position, and he wrote him a long letter about it the day before the meeting.

> I like your Paper very much, & think very highly of it, tho' you really are wrong about Br.g's Xtianity.
> It's quite true that several times dramatically he has spoken as a Xtian, more especially during his wife's life, & while her influence lasted strong upon him. But he is a Theist, & is *not* a *Trinitarian*; he does *not* hold Christ to be God.

Letting alone the fact that no doctrinal Xtian could have written *La Saisiaz* without putting his definite Xtian doctrine into it, my friend Mrs. Orr (Sir F. Leighton's sister) who has known R.B. as a sister for 12 years, has heard him discuss the subject with friends; & he has distinctly said that he holds Xt to be a man & *not* God. He'd willingly go on his knees to Xt as one of the best, if not the best, of men, but not as God. There is nothing in his poetry—*Saul* or anywhere else—that can't be explained by B's dramatic Xtianity & his intense belief in a personal God, in immortality, & the ultimate redemption [of] every human soul.

Miss Lewis [who was also to deliver a paper on January 27] had a strong Xtian bit in her Paper. By the arguments of me & others, she has been at least so shaken in her point that she has cut out the Xtian section. I wish I c[oul]d have a chance of arguing the point with you before your Paper is read. If you'll send me a card to-night, I'll come to you at any time on Friday.[31]

Thomson was naturally in no condition to discuss theology with Furnivall, and the paper was read at the meeting as written, by Furnivall himself, who complained that he was obliged to deliver it too rapidly for lack of time. "Nevertheless it was most heartily applauded at the end," he reported to Thomson a few days later, "& all your humorous bits were caught up at once & cheered & laught with. Miss Hickey, Mrs. Orr, [J. T.] Nettleship, & all our folks agree that yours was the best Paper we had had." [32] Miss Hickey did indeed like the paper: she wrote on February 3 to Professor Corson that it "pleased me more than any we have yet had." [33] Another admirer present at the meeting was H. H. Hood Barrs, who sent this account of it to J. W. Barrs on January 28: "Went to Browning Soc[iet]y last night. Had a maudlin spinster's [Miss Lewis'] paper to begin with, & then B.V.'s wine of the gods—B.V. rather startled Canon [F.W.] Farrar with his paper. Of course the author was *not* there. He is however *much* better." [34] In fact, the only voice of dissent at the meeting was that of Furnivall, who predictably registered an anti-Christian protest after he read the paper. Despite his personal reservations, however, he was able to tell Thomson later that even Browning was "very pleazd at your kind words about him." [35]

Furnivall, recognizing Thomson's desperate financial state, made repeated efforts to publish the paper in some periodical. He submitted it to the *Fortnightly Review, Contemporary Review, Temple Bar*, and *Fraser's Magazine*, in each instance unsuccessfully.[36] Thomson on March 10 wrote to Bertram Dobell, "Furnivall, having vainly proposed my Browning Notes in the most zealous way to various periodicals, is going to print them at length in Society's transactions." [37] Yet if Furnivall was generous in his attempts to help Thomson, he was also remarkably insensitive to the seriousness of Thomson's illness. On February 28, for instance, he wrote to Thomson, who was once again with the Barrs family at Leicester, and urged him to start a branch of the Browning Society there[38]—this at the very time Thomson was on the verge of his final illness and was alienating himself from the only friends he had who could have helped him. He returned to their home one evening so intoxicated that Harriet Barrs refused to let him in and forced him to spend the night in the coach house. The next morning Thomson, stricken with embarrassment and remorse, left hastily for London. There his drinking became so uncontrolled and his behavior so violent that he was soon beyond the aid of even the Barrs family. He died a sordid, agonizing death on June 3, 1882.

The paper on Browning, then, was written during the last creative phase of Thomson's erratic career. He was, of course, in this instance a most reluctant critic, and there is an appropriate irony in the fact that the Browning Society's *Papers*, to which he had contributed so unwillingly, published one of the few tributes that appeared after his death.[39] But there is no real incongruity in Thomson's final rhapsodical praise of Browning, whom he had long admired for intellectual and spiritual qualities he himself lacked.

Dr. Edward Berdoe (1833–1916)

At the sixth annual business meeting of the Browning Society on June 24, 1887, it was announced to those present that a novel "full of Browning teaching" was in the press and would be published in September.[40] Written under the pseudonym "AEsculapius Scalpel," *St. Bernard's: The Romance of a Medical Student* recounted the experiences of a noble and religious young man who falls among evil companions; he is exposed, furthermore, to such "abuses" of the medical world as vivisection and advanced religious views. Just as he reaches his moral and emotional nadir at the end of a night of dissipation, some inspiring lines from Browning's *Paracelsus* flash into his troubled mind. His childhood faith and his former rectitude are promptly recovered, and soon order is restored to the wayward life.

The author of this curious novel was none other than Dr. Edward Berdoe, who was described during his lifetime as "the greatest authority on Browning that we have";[41] and if the plot of *St. Bernard's* seems implausible, we must remind ourselves that it is almost entirely autobiographical: Dr. Berdoe was, by his own testimony, drawn back to the Christian faith through hearing a lecture on *Paracelsus*. To a

REPRESENTATIVE BROWNINGITES — I   / 61

twentieth-century reader, such a conversion will perhaps seem to be a grotesque fulfillment of Matthew Arnold's prediction that poetry would someday assume the functions of religion; but Berdoe's experience was so characteristically the experience of a Victorian Browningite that an examination of it will reveal much about the religious temper of the time and about the peculiar influence that Browning exercised over his more enthusiastic readers.

Like the protagonist of *St. Bernard's*, Berdoe abandoned Christianity, despite his early training for the dissenting ministry, after an exposure to agnostic scientific thought in medical school. Having served as a physician in both the Crimean War and the American Civil War, he then set up a practice in the East End of London, though his services were also in demand in the more fashionable areas of the city.[42] Sometime during 1883, however, a small event changed the course of his life. Moncure Conway, the American Unitarian minister who held the pastorate of South Place Chapel (where Browning's friend W. J. Fox had formerly preached), spoke frequently on Browning's poetry, for he was a zealous Browningite and a familiar figure at the society's meetings. Berdoe one day listened to Conway lecture at South Place on *Paracelsus*, a poem perfectly calculated to interest a physician. The effect upon Berdoe, as he tells the story, was immediate and profound:

> On the following day I purchased a set of Browning's works. The first poem I read was *Saul*. I soon recognized that I was in the grasp of a strong hand, and as I continued to read *Paracelsus, Men and Women*, and *A Death in the Desert*, the feeling came over me that in Browning I had found my religious teacher, one who could put me right on a hundred points which had troubled my mind for many years, and which had ultimately caused me to abandon the Christian Faith.[43]

Instead of attending religious services, as most converts would have done, Berdoe turned for instruction and inspiration to the meetings of the Browning Society. He wrote promptly to Miss Hickey, who recognized an extraordinarily ardent Browningite and put him at once on the society's committee. He was soon lecturing at South Place Chapel and elsewhere on "Browning's Message to His Time," and on March 30, 1883, he made his first recorded remarks at a Browning Society meeting—remarks that reflected his own strange conversion: Browning's poems, Berdoe said, were "the best work on modern theology." [44] Later in one of his books he was to boast that he had "attended nearly every meeting of the Browning Society from its inauguration" [45]

—a claim that amused many reviewers—and it must surely be true, for the society's published transactions record more contributions, both papers and informal observations during the discussion periods, from Berdoe than any other member except Furnivall and possibly William Revell.

At the meeting of January 25, 1884, Berdoe revealed a new interest. Turning aside for the moment from Browning's theological teachings, he delivered a "medical man's view" of Paracelsus.[46] As chairman at the next meeting he continued to expand the idea: Browning, he told his listeners, "is the scientific poet of the age." [47] Though none of the other speakers that evening agreed with him, Berdoe was not to be discouraged. This interest—or rather compulsion, for he brought up the subject incessantly—culminated in a paper which he delivered to the society on April 24, 1885, "Browning as a Scientific Poet." Berdoe held that in Browning's works the poetic and scientific methods "are truly combined." Browning is "intimately acquainted with the physical sciences," as every poet of the future must be, and therefore he is especially equipped to teach us that agnosticism is "far less in harmony with the truly scientific habit of mind than the broad and noble conception of Christianity" [48] which he presents to us. Bernard Shaw, who consistently played the role of devil's advocate within the society, replied to Berdoe's thesis that evening with particularly devastating force. He remarked that "though he had hitherto regarded himself as an arrant sciolist in scientific matters, he had picked up in the course of his general reading all the knowledge of the undulatory theory of light, the phenomena of double refraction, &c., which Dr. Berdoe had praised Browning so highly for possessing." [49] Browning himself, after reading the paper in its published form, wrote a friendly but slightly evasive letter to Berdoe in which he praised his disciple for "the Paper in which you so generously estimate my attempts to make use of the few materials of a scientific nature I have had any opportunity of collecting: would they were of more importance! . . ." [50]

If this episode clearly demonstrates Berdoe's lack of any sense of proportion, his behavior at a later meeting of the society shows a surprising absence of Christian charity as well. During the early months of 1888, Berdoe's views on Browning and the Browning Society came under increasingly frequent attack from another member, Edward Gonner, who, like Shaw, delighted in annoying the pious. For example, when on January 27 Berdoe suggested that occasional simple papers be read for the benefit of new members, who were young and inexperienced in the mysteries of Browning, Gonner retorted that "he really did not think they were constructed on the plan of an Elementary Board school. Their object was to investigate, not to teach new members." [51] Gonner often complained about Berdoe's religious preoccupations and "deprecated the introduction of theological discussions in this Society." [52]

The quarrel at last came into the open on June 29, when, at the society's annual business meeting, Gonner introduced an amendment that the society be disbanded at the close of the 1888–89 session.[53] "He had an idea that this Society was instituted with something of a literary aim and basis," Gonner said; "but if it was as a kind of auxiliary missionary society for spreading abroad the gospel of Browning, then he would regard himself as being out of place as a member of it." Besides, he added, he still possessed sufficient reverence to object to the bandying about of sacred subjects in their meetings. Berdoe, who at once interpreted this speech as yet another harassment from an agnostic enemy, responded by savagely attacking Gonner's character. He declared that Gonner, though he had "sneered without exception at every paper" and "had dealt very unkindly with the Society from first to last," had never read a paper of his own; he was therefore unqualified to make any complaints. Shaw, however, came to Gonner's defense by seconding the amendment, though

> on some points he wished to dissociate himself from Mr. Gonner. Mr. Gonner spoke of his strain of reverence. He (Mr. Shaw) had not a spark of reverence, and he did not like good taste. He liked Dr. Berdoe because he always spoke in bad taste (laughter).

Berdoe's bad taste in this instance had a damaging effect upon the society, even though Gonner's amendment was soundly defeated. Gonner himself, long a leader and supporter of the society, dropped out of its activities very shortly, as did several of the other most intelligent members, and until its dissolution in 1892 the discussions at the meetings became more and more aridly theological. Berdoe told a journalist years later that "the Browning Society was broken up through some of its members taking up and maintaining [the] theory" that Browning "was a great religious teacher and theologian." [54] The truth is, of course, that his own spirit of violent, intolerant partisanship was partially responsible for destroying the society.

Berdoe's bad taste, in a critical rather than a personal sense, revealed itself on other occasions in the Browning Society and in his books. Probably his most conspicuous weakness as a critic was his inability to admit that Browning had any faults: if Browning's plays would never be popular, the contemporary stage was to blame; if

Berdoe found *Fifine at the Fair* difficult to understand, he "must not confess before this audience [the Browning Society] that Browning was unintelligible"; if the later poems seemed "hazy," it was because Browning "had an enlarged vision, and saw more round things than formerly." [55] Yet the number of Browning's poems that he rejected is startling. "James Lee's Wife" he found "not, as a whole, satisfactory." [56] The subject of "Ivàn Ivànovitch" was "extremely terrible" and therefore distasteful.[57] "Mr. Sludge, 'the Medium'" was not one of his favorite poems.[58] He thought "In a Balcony" "one of the most idiotic love-stories he ever read," and he of course disliked all love stories, good or bad.[59] "Andrea del Sarto" was an especially repulsive poem:

> As for the man Andrea, he had the most profound contempt for him; he seemed to him a drivelling imbecile. Just imagine painting a picture for one's wife's lover, who was whistling outside! He (Dr. B.) would have kicked him! [60]

Some years later, in fact, Berdoe made what must surely be the most damaging admission ever uttered by a leading Browning critic:

> I own his style is very rough; I don't always like it. Indeed, I sometimes think I like him so much, just because at times he isn't a poet, for *poetry, as such, doesn't appeal to me greatly.* I like scientific men because they teach. Browning is a philosopher and a scientist, and I like his philosophy and science. [Italics supplied.] [61]

Yet if Berdoe's admiration for the poetry was not unqualified, his extravagant regard for Browning as a religious teacher never flagged. Indeed, at times Berdoe's rapturous praises of Browning seemed almost to border on blasphemy. Commenting on another literary critic, he wrote: "He does not attempt to force upon his readers any strained construction of his own but sinks himself in his Master [Browning] & makes us know that we are hearing *him.*" [62] The capitalization of "Master" would, to most Christians, suggest an allusion to Christ himself, but Browningites like Berdoe always capitalized it when referring to Browning as well. In a similar vein, he once advised E. H. Blakeney that his students, when "trials come & doubts assail" in the future, would be thankful for "this learning [Browning's poetry] more than any other save the Holy Scriptures." [63]

Berdoe wrote four books on Browning, as well as editing another, and these, like his remarks at the Browning Society, are curiously phrased in the language of muscular Christianity spiced with occasional medical jargon. The first of them, *Browning's Message to His Time* (1890), consists largely of his Browning Society papers, with the chief emphasis on Browning's "scientific" and religious ideas. It is gratifying to discover that contemporary reviewers remained unconvinced, as had the members of the society, that Browning was a "scientific" poet, though all readily agreed that scientific lore sometimes appears in his work.[64]

The Browning Cyclopaedia (1892), on the other hand, was a more ambitious volume: Berdoe described it as the first "serious attempt that has been made to deal with the whole of Browning's published works." [65] In actuality, the *Cyclopaedia*, though it contains some useful paraphrases and information, is a digressive, pedantic exploration of all the byways of Browning scholarship, a huge, inchoate mass of historical and philological materials compiled by a man who was obviously industrious but lacking in all sense of proportion.[66] It is especially notable for its reflection of Berdoe's private demonology: the article on "vivisection," for example, is twice as long as that on "My Last Duchess," and the sinister cripple in "Childe Roland" is seen as an atheistic vivisectionist. The book, furthermore, is riddled with errors and wild conjectures. E. K. Chambers, complaining in a letter to the *Academy* about Berdoe's faulty knowledge of Greek, alluded sarcastically to his boast of having attended all the Browning Society meetings: "I venture to think that his time would have been better occupied in acquiring the rudiments of the Greek language." [67] Astonishing as it may seem, however, the *Cyclopaedia* is still in print today, and one can only conclude that its very bulk and pedantry have succeeded in intimidating many readers.

Berdoe's other books are shorter but reveal with equal clarity his deficiencies as critic. In 1895 he edited *Browning Studies*, a selection of the Browning Society's papers, which of course included only those papers with a heavily philosophical or moral content (as well as one paper by Mrs. Glazebrook with which Browning had publicly disagreed). Similarly, *Browning and the Christian Faith* (1896) is such a blatant example of message-hunting in poetry that another Browningite of unquestioned loyalty, Helen Clarke, was compelled to say of it:

> He chooses a certain number of passages from Browning as texts, having divorced them utterly from their connection either as links in an argument or as the expressions of opinion of individual characters, and builds upon these texts a system of theology which he bolsters up with quotations from various theological authorities.[68]

Berdoe's last work, in contrast, can only be regarded as a belated attempt to make his own *Cyclopaedia* readable. Entitled *A Primer of Browning* (1904), it is simply a brief, poem-by-poem survey of the poet's work.

It is clear to us today that Browning's reputation ultimately suffered from the work of intemperate enthusiasts like Berdoe. As the quarrel with Gonner so graphically illustrates, his militant championing of the poet tended to drive away more sober thinkers. Furthermore, Berdoe's "religion," upon closer examination, proves to bear little relationship to traditional Christianity; it seems nearer in spirit to the Positivist variety of idolatry, the worship of secular saints. Even his obsession with vivisection, amusing though it might seem, reveals the unbalanced mind of a fanatical crusader. Despite his liabilities as critic (a critic of poetry, let it be observed, who disliked poetry), it is a fact that undergraduates in the United States still pore over Berdoe's *Cyclopaedia* as if it were the latest and most authoritative word on Browning. The book's prolonged popularity affords melancholy proof that the worst of the early Browningite scholarship and criticism has not yet been displaced.

J. T. Nettleship (1841–1902)

"I have got two designs of Nettleship's," Edward Dowden wrote Miss Elizabeth D. West in 1873. "They are characteristic of his work and of the man. . . . very beautiful, but hopeless." [69] The exasperation Dowden obviously felt in trying to define the weakness of John Trivett Nettleship as an artist is familiar to us today; for Nettleship, as the author of the first book devoted solely to Robert Browning's poetry, is an infuriatingly bad critic (F. G. R. Duckworth commented that his essays on Browning "vary widely from mediocrity relieved by occasional flashes of real insight to sheer stupidity" [70]), a critic, moreover, whose badness often defies analysis. Nettleship as a Browning critic, however, deserves our attention, not only for his chronological position among Browningites, but also for his later role as a leading figure in the Browning Society.

Though Nettleship practiced for a few years as a solicitor, his interests were largely literary and artistic, and by the age of thirty he had turned to painting for a livelihood.[71] Nettleship was at this time a sprucely dressed young man who sketched "gods, and angels, and lost spirits," but when W. B. Yeats called upon him at his home in Wigmore Street a quarter of a century later, he found a silent, balding, gray-bearded old man who was "now a painter of melodramatic lions." For twenty-seven years (1874–1901) Nettleship, whose imagination had once created a Blakean spirit world, maintained a shabby Bohemian existence by exhibiting, at the Royal Academy, huge paintings of the animals at the Zoological Gardens. Now, sipping cocoa moodily from an enormous teacup, he tried to justify to Yeats the betrayal of his youthful artistic ideals. " 'Rossetti used to call my pictures potboilers,' he said, 'but they are all—all'—and he waved his arm to the canvasses—'symbols.' " When Yeats urged him to return to the earlier imaginative designs, Nettleship's only reply was, "Nobody would be pleased." [72]

His interest in Browning, however, had developed before the days of the melodramatic lions. In 1866 Nettleship helped to establish in London the Fetherstone Club, a small literary group, before which he read a paper on Browning's poetry;[73] and this paper was to be the beginning of the *Essays on Robert Browning's Poetry* published two years later. Though it is the first book-length treatment of Browning, there is little else to distinguish his *Essays* from the books of, say, Berdoe near the end of the century: it was addressed to "students of Browning" (a phrase which already possessed cultist implications); it sought to discover in Browning's poetry a "wide and life-giving philosophy"; and it abounded with expressions of uncritical adulation. Like Browningites of the following generation, he devoted much space to "Saul" (because of its religious content) and *Sordello* (because of its fascinating obscurity). The chapter most directly prophetic of the later vagaries of the Browning Society, however, was the one which treated "Childe Roland." "I know that it is no light thing to attribute meanings to a poem which the maker of it would disclaim," Nettleship wrote; "but the present romance is so full of suggestiveness and possibility of second meaning that I should not feel justified in passing it by in silence or with only a slight comment" (p. 120). The poem he interpreted as an allegory of man's loss of faith in God, with a careful gloss describing the significance of each detail. Even the old blind horse which Browning's knight passes is seen as teaching readers of "sin and suffering, earned by sin" (p. 144). (It is amusing that in 1882, after hearing the Reverend Joshua Kirkman read another allegorical interpretation of "Childe Roland" at a Browning Society meeting, Nettleship remarked in the discussion which followed that "an attempt had been made to get a psychological study out of what was a mere romance." [74]) A perceptive reviewer in the *London Quarterly Review* detected the essential weakness of Nettleship's book. "In the effort to popularise a poet," the reviewer wrote, "the critic must remember before all things, that, while it is of the utmost importance that the poet's moral teaching be of the purest, his works are not generally consulted as text-books of morality, or even as Chinese puzzles from which moral sentiments are to be hunted out." [75]

By 1881, when Furnivall and Miss Hickey founded the Browning Society, Nettleship's critical tastes had changed considerably. Just as he had abandoned the ethereal sketches of his youth for more substantial subjects like lions and tigers, so the spiritual allegories of his early criticism had yielded to such prosaic interests as line-counting[76] and the classification of Browning's poetry according to its subject matter.[77] Nevertheless he was still a Browningite, even if the rhapsodical tone was absent, and he was active from the beginning in the Browning Society. Furnivall, in fact, alluded to him in his opening address to the society as one of England's leading authorities on Browning.[78] Nettleship attended most of the society's meetings, and he served as a member of its committee from 1881 to 1887.

His first paper before the Browning Society, delivered February 28, 1882, revealed his new analytical bent. Attempting to separate the "truth" from the "sophistry" of Browning's *Fifine at the Fair*, the paper provided an elaborate paraphrase of the poem, with every statement labelled by Nettleship as either "S" (sophistical) or "T&S" (mixture of truth and sophistry). *Fifine* was perhaps the most striking instance of Browning's casuistry, which so troubled the society. The speaker (a modern Don Juan), after all, sounded uncomfortably like Browning himself at times; and, if the poet was unwilling to do so, surely somebody had to distinguish the true from the false. Hence the absurdity of Nettleship's paper was scarcely noticed by his listeners. Only F. D. Matthew protested mildly that *Fifine* was a dramatic monologue rather than a personal utterance by Browning. Furnivall, on the other hand, praised Nettleship's willingness to take time away from his latest paintings, "a grand Lion roaring over his wounded and dying Lioness, a snow Leopard trying to rescue its cub from a Vulture who had carried it off, and a Navvy's sweetheart stopping him from seeking a bloody revenge." The tone of the discussion was, in fact, set by Miss Louisa Drewry, who expressed her certainty that *Fifine* contained "much philosophy of life." [79]

Nettleship read two more papers before the society, neither as misguided as the first but both eliciting equally irrelevant responses from the audience. In "Browning's Intuition, Specially in Regard to Music and the Plastic Arts" (February 23, 1883), he linked artistic intuition with a religious faith in the hereafter, though this was hardly the major idea advanced in the paper. The members of the society, however, immediately seized upon this observation and launched into a lengthy, incoherent discussion of the possibility of a future life. The agnostics, led by Furnivall, lined up on one side of the issue; the Christians, led by Miss Drewry, lined up on the other; and Nettleship's paper was hardly mentioned again during the rest of the meeting.[80] The third paper, "On the Development of Browning's Genius in His Capacity as Poet or Maker" (October 30, 1885), touched off a long discussion of Browning's plays versus Shakespeare's. Then Dr. Berdoe, objecting to the word "development," insisted that Browning had possessed from birth the powers of a Buddha. Shaw, on the other hand, sarcastically demanded a definition of "soul." He added that the paper had been too long and that it showed evidence of Nettleship's having read Browning too exclusively.[81]

Nettleship was a shy, proud man who must have been dismayed by these unexpected attacks upon his views. Furthermore, his remarks at the society's meetings show annoyance with the excessively subtle readings of Browning's poems provided by other members. After listening to a paper on "The Flight of the Duchess," he said, "Mrs. Owen has given us a very beautiful and ingenious interpretation of her own; but the finding of secondary meanings in such works of Art is apt to be a dangerous habit, the more so because it is seductive." [82] He at last dropped out of the Browning Society early in 1887. Though he had promised earlier to write a paper on "Browning as a Landscape Painter," he now refused to do so.[83] He wrote to Furnivall on May 27 of that year: ". . . I must with all the respect due to you as the Founder, and to the members generally, of the Browning Society, decline to read a paper at any one of its meetings; my promise was surely cancelled when any connection with you ceased." Furnivall, annoyed, wrote at the bottom of his letter: "But he made the promise some months after he'd left the Society. I tell him this." [84] However, the paper was never written. Two years later Nettleship evidently complained to Browning himself about the society's proceedings, for Browning replied that he thought Nettleship was "hard on the Society,—*not* for the vagaries of the gnostic papers—those marked by the 'overknowingness' you animadvert upon most justly— but because I never understood that the Society was originally instituted for the purpose of even elucidating dark passages or disinterring deep meanings. . . ." [85]

Though he was no longer a member of the Browning Society, Nettleship's enthusiasm for Browning's poetry never waned, and he published in 1890 a much enlarged edition of his book, this time entitled *Robert Browning: Essays and Thoughts.* The second half of it was entirely new, mostly comprised of the Browning Society papers which had been so ill-received by its members. Needless to say, the old and new parts of the book were greatly dissimilar in tone and subject matter; Nettleship admitted in a Prefatory Note that the essays did not form "in the ordinary sense a continuous whole." The book was not well-received by reviewers, but it went into several editions.

Browning was dead, of course, by the time *Essays and Thoughts* was published, but it was dedicated to him "with his permission." Browning had known Nettleship since 1866, when he was shown the manuscript of the first book,[86] and he expressed gratitude on more than one occasion for Nettleship's "appreciative estimate." [87] Yet Browning's reaction to Nettleship's paper on *Fifine* (it caused him to read his own poem again for the first time in ten years[88]) is, to say the least, ambiguous. An unkind way of interpreting it would be to say that Browning was so puzzled by the paper that he found it necessary, probably shaking his head all the time, to consult the poem itself.[89]

Even Browning, despite his characteristic generosity, was led on one occasion to allude to that curious mixture of talent and obtuseness which Dowden had remarked in Nettleship's paintings and which characterized his literary criticism as well. "I went yesterday to see Nettleship's pictures—fine and forcible, I thought—especially a life-size tiger," Browning wrote to his son in 1889. "He is a clever fellow but 'wanting is—what?' " [90] Browning's self-quotation asks the question that still puzzles us. That Nettleship was a man of intelligence and discrimination needs no further proof than his early recognition of Browning's genius; but it is equally certain that his literary criticism, which moved uneasily from irresponsible allegorizing to ludicrous schematizing, typifies many of the deficiencies of Victorian critical attitudes toward Browning.

CHAPTER IV

SOME REPRESENTATIVE BROWNINGITES—II

=≋=

These books [Symons' *Introduction to the Study of Browning*, Wise's *Pauline* facsimile, Kingsland's *Robert Browning: Chief Poet of the Age*, and Corson's *Introduction to the Study of Robert Browning's Poetry*] belong to the very considerable literature of *Browningismus* which the exertions of the Browning Society are heaping about the poet (whether as men in the East brick up a troublesome visitor or not opinions differ).

—*Saturday Review* (1887) [1]

Arthur Symonds (1865–1945)

ARTHUR SYMONS is most often remembered today for his literary activities during the 1890's, when he was editing the *Savoy*, interpreting the Symbolist movement to the English reading public, and moving in a circle that included Yeats, Dowson, and Beardsley; but our view of his long career as poet and critic is surely distorted if we restrict our attention to those few years when his fame was greatest and his labors most intense. If we turn instead to the 1880's, we will see him in quite a different light: not yet the champion and practitioner of decadent, *fin-de-siécle* poetry, Symons was during this decade a zealous Browningite, still struggling to break away from a home filled with evangelical piety and still trying to find his place in the London literary world. It was during this decade, too, that Symons met—chiefly through his membership in the Browning Society—the men who were to help him launch his career.

Symons' initial introduction to the larger world of London must have been managed at least partially by Dr. Furnivall. In the early eighties Symons began corresponding with Furnivall, who, with his usual generosity and impulsiveness, assigned the inexperienced Symons the task of writing the introduction to the facsimile edition of the First Quarto *Venus and Adonis* (1885). However, Symons did not meet Furnivall personally until August, 1887, when they spent a day together in the country. Symons found him altogether delightful:

> We chatted of innumerable things, & his graphic anecdotes have quite set me up in current biography. Of Meredith he has some capital tales, & of course of Browning. I set him off on Swinburne,— & you know what I should hear of "the little brute", as he generally calls him. He spoke very kindly of Pater. . . . I was immensely entertained with him, & pleased even beyond my anticipations.[2]

In December, 1888, he recorded another encounter with his irrepressible friend:

> I saw in London, too, the ever-vivacious Dr. Furnivall, who is as brisk, light-hearted and vigorous as ever. His last argument is to show that Shakespeare was *not* born at "Shakespeare's Birthplace", and detailed it to Dykes Campbell and me with infinite detail and equal assurance.[3]

It is amusing, though not untypical, that when Furnivall read Symons' first volume of verse, *Days and Nights* (1889), he immediately expressed his disapproval of it;[4] Furnivall's warmth and helpfulness to young writers were exceeded only by the bluntness with which he expressed his views. Yet Symons could observe on another occasion, with perfect truthfulness, that "no one, I am sure, is so indebted to Dr. F. as I am—in an infinitude of ways."[5]

The other scholar to play a large role in Symons' literary initiation was Dykes Campbell, who during this decade served as Symons' chief confidant and literary adviser (the course of their friendship is recorded in several hundred unpublished letters from Symons to him in the British Museum[6]); and it was he who, in 1889, introduced Symons to Browning.

In February, 1881, Symons, though only a schoolboy of sixteen in rural Devonshire, had already written his first essay on Browning, who was to be for many years his primary literary idol.[7] He submitted an article on Browning in 1882 to the *London Quarterly*, which declined to accept it because of "its excess of enthusiasm";[8] but shortly thereafter he did succeed in publishing another article, entitled "Robert Browning as a Religious Poet" in the *Wesleyan Methodist Magazine*.[9] Though the tone of the piece was appropriate for its audience

("Browning's conception of heaven is very beautiful and encouraging"), even at this early date Symons' critical acumen is evident in his insistence that "Browning is a dramatic poet, and as such he gives utterance, dramatically, to all manner of opinions." This idea, elementary as it may seem, was never understood by the majority of Browning's readers, who insisted upon treating his poetry as if he were a dissenting preacher in poet's clothing. At a very young age, then, Symons showed himself to be an enthusiastic expositor of Browning's verse, yet this first article (which brought him his earliest income—one guinea—from writing[10]) also revealed his ability to make a subtle but important distinction that eluded most other Victorian Browningites.

Because of his friendship with both Furnivall and Campbell and because of his own youthful passion for Browning, Symons was as early as 1882 a member of the Browning Society, and by 1885 he was drawn more fully into its activities. His first paper, entitled "Is Browning Dramatic?", was read before the society on January 30 of that year, though the author, who still lived with his family in Devonshire, was not present. The paper did not treat Browning's plays; instead, Symons surveyed the dramatic qualities of the poet's monologues, each of which he described as a "drama of the interior, a tragedy or comedy of the soul." Though Symons' paper was intelligently and sensitively written, its very subtlety bewildered the Browning Society members, who were more accustomed to lectures on "Browning as a Religious Teacher" or "Browning's Philosophy of Life." The discussion that followed the reading of the paper, in fact, centered entirely upon Browning's plays: were they or were they not successful?[11] On February 9 Symons, at Campbell's invitation, wrote a reply, printed in the society's transactions, in which he protested that his use of the term "dramatic" had been misunderstood.[12] One can only conclude that Symons' paper had simply passed over their heads and that the members of the society were victims of their own thought-clichés about Browning's plays, which they never tired of discussing.

Undeterred by this somewhat unintelligent response to his first paper, Symons next contributed to the society's transactions a note in which he compared the careers and artistry of Browning and George Meredith,[13] for the latter of whom he confessed "a quite uncontrollable enthusiasm," [14] and on June 22, 1885, he wrote to Furnivall that he would be willing to serve on the Browning Society's committee,[15] a post which he held until 1892. Though he continued to send in occasional notes for the Notes and Queries column in the *Papers*, he soon realized that the critical opacity of the members was evident even here. "Most of the queries that I have seen might be solved by two or three minutes' study of the context," he complained, "but could only be *explained*, in writing, at an unreasonably great length." [16] Nevertheless, he promised another paper for the society in March, 1886, even though, as he told Furnivall, "the magazines, &c, are beginning to give a little more heed to my enchantments, & I have consequently rather more work on hand (tho not nearly so much as I should like)." [17]

Symons worried a great deal about his newest assignment—at one point he feared his topic was too similar to that of another paper to be read that session[18]—but at a meeting of March 26, 1886, the chairman announced that Symons' paper on "Browning's Metrical Development" had not been completed because of his work on a "Browning Primer." [19] This was a reference to Symons' *Introduction to the Study of Browning*, published by Cassell in the autumn of 1886, which was distributed to every member of the Browning Society. Dedicated to Meredith (who had seen the dedication in proof and insisted that the phrase "greatest of living novelists" be deleted [20]), the slender volume, Symons' first, had nothing but high praise for Browning's art and thought. "I have made the Preface as brief as I could," Symons told Campbell; "I took my cue from Dr. Furnivall's remark that the book was rather too much of a paean, & have tried to anticipate that objection, just in a word." [21] Campbell, incidentally, read the proofs and suggested occasional revisions, which Symons duly made.[22]

Symons' technique was to provide an introductory discussion of the characteristics of Browning's poetry, followed by explications of individual poems. Though the book, like his first article on Browning, is marred by an "excess of enthusiasm," it is in many respects brilliant and perceptive, displaying that fine critical tact which was to characterize his subsequent prose writings. Symons was one of the first to recognize, for example, that "nearly all of the miscellaneous poems, long and short, are monologues." It is Browning's "frequent practice," he added, "to reveal the soul to itself by the application of a sudden test, which shall condense the long trial of years into a single moment" (p. 9). Symons also handled deftly the thorny questions of Browning's "obscurity" and "harshness," and he saw, as few other Browningites did, that *Men and Women*, not the later didactic works, "represents Mr. Browning's genius at its ripe maturity, its highest uniform level" (p. 91). A careful examination of the *Introduction* shows it to be, in fact, the finest book written on Browning's poetry in the nineteenth century; by comparison, the works of his contemporaries (such as Berdoe and Nettleship) seem filled with pedantry and tedious message-hunting.

Symons' book was reviewed favorably and went through a first edition of two thousand copies within four months.[23] James Russell Lowell, who had been sent a copy by Campbell, thought it "exceedingly well done. Indeed it seems to me the best of its kind that I have seen. It has the insight that comes of loving enthusiasm which is always cheering." [24] Symons also sent his *Introduction* to Walter Pater, the third member—with Browning and Meredith—of the holy trinity which he was worshipping during the eighties. Pater replied by thanking for the "interesting and useful volume on Browning, one of my best loved writers," and by inviting Symons to visit him in London.[25] One particularly flattering review, which appeared in the *Guardian*, caught Symons' attention:

> We find in Mr. Symons the thoughtful and practised yet enthusiastic student in literature—in intellectual problems; always quiet and sane, praising Mr. Browning with tact, with a real refinement and grace; saying well many things which every competent reader of the great poet must feel to be true; devoting to the subject he loves a critical gift so considerable as to make us wish for work from his hands of a larger scope than this small volume.[26]

He was astonished to discover shortly thereafter that the author of the review was none other than Pater. The news, he told Campbell,

> set me in a state of great exaltation, from which I am but slowly recovering. Pater to have written a review of my book, and *such* a review! Why did he never tell me? Do you know, when I read that review first I said to myself, "This is rather nicely written: I wonder who wrote it? Evidently one of Pater's disciples." The thought never occurred to me for a moment that he had done it himself.[27]

Browning's most recent volume of verse, *Parleyings with Certain People of Importance in Their Day* (1887), prompted Symons' last paper for the Browning Society. After deciding to add an appendix on *Parleyings* in the second edition of his *Introduction*, Symons promised also to write a paper "if I have anything more to say on the subject." [28] Furnivall, despite his confession that he didn't "care for [*Parleyings*] a bit," [29] scheduled the paper for the April 29, 1887, meeting. By the end of March, Symons had finished the assignment. "I hope, if you are there to hear it," he wrote Campbell, "you will come down on it for its scrappiness & want of connection, & that you will state as your opinion that there is a rather nice bit on the poetic interpretation of nature." [30] Campbell, in the end, read the paper for Symons, who was again absent from the meeting, and despite Symons' assertion that Browning must be regarded as a poet rather than a philosopher, the discussion that followed turned upon the society's chief preoccupation, Browning's theology.[31]

Thereafter Symons' connection with the Browning Society became more tenuous, for he was finding literary work elsewhere. "I am afraid there is no chance of my being able to do a paper for the Browning Society's next session," he informed Furnivall on May 29, 1889;[32] nevertheless, in the previous month he had made his only recorded appearance at one of its meetings, in order to hear a paper read by his friend, Mrs. Alexander Ireland. When Symons, during the discussion period, compared Browning's "A Toccata of Galuppi's" to a painting by Watteau,[33] it should have been clear to everyone present that he had now moved into the world of Pater and out of the quite different world of the Browning Society. Symons' last correspondence with the society's leaders took place in 1895, three years after it had become defunct, when E. E. Davies, the last honorary secretary, sent out a plea to former members of the committee for new subscriptions so that the remainder of the society's transactions might be published. "It is an infernal imposition—I, for instance, was never more than nominally a member of the committee, & latterly never even paid my subscription," Symons complained to Campbell. "Is one however legally bound to pay? Please advise me in the matter." [34]

If Symons had grown disenchanted with Dr. Furnivall's band of Browningites, however, he would remember with gratitude for the rest of his life that it was his connection with the society which had enabled him to meet Browning himself. As early as 1882 Symons had received a sort of indirect communication from the great man. In that year he sent to Furnivall a published poem entitled "Unanswered Yet," allegedly by Browning, who was then shown the poem by Furnivall and denied its authorship. Furnivall sent on to Symons Browning's reply, with this note on the back of the letter: "I thought you'd rather have R.B.'s answer than mine. And here it is." [35] For Symons, it was "a Red-letter-day": "Is not that a treasure for me?" he wrote a friend. "I had long wanted to get Br.'s autograph and *now have it* under such interesting circumstance, the letter being written solely for my benefit." [36]

Symons at last received a letter addressed to himself from Browning when, in 1886, the proofs for his *Introduction* were sent to the poet by Cassell.[37] Browning, who was vacationing in Wales, made a few corrections in the proofs, granted the necessary permission to quote his poetry, and thanked Symons for his "patient attention to all these poems" and for so thoroughly entering into "the spirit in which they were written." [38] Symons also had the satisfaction of learning a year later from Campbell that Browning had read his poem "The Revenge" and had thought it "*very* good, very good *indeed*." [39]

On July 21, 1887, after a short visit to London, Symons described to Campbell his first glimpse of Browning:

> I must tell you of a piece of extraordinary good luck which befell me a few minutes after I had left your house on the pleasantest of all possible Tuesdays. I started as you directed me, cleared the Albert Hall, & had walked a very little way onwards, when, as I was looking about for a bus, whom should I see, driving quietly along, but—of all men in the world the one I would have given most to see—Browning! It was my first sight of him, but I would wager anything that I could not possibly have been mistaken. There were three ladies with him, all I think elderly & dressed in black. . . . He was just precisely like the photograph hanging before me as I write— the large one issued by the Browning Society. Now was not that a singular piece of good fortune?—quite, by itself alone, worth coming to London for.[40]

Symons was becoming increasingly impatient to meet Browning and began to ask his friends to arrange the introduction. "[Norman] MacColl [editor of the *Athenaeum*] told me that Browning had also been speaking to him about me—which I thought was very kind, as he does not know me," Symons wrote to Furnivall in May, 1889. "I wish he did—or rather that I knew him." Would Furnivall take him to see Browning? [41] "Get along with you!" answered Furnivall; Symons could call upon the poet alone—and "that is just what I shall not do," said Symons, whose shyness would not permit him to visit Browning "unasked and unintroduced." Symons then wrote to Campbell with a proposition: if Campbell would introduce him to Browning, Symons would reciprocate by introducing Campbell to Olive Schreiner, the South African novelist.[42]

At last, on August 25, Campbell took him to 29 De Vere Gardens, telling Symons on the way that Browning had said he would be "*particularly* glad to see Mr. Symons." [43] Years later Symons recalled Browning's "violence of voice; it had the whole gamut of music, it vibrated, it thrilled me, by certain touches of rare magic in it." The only other detail of the interview which the awed disciple could remember was that they had discussed Poe's "The Raven" and that Symons had championed Poe's theory of the superiority of the short poem—until he realized, with some embarrassment, that he was talking to the author of *The Ring and the Book*. As they left, their host urged Symons to visit him again; but within four months Browning was dead in Italy.[44]

Symons attended Browning's funeral in Westminster Abbey on December 31, 1889, an event he alluded to in his review of Browning's last book, *Asolando*, which appeared in the *Academy* on January 11: "Reading *Asolando* once more, and remembering that coffin one had looked down upon in the Abbey, only then quite feeling that all was indeed over, it is perhaps natural that the book should come to seem almost consciously testamentary, as if certain things in it had been really meant for a final leavetaking." [45] He also wrote a poem entitled "Dead in Venice," one stanza of which bore witness to Browning's lasting influence upon him:

> Dead? But to me that cannot be—
> Who loved him when a boy, nor still
> Can read that name without a thrill
> Which once was all-in-all to me.[46]

At the first meeting of the Browning Society after Browning's death, January 31, 1890, Dr. Furnivall read a formal statement of the society's sorrow which he himself had written, though he added that these sentiments had first been expressed by "Mr. Arthur Symons, . . . a younger and more eloquent writer than myself," but the draft had been accidentally misplaced.[47]

One must regret that we have lost this tribute to Browning by Symons; yet we do have another document, perhaps as interesting in its own way, that nicely sums up Symons' ambiguous relationship with the Browning Society and his worshipful attitude toward Browning. On December 13, 1884, there appeared in the *Academy* a poem by Symons called "A Fancy of Ferishtah," full of obvious allusions to Browning's *Ferishtah's Fancies*, which had been published just the month before.[48] In Symons' allegory Ferishtah (that is, Browning), a Persian poet, is surrounded by disciples (clearly the members of the Browning Society) who come "to gather up his words / And question him of matters near and far." Instead, Ferishtah asks them a question: "What claims to thanks or love hath work of mine?" After many of his listeners (some of the less intelligent Browningites?) babble "windy thanks of words," one tells of having seen a youth (Symons) reading Ferishtah's poetry, with his heart throbbing "to the music of his verse in time." Upon being questioned, the youth confesses to an ambition:

> He told me likewise with a modest air,
> Himself had written verse: small skill had he,
> (There, I believed him!) yet, of what he had
> No little had Ferishtah taught him; hoped,
> Likewise, he told me, to make someday some
> Small, small, however small name for himself,
> And thanked Ferishtah as a candle might
> The Sun that shines and shows it how to shine.

The answer satisfied Ferishtah, and Browning, who saw the poem in manuscript, was evidently satisfied too. "By the kindness of Mr. Furnivall," he wrote Symons,

> I received your gracious poem last evening. All I can say in acknowledgement is that if "Ferishtah" has produced such a pupil he is happy indeed—a happiness quite unalloyed by dissatisfaction that the pupil treads so closely on the heels of the Master—who bids him "I *pede fausto*"—or, in the vernacular, "Go a-head," with all his heart.[49]

Symons did indeed go ahead, so much so that by the next decade the ideas and attitudes expressed in his own verse would no longer have been acceptable to his former master; one feels that the decadent verse of the nineties would surely have seemed repulsive to Browning. Nevertheless, Symons' sojourn amidst the Browningites during the 1880's provides us with the amusing and edifying spectacle of a talented young critic, still naive and inexperienced, yet already too sophisticated in his literary perceptions for the earnest members of the Browning Society; and, what is perhaps even more interesting, we see in this experience Symons' growth from an adolescent infatuated with Browning to a mature student of literature whose interests were widening to include all aspects of European culture. Arthur Symons' encounter with Browning and the Browningites constituted, in short, his literary apprenticeship: by the nineties he was able to emerge with fully developed powers as the chief literary spokesman of that decade.

Thomas J. Wise (1859–1937)

The career of Thomas J. Wise, possibly the most distinguished bibliophile of this century and also the most notorious bibliographic forger, continues to fascinate laymen and scholars alike. Not until a few years before his death were his amazing deceptions exposed; but since 1934, beginning with Carter and Pollard's *Enquiry*, a seemingly endless series of books about Wise has appeared.[50] Except for Wilfred Partington's biography, these volumes have been highly technical bibliographic studies of the Wise forgeries and the few shreds of evidence about them that literary detectives have been able to piece together. Behind the elaborate investigations of type fonts, false imprints, and watermarks, however, lies an essentially psychological problem: what sort of person could be simultaneously a collector of international stature and one of the most clever criminals of our time? Since most of the forgeries were produced and distributed while Wise was still a relatively young man, we must seek an answer to the question by examining this part of his life; but here new problems arise, for, as Partington discovered, little is known or can be learned about Wise's youth. The founder of the Ashley Library had discreetly covered his own tracks. Nevertheless, Wise was active in both the Shelley and Browning societies, and through a painstaking scrutiny of his activities in the latter, we can catch an occasional, tantalizing glimpse of the man whose Jekyll-and-Hyde personality was later to dominate and then bring infamy to the book world.

It should be made clear at the outset that Wise was a book-collector of the purest variety—that is, his interest in books was limited almost entirely to their physical form and value; their literary content was a matter of no concern to him. His imperviousness to the values of literature, in fact, contributed to a narrow outlook and singular lack of charm;[51] but his acquisitive instinct and his subtle business sense were already during the eighties giving him a formidable reputation among the booksellers and collectors of London. Though he was still living with his parents on a modest clerk's salary, his magnificent capacity for bluffing (which carried him through every difficulty until Carter and Pollard began their investigations) persuaded booksellers that here was an influential and rising bibliophile indeed. As Partington has already observed, his membership in the Browning Society was part of his total plan of conquest, for at its meetings he knew he would meet other collectors and scholars who could provide useful information or introductions.

As for Browning's poetry, there is no evidence that Wise read it very often. At least he delivered no papers to the society, almost never joined in the discussions, and made only infrequent contributions to the Notes and Queries section in the *Papers*. The longest of these, a highly laudatory review of Kingsland's brief book on Browning, sounds vaguely sarcastic, though probably it was merely one of Wise's rare attempts at humor: "Altogether this little booklet deserves to be made widely known," he wrote; "and those readers who wish to initiate their friends into the mysteries of Browning-Worship, should obtain copies for the purpose of distribution." The note ended, however, with a distinctly commercial ring ("The volume . . . is published at the nominal price of *one shilling*"), and it is not surprising to discover that Wise had published the book at his own expense.[52]

Wise's first recorded appearance at a Browning Society meeting was on July 7, 1882,[53] and the following November he was listed as one of its members. However, it is clear that he had been active in the society since its very inception, because the annual report of 1882 mentions a Browning concordance which he had already promised to prepare.[54] A year later the plan was abandoned for lack of funds.[55] Although he was silent (or perhaps not present) at most of the society's meetings, the occasional appearance of his name in the annual reports demonstrates that he was working busily behind the scenes: from 1883 through 1886 he audited the accounts, in 1885 he became a member of the committee, and in the next year he completed his most ambitious project to date—a facsimile reprint of Browning's *Pauline*.

Probably the *Pauline* facsimile—a work of crucial significance in Wise's introduction to the art of forgery—was inspired by a memorable first visit to Browning's home in early March, 1886.[56] Accompanied (of course) by Dr. Furnivall, Wise was quite unlike those Browningites who, after such a pilgrimage, gushed in print about the "spiritual experience" of meeting the poet in his natural habitat. He was much more the detached and impassive observer—but what he saw that day was enough to make any aspiring young collector's blood run cold. As they entered Browning's front room, their host was seated before the fireplace, and, making cheerful small talk all the while, he methodically pulled out of an old trunk bundles of letters and documents and threw them into the fire. A packet of letters from Carlyle . . . the manuscripts of Browning's early unpublished poems . . . one by one they fell among the flames, and Thomas Wise sat watching, inwardly writhing in exquisite agony. It was a collector's nightmare. Then Browning groped in the trunk and brought forth two copies of *Pauline*, his first published work, which, a month after its appearance in 1833, was withdrawn; Browning himself claimed that not one copy had ever been sold. Wise was tantalized by a wishful idea: would Browning perhaps give him one copy of this rarity?

But for once Wise was not sufficiently brash to ask the vital ques-

tion, and the opportunity passed as Browning put the books aside.
After they left the house, he revealed his frustrated desire to Furnivall, who was both amused and impressed by Wise's curious inten-
sity. Furnivall, though, had a sensible suggestion: that Wise write to
Browning, asking for one of the copies of *Pauline* and offering to send
any sum of money to a charity of Browning's choice. A few days later,
at Dykes Campbell's apartment, the books were again mentioned with
both Wise and Browning present, but this time Wise was momentarily
silenced by the poet's unexpected offer to give one of the copies to
Campbell. The next day Wise followed Furnivall's advice and wrote to
Browning, who replied that he must keep the other *Pauline* for his
son.[57]

It was an exasperating experience for Wise; to make matters
worse, he had to spend £22 10s in order to purchase a copy of *Pauline*
from a bookseller two years later.[58] The frustration of losing the *Pauline*, however, was not without its hidden benefits, for the entire episode made Wise conscious of the book's excessive rarity and of its
interest to Browningites; Browning had, of course, reluctantly reprinted its text in 1868, but the first edition, a bibliographic and literary curiosity, continued to hold a special appeal for collectors. Why
not, Wise decided, make a *facsimile* reproduction of that first edition
for the benefit of Browning Society members? Furnivall agreed to let
the society sponsor the project, Browning gave his consent, and Wise
set to work on it at the London printing house of Richard Clay and
Sons. It was an important moment in Wise's career, for the technical
skill he acquired in reproducing the original typography of *Pauline*
prepared the way for the bibliographic forgeries which he began to
create within a year or two.[59] The *Pauline* itself, needless to say, was
not a forgery. Each of the 429 copies distributed to Browning Society
members said plainly on the title page that it was a "Reprint of the
Original Edition of 1833," though ironically Wise complained many
years later in the *Bookman's Journal* that copies of the *Pauline* facsimile had been altered and "faked up" by others and sold as origi-
nals.[60] Wise's own fabrications were much less crude than that, but
their very sophistication owed much to his apprenticeship in the
Browning Society.

Browning's correspondence with Wise while the facsimile was being prepared for publication—which correspondence Wise himself
later printed—reveals with appalling clarity the young collector's persistent badgering of Browning and Browning's notable lack of enthusiasm for the project. Though Wise was to boast in his old age of his

acquaintance with Browning, implying that it was of an intimate nature,[61] the letters tell another story. On July 6, 1886, Browning wrote, "If it really *does* interest you to have my statement in 'black and white,' I willingly repeat that to the best of my belief no single copy of the original edition of *Pauline* found a buyer." [62] Browning's statement in "black and white" naturally was then added to Wise's personal collection of impressive literary documents; from his point of view, asking naive questions had its rewards. On August 8 Browning wrote again, this time declining to provide an introduction to the *Pauline* facsimile; and in November he refused to read the proofs.[63] The few other letters addressed to Wise are equally perfunctory: acknowledgements of Shelley Society[64] publications (in 1888, for instance, Wise did a facsimile of the first edition of *Adonais* for that organization) or routine answers to inquiries. One particular query provoked an unusual outburst of wrath from Browning, and another one sought an endorsement from the poet of Wise's forged "first edition" of Mrs. Browning's *The Runaway Slave*.[65] Browning's most cryptic missive was a postcard sent upon learning the price Wise had paid for an original *Pauline*: "Thanks, unwise Wise!" [66] Browning, in fact, was highly suspicious of the current obsession with first editions, which was being fostered by Wise, and he observed sardonically that Wise's copy of *Pauline* had been purchased "at about two-thirds of the price paid for printing the whole edition fifty-five years ago." [67]

Wise attempted to answer such objections by explaining in his preface to the *Pauline* facsimile that since "the little volume has now become so scarce that very few of the numerous collectors of Browning Ana can ever hope to possess a copy, the need for its reproduction is beyond question." Except for the paper, he wrote, his facsimile was a "very good and precise representation" of the original; and he justified this strange concern with a book's physical form by adding that a certain sentiment was wanting when *Pauline* appeared in "another dress." It was not an especially convincing argument, but its shakiness was not observed by the Browning Society. The annual report of 1887 described the facsimile as "a charming little volume." [68] On the other hand, the *Saturday Review*, while generally applauding Wise's effort, complained of his attempt to reproduce the original in every respect. A true book-lover, it claimed, despises nothing more "than a sham original—scagliola aping marble, graining aping natural wood, leatherette aping good sound calf skin." [69] "Forgeries aping true first editions," the *Saturday Review* might have added, had it possessed the gift of prophecy.

The most curious aspect of Wise's relationship with the Browning Society is that he seems actually to have become a more powerful figure in it after its formal dissolution. The society's last public meetings were held during the 1891–92 session, but for several years thereafter private meetings were conducted in members' homes, and there were fitful attempts to raise subscriptions for certain publishing ventures; it was during this period of lingering decline that Wise was known as the society's honorary secretary, though that is surely too grandiose a title for his occasional responsibilities. On May 1, 1895, for example, Wise issued a circular[70] to all former members asking for two subscriptions from each in order to complete some projects: (1) Part VI of the *Papers*, which was to include an index to the other twelve parts; (2) a revision by Wise of Furnivall's Browning bibliography; (3) the publication of some Browning letters; (4) a new series of *Illustrations to the Life and Writings of Robert Browning*; and (5) the publication of "The Old Yellow Book," a collection of legal documents which was the source of Browning's *The Ring and the Book*.

Part VI of the *Papers* was never published, though Wise later claimed that he had completed it in manuscript.[71] (Significantly, the index was not found among Wise's papers when they were acquired by the British Museum; nor, incidentally, did his copy of the *Papers* show much wear. Most of the pages were uncut.)[72] The bibliography, which had already been published in the *Athenaeum* the previous year, was reprinted and augmented in *Literary Anecdotes of the Nineteenth Century*, edited by Wise and W. R. Nicoll, in 1895.[73] Wise, however, did succeed in raising some money, for that year there was published under the imprint of the Browning Society the first volume of *Letters from Robert Browning to Various Correspondents*, edited by Thomas J. Wise.[74] Though financed by Browning Society subscriptions, the book resembles the countless other privately published collections of literary correspondence which Wise issued; the only difference is that this time someone besides Wise was paying the expenses. Dykes Campbell—and probably the other former Browning Society leaders as well—would have much preferred that Wise use the money for Part VI of the *Papers*. On April 28, 1895, for instance, he sent this note of advice to Wise:

> I cheerfully become a member for the next two years until you get all that *necessary* work done to the Br. Soc. papers. But I am not so sure about the Browning Letters—there you would constantly come into risky collision both with Pen and G. Murray Smith. Think it over well.[75]

ROBERT BROWNING   This photograph was issued in three sizes in 1881 to members of the Browning Society. Arthur Symons, after his first glimpse of Browning in 1887, wrote to James Dykes Campbell: "He was just precisely like the photograph hanging before me as I write—the large one issued by the Browning Society."

Nevertheless, Wise published four volumes in all of Browning's letters; taken together, they formed the core of the important 1933 Hood edition of Browning correspondence.[76] As Furnivall explained to Slater in 1895, Pen Browning "w[oul]d never consent to my printing his father's letters. When Wise or any one else does it privately, he never hears of it, I suppose; & if he does, doesn't care to take action against a stranger." [77]

For a time, Wise and Campbell contemplated an even more ambitious project: a facsimile reproduction of the Latin documents in "The Old Yellow Book," which was owned by Balliol College. Campbell estimated that the work would cost about £100 and suggested that the Browning Society's publisher make arrangements for the reproduction at the Bodleian;[78] but Campbell died a month later, and Wise apparently did not carry out the project.

Despite Wise's evident pursuit of his own interests above those of the organization, his contributions to the Browning Society were substantial. Nor can one overlook his magnificent collection of Browning correspondence and his several Browning bibliographies and catalogues, as well as his later generous assistance to scholars and writers. Unfortunately, all of Wise's achievements, in this area as well as others, were marred by his occasional dishonesty and treachery. The bibliographies, excellent as they are, can be used only with extreme caution nowadays, for embedded in them are numerous small falsifications as well as the titles of Wise's five Browning forgeries.[79] One is also saddened by Wise's subsequent attacks upon Furnivall—after the latter's death, of course, since normally the victims of Wise's slanders were in the grave and hence unable to defend themselves. Of Furnivall's Browning bibliography he made the following claim:

> Although the name of Dr. Furnivall alone appeared on the title-page as the compiler of the Bibliography, the spade-work was done almost entirely by me under his direction. It was my first lesson in bibliography. But it was always Dr. Furnivall's habit to take full credit for any undertaking in which he was the smallest degree concerned. In the present instance Dr. Furnivall's share of the labour consisted in "compiling" and annotating the work done by Mr. J. T. Nettleship and myself.[80]

It is an absurd charge, since Furnivall specifically acknowledged the assistance of eleven helpers in his bibliography (including Nettleship),[81] and Furnivall's contemporaries testify unanimously that he was remarkably uninterested in any personal honor which might be attached to scholarship. Furthermore, Furnivall's own interleaved copy of the bibliography, which he revised for many years in planning a second edition, provides compelling evidence that he was in fact its true author.[82]

Wise's antagonism toward Furnivall showed itself in less obvious ways even during the eighties. Though he evidently played some small part in organizing the "Furnivall Fund" after the Outram libel trial, Wise displayed little enthusiasm for the cause. William Michael Rossetti, sending his contribution to Dykes Campbell on February 23, 1888, offered this explanation for being so late in coming to Furnivall's aid:

> I fear I may have appeared a little negligent in the matter: but the fact is—what I asked Wise a fortnight or so ago to tell me was the proper address to wh[ich] I ought to send any subscription; & to this query W. has not yet replied, neither does he let me know anything about the Mr. Slater named in your note. As I don't know anything about Slater's address, you will excuse my forwarding the cheque direct to you.[83]

And in 1886 when Andrew Lang published a poem mocking Furnivall's "He was my father's friend!" remark at the Shelley Society's opening meeting, Wise gleefully reprinted it in a "private edition"—without Lang's permission.[84]

It is a striking commentary upon both Furnivall's generosity and his lack of perception that he seemed unaware of Wise's hostility. For his part—in a letter to Slater, dated August 18, 1896—he could only praise such an obviously industrious young man:

> How our friend T.J.W. is coming out! We shall soon have him as one of the most prominent Victorian literary men, quite cutting out us poor quiet fellows.
> I'm glad of his success for he is a genuine worker, & really loves his subject.[85]

The prophecy of Wise's rise to fame was accurate, but in another respect Furnivall was wrong. Wise did indeed achieve a spectacular success in his lifetime—his name is one of the few among the Browning Society members that most readers today would instantly recognize—but eventually his fame was transmuted into notoriety; and in his early activities among Furnivall's Browning enthusiasts one can already see the portents of disaster.

William G. Kingsland (1848-1933)

A visitor who attended a Browning Society meeting for the first time on January 25, 1884, wrote later that he was greeted "in the most cordial and courteous manner" by William G. Kingsland, a modest, unassuming man who nevertheless played a vital role in the society's affairs.[86] That a stranger should have been welcomed by Kingsland is not surprising, since, as the official reporter of the discussion periods, he must have attended nearly every meeting. Judging by the reports of the meetings that appear in the *Papers*, one can guess that Kingsland had a good ear for dialogue, though he transcribed the discussions in longhand. There was in fact occasional dissatisfaction with the incompleteness of his minutes, and the society appealed for a new volunteer who was familiar with shorthand; but Kingsland continued to serve as an unpaid reporter, even though the society did sometimes hire a professional stenographer when special speakers were on the program.[87] The shorthand reporters, too, were sometimes unsatisfactory, as the following characteristic note from Shaw to Campbell in 1884 shows:

> I send you a report of my speech from memory. The notes you sent me made my blood run cold until I came to a few blunders which convinced me that I had not really talked such nonsense, but that your stenographer, instead of reporting me verbatim, had made a few inaccurate notes of my speech in shorthand, and transcribed them wrongly. I am a poor phonographer myself; but I think if I took down a speaker as having uttered the words "epic poet," I could make a saner transcription of my own notes than "block poet." The fellow was thinking of his own head.[88]

As for Kingsland's reports, the few proofs of them which have survived show no major corrections by speakers or chairmen;[89] probably the most damaging complaint that can be brought against his transcriptions is not that they are verbally inaccurate but that occasionally the discussions moved beyond Kingsland's intellectual grasp, so that consequently the fine distinctions of certain speakers are not adequately reported in the *Papers*. At the same meeting (January 25, 1884) when he displayed such memorable hospitality to the visitor, for example, Kingsland confessed during the discussion period that the speaker, Miss Arthur, "had gone far beyond his depth in her philosophical analysis" of *Paracelsus* and that he himself "preferred to look at this great work in its more human aspects." [90] And, to put it simply, the human aspects of a poem were for Kingsland its religious aspects. He was strongly opposed to any sort of literary analysis of Browning's poetry, for that might lead to adverse criticism of it, which in turn could cause one to neglect its great spiritual lessons which Browning had provided for one's personal guidance.[91] Browning seemed to Kingsland a great moral teacher:

> From him we might gather lessons on all the great problems of life here, and life to come; and also something even rarer, strength, bracing for every-day duties. . . . Browning had not only been a teacher to him [Kingsland], but had been a great spiritual influence —an influence which grew upon him with each succeeding year.[92]

He agreed with Dr. Berdoe that Browning "had a clear gospel for the age," [93] a gospel which he found chiefly in "Saul," "Rabbi Ben Ezra," "A Death in the Desert," and *Paracelsus* (a poem he was reading for the fifth time shortly before his death).

Kingsland could also be charmingly naive, as when, after hearing a hostile analysis of the theological views in *Ferishtah's Fancies*, he demanded to know "why, if [*Ferishtah*] were so bad a book, it had reached a third edition in a very short time." [94] When, at another meeting, he claimed that "the test of true poetry" was whether it made one feel good after reading it, Dr. Furnivall pounced upon this *non sequitur* and retorted that "Dr. Watts's hymns &c. might make you feel better, but they were not works of genius." [95] It is probably true, as an acquaintance of Kingsland's wrote after his death, that "his attitude of mind was probably more Victorian than modern, but less rigid and more tolerant." [96] Therefore, unlike his more militant fellow-believers in the Browning Society, he was not inclined to pronounce anathema upon agnostics and atheists who did not see Browning as a Christian poet. "It did not much matter to them [Browning's readers] what Mr. Browning himself *believed*, or what he was *supposed* to teach," said Kingsland. "Each of us could get out of Mr. Browning's poems whatever helped us or gave us any comfort—and that was all we needed." [97]

Other remarks Kingsland made at Browning Society meetings mirror his own social background and concerns. Browning, he said, "taught . . . that one kind of honest work was as good as another, if only it fitted to the capacity of the worker, for spiritual training." [98] At another meeting he described Browning as "the *teacher of teachers*," one who especially inspired those who were engaged in instructing "the people"—i.e., the poor.[99] It is not an exaggeration to say that in these two statements one can see the exact outlines of Kingsland's life. The largely self-educated son of a carpenter, he was a proof-reader for the *Army and Volunteer Gazette*; but his chief energies were reserved for Sunday school work at Offord Road Chapel, Barnsbury (on the northern edge of London), where he taught for 62 years.[100] Though a quiet and reserved man, he also gave frequent private Browning readings and public lectures on Browning's verse. The *Islington Gazette* reported in 1877 that at the weekly meeting of the Offord Road Young Men's Christian Debating Society, Kingsland took the affirmative side of the proposition, "The poems of Robert Browning are of a higher order than those of Alfred Tennyson." Kingsland, characteristically, argued that Browning is a greater poet because he is an outstanding religious teacher who writes poems with "profundity of thought," while those of Tennyson have a "vague, dreamy, shadowy character." His opponent made the usual complaint about Browning's obscurity, but Kingsland appears to have carried the day, since his arguments are reported in much greater detail than those of his opponent.[101] (On the other hand, it should be borne in mind that Kingsland himself probably wrote the article.)

He was also given to composing effusive sonnets dedicated to Browning and devotional-style articles about his poetry for the *Islington Gazette*.[102] In 1890, with the help of the Reverend J. S. Jones, he founded the Islington Browning Society, one of the larger branches of the London organization, and became its first honorary secretary;[103] and in 1889, when two American Browningites, Helen Clarke and Charlotte Porter, founded *Poet-Lore*, a journal which served at first as a newsletter for Browning and Shakespeare societies in the U.S.A., Kingsland became a regular contributor. Until 1903 he was listed on the masthead as an honorary associate editor, in which capacity he wrote occasional articles and a "London Literaria" column, both of which often treated Browning matters. Since Kingsland, who was only a proofreader, did not have access to much genuine literary gossip, he relied heavily on a few sources of information, particularly Thomas Wise. Hence we find him revealing breathlessly in *Poet-Lore* in 1894 that a group of rare Browning first editions had recently come to light (Wise forgeries, of course);[104] and in the same year he reported that he and Wise were preparing a Browning bibliography for publication in the *Athenaeum*.[105] Not surprisingly, the bibliography was published under Wise's name alone, and Kingsland's labors went unnoticed except among readers of *Poet-Lore*. (The episode, incidentally, acquires a delicious irony when one recalls Wise's complaint that *his* contributions to *Furnivall's* bibliography had been unrecognized.)

Kingsland's friendship with Browning began in 1868, when a short note of praise for his poetry had elicited from Browning a remarkable letter in which he insisted that although he did not deliberately puzzle his readers, neither did he pretend "to offer such literature as should be a substitute for a cigar, or a game of dominoes, to an idle man." [106] From then until his death in 1889, Browning corresponded occasionally with Kingsland and sometimes even visited his home. To Kingsland, who could never forget his low social station, it was an overwhelming demonstration of Browning's generosity that he should call himself the friend of a humble proofreader.[107] Hence his later published remarks on Browning all bear the unmistakable imprint of the self-abasing disciple who enters into an epiphany of joy and worship whenever he is brought into the presence of his adored poet.[108] The reverential tone is even more strikingly evident in a note which Kingsland wrote immediately after returning from Browning's home on Sunday, April 12, 1888. The note concludes: "Going out from his presence this Sabbath morning, I felt that I had been in the company of a man of God, of a denizen of another sphere, of one who lived in the world, yet was out of it." [109] Like Dr. Berdoe, Kingsland seemed always to be skirting the edge of deification in writing about Browning.

Browning, for his part, found Kingsland a pleasant companion, though (if Kingsland is to be believed) they spent much of their time together discussing Sunday school and temperance activities. It must be a sign of Browning's virtuosity that to Kingsland he appeared an ardent supporter of Sunday schools, while to Berdoe he was an antivivisectionist, and yet to the majority of his friends he was simply an amiable, sophisticated man of the world. It was not only in his dramatic monologues that Browning could persuasively speak through many differing characters; in his own relationships with other people he seems to have relished playing a variety of roles, and consequently his acquaintances always found in Browning a reflection of their own views. Furnivall and Mrs. Orr, for example, were convinced that Browning was a theist, while to Kingsland it was transparently obvious that the poet was a Christian—and an evangelical Christian at that.

For the rest of his life, even after the Browning Society was dissolved, Kingsland continued to worship at the shrine of Browning: he named his only son William Browning Kingsland; he brought out in 1890 a second and enlarged edition of his book *Robert Browning: Chief Poet of the Age*; and in his last years he corresponded frequently with the director of the Browning Library at Baylor University. It must also be added, in all fairness, that Kingsland's writings on Browning, despite their excess of piety, provide many valuable anecdotes about the poet's later years and record his interesting observations about his own poetry. Kingsland, in other words, cannot be dismissed as merely a crank or sycophant; his awe of Browning was unfeigned, and his writings show him to be bright and observant. Nevertheless, Kingsland must be regarded as what one might call a limited observer—that is, much of the interest in both the society's transactions and his own memories of Browning lies in the obvious discrepancy between what he heard and what he understood. From a novelist's standpoint, this kind of character is a means of producing irony and of suggesting the limitations of human perception. If, therefore, when reading the records of discussions in *The Browning Society's Papers*, we are puzzled or charmed by their naïveté, we must call to mind the startling combination of intelligence and restricted viewpoint which William Kingsland represented.

Hiram Corson (*1828–1911*)

In former years, before American universities became the impersonal educational machines they now are, nearly every campus could boast of some particularly flamboyant personality among its faculty, a tireless promoter perhaps, or an eloquent speaker, who frequently possessed greater actual authority than the university president himself. A surprising number of these men were also professors of English who promoted the gospel of Browning: Baylor University had its Dr. A. J. Armstrong, Yale had its William Lyon Phelps, and Cornell had one of the earliest Browningites of all—Professor Hiram Corson. Corson, who had come to Cornell in 1870 as Professor of English Literature, was a tall, handsome man who wore impressive velvet vests and spoke in a rich, sonorous voice. The technical aspects of literature interested him not at all; he believed that the "spiritual message" of a poem could be understood only when it was read aloud, and therefore much of his time was devoted to public recitations of poetry. He thundered Browning, Tennyson, and Shakespeare to his classes, to women's literary circles, and to the Cornell students every Saturday morning, often accompanied by soft organ music in the campus chapel.[110]

To Corson must go the credit of organizing the earliest known Browning Club, a small study group of Cornell faculty members and their wives who first met in 1877.[111] The members spent two years on *The Ring and the Book*, but *Sordello* evidently presented more serious difficulties, because in 1883 they were still pondering its mysteries.

Through Corson's missionary efforts, Browning clubs were also set up in Philadelphia, Syracuse, and Baltimore.[112] No doubt much of his success resulted from his remarkably eloquent voice, which so accurately interpreted Browning's verse, according to one who heard it, that "no papers from the Browning Society, no comments of any scholar were necessary in order to understand the spiritual meaning of 'Childe Roland to the Dark Tower Came.'"[113] Moses Coit Tyler, who met Corson on board a steamship to London in June, 1882, left this record of the encounter in his diary:

> I have never travelled with a more delightful companion. He is an inexhaustible source of entertainment. His mind is a magazine of anecdotes and literary quotations; his wit is brilliant; he has been in gay spirits most of the time; and I have had some of the finest talks with him I ever had with anybody. He quotes Shakespeare or Tennyson by the hour; you mention a word and he has a passage of poetry to quote in which the word occurs.[114]

Corson was going to England that summer in order to fulfill a promise he had made there the previous June in 1881, when he had visited Browning for the first time, and, later the same day, joined one of Dr. Furnivall's famous boating parties up the Thames. A few days earlier Corson had already discussed with Furnivall his newly formed Browning Society and had agreed to deliver a paper in June of the following year.[115] The paper, entitled "The Idea of Personality, as Embodied in Robert Browning's Poetry," was so long, however, that in April, 1882, Corson wrote to Furnivall asking if he could not have *two* evenings. Somewhat alarmed, Furnivall replied that this would be impossible, since June 23 was the last meeting of the 1881–82 session, and probably few members would attend the second evening; besides, he added bluntly, "as you treat only one point in B's poetry, surely you can get what you want to say into that time [an hour and forty-five minutes]."[116]

Corson decided to settle for one evening, though it must have been a long meeting, as "The Idea of Personality" in its published form occupies more than twenty-eight pages in the *Papers*.[117] The thesis of Corson's paper was that the human soul, which transcends the rational intellect in both its claims and powers, is transformed through exposure to a powerful personality. "A cardinal idea in Browning's poetry," said Corson, "is the regeneration of men through a personality who brings fresh stuff for them to mould, and prove right,—new feeling fresh from God—whose life reteaches them what life should be, what faith is, loyalty and simpleness. . . . The intellect plays a secondary part." The corollary of this idea is that "literature and all forms of Art are but the intermediate agencies of personalities. The artist cannot be separated from his art." Such, he said, was Browning's view of the nature and function of poetry.

The discussion which followed at the meeting was composed chiefly of fulsome praise of Corson,[118] and six weeks later Furnivall wrote to him that Browning "liked your Paper better than anything else that had been written on him since the Society started." [119] Furnivall himself, however, questioned the soundness of Corson's assertions, and on August 11 sent him the following private critique of his paper:

> I have read your Paper again this morning, & think it a very fine one, full of true ideas & words. But I've not been able to stop myself from feeling & saying, "Is this view fairly Browning's, got out of him by Corson; or is it Corson's view, justified by what little he can find in Browning to back it up?" And I confess that the latter alternative is the one that such little knowledge as I have of Br. compels me to adopt.
>
> Undoubtedly you've hold of a great truth in this doctrine of Personality; & as undoubtedly your declaration that it is the centre of B.'s teaching *calls up no response whatever in my mind.* I admit that you have made out a case, but that is all. I rebel against the view as true of B. altogether.
>
> Where is it in his Essay [on Shelley], in his statement of the object of Poetry; where in the *character* of Sordello, Paracelsus, the Fifine Man, or any other of his leading personages? Even in Caponsacchi the regenerating element is Love. And if you say Love *is* Personality, then all poets—many more than Br.—preach it.
>
> Next, if Art is the agency of Personality, & Art expresses itself by words, surely something should be said on Br.'s verse—which you so justly, tho' with cruel unconsciousness, print as prose.[120]

Despite this clear-eyed exposure of the paper's weaknesses (the point about Corson's printing the poetry as prose is especially telling), Corson continued to use it in America as the basis of lectures to many small literary groups, and when in 1886 he published a book entitled *An Introduction to the Study of Robert Browning's Poetry,* the paper, somewhat revised, became its second chapter. Because Corson corresponded regularly with the Browning Society leaders in London, they regarded him as their staunchest American ally, and his book caused a considerable stir among English Browningites.[121] Even before it was published, Dykes Campbell wrote to Corson urging that the title be changed so that it would not be confused with Arthur Symons' *Introduction to the Study of Browning*, which was also about to be issued.[122] Corson retained his original title, however, with the result that most periodicals reviewed his book and Symons' in the same issue. Actually, the books were not identical in format: Symons provided an analysis of each of Browning's volumes, whereas Corson, after several introductory chapters on "obscurity" and other such familiar matters, merely printed a selection of Browning's poems. Nevertheless, the similarity of titles invited comparison, and most reviewers found Corson's *Introduction* less satisfactory than Symons'; they complained that the introductory essays were fuzzy, irrelevant, and thesis-ridden. The *Saturday Review,* which always approached books about Browning with homicidal intentions, made this terse observation: "Suffice it to say that, if anyone will imagine a weak aftergrowth of Boston Transcendentalism applied to the purpose of poetical criticism, he will not have a bad idea of the Cornell critic." [123]

Symons, when sent a copy of the book by Campbell, managed to take an amiable view of the critical shortcomings of his American rival:

> I have read what was new to me, & glanced here & there among the Selections, not being able, I regret to say, to stay my hand occasionally from putting a query or a denial against certain singular statements. I can hardly tell you what my impression of the whole is. The Selections are good, & most of the notes, & so, I should think, are the "Arguments," if one must have such things at all. "B's obscurity" is very practical & sensible. But I can see nothing much in the first chapter ["The Spiritual Ebb and Flow exhibited in English Poetry from Chaucer to Tennyson and Browning"], viewed from any point, & it has certainly nothing to do with Browning. I remember that the "Personality" paper contained much that is excellent, but I doubt if it is what people want as an "Introduction to Browning." The book is much too composite & compiled: worst of all, it gives not the slightest idea of B's career as a poet, his works in general, or his later works in any degree whatsoever. But in the parts I have spoken of there is much that is telling and stimulating.[124]

And Furnivall, while regarding the book as a "great service to students of B.," complained to Corson about his decision to "put such a big choker as the *Flight of the Duchess* so early in the book. It takes up the room of 8 or 10 shorter & more attractive pieces of greater artistic —if not spiritual—worth," Furnivall added. "I only hope that most readers'll skip it till they've read the rest of the vol., & then take it last." [125] Browning, on the other hand, was uniformly gracious to his admirers, no matter how misguided they might be. He wrote an eloquent letter of appreciation to Corson and made minor corrections in the text, both of which appeared in a second edition of the *Introduction*.[126]

Another paper by Corson, "The Conditions of Spiritual Vitality and Development, Exhibited in Robert Browning's Poetry," was scheduled to be read at the Browning Society meeting of March 25, 1887,[127] but he did not send it, and thereafter he is not mentioned in the *Papers*, though he did remain on the society's committee until 1888. Throughout the eighties Corson and his wife continued to visit Europe occasionally, each time paying their regards to Browning. In the autumn of 1889 the Corsons were spending an academic sabbatical in Italy, where for a week in November they enjoyed Browning's cheerful company while sight-seeing in Venice. Browning impressed Corson with both his youthful vitality and his detailed knowledge of the city; but a month later Browning was dead, and when the news reached Corson in Florence, he was stunned. Within a few days he sent off an account of his last meeting with Browning to the *Nation*.[128]

And there, it would seem, any description of Corson's relationship with Browning would have to end, but such is not the case. After the turn of the century, Corson's lifelong interest in the spiritual world was transformed into an obsession with spiritualism. By 1906, according to a contemporary, Corson was communing daily with Tennyson, Browning, and Milton, and living "on the most intimate terms of familiarity with his dead wife." [129] Corson was during these years also writing his reminiscences of Browning, for which he never found a publisher,[130] and at one of his seances he treated Tennyson, Whitman, Longfellow, Mr. and Mrs. Browning, and sundry other spirits to a reading of a chapter from his projected book on Browning. "At the close of the reading," Corson wrote to his son (who was alive, let it be hastily noted), "there were loud raps by Browning which I took to signify his approval of the paper." [131] At other seances Browning's messages seemed even more explicit to Corson: the poet expressed his approval of Lilian Whiting's book *The Florence of Landor;* he regretted having written "Mr. Sludge, 'the Medium' " (but then what else could a spirit say about a poem which seemed to condemn spiritualism?); and he praised G. K. Chesterton's interpretation of "Sludge." [132] (Chesterton had written in 1903 that the poem is not an attack upon spiritualism but only upon its perversion by Sludge!)[133]

It was a grotesque closing note for Corson's remarkable career, yet one is tempted to find a lesson in it. Browning was beyond question one of the greatest English poets of the nineteenth century, and among his readers he could count the most intelligent and perceptive segment of the Victorian public; but the inescapable fact remains that his most ardent admirers were often tinged with fanaticism. They saw in him not merely an excellent poet, but an answer to their spiritual ills, an embodiment of Christian values, and a link with the unseen world. Corson's seances were, of course, the *reductio ad absurdum* of this view; but in the pathetic, slightly ludicrous figure of the old Cornell professor sitting across the room from an empty chair, awaiting messages from the great poetic seer, we can come very close to a definition of the archetypal Browningite of the last century.

CHAPTER V

THE BURDEN OF CRITICISM

In fact, commentaries on Browning generally bear a close
resemblance to foghorns. They proclaim the existence of a
fog; but they do not disperse it.
                                                    —T. R. Lounsbury[1]

THE WIFE of Mark Pattison, the dour Rector of Lincoln College, has
left us a delightful record of one meeting of the Oxford Browning
Society in 1883, a meeting which symbolizes graphically the weaknesses of all the Browning societies. The members met in the Patti-
sons' home, and Mrs. Pattison—who was a close friend of Browning's
—was first accosted by an anonymous youth who said, "I fear that you
are not an admirer of our great poet." When she protested, he explained, "Had you appreciated Browning, I should have supposed that
you would have become a member of this Society." Then the meeting
began:

A lady [Miss Elizabeth Wordsworth?] . . . read a bit from "Balaus-
tion's Adventure," and made a remark to which no one responded;
she then tried a second, which she addressed to the Chairman, and
which he received in dead silence. I turned to D—— M—— [D. S.
MacColl?] (Newdigate prizeman) and asked if the discussion was
always as flat as this, to which he, "I was just thinking that I had
never been present at so brilliant a discussion since the foundation
of the Society." [2]

Mrs. Pattison's reply is not recorded.

The lopsided zeal of most Browningites gained notoriety for them
even in their own time. Matthew Arnold, the leading critic of the age,

repeatedly declined to review Browning's books because he knew that any deprecatory remarks would call down upon his head the wrath of the disciples. The verse of Browning unfortunately lacked lucidity, Arnold explained to John Llewelyn Davies (himself a Browningite of more temperate outlook), yet he "could not in conscience review him without saying this, and the public would inevitably seize upon this, and neglect all one said about Browning's genius—so that I should do his vogue no good." [3] Impartial criticism was clearly impossible in the case of a poet whose followers spoke of their admiration for him as "the faith" and designated all others as "outsiders." Little wonder, then, that the Browning Society often failed in its primary task, the discussion and elucidation of Browning's poems.

Anecdotes about the critical ineptitude of the Browning societies of London and elsewhere have, in fact, become part of the literary folklore of both England and America. *Punch*, in a parody of the London society's gatherings, reported that one meeting closed with an appropriate suggestion from a new member that they play a game of blindman's buff.[4] The *Athenaeum* announced that a Boston Browning club, while struggling with a difficult passage in "A Toccata of Galuppi's," pondered the merits of playing Galuppi's composition in order to resolve the poem's ambiguities.[5] And a short story entitled "A Browning Courtship," which appeared in the *Atlantic Monthly* in 1888, affords an enchanting glimpse of the proceedings of a small New England Browning club. The discussion centers around these lines: "The morn when first it thunders in March, / The eel in the pond gives a leap, they say—"

"My dear madam, it is a matter of the utmost importance that we understand each line perfectly before we proceed to the next," observed the colonel.

"Yes," assented Miss Niles. "Do you consider that passage allegorical, Mr. Brown? Does the leaping of the eel in the pond symbolize the struggles of Italy for freedom?"

"I will get the encyclopaedia and look up eels," said Mr. Ellis. "I should like to know whether all eels leap in all ponds when it first thunders, or whether this habit is peculiar to Italy."

"Don't you think it is just a local superstition," suggested Annie mildly, "and hadn't we better go on to the more important part of the poem?"

"It is all equally important," said Colonel Parmington gravely. "Each word that Browning ever wrote is of equal importance with every other word."

After considerable discussion in the same nonsensical vein, the group votes to move on to the following lines and appoints a committee to bring back a report on these first lines at the next meeting.[6]

Though apocryphal, the stories illustrate precisely the chief short-comings of the London Browning Society's critical output: its penchant for allegorical interpretations, its urge to identify every allusion (no matter how trivial), its fundamentalist confidence that each line of Browning's text is divinely inspired, and—alas, it must be admitted —its amiable confusion. But let it be said in their defense that the members of the Browning Society were confronted with an enormously difficult task. While Browning was still alive and before the passing of time had done its inevitable sifting and winnowing, they attempted to comprehend the great, confusing mass of Browning's poetry, which by his death in 1889 had filled seventeen volumes. They had to sort out and evaluate it, explain it, define it, describe it, defend it, compare it, investigate it—and all this was to be done by a comparatively small group of people who were not, for the most part, trained or experienced in the techniques of literary criticism. It was an undertaking of such scope, Augustine Birrell playfully remarked, "as, in the language of joint-stock prospectuses, 'to transcend individual enterprise,' and consequently, as we all know, a company has been recently floated, or a society established, having Mr. Browning for its principal object." [7]

The society's major liabilities, aside from its evangelical fervor, were a lack of any definite critical method (most of the papers were either sloppily impressionistic or moralistic) and an ignorance of the biographical background of many of Browning's poems. For the latter sin of omission the Browningites could not be held really accountable, of course; the details of a man's life generally become well-known only after his death. But this ignorance betrayed the society into some very curious interpretations of (for example) *Fifine at the Fair*, when an awareness that its bitter mood was occasioned by Browning's unsuccessful proposal of marriage to Lady Ashburton in 1869 would have spared the society such absurdities as Nettleship's paper on *Fifine*.[8] Still, one can scarcely demand of a poet's contemporaries that they possess hindsight. In fairness to the Browning Society, it should also be observed that fashions in critical approaches and terminology are short-lived, and no doubt our Freudian and Marxist interpretations of literature today will seem as quaintly old-fashioned to readers of the twenty-first century as does the Victorian search for moral uplift in poetry.

Nevertheless, having said all this, one must admit that much of the Browning Society's literary criticism was very, very bad. One reason for this was that the society, instead of exploring new approaches to Browning's poetry, was content to discuss the issues which had already become critical clichés half a century earlier. Was there any more threadbare topic, for example, than Browning's obscurity? Browning himself called it "the old convenient verdict on my poetry—'unintelligible.'" [9] And indeed Browning's verse *was* often obscure, though the cries of outrage by his first readers seem exaggerated to those today who have wrestled with the tortured syntax of Dylan Thomas or E. E. Cummings. The Browning Society, however, simply talked the subject to death, and in the end the platitudinous conclusion was always the same: Browning was obscure but rewarding.

Frequently this truism was expressed in metaphors. The members of the society, in fact, exercised a depressing ingenuity in inventing new figures of speech to describe Browning's lack of clarity in verse. Edward Gonner said that "before we were rewarded by a magnificent sunset, we had to wade through herbage and leafage innumerable." [10] Dr. Berdoe quoted Augustine Birrell as saying that *Sordello* was a palace without a staircase. Berdoe himself remarked that the poem was "as full of beauties as a tropical forest, [but] it was as difficult to explore." [11] Joshua Kirkman compared Browning's works to "volumes of cobwebs strung with innumerable pearls glittering in a light beyond our ordinary powers of vision." [12] The metaphors, however, could be used to condemn as well as defend. "Language is for [Browning] a conquered province rather than an inherited kingdom," Dr. John Todhunter observed.[13] J. B. Oldham claimed that the "structural deformities" threatened to suffocate Browning's poems with "their weed-like growth." [14] The most elaborate figure of all was invented by Mrs. Ireland:

> We wander vaguely through the palace of the Master's thought, and we lose our way. But some of us have caught a strain of distant music, a glimpse of a flying figure, we seem to hear a dim echo as of multitudinous footfalls, we have seen a wondrous light stealing below massive portals. Eagerly, blindly, we press on and on! [15]

A few of the most devoted Browningites, of course, could be relied upon to deny that Browning was ever difficult to understand. "They should not be too hasty in accusing Browning of obscurity," said Walter Slater. "It was possible the obscurity existed in the mind of the reader, and what was unintelligible to one mind might be quite clear to another." [16] James Cotter Morison advanced the same idea, though in slightly more sophisticated language:

> It is no tenet of ours to deny that Browning is obscure to—those who have not the means of understanding him. He takes no pains to write down to the meanest capacity of all possible readers. . . . But that he is obscure to the reverent and patient gaze of the fitly-prepared student, is what we peremptorily deny.[17]

Freely paraphrased, Morison's statement seems to suggest that anyone who does not understand Browning is either irreverent, impatient, or ill-prepared. It remained for Dr. Berdoe, however, to put the finishing touches upon this circular argument: the obscurities, he suggested, were like the prickles on the prickly pear, which kept birds from eating the seeds so that the fruit might be preserved for the higher animal, Man. "It was possible," he continued, "that these difficulties in Browning's poems might serve a similar purpose—to keep off some of the idle, silly people who read only for amusement." Shaw, who was present at this particular meeting, spoke a few minutes later. Browningites who held such a view, he observed wryly, "seemed to have a notion that Browning thought out a thing quite clearly and then immediately sat down and thought how he could make it unintelligible and prevent anybody from reading it." [18] The deflating hiss of that theory should have been audible to everyone in the room.

Fortunately, not every discussion ended on such a comic note, and many just and penetrating observations were made at the Browning Society meetings on the subject of poetic obscurity. Miss Lewis, for instance, hazarded the guess that the main source of Browning's occasional obscurity was his inability "to gauge the apprehending power of the ordinary mind." [19] Had she added that Browning's haphazard, informal education left him unaware of what most readers could be expected to know, her explanation would probably satisfy many critics of Browning today. Other theories were also offered. James Thomson thought that *Sordello* was obscure not because of its language but as a result of its "abrupt transitions, the rapid discursions, and the continual recondite allusions to matters with which very few readers can be familiar." [20] At an early meeting of the society F. W. Farrar made a valuable distinction between difficulties of thought and difficulties of exression (only the latter, he felt, were reprehensible),[21] and several years later J. B. Oldham, in a paper devoted to the subject, offered an expanded explanation of the varieties of obscurities present in Browning's poems: ". . . those which obviously arise out of the nature of the subject-matter of the poems; . . . those which arise out of the poet's method of treating that subject-matter; . . . those which arise out of the poet's characteristic and often eccentric modes of expression. . . ." [22] Oldham's paper constitutes a full and useful discussion of the issue; indeed, it was censured by conservative Browningites for the candidness with which it enumerated Browning's specific ambiguities.

It has been often claimed that the Browning Society people revelled in his obscurity, that it held for them the fascination of a Chinese puzzle or the exclusive delight of a Masonic password. Doubtless some were attracted by this promise of the mysterious, but to most members, the obscure quality of Browning's poems was simply annoying, for they felt that it interfered with his function as a moral teacher of the masses. How could he preach a "clear gospel for the age" in cryptograms? Edwin Johnson said that "it appeared to him that Browning was to be complained of for throwing these repeated enigmas before his admirers, and giving no clue to their solution." [23] Dr. Furnivall stated the case even more emphatically: "He could not also get over Browning's obscurity in many of his poems; and he thought if the poet would only take counsel with others on the subject, his work would be better." [24] But eventually even Furnivall, with all his common sense, had to fall back upon a metaphor typical of him:

> When you were rowing or hunting for the first time, you wanted hints as to which bank to steer by, or which way the quarry was likely to take. Well, those who had studied Browning knew that he was hindered in getting hold of people by a good many obscurities, and it was the Society's duty to face these obscurities, to acknowledge them and to investigate their causes.[25]

If Browning's poetry was obscure, it was also often harsh and rough. Readers of Arnold's poems might lament a line like "Who prop, thou ask'st, in these bad days, my mind?" ("To a Friend"), but what were Browningites to make of entire volumes of seemingly grotesque, jingling verse? If they were uncompromisingly honest like Furnivall and William Revell, they might call Browning's form "execrable" and add that posterity would have an even lower opinion of it;[26] but naturally most of them preferred to defend the harshness, and once again, when logic failed them, they appealed to metaphor. "The verse may be rugged, ear-splitting, teeth-splitting . . . , but don't mind that," said H. J. Bulkeley; "read on, break through the crust, burrow down and get at the golden thought." [27] The members of the Browning Society, it should be pointed out, excelled at the mixed metaphor. Bulkeley, though, is put to shame by Thomson, who came up with this wonderfully incoherent figure:

> [Browning's] strong, intensely original, and many-sided individuality has, among finer savours, a keen relish for the odd, the peculiar, the quaint, the grotesque; and when these offer themselves in the subject-matter, his guiding genius is apt to throw the reins on the necks of the vigorous talents and eager perceptions, which run risky riot in language as quaint and grotesque as the theme.[28]

Alternately, Browning's lack of melody might be compared with a steep, rugged mountain, beyond which lay a "rich country" (the Promised Land?) or at the foot of which ran "the gently murmuring streams of more melodious poets" (Tennyson? Swinburne?).[29] For if Browning's harshness hid philosophical profundity, it necessarily followed—and this is implied in most of the figures—that more fluent writers were shallow and unspiritual. "It may be better in these oily days of minds as well as railway-trains advancing without friction, to be somewhat rugged with Browning, Isaiah, Carlyle, &c.," remarked the Reverend Mr. Kirkman, "than ever smooth with the more popular prophets of lies and delusions." [30] His nuggets may be rough but they are golden (as the Reverend Mr. Haweis affirmed); he gives us solid, nourishing mutton (so said Furnivall), even if it does lack some tasty currant jelly.[31]

The same line of defense—that the harshness is the necessary concomitant of Browning's intellectual depth—is present in most of the nonfigurative arguments as well. The Reverend Mr. Forsyth gave typical expression to this viewpoint when he said that "much of the roughness of verse so often complained of was inevitable in the expression of the intricate thought, and in no case did he ever come away from his study of Browning cloyed and with his mind diluted, as sometimes happened after a course of smoother versification." [32] (Another slighting reference to the Tennyson school of poetry.)

On the other hand, at least two members suggested ideas worth serious consideration even today: Bulkeley investigated several poems charged with "undue ruggedness and grotesqueness," and he found that in every instance the lack of "smoothness" was in some way related to the dramatic situation of the poem; and Shaw conjectured that "novelty of treatment and strong individuality of style quite commonly made critics of unquestionable knowledge and taste deaf to melody, rhythm, and harmony. If Dr. Furnivall and Mr. Gonner were wrong about Browning, they were no more deceived than Spohr and Weber were about Beethoven." [33] Clearly Browning's racy, colloquial style, which contributed much to his reputation for "harshness," *was* new and prefigured in some manner the language and sensibility of Pound and Eliot in our own century. That we have not yet fully charted Browning's achievement in this area may perhaps be attributed to the bad example of the Browning Society, which rarely was able to move beyond the banal formulation that philosophical content produces crabbed form in poetry.

The Browningites were prone, as we have already seen, to compare Browning with other writers, usually to the detriment of the latter. At various times they cited his similarity—or perhaps superiority —to Emerson, Ruskin, Scott, Meredith, and Chaucer;[34] but above all, with maddening regularity, they spoke of Browning in relation to Tennyson and Shakespeare. Dr. Berdoe confessed that "Browning's words acted as a tonic—and he often put Tennyson aside to get some of the high and bracing thoughts of Browning." [35] Tennyson was the best known of the "smooth" poets, and so of course one could assume that his metrical facility concealed superficial or unsound ideas. His attitude toward women, for example—was it not true, Furnivall insisted, that he was a prig and that "Browning's view of love was a distinctly superior one"? [36] (Furnivall, who earnestly sought the emancipation of women, particularly in education and sports, was enormously distressed by the antifeminist implications of Tennyson's *The Princess*.) If one were daring one might even argue, as did the Reverend Mr. Kirkman, that Browning was superior not only intellectually but also artistically, that "he has a far wider and more commanding versatility of rhythm than Tennyson." [37]

But Furnivall generally discouraged such explicit comparisons with a living contemporary, perhaps because he was also a friend of Tennyson's, and perhaps too because he saw that such comparisons fostered unpleasant rivalry and partisanship. He had neatly skirted the issue in his original Browning Society prospectus by writing: "Without entering on the next question of who is the greatest living poet, Mr. Browning's admirers are content to accept the general verdict that he is both one of the greatest, and *the* most thought-full." [38] In his bibliography, when Furnivall quoted a statement by James Thomson that Browning was superior to Tennyson, he discreetly omitted Tennyson's name.[39] Yet it should be added that the very founding of the Browning Society was prompted in part by a sense of competition with another contemporary. "One main motive with me for taking this step," Furnivall wrote some years later, "was some talk and writing of a certain cymbal-tinkler [Swinburne, no doubt] being a greater poet—that is, maker, creator of men and women—than Browning. I couldn't stand that." [40]

However, if invidious comparisons with living poets were somewhat suppressed, it was always open season for Browning-Shakespeare analogies. Naturally many were quick to point out that Browning and Shakespeare had to be judged by quite different standards, even assuming that one were discussing *plays* in both instances. Arthur Symons, for one, perceived that Browning differed radically from Shakespeare in being more subjective, more analytic, and therefore more modern; similarly, J. B. Oldham contrasted Shakespeare's dramatic method and Browning's psychological approach.[41] Furnivall also questioned the relevance of such comparisons: "The method of Browning, writing for the eminently subjective nineteenth century, necessarily differed from that natural to Shakspere writing for the eminently objective England of the sixteenth century." [42]

Nevertheless, Shakespeare continued to be the standard of reference: J. D. Williams contributed a brief paper comparing Browning's Guendolen and Shakespeare's Beatrice; Professor P. A. Barnett gave a paper on "Browning's Jews and Shakspere's Jew" (to which the perpetually splenetic Edward Gonner replied by announcing that "with regard to the general question of a comparison of Shakspere and Browning, he was happy to throw himself on the side of the former"); J. J. Britton thought that Browning understood women just as thoroughly as did Shakespeare; and Furnivall himself admitted that "Browning went deeper into the subject of music than did Shakspere." [43] On occasion Furnivall had to restrain the enthusiasm of his Browningites, as when Elizabeth Dickinson West insisted that Browning's villains were more lifelike than Shakespeare's. "Miss West can see the facts when she is dealing with Browning," Furnivall retorted. "Her eyes are darkened when she looks at Shakspere. The truth is that Browning but follows Shakspere—at what distance, he knows better than we—in creating Men and Women." [44] For once, sanity prevailed at a Browning Society meeting.

The excessive praise of Browning reached such heights in the first few months after his death that Appleton Morgan, president of the New York Shakespeare Society, felt obliged to explain in print the differences between Shakespeare societies and Browning societies. The Shakespeareans, he said, took for granted Shakespeare's greatness and devoted their time to a study of the materials with which he worked in his plays, whereas the Browningites, uncertain of Browning's real stature, were constantly making extravagant claims on his behalf. Furthermore, the Shakespeare societies had offered no such pretentious nonsense to the world as papers on "Shakespeare as a Religious Teacher." [45]

Yet in their insistence upon Browning's unique achievement as a "religious teacher," the members of the London Browning Society were troubled by one uncomfortable fact: that the most remarkable personalities in his poems were almost invariably deeply tainted with evil. Sludge, the Duke of Ferrara, Caliban, Guido, Don Juan—as Shaw said of the characters in Shakespeare's plays who display an interest in music, if they were to attend the Philharmonic concerts, "you would have an audience in St. James's Hall of which I certainly should not care to form one." [46] What was even more distressing to loyal Browningites was that these repulsive figures were often endowed with great intellectual gifts which enabled them to plead their cases with the very theories about God, man, and art which Browning himself held. Edwin Johnson summed up the problem thus: "Browning certainly endows his scoundrels with so much of his own nature that he oversteps the bounds of dramatic consistency; and in this monologue ['Sludge'] a dissolving view is constantly before us: Sludge melting into Browning, and Browning into Sludge [in] a manner that is fairly baffling." [47]

As usual, the members were prompt to find excuses for this unseemly habit. The easiest solution was to dismiss the charge of casuistry and say that Browning was merely entering "into the varying moods" of his protagonists; but this answer seems to have satisfied nobody except Dorothea Beale.[48] Or, like Roden Noel, one could hold that although Browning "stirs up the rottenness of [life] a little too curiously," his evil characters are offset by ones of shining purity, as in the opposition of Guido and Pompilia in *The Ring and the Book*.[49] One might also argue, as several members did, that "Browning can enable us to understand our fellow-men better, [and] can show us good ground for pitying or loving a fellow creature whom we otherwise could only hate." [50] James Cotter Morison suggested that Browning was drawn to grotesque figures like Caliban and Sludge because of his "gift of humour." [51] Miss West, in a useful paper on Browning's villains, offered the curious but intriguing explanation that the poet's mystical tendencies were balanced by tendencies to deal with inferior creatures. "To these mechanic's-propensities of his he can only give the satisfaction of exercise by thus occupying them with things which, being devoid of spiritual beauty, do not engage his mystical faculty," she wrote. "To meet this requirement, he chooses sometimes the grotesque, sometimes the morally ugly, for his subject matter." [52]

The most intelligent discussion of the topic was provided by Edward Dowden, who, it will be recalled, was not a regular member of the society. Dowden said that it did not seem a matter of wonder to him "that an optimist thinker should make strict inquisition of evil, for the vivid conception of good demands the conception of evil, which must be studied in order to be mastered and set aside"; and he then traced the treatment of villainy and evil in European literature of the past.[53]

Furnivall, on the other hand, adopted a much less complicated attitude toward Browning's fondness for casuistry. From his point of view, Browning was merely "whitewashing a blackguard." He took strong exception to the sentimental notion that such an operation would somehow broaden our sympathies, and he ridiculed the opinions of some other members by translating them into Furnivallese: "If you could show by lying and misrepresentation that a blackguard had some fine qualities, then you were conferring a benefit on humanity! Dr. F. confessed he was not prepared to accept that position." [54] The solution, Dr. Furnivall thought, was to persuade Browning to abandon these impostors and spend his time instead on nobler subjects.[55] If only Browning would take the advice of others! It was very troublesome, after all, when the poet insisted upon putting great spiritual truths in the mouth of *Fifine*'s Don Juan, because even Furnivall had to write Browning "to ask what really was his idea." [56]

But Furnivall's habit of dashing off a letter to Browning every time a problem of interpretation arose eventually created still another critical issue, one with which the Browning Society wrestled unsuccessfully for years. The dilemma was this: to what extent should a poet's conscious intent be taken into account in interpreting his poetry? Specifically, if he disagrees with his critics about what a poem means, who is to be believed? The poet? He did write it, after all. The critics? Perhaps, it is argued, they see some pattern or significance in the poem of which the poet himself was not aware. The latter view has been persuasivly advanced in our century by W. K. Wimsatt and Monroe Beardsley, who condemn excessive reliance upon a poet's statements about his own poetry as "the intentional fallacy."

A majority of the Browning Society members also subscribed to this view, though not always with the best motives. The religiously inclined, such as Miss Beale, used it to justify their selecting from Browning only those portions of his poetry which supported their own theological attitudes—or, as Miss Beale put it, bringing out "from the poems some of the treasures by which we feel our spiritual nature has been enriched." [57] Others, like Miss Drewry, felt free to interpret Browning in any way they wished because they saw him as the unconscious medium of divine truths:

> Miss Drewry said,— . . . I wish to express my strong conviction that the poet is a specially inspired being, who comes by a sort of instinct at that which it costs others much labour in thought and investigation even to appreciate. . . . [Each reader will find a different message, according to his needs] . . . and this whether the poet himself recognizes it as his conscious and purposed meaning or not.[58]

Arthur Symons expressed the same idea, in nonreligious terms, when he quoted Plato as saying that "poets utter great and wise things which they do not themselves understand." [59]

Most Browningites, however, accepted the "intentional fallacy" theory because it lent authority to their extremely allegorical readings of Browning's poems. If his word were taken as the final authority on "Childe Roland," for example, that poem would be nothing more than a "romance" inspired by some figures on a tapestry; whereas in fact every Browningite had his own explanation of the poem's "spiritual meaning." The Dark Tower was Truth, or Death, or Life, or Religion, or Materialism, or . . . well, whatever one chose to make of it. After a paper on "Childe Roland" by Joshua Kirkman (he belonged to the Death school of thought), Dr. Furnivall dropped a bombshell ("a charge of dynamite," he called it) into the discussion. Browning had on three separate occasions told him, Furnivall announced with wicked glee, that the poem had no allegorical significance. There was no harm, he added, in using "Childe Roland" to "signify whatever image it called up in [the reader's] own mind. But he must not confuse the poet's mind with his." Kirkman reacted to this news with dismay. If the Dark Tower did not represent death, it *ought* to, he said; and besides, if Dr. Furnivall were continually to ask Mr. Browning what his poems meant, there would soon be no need of a Browning Society![60]

This doleful prophecy was very nearly fulfilled at a meeting in 1889. Mrs. Glazebrook wrote a paper in which she declared that the nymph in "Numpholeptos" represented "the ideal woman—a modern Beatrice or Laura," but Dr. Berdoe and others emphatically disagreed,

THE BURDEN OF CRITICISM

and therefore the members present voted that Furnivall (so a note in the transactions says)

> should ask Mr. Browning whether his poem was an allegory only, or meant to represent any type of woman present or past. This has accordingly been done; and as the author's own interpretation follows, the printing of the discussion becomes needless. So (it may be said) is the printing of the paper. But as that was set before the meeting, and contains a view that may be fairly taken in the absence of authoritative exposition, the paper is not cancelled.[61]

Appleton Morgan might well have added, in his article contrasting the Shakespeare and Browning societies, that Shakespearean critics were secure in the knowledge that their poet was in the grave, and they could not hear him laughing at them—"a contingency too possible in the case of Mr. Browning," as Roden Noel wittily observed.[62]

*   *   *

These, then, were the critical issues that divided the Browning Society. But there was one assumption upon which they could all agree: that Browning was the greatest thinker and philosopher of all living poets. For readers in our century, this one pervasive assumption of the society is especially distressing, because many no longer willingly accept the notion that poets are repositories of great spiritual and intellectual truths; our literary criticism implicitly denies this when it focuses upon the technique of a poem, its language, its texture, its surface brilliance. Our rejection of the "poet-teacher-prophet" ideal, so commonly held by the Victorians, has led to considerable neglect by modern critics of such didactic poets as Tennyson and Browning. Browning in particular has suffered from this shift in critical values, since his ideas seem badly discredited today. His admonition to live life joyously, impulsively, and vigorously—what was it, George Santayana demanded in 1900, except barbarism, "a thought and an art inchoate and ill-digested, . . . a volcanic eruption that tosses itself quite blindly and ineffectually into the sky"?[63] Santayana's charge that Browning possessed visceral attitudes rather than a "philosophy" has not yet been completely answered and has been often repeated by readers dissatisfied with Browning.

In the eighties, however, except for a few renegades, almost nobody in the Browning Society was questioning the validity of Browning's philosophy. Needless to say, philosophy did not mean to them an organized system of thought; rather it meant Browning's admirable optimism and heartiness, his assurance that apparent failure may be success in the eyes of heaven, his glorification of romantic passion, and above all his Christianity. The curious thing about this situation is that even the agnostics and those who questioned his philosophic premises joined in the chorus of praise for Browning as a thinker. Furnivall, who repeatedly explained at the meetings that he disagreed with Browning's religious views, nevertheless defended him in print as "the greatest Christian philosophic poet now living." [64] And at the same time that he was protesting the obsessive concern with Browning's "message," James Cotter Morison admitted that he was the greatest "union of poet and philosopher" in the history of the world.[65]

Yet even in the society's early years there were some occasional rumblings of discontent, for if all agreed that Browning was a great thinker, some at least tired quickly of the steady diet of papers which treated only the didactic elements in his verse and neglected almost entirely its literary qualities. Morison sounded the first note of dissent at the meeting on April 28, 1882, when he complained mildly that their preoccupation with Browning's philosophy was interfering with their enjoyment of his poetry.[66] After the meeting he contributed a short note to the *Papers* entitled "Of What Concern to Us Is a Poet's Philosophy?" Part of it is worth quoting, since it represents an important minority viewpoint within the Browning Society:

> Attempts to turn great Poets into Philosophers, and to deduce from their works a more or less consistent system of thought, have been frequently made at different times. Homer, Vergil, Dante, Shakespeare, Goethe, have been treated in this manner, with results more than questionable. . . . How indifferent we are to the Poet's creed, philosophical or religious, is shown by the manner in which we enjoy Homer, Lucretius, Dante, and Shelley, to take obvious types for example. The Polytheism of the first, the Epicurean philosophy of the second, the Catholicism of the third, the Pantheism of the fourth, are never allowed by a lover of poetry to interfere with, or in any degree affect, his appreciation of the *poetry* of any of them. . . . One might almost say that we are no more concerned with a poet's dogmatic creed than with his personal appearance. We take his creed for granted, whatever it may be, and are wholly indifferent to it.[67]

That this was a minority opinion, though, is shown by the continuing didactic emphasis of the Browning Society papers. At the meeting held the following October, for example, the society heard papers by

Miss Beale on "The Religious Teaching of Browning" and Edwin Johnson on "Conscience and Art in Browning"; and after they were read, the chairman, Francis Storr, announced that "Professor Johnson had vindicated, against the objections of the previous Chairman [Morison], the legitimacy of deducing or expounding the philosophy of a poet. The same argument would hold good of the religion of a poet." [68]

Furnivall himself certainly had no objections to philosophical and theological discussions at the meetings. "If the orthodox people trotted out their beliefs as facts," he commented in his inimitable way, "those of the other side were bound to tell them they were delusions." [69] He even threatened once to write a paper detailing his own disagreement with Browning.[70] By the middle of the decade, theology had become the all-consuming passion of the society. It was like a boomerang, said Dr. Berdoe; "they were constantly throwing it away with all their might, but it always returned." [71] The Browning Society was fast becoming, as Shaw said later, a conventicle where devout and aging ladies discussed their religion with Furnivall.[72]

This resulted in an increasing polarization of the agnostic and Christian elements of the society, for by 1887 nearly every meeting was turning into a pitched battle, with salvos of Biblical texts coming from one side of the room and barrages of sarcasm and rhetoric from the other. The standard-bearers for the agnostics were Shaw and Gonner, while the Christian believers were led by Berdoe, Miss Stoddart, and Miss Whitehead. As early as April 30, 1886, Shaw had "deprecated the introduction of the theological element" into their meetings,[73] but war was not really declared until February 25, 1887, when Gonner, with sardonic humor, "remarked on the difficulty of keeping out personal theology in the discussion. One of the objects of our meetings," he continued, "was to discover Browning's theological bias; but we confuse *our* opinions in the matter, and so convert the discussion into something that might suit the chambers of the Christian Evidence Society." Miss Whitehead immediately retorted that the poem they were discussing, "A Death in the Desert," perfectly summed up Browning's belief in Christ, and "she considered the poem most helpful to our faith." [74]

The dissension within the society finally reached crisis proportions at the meeting of May 25, 1888, following a paper by Miss Stoddart on "Saul." Furnivall, who ignited this explosive discussion, seems, as usual, to have played an ambiguous role: as an agnostic, he enjoyed sniping at the Christians, but it was all done in good humor, and he always appeared greatly astonished when the orthodox became angry.

In this instance, he objected to the view held by Miss Stoddart (and Browning too, for that matter) that David had prophesied the advent of Christ, and he blandly dismissed it as a "poetical fancy." Dr. Berdoe protested that David had indeed looked forward to a Messiah; and "speaking as a medical man," he observed that Christians bore their trials more cheerfully than unbelievers. Annoyed by the evangelical overtones of this last assertion, Shaw then proceeded to condemn both Christianity and capitalism in one sweeping speech:

> He [Shaw] had some experience as to how Christianity enabled people to endure sorrow. He must say that they bore the misfortunes of others with the most extraordinary magnanimity. . . . he thought if Christ were to come on the earth and see what was taking place, he would be very greatly hurt to be told that it was the influence of his spirit, for he thought this was the most desperately mean, sordid, selfish, rascally, dastardly century that any one could wish to live in. They found wretched men, women, and children working and sweating from twelve to eighteen hours a-day for a bare subsistence, in order to produce the dividends on which these very Christian people lived pleasantly, and went to church on Sunday to thank God that they were not as other men.

After some brief remarks by the Reverend Mr. Graham, in which he praised Miss Stoddart for having written a better sermon on the poem than he could have, Gonner stood up and angrily attacked the logic of both Berdoe and Miss Stoddart, who had, he said, "thrown down a distinct challenge to one party, and the other side were quite justified in taking up the challenge." Kingsland replied that she "had simply taken Mr. Browning's opinions as laid down in *Saul*"; Miss Whitehead accused the agnostics of courting abuse; and at last Miss Stoddart spoke in her own defense. She "had certainly thrown down the gage," she said, "and was perfectly ready to hear the arguments on the other side—and she had heard none." Furthermore, she wished "to make an especial stab at Mr. Shaw; he made the most singular statement she had ever heard." [75] As Professor Donald Smalley has said of her remarkable speech, Shaw had scratched a Methodist to find an Amazon. [76]

If this meeting ended on a note of perfect confusion, the next one, on June 29, 1888, was even more tumultuous, for then Gonner introduced his amendment recommending that the society be disbanded. This was in part, as we have seen earlier, a result of the antagonism between Berdoe and Gonner; but it also brought out into the open a most important question: should the Browning Society spend most of its time debating Browning's religious views? "They were aware of his aversion to theological discussions," Gonner told the members. "It seemed to him that when to enthusiasm they joined profound ignorance, they were likely to have [a] little unpleasantness. . . . He contended that in printing discussions which would not disgrace the pages of the *Christian Globe*, the Society was not performing its work." Gonner's proposal had approximately the same effect as a drunkard's announcement of his presence at a temperance rally. For the rest of the meeting, one earnest Browningite after another arose to proclaim his belief in both Browning and Christianity, and to express his horror at Gonner's heretical ideas. Miss Stoddart felt certain "that her paper had been especially aimed at in the amendment. . . . If theological poems were to be put in the shade," she demanded to know, "what poems were left?" The transactions report that the conclusion of her speech was punctuated with cheers from the other members. Miss Whitehead said she had discussed the entire problem with Dr. Furnivall a year before, and his solution was "hang the theology!" ("Laughter," note the transactions.) But the members decided, in effect, to hang Gonner's amendment instead; besides Gonner and Shaw, only Dykes Campbell voted for it.[77]

For the rest of the society's brief history, theology continued to hold sway, and if there were no further public fights over the matter, that was because Shaw and Gonner shortly dropped out of the society. The forces of orthodoxy were firmly in control.

When in 1891 *Poet-Lore*, the American Browningite journal, heard the news of the Browning Society's impending dissolution (this time it really happened), its editors attempted to assess the society's achievements and to discover what had gone wrong in recent years. Every student of Browning, the editors wrote, goes through several phases: first, "he considers himself the divinely-appointed interpreter of Browning obscurities"; second, he proclaims Browning to be a great philosophic and religious teacher; and third, it at last dawns upon him that Browning is an essentially dramatic poet, a discovery which opens up entirely new areas of criticism. "The London Society," they concluded cryptically, "has hardly got beyond the second stage, and its outlook has in consequence been somewhat circumscribed." [78] It is a shrewd observation. The Browning Society, in making Browning's poetry subserve a religious purpose, produced a large body of criticism which, if not an outright failure, is most uneven in quality. By 1892 nearly 100 papers had been produced under the society's auspices, not to mention the other materials printed in the transactions; but because of their single-minded determination to find moral inspiration in Browning, often to the exclusion of literary values, many of these papers possess little more than historical interest today. If one were to draw a moral (as the Browningites were so fond of doing), it would be that although, to paraphrase T. S. Eliot, literary criticism may be supplemented by criticism from a definite ethical and theological standpoint, nevertheless the literary considerations cannot be abandoned altogether.[79] If they are, criticism is no longer an act of judgment or explication; it becomes merely an instrument of religious propaganda.

CHAPTER VI

THE MEETINGS, 1881-84

The poetry of Mr. Browning has had singular fortunes. Rejected at first by the world, his poems became the possession
of a few friends of romance; then a wider public was induced
to read them; finally they fell into the hands of people who
have overbuilt the fairy plot of ground with "societies," and
who squabble about texts and meanings like scholiasts or Biblical commentators. The last estate of the poems has been worse
than the first.

—Andrew Lang[1]

THE BROWNING SOCIETY sponsored a variety of activities—including
the writing and publication of books, the production of plays, and the
planning of public lectures on Browning—but its *raison d'etre* was the
monthly meetings at which papers were read and discussed. Held on
the fourth Friday evening of each month between September and
June or July (though there were occasional departures from this
schedule), the meetings were at first conducted in the Botanic Theatre of University College; but the society soon moved to a smaller
room, because the size of the lecture theatre tended to discourage free
discussions. It is difficult to determine how many attended the meetings, because figures were recorded in the transactions only when the
audience was exceptionally large. At the opening meeting, for example, more than 300 were present, but we may be certain that this
figure was never surpassed and perhaps not even equalled at subsequent meetings, for after the first year they were no longer open to the
public. (Each member could, however, bring one visitor.) When the
society fell upon evil days near the end of the decade, some of the
meetings were undoubtedly very sparsely attended.

No matter how many or few members came, seldom did more than a handful actually participate in the discussion periods, and those who did speak generally made themselves heard at every meeting. At their worst, these exchanges resembled nothing so much as a bad imitation of Dickensian fiction, with each puppetlike personality mumbling a few phrases that serve to characterize him: Dr. Berdoe would denounce vivisection, Dr. Furnivall would snort at the illogicality of Christians, Miss Stoddart would allude to life's spiritual values, Kingsland would murmur that Browning was a great teacher . . . and so it went until, as the transactions so often say, the meeting would end with a "conversation of a general nature." In reality, the discussions were not fully spontaneous, since the papers were often issued before the meetings in "proof" form, and some members were therefore ready to deliver carefully prepared speeches after the papers were read. At one meeting, following a paper by Mrs. Ireland, Dr. Berdoe announced that as soon as he had heard her American accent, he knew they would have a good paper. When Mrs. Ireland immediately protested that she was not an American, Berdoe apologized but added blandly that "as he had prepared something very nice to say about America and the Americans, he was going to say it—it must not be wasted." [2]

There was considerable disagreement among the members about what categories of papers ought to be read. A few favored the pattern followed by the Oxford Browning Society—i.e., the presentation of a brief, simple paper on a single poem, followed by a general discussion of the poem itself. If Mrs. Pattison is to be believed, however, this approach produced rather dismal results, and Edward Gonner, at the June meeting in 1888, provided additional testimony that the "Oxford Plan," as it was known among Browningites, was not a success. [3] Furnivall, on the other hand, wanted papers that provided intensive analyses of individual poems—"going through a difficult poem of Browning's and bringing out beliefs as to the purpose at the bottom of the poem." [4] But the majority of the members admired precisely those papers which Furnivall deplored: superficial surveys of the "general characteristics" of Browning's verse or of its "spiritual teachings." It is significant that when Miss Helen Ormerod, at Furnivall's request, presented a brisk, factual biography of Abt Vogler, her audience protested in unison that she had neglected the religious qualities of Browning's poem. In vain did Gonner defend her paper as one that the society "would be proud to print"; clearly most Browning enthusiasts valued inspiration rather than information. [5]

If this axiom is correct, then the inaugural address at the meeting of October 28, 1881, by the Reverend Joshua Kirkman (1829–1904) must have been one of the most popular ever delivered, for few of the subsequent papers were able to climb to its dizzying level of generality. For thirty-three years vicar of St. Stephen, Hampstead, Kirkman possessed no obvious qualifications for his assignment except that he had delivered a series of lectures on *Sordello* in Hampstead during the sixties;[6] but of course, as the unceremonious Furnivall confessed at that first meeting, Kirkman was "the only real Browning scholar" he knew in the summer of 1881.[7] The earlier lectures had attracted Browning's attention at the time, and the Browning Society address also provoked a cordial response from the poet when he saw it in print.[8]

Kirkman said he had wanted to call his address "Browning Made Easy," and the gist of it was simply that beginners in Browning should avoid the long, difficult poems and start rather with simple ones like "Rabbi Ben Ezra," "Prospice," and (somewhat unexpectedly) "Childe Roland"—a "splendid trilogy" which he was still praising sixteen years later in the *Hampstead Annual*.[9] This was hardly novel advice —the more sensible Browningites had been saying as much for years —but Kirkman had a knack for stating the obvious in grandiloquent terms. "*We must first divide Browning's work into two great classes*," he announced with a flourish. "First, *those works which may be understood and enjoyed*. Second, *those which never will be*." [10] (Furnivall, a few minutes later, interpreted this as meaning "1. the poems which Mr. K. liked; 2. those which he didn't like." [11]) Kirkman went on to discuss Browning's verse in relation to music, art, and Christianity, claiming, under the last heading, that Browning was "preeminently the greatest Christian poet we have ever had" [12]—an assertion that appears to overlook the existence of Donne and Milton. It was, as the *Echo* pointed out, a speech filled with "extravagant laudation." [13]

Kirkman concluded by suggesting specific tasks which the Browning Society might profitably perform: papers on individual poems that were especially difficult; treatises on such topics as Browning's humor and his attitude toward science (Berdoe later explored this subject with disheartening regularity); short "Arguments" prefixed to the poems (Furnivall favored these also, but Browning would not agree to them[14]); a lexicon of names and allusions in his poetry (Berdoe's *Browning Cyclopaedia*?); the organizing of public lectures on Browning (this was done, and Kirkman himself was among those who spread abroad the Browningite gospel[15]); and a digest of reviews (this function was assumed by Furnivall's bibliography and the Notes and

Queries column in the *Papers*). The latter part of Kirkman's address, in other words, outlined a program of action for the Browning Society, many details of which were actually carried out. But the chief effect of his speech as a whole was to "shoulder Browning up into a factitious popularity"—which Kirkman warned against—"that would be sure to become extinct like fireworks." [16] In describing Browning as "the profoundest intellect, with widest range of sympathies, and with universal knowledge of men and things, that has arisen as a poet since Shakespeare," [17] Kirkman set a bad precedent for all the idolatrous Browning Society papers which were to follow. It is no wonder that Browning felt like "a poor sinner indeed" after reading such heady praise.[18]

Both before and after Kirkman's address, the October 28 meeting was dominated by Furnivall, who explained why he had founded the Browning Society and attempted to trace Browning's poetic development. The liveliest remarks offered at the meeting, however, were by Moncure Conway (1832–1907), an American Unitarian minister who made a career of championing liberal causes, lecturing, and writing. Shortly after he arrived in London in 1863, the gregarious Conway discovered that he was Browning's neighbor, and soon he began to take long walks with the poet, enlist his support for abolitionism, and publish reviews of his books from proofs supplied by Browning.[19] Though a man of energy and intelligence, Conway possessed little judgment and even less respect for factual accuracy, as Browning, to his consternation, quickly discovered. Using information supplied by the poet, Conway produced a review which Browning described as an "unwise piece of picturesque narration." "He means well, of course," Browning went on. "He said I was very intimate with the [G. H.] Lewes's—i.e., I dined once, and spent two evenings there." [20]

Conway's remarks at the first Browning Society meeting were likewise a jumble of personal recollections and spurious anecdotes about Browning's early reception in America. His prize anecdote, which he repeated years later in his autobiography, described James Russell Lowell as saying in 1854 that he would give his copy of *Sordello* to anyone who could honestly claim to understand it.[21] Furnivall, after the meeting, sent Kingsland's minutes to Lowell, who was then living in England, and Lowell promptly dismissed Conway's story as apocryphal:

> If I ever offered to give away my copy of *Sordello* (as Mr. Conway says) it must have been an outbreak of humourous petulance called forth by some bore [Conway?] who was talking nonsense

about the poem & endeavouring to make a convert of me to his misunderstanding of the poet—*me* who had been an almost passionate
admirer of him ("this side idolatry") for years. . . . One thing is
certain—that I still own & value my original edition of *Sordello*.[22]

As a result, this part of Conway's remarks was not published in the
society's transactions.

The second meeting, on November 25, 1881, affords an interesting contrast between the two most common types of papers which the
society was to hear thereafter: a general survey of Browning's works,
and a study of a particular poem. Two papers were read, the first of
which was a sketchy but intelligent summary of Browning's poetic
output by George Barnett Smith (1841–1909), the author and journalist whom Browning so respected that he gave him advance proofs
of his books for reviewing purposes.[23] The other paper, by the Reverend John Sharpe (1846–95), a classical scholar who became in 1883
Rector of Elmley Lovett, Droitwich,[24] was a close reading of "Pietro of
Abano," which Sharpe tersely paraphrased and explained. This latter
paper pleased Furnivall enormously, for it represented the kind of
specific study he felt Browning's poetry needed, and during the following year he occasionally cited it in print as the finest piece yet written
on one of Browning's poems.[25]

But at the next meeting (January 27, 1882) both papers were
much more diffuse than Sharpe's. The chairman of the meeting, Frederick W. Farrar (1831–1903), had declined to join the Browning Society but readily agreed to take the chair, for he had long known
Browning and was fond of larding his sermons with Browning quotations. Farrar, Archdeacon of Westminster and after 1895 Dean of
Canterbury, was the author of a highly popular life of Christ and other
studies of early church history (one of which was dedicated to Browning); like most clergymen, he seems to have been drawn to Browning
primarily because of a few explicitly religious poems such as "Saul"
and "A Death in the Desert." [26] The first paper which Farrar introduced that evening was by Miss Mary A. Lewis (d. 1905), author of
inspirational fiction for the Christian Knowledge Society and daughter
of Sir George Cornewall Lewis (1806–63), the distinguished scholar,
editor, and statesman.[27] Her paper, it must be said, was a rather disappointing performance. Entitled "Some Thoughts on Browning," it
was a rambling discourse upon the moral aspects of Browning's verse
and upon "his strong, hopeful philosophy of life." At the insistence of
Dr. Furnivall she had struck from her paper "a strong Xtian bit," [28] but
even so she retained a peroration in which she acclaimed Browning as

the great religious teacher for whom England had been waiting "many a long year." [29] The real highlight of the evening, however, was the next paper, James Thomson's eloquent and moving tribute to the poet he had admired since his youth. A number of young men had come (in vain) from Cambridge that evening solely in order to see the author of *The City of Dreadful Night*.[30] Miss Lewis' paper probably did not soften their disillusionment.

Though the papers delivered at the next two meetings (February 24 and March 24, 1882) were sharply focused studies of individual poems, they produced discussions marked by glorious confusion. At the February meeting, chaired by Peter Bayne (1830–96), an angular Scottish journalist who had once edited the unsuccessful London *Dial*,[31] J. T. Nettleship made his lamentable attempt, described in an earlier chapter, to separate neatly the truth and the sophistry in *Fifine*. It was such a curious performance that it left the members rather puzzled. Was the poem a vehicle of spiritual truth or was it merely a gigantic practical joke by Browning? No one seemed quite certain, though Furnivall insisted that "Mr. Nettleship has given us all great help." [32] At the March meeting the chair was occupied by Roden Noel (1834–94),[33] who introduced Joshua Kirkman's paper on "Childe Roland" with a warning: let us not, he said, attribute to Browning our own fanciful interpretations of his poetry. His advice, alas, was not heeded by either Kirkman or his listeners. The rest of the meeting was devoted to the question of whether the Dark Tower in the poem represented Death (as Kirkman said) Truth (as Miss Drewry said), or nothing in particular (as Furnivall said). The problem was not resolved to anyone's satisfaction.

The paper read at the April 28, 1882, meeting by John B. Bury (1861–1927) represented one of the first literary efforts of a student at Trinity College, Dublin, who was later to become one of the most eminent historians of the day.[34] The honorary secretary of a local Browning Society at Trinity, Bury had written to Furnivall the previous autumn about certain similarities he saw between the ideas of Browning and those of Hegel. Browning, when he saw the letter, was delighted, though he admitted to Furnivall that he had never read Hegel.[35] Browning was equally pleased when he inspected a proof of Bury's paper, which treated "Browning's Philosophy" in Hegelian terms.[36] The members of the society were not satisfied with it, however. "He did not think it a special joy to have to master Hegel before we could understand or enjoy Browning," said the chairman, James Cotter Morison (1831–88), a brilliant scholar whose home in Paris was a social center for French and English Positivists.[37] "It seemed to him that Browning was better when not diluted with Hegel." W. C. Coupland said he wished that Bury were there to explain his own paper, and Ernest Radford called him a "plain-spoken Agnostic." [38] Though the Browningites spoke often of Browning's "philosophy," an excursion into formal philosophy did not appeal to them.

The problem of Browning's casuistry came up again at the next meeting (May 26, 1882) in a paper on "Bishop Blougram's Apology" by Edwin Johnson (1842–1901), a literary scholar and historian who since 1879 had been Furnivall's neighbor on Primrose Hill. Furnivall, who thought him one of the most stimulating thinkers he had ever met, persuaded Johnson to write occasional papers for the Browning Society as a relaxation from his more strenuous labors in connection with the early history of the Christian church.[39] His paper on "Blougram" was a clever one, consisting chiefly of a defense of the bishop's character, though afterwards the chairman, the Reverend Mr. Haweis, made the surprising observation that he admired Gigadibs, the supercilious young journalist, more than he did Blougram. The evening concluded with a fairly brief paper on "Browning and the Arts" by William Sharp (1855–1905), the Scottish poet and editor who subsequently achieved a curious sort of fame by writing under the pseudonym of "Fiona Macleod." [40]

Shortly after the June meeting, at which Professor Corson read his "Personality" paper, the Browning Society held its first annual business meeting, on July 7, 1882. The 1881–82 session had been prosperous and active: the society had heard papers by such notables as Thomson and Corson; membership had doubled; and several books were either in preparation or already issued to members. These annual reports, distributed at the last meeting of each session and written in Furnivall's inimitable style, provide a useful index of the society's changing fortunes and goals. The later ones must be used with caution, however, for as both morale and membership began to sag, the reports acquired a sort of obliqueness; they seem designed to conceal rather than reveal the society's true condition. After 1889 they did not even include membership figures, and there were increasingly urgent appeals for promptness in paying back subscriptions. Even when, in June, 1891, the annual report announced the society would disband within a year, the real reasons for its collapse were not disclosed.

The second session of the Browning Society began on October 27, 1882, with papers by Miss Dorothea Beale (1831–1906) and Edwin Johnson. A short, stern-looking woman, Miss Beale was principal of Cheltenham Ladies' College and since the middle of the century had been one of the leaders in preparing women for higher education in England. As a reformer and despot at her school, she usually seemed distant from her students except during the second half of the summer term, when she would give a series of emotion-charged readings of Browning's poems to the older girls.[41] Like so many other readers of that decade, she valued Browning primarily as a source of spiritual consolation in an age when religious values seemed to be disappearing. "When the sense of failure and discouragement had taken hold of her," Miss Beale told Furnivall privately, "she turned to Browning all buoyant with faith and hope, and found in him the very thing that uplifted her above the sense of failure, and encouraged her in all her work." [42] Her constant companion at the Browning Society meetings was a fellow-reformer, Miss Frances Buss (1827–94), principal of the North London Collegiate School for Girls, who was asked by a friend after one such meeting why she went out in the evening after a hard day's work. "I can do more good for the school often in an evening like this," replied Miss Buss, "than by a whole day at my desk: one can see people and talk to them." [43]

Miss Beale's paper, "The Religious Teaching of Browning," which she had also read to the Cheltenham Browning Society just the month before,[44] described Browning as "a prophet whom God had given to our storm-tost age, a pilot who has learnt by long experience the hidden rocks and sandbanks on which the vessel of faith may be wrecked, now that the old anchor chains are burst asunder." [45] When the chairman of the meeting, Francis Storr (1839–1919), subsequently editor of the *Journal of Education*,[46] suggested that Browning could better be called a poet of casuistry rather than a religious poet, Miss Beale rejected this opinion vigorously. She explained that she had "proposed not to dwell on what seemed the faults of our poet— the world does this quite sufficiently—but to bring out from the poems some of the treasures by which we feel our spiritual nature has been enriched." [47] The paper by Edwin Johnson which followed, "Conscience and Art in Browning," was of course less earnest in tone, but it too emphasized the didactic element in Browning's verse.

The chairman of the next meeting (November 24, 1882) was the most active of the society's vice-presidents, the Reverend John Llewelyn Davies (1826–1916), a genial broad-churchman whose sermons Browning read with interest.[48] Davies had the unenviable task of presiding over the discussion of a paper by Mrs. Frances Mary Owen (1842–83), honorary secretary of the Cheltenham Browning Society and enthusiastic leader of countless local literary and humanitarian activities.[49] Her paper, entitled "What Is the Flight of the Duchess?", brought the society face to face again with what one might call the "Childe Roland" dilemma: is it legitimate to apply to a poem allegorical interpretations which were obviously not intended by the poet? "It does not spoil a work of art that those who look at it should see more than the artist had designed they should see," Mrs. Owen declared firmly, and she proceeded to explore the poem from this point of view.[50] J. T. Nettleship sullenly demurred, but Furnivall, who was a very religious agnostic indeed, observed that "all things were potentially vehicles for the carrying of spiritual truth." [51] The second paper of the evening, which is inexplicably not printed in the transactions, was John Sharpe's discussion of the dramatic relevance of the songs in *Pippa Passes*. If one can judge by the abstract which appeared in the *Academy*, this paper must have been one of the most discriminating of the entire session.[52] That it is absent from the same volume in which Dorothea Beale's paper occupies fifteen pages is yet another symptom of the society's critical myopia.

On January 26, 1883, the female members were out in force to hear a paper on "The Part Played by Women in Browning's Poems" by William G. Martley (1860-1920), then a student at Balliol and within a few years a clergyman.[53] It was, as Furnivall said, "a bachelor's Paper," [54] and it treated marriage as a form of religious conversion in which woman's influence made man's true development possible. After surveying Browning's heroines, Martley concluded that the poet looked forward "to a future of increased usefulness and knowledge for Woman." [55] The paper was praised by the ladies present and by the chairman, William C. Coupland (1838-1915), a former Unitarian minister who was, appropriately, Professor of Mental and Moral Science at Bedford College for Women, London;[56] but Furnivall expressed alarm at the antifeminist note in Browning's poetry. "No doubt the self-abnegation of woman to man had impressed itself on Browning," he said, "but it belonged more to the passing generation than the present—they asserted their own individuality now more than they used to do." [57]

The highlight of the February 23 meeting was not the paper on "Browning's Intuition, Specially in Regard of Music and the Plastic Arts" by J. T. Nettleship, but rather the appearance in the chair of William Holman Hunt (1827-1910), the famous Pre-Raphaelite painter whose works had aroused public controversy thirty years before and were still regarded with lingering hostility by the Royal Academy, though their strong literalism appealed to most Victorians.[58] Hunt's speech consisted chiefly of pleasant recollections of early days in the Pre-Raphaelite movement, when Hunt, Dante Gabriel Rossetti, and the other members of the Brotherhood were excitedly discovering Browning's poetry. (In correcting a proof of his remarks at the meeting, incidentally, Hunt qualified his statement that "he was first among painters who had studied [Browning], and received inspiration from him" by adding that he could not have made this assertion until the death of Rossetti twelve months before.[59]) Hunt, himself a highly didactic artist, praised especially the religious qualities of Browning's verse and his "belief in a future life." [60]

Hunt's comment reminds us that until this point in the society's brief history, no paper had openly attempted to represent an agnostic viewpoint, but at the March 30, 1883, meeting, a pleasant unbeliever by the name of William F. Revell (d. 1911) delivered some unorthodox remarks on "Browning's Poems on God and Immortality as Bearing on Life Here." In all, Revell wrote five papers for the Browning Society (more than any other member) and later published a book entitled *Browning's Criticism of Life* (1892); the substance of all his observations on Browning was that the poet's religious position ought to be described as theistic rather than Christian. As Shaw commented in 1888, Revell "had over and over again got Browning in a corner" on the question of his religion.[61] Yet in temperament and outlook Revell was closer to Furnivall than to Shaw or Gonner, for although he emphasized theological inconsistencies in Browning's poems, he thought religious topics "the most interesting with which they had to deal in their way through life," [62] and he bore down as heavily as any Christian on the concept of Browning as a moral teacher.

Nevertheless, this first paper of Revell's was more than successful in provoking the faithful to wrath. "It seems to me a mistake," he said, "to be forever insisting on Browning's being a sort of 'Christian Evidence Society' agent." Browning's poems were like the Bible, he continued: one could cull sentences to support any viewpoint. The remainder of the paper was comprised of "some good points [which] might be made by anyone who chose to dispute Browning's orthodoxy." [63] The chairman of the meeting, James Cotter Morison, was delighted, and so was Furnivall:

> Mr. Furnivall could echo the words of the Chairman. He was specially glad to hear them, because he (Mr. Furnivall) had been condemned for not holding Browning's belief. . . . He (Mr. F.) had been glad that the orthodox should have been enabled to make the best of their case; they had done so, and it seemed to him that the best of them were willing to admit that Browning's creed was a strong Theism, not a definite Christianity. At any rate, he could

answer for one or two who had considerably modified their former views.

A more representative reaction to the paper was that of Samuel Rowe Bennett, a poet and biographer, who thought Revell had "attacked" Browning.[64]

The chairman of the following meeting (April 27, 1883) was the Reverend Henry John Bulkeley (1841–1922), honorary secretary of the Border District Browning Society and an energetic popularizer of Browning's works.[65] Originally Edward Dowden (1843–1913), the well-known Shakespearean scholar of Dublin University,[66] had been scheduled to take the chair that evening, but at the last moment he declined to do so, probably because of his intimate relationship with the author of the paper. He did attend the meeting, however, and contributed at length to the discussion. The paper, "One Aspect of Browning's Villains," was by Miss Elizabeth Dickinson West, daughter of the Dean of St. Patrick's, Dublin, and a former student of Dowden's (as well as his future second wife). Until Miss West was introduced to *Christmas Eve and Easter Morning* by a school friend, she had read only Mrs. Browning's verse,[67] but in 1871 she wrote an article on "Browning as a Preacher," which appeared in *Primitiae*, a collection of essays by students of Alexandra College, Dublin. Dowden passed the book on to Browning, who read her work with pleasure and immediately wrote to her about it.[68]

Encouraged by this response, Miss West sent Browning a copy of the entire essay (only the first half had been published in *Primitiae*) when it was reprinted in the Oxford magazine *Dark Blue* later that year.[69] "Through all those interesting years," she wrote near the end of her life, "I always regarded Mr. Browning as a *friend*, though we never saw each other." [70] When the Browning Society came into being, Miss West's interest in his poetry was again quickened: she published in the *Academy* a sonnet dedicated "To Robert Browning, on Rereading Some Poems Long Unread," [71] and she announced to Browning that she intended to prepare a paper for the society.[72] Her paper on Browning's villains, which was read by Miss Hickey, was an almost unqualified success. Edward Dowden congratulated the Browning Society "on having moved one of Browning's most admirable interpreters to return to the study of his works, and set forth so thoughtfully and truly one special aspect of them." [73] Dowden afterwards reported to Miss West that M. Milsand, Browning's friend, who was present at the meeting, had also privately praised the paper.[74]

On May 25, 1883, the Reverend Mr. Bulkeley, who had presided over the previous meeting, delivered a paper on "James Lee's Wife" which was little more than an industrious paraphrase of the poem and provoked a particularly dull discussion. Making one of his last public appearances that evening was the chairman, Mark Pattison (1813–84), who was Rector of Lincoln College and a scholar of such austere demeanor that he is said to have been the model for a whole series of arid pedants in Victorian fiction, most notably Mr. Casaubon in George Eliot's *Middlemarch* and Squire Wendover in Mrs. Ward's *Robert Elsmere*.[75] Nevertheless, his aloofness concealed one of the most brilliant minds of the age, and it was one of the triumphs of the Oxford Browning Society that he had been persuaded to join in its activities. The London Browning Society also hoped to hear a paper by Pattison the following March, but his final illness prevented its completion.[76]

For the first time, at the June 22, 1883, meeting, a scheduled paper (by Cyril Leslie Johnson) was not ready, and Dr. Furnivall fell back upon an expedient which was to tide him over many crises in the final years of the society's existence, when papers failed to materialize at one meeting after another: he read part of a paper which had already been published or delivered elsewhere. In this instance he used an appendix, comparing Browning's Guendolen and Shakespeare's Beatrice, of a paper recently read to the Cambridge Browning Society by the Reverend J. D. Williams (1829–1904), Vicar of Bottisham, who pursued classical studies and corresponded occasionally with Browning.[77] Another brief paper, this one by Mrs. Francese H. Turnbull on "Abt Vogler," followed; neither inspired much discussion. Mrs. Turnbull, subsequently the author of two historical novels, expressed her admiration of Browning's religious attitudes in familiar language: "In an age like the present," she wrote, "when the faith of many is drifting, anchorless, when dull grey clouds of doubt have settled down on most of our noblest intellects, have we not indeed cause for thankfulness that Browning is among 'the last who believe'?"[78]

The 1882–83 session closed with a meeting on July 6 at which the Reverend John Samuel Jones (d. 1896), a prominent Wesleyan minister who lectured frequently on Browning, presided.[79] The second annual report, which was read by Miss Hickey, was again cheerfully optimistic, recording an increasing number of activities by the society and a membership that had now reached nearly two hundred. It contained, however, one disquieting paragraph which said that some members (particularly Mrs. Orr) felt a terminal limit, perhaps of five years, ought to be placed on the society's existence. The matter was discussed at the meeting, and most members seemed to agree with

Furnivall's blunt observation that "if old Members got tired of it, let them clear out, and make way for new ones, not seek to shut the Society up." It caused hardly more than a ripple in the placid waters as the society quietly rejected the proposal; but the discussion was an omen of the much more violent reactions which Gonner's similar suggestion was to evoke in 1888. Mrs. Orr conceded that few favored her idea but added that "she thought it would be better to kill the Society while it was in full vigor, rather than let it dwindle away," a remarkably accurate prophecy of what was actually to happen.[80] The rest of the meeting was devoted to a paper on "Saul," which amounted to nothing more than a prose summary of the poem, by the Reverend H. C. Beeching (1859–1919), Curate of St. Matthew's, Mossley Hill, Liverpool, and subsequently Dean of Norwich. Beeching, who had long displayed a special interest in contemporary writers, was a poet and essayist of considerable charm, but this paper was not one of his better efforts.[81]

For the first meeting of the new session (October 26, 1883), Furnivall found a speaker who was a minor literary celebrity, Dr. John Todhunter (1839–1916), an Irish physician who had moved to London during the late seventies and devoted his time to literary interests. A poet and playwright, Todhunter was a participant in the Celtic literary revival, with which the names of Yeats and Synge were associated near the end of the century.[82] His paper, a discursive study of *The Ring and the Book*, was unremarkable, but his very presence at a Browning Society meeting poses some interesting questions. How, one is tempted to ask, did the society—that bastion of piety and evangelical sentiment—attract men of such diverse backgrounds as Todhunter, or Bernard Shaw, the brilliant, red-bearded exponent of Fabian Socialism and Ibsenism, or Ernest Radford, the secretary of the Rhymers' Club? Part of the answer must lie in the breadth of Browning's appeal; but, beyond that, we must seek an explanation for the society's heterogeneous membership in Furnivall's wide range of acquaintances. At the British Museum Reading Room, where he spent most of his time, Furnivall came to know nearly all the writers and scholars of note in England, for the Reading Room was then, as it is now, one of the important centers of literary research in Europe. Sooner or later every reader there met the jovial, bearded, industrious gentleman who labored so cheerfully over old literary texts; and then he would join Furnivall some afternoon at his favorite tea shop on New Oxford Street, and in time, when the friendship was established, he would be asked to participate in the activities of one of Furnivall's societies, perhaps by editing a text, preparing a concordance, or delivering a paper. It was an effective means of recruiting new talent, but the strange confrontations it produced in the Browning Society between the advanced thinkers of the age and evangelical spinsters and clerics were sometimes startling.

The society on the evening of November 23, 1883, heard a paper by John Sharpe on *Jocoseria*, which Browning had published only the previous March. Though intelligently written, Sharpe's paper was the sort that inspired laughter among the unbelievers of the world, for the idea of Browning's disciples following close upon his heels, turning out massive commentaries on his poetry as soon as it was printed, struck some observers as very amusing indeed. Dykes Campbell also read his translation of a French review of *Jocoseria* at the meeting. The chairman was Richard Garnett (1835–1906), the shy, learned Keeper of Printed Books in the British Museum.[83] Garnett was keenly interested in all of Furnivall's societies and was an acquaintance of Browning's as well; besides serving as chairman of three Browning Society meetings, he made certain that the British Museum was receiving the society's publications even though no copyright application had been made for most of them.[84]

Miss Louisa Drewry (d. 1916), an intensely religious member who spoke often at the meetings and recited Browning's verse for society entertainments, presided at the meeting of January 25, 1884. The evening was less memorable for its paper, an earnest study of the ideas of *Paracelsus* by an otherwise unidentified Miss Arthur, than for the remarks of Shaw, who mockingly announced that he had been "terrified" by the erudition of the paper.[85] Shaw was in good form that evening, though he had made his first speech at the Browning Society only two months earlier; and hereafter he intimidated and enraged the members by gleefully displaying irreverence toward all that Browningites held sacred. At the February meeting, for instance, he must have left the others reeling in shock when he proclaimed that they would be better off if they stopped discussing and went home to read Browning instead. To accuse a Browningite of not knowing his Browning was a supreme insult, and it is interesting to observe that Kingsland's minutes of the meeting end abruptly at this point.[86] Aside from the joy that came from producing mayhem, why did Shaw join the society? Once again the answer must be that Furnivall's net occasionally pulled in some very queer fish indeed. Shaw undoubtedly met Furnivall at the British Museum, where both of them did their writing, and Furnivall was soon giving him advice on where to submit the manuscripts of his novels,[87] assigning him some indexing work (which Shaw never completed),[88] and enrolling him as a member of the New Shakspere Society ("the Old Spelling Society," Shaw called it), the Shelley Society, and the Browning Society.

Shaw had never read a word of Browning, though he was full of Shelley and Shakespeare, and many years afterwards he could not remember even having paid any subscriptions to the societies. (Actually, as a surviving letter to him from Slater shows, he did send at least one subscription to the Browning Society.[89]) Shaw was a willing joiner because the societies gave him an opportunity to practice speaking in public, which so terrified him at this time that afterwards he scarcely knew what he had said; and Furnivall wanted Shaw at the meetings because he could be depended upon to enliven the discussions.[90] Shaw has also left us some of the most witty recollections of the Browning Society's foibles, as in these retrospective comments of his upon the Browningite craze of the eighties:

[Furnivall], who began as an ardent Tennysonian, but got tired of it and took to Browning, worked the Society for the ladies, but had no consideration for their faith, being himself a muscular Christian agnostic.[91]

Societies have been established to discuss Browning; and they would not have held a meeting the less if Browning had been a revivalist preacher who had never penned a Rhyme in his life.[92]

The oddity of these bodies [Shelley, New Shakspere, and Browning societies] was that Furnivall's crowd was a Browning crowd to whom Browning was a religious leader; and Furnivall openly scorned Jesus because, as he put it, "the fellow let himself be spat upon without at least giving the spitter a black eye." I and the late E. C. K. Gonner, still in our mischievous youth, used to egg him on to horrify the pious old ladies whose subscriptions kept the Societies going.

They followed him into the Shelley Society in all innocence; and when I, at the first meeting in the lecture theatre of University College, announced that as a good Shelleyan I was a Socialist, an Atheist, and a vegetarian, two of them resigned on the spot.[93]

Thus, in later years, did Shaw look back with amusement on the Browning Society; but time had its revenges, and near the end of his life Shaw societies sprang up in England and America, with elaborate constitutions, regular meetings, and even—to make the parallel complete—papers on Shaw's religion! "Where be your jibes now?" as Hamlet demanded of poor Yorick. "I am not a Shavian," Shaw is reported to have said; but Browning too, confronted with the idolatry of the Browning Society, was at last moved to announce, "I am quite other than a Browningite." [94]

Despite Shaw's harassment, the society lumbered on, and at the February 22, 1884, meeting it heard papers by two young men from King's College, Cambridge: Arthur Christopher Benson (1862–1925) and Walter Alexander Raleigh (1861–1922). Both were at the beginning of remarkable careers as educators and literary critics, and their contributions to the Browning Society demonstrate once more that the society held a special attraction for bright young men on their way up in the world (this category would also include, for example, Shaw and Gonner), though, as we have seen, in the end it was the less fiercely intellectual, more religiously conservative older members who established the dominant tone of the organization. Benson, a member of a distinguished literary family and later associated for many years with Magdalene College, Cambridge, first as Fellow and Lecturer and afterwards as Master,[95] contributed a short paper on "Waring," in which he claimed to see a romantic renunciation of modern civilization. The paper by Raleigh, who later wrote important studies of Wordsworth and Shakespeare,[96] was entitled "On Some Prominent Points of Browning's Teaching," yet behind this conventional title lay a relatively novel idea (novel at least in the Browning Society): that Browning's "teaching" was unsystematic and existential rather than intellectual in nature. "My moral," he concluded, "enjoins the reading of Browning, rather than the discussion of conclusions to be drawn from his works. The teaching of his poetry is transitory, and cannot be stereotyped; indeed, its best effects are expressible in terms of experience rather than of learning." [97] Such an approach to Browning's ideas might have been discussed with profit by the Browning Society, but unfortunately the chairman, Dr. Berdoe, led the group instead down his favorite blind alley—Browning's claims to be called a scientific poet.

A much more ordinary paper was delivered at the next meeting (March 28, 1884) by the Reverend J. S. Jones on "Browning's Ecclesiastics." It was a topic which would of course appeal to Jones, who was a member of the committee that met annually to arrange appointments of Wesleyan Methodist ministers,[98] but his survey of the clergymen who appear in Browning's verse rarely moved beyond superficiality. It produced, moreover, ritual responses from both Christians and non-Christians: Furnivall interpreted the paper as saying that priests "in the lump are bad," while Kingsland praised the words of Rabbi Ben Ezra as being "full of the truest teaching, and of deep spiritual experience." [99]

For most Browningites, the climax of the 1883-84 session was the appearance in the chair on April 25 of James Russell Lowell, the poet who to English minds represented the best product of American civilization. Though Lowell, then the American ambassador to the Court of St. James, had been apprehensive about "running" a meeting and had even feared for a time that another appointment would prevent his attending it,[100] he cheerfully accepted the chairmanship because of his intimacy with both Furnivall and Browning. An honorary secretary of the New Shakspere Society and since 1870 a member of the Chaucer Society, Lowell warmly admired Furnivall's labors on behalf of literature. "You have done for the English Language what no man ever did or thought of doing . . . ," Lowell wrote him on learning of the Civil List pension awarded to Furnivall in 1884.[101] Browning he had known even longer, for they first met in England in 1852, frequently thereafter corresponded, and, when they were both living in London in the eighties, dined together.[102] From the time in the early 1840's, in fact, when Lowell saw a brief excerpt from *Pippa Passes* in an American newspaper, he had been proclaiming Browning to be one of the chief poets of the century. It was an opinion he did not abandon. Immediately after Browning's death in 1889, Lowell wrote to a friend: "There was no man who had more of the living energy of poetry in him or was more virile, though I think the molten metal often over-ran the mould & hardened in fantastic or even unsightly splashes. But it had been molten, which is the main thing." [103]

Lowell's speech to the Browning Society, which drew a large audience and which Browning afterwards described as "clever," [104] began with an explanation that although he did not regard the Browning Society as necessary for the understanding of Browning (he had refused to join it in 1881), he was there that evening "to confess a debt of gratitude which has gone on increasing for now more than forty years." [105] In reality, Lowell's views on Browning had changed little since 1848, when he had written a lengthy, discursive study of his poetry for the *North American Review*.[106] Then, as now, he had stressed Browning's objectivity and the unique achievement of his plays; but in the reverent atmosphere of the Browning Society even Lowell felt compelled to soften some of his previous unflattering remarks on the poet's unconventional style. Yet Lowell did have the courage to caution the members against partisanship, of which, he said, he had seen symptoms in recent years (meaning, perhaps, the society itself); then he concluded on a happier note by praising Browning's moral teachings.

The meeting continued with a paper by James Cotter Morison on

"Caliban," which he interpreted as an attack upon natural theology. The paper was one of the shortest ever read to the society, for Morison, who was convalescing in southern France from a bronchial irritation, had submitted it only at the last minute, and then under protest; he claimed that he had never promised to write the paper, though Dykes Campbell thought he had.[107] Nevertheless, the evening was a full and lively one, for in addition to Lowell's remarks from the chair, the society heard a long speech by Furnivall as well as an onslaught by Shaw against every sacred cow in sight:

> Browning's *Caliban* is a savage, with the introspective powers of a Hamlet, and the theology of an evangelical Churchman. I must confess that I cannot conceive an evangelical Churchman possessing the introspective powers of a Hamlet. (Great laughter.) Although this character of *Caliban* is very interesting, and is, in fact, one of my Browning favourites, I am compelled to say that it is unnatural, impossible, and radically undramatic. (Applause.)

On an occasion of such general good will, even Shaw, with all his blasphemies against orthodox Browningite doctrine, could get a hearing, although the next speaker, George Barnett Smith, said that he trusted that "the gentleman who has just spoken will live to revise his opinion as to what is, and what is not, dramatic poetry." [108]

The last two meetings of the 1883–84 session brought the third year to a close with the Browning Society in a complacent and self-congratulatory frame of mind. On May 23 Miss Drewry, advancing the familiar Browningite theory that criticism destroys the best values of poetry, presented a deliberately uncritical summary of *Luria*. In the chair was Moncure Conway, who repeated the same Browning anecdotes, by now rather stale, which he had told at the first meeting of the society. At the July 4 meeting, in addition to a sketchy, impressionistic paper on "In a Balcony" by Mrs. Turnbull, the society listened to an annual report which exuded pride in past achievements and confidence in the future. Membership had increased to more than two hundred; Browning's books could now be purchased at less than half their former price; and the society had become, according to the report, "a central body to which [the Browning student] could apply for help in solving doubts, for sympathy in his work, for aid in the spread of Browning's influence." [109] Dr. Furnivall's remarks at the meeting reflected the report's blithe optimism. "As to the Society's future," he said, "they had only to work on the same lines, and extend them in the same spirit." [110]

There were minor disappointments, of course. Furnivall had been trying since 1882 to persuade George Meredith, who was already a member, to join the committee or write a paper; but twice, in May and July, 1884, he repeated his refusal because of "a continued state of lowered health." [111] Yet to a close observer it might have appeared that the health of the Browning Society itself was in a precarious state, for behind the expansive mood of the annual reports were concealed some unpleasant facts: membership gains were levelling off, critical attitudes were hardening into rigid orthodoxies, and the interests of the society seemed to be focusing more and more upon Browning's theological views. But in July of 1884 the perils of the future went unnoticed as the society bustled about, a bit self-importantly, in preparation for another triumphant session. Browning's plays would be performed, his poems would be set to music, a shilling primer would be written, public lectures on Browning would be organized, and soon, it appeared, every Browningite would become a missionary to an infidel world. "The position of the Society," said Dr. Furnivall, "is now sounder and more influential than it has ever been. All its difficulties, within and without, have been happily tided over." [112]

CHAPTER VII

THE MEETINGS, 1884-92

> But [this] raises the question, on which I hope there will be
> some discussion, whether we are more to address ourselves to
> the select circle of ourselves who do already love and value
> Browning far beyond the measure of conventional acknowl-
> edgment, and desire to help each other to study him more and
> know him better; or whether we are not rather to appeal to
> the far larger circle of those who may wisely be attracted to
> discover and appreciate him for themselves.
>
> —Joshua Kirkman (1881)[1]

FROM THE VERY BEGINNING, as the above statement from the Reverend Mr. Kirkman's inaugural address suggests, the Browning Society's
goals were not clear. Browning's admirers, both within the society and
without, sensed uneasily that their favorite poet had long been ignored by the public at large, and they wished to increase his fame so
that he would be as widely quoted and read and discussed as Tennyson or Shakespeare. But by a cruel irony the Browningites felt obliged
to adopt the stance of an embattled minority, and hence their efforts
to popularize Browning's poetry failed, because, as the *London Quarterly Review* said, the wicked world resented their tone of superiority.[2] The Browningite cause became for many a holy crusade: zealous
partisans labored among the heathen (i.e., those who rejected or were
ignorant of Browning's poetry), and when lack of success discouraged
them, they turned to one another's company for consolation and advice. Increasingly, therefore, the Browning Society saw itself as a
haven of rest where weary Browningites could refresh themselves by
meeting with fellow-believers and where plans for new missionary
ventures could be laid. Its thoughts turned in upon itself, and, in common with other sects, the society began to marvel at the contrast be-

tween its own purity of spirit and the dark, polluted world where Browning's spiritual message had not yet penetrated. "At a recent meeting of the Browning Society a complaint was made [by Edward Gonner] that it was rapidly degenerating into a third-rate missionary society," Dr. Berdoe observed from the chair in January of 1889. He continued:

> The only objection to that description was the adjective "third-rate;" he had been flattering himself that they were a "first-rate" mission- ary society. He thought such a lecture as they had had that night was a very good specimen of the kind of missionary work that might be carried out by the diffusion of Browning's works.[3]

Clearly such a call for poetic evangelism would alienate those members who insisted upon seeing Browning as a poet rather than a prophet; but by 1889 such members comprised a dwindling minority, for most either had withdrawn altogether from the society or were still licking their wounds after the attack upon Edward Gonner and his plea for a more distinctly literary viewpoint the previous summer.

However, the religious forces which Dr. Berdoe represented were able to suppress heresies with a heavy hand only in the society's years of decline; in 1884 there was still a diversity of new faces and new ideas coming into the Browning Society. During the session which began that autumn, for example, the names of William Michael Rossetti, Arthur Symons, and Augustine Birrell—all writers of some degree of distinction—appear for the first time in the *Papers*.

A modest, self-effacing civil servant who seemed out of place among the colorful bohemians who clustered around his brother Dante Gabriel, Rossetti had known Browning since 1853, and even before making his acquaintance had praised his *Christmas-Eve and Easter-Day* in the pages of the short-lived Pre-Raphaelite journal, *The Germ*. Later, in the sixties, Rossetti assisted Browning in preparing a frontispiece—without much success, it should be added—for a new edition of Mrs. Browning's *Aurora Leigh*.[4] When Dykes Campbell asked him in June of 1884 to write a paper for the Browning Society, therefore, Rossetti was inclined to accept the invitation, "having always been on certain grounds," as he pointed out, "a fervent Browningite." But with characteristic self-distrust, he decided that his knowledge of Browning's poems, especially the later ones, was inadequate for the task and asked instead for a list of the papers which had already been read, as it "might possibly furnish me with a hint as to what subjects remain advantageously open to treatment." [5]

He did, however, accept the chairmanship of the October 31, 1884, meeting, at which Moncure Conway was to speak on *Sordello*, but by two weeks before that date he admitted to Dykes Campbell that even this small assignment left him terrified:

> I feel as yet as if I have really nothing to say—worth saying—on the subject of Sordello: but this is a state of feeling wh[ich] constantly besets me in such matters until the moment for acting comes, & then I get on less badly than I was expecting. Let us hope that such will be the case this time.[6]

Speaking from notes at the meeting, Rossetti introduced Conway's inconsequential paper with considerable charm, referring to his own youthful enthusiasm for *Sordello*; but these notes (which are in the British Museum today) contain a telling phrase that was omitted from the published account of his speech: "Gabriel, *much more important than myself*, was one of the earliest admirers & preachers of S[ordello]." [7]

Because of a society entertainment in November, the next regular meeting was not held until January, at which time Arthur Symons read his first paper, "Is Browning Dramatic?" The plays of Browning were also under discussion at the meeting of February 27, when Benjamin L. Mosely (d. 1916), a barrister,[8] delivered a paper entitled "On Miss Alma Murray's Creation of Constance, in *In a Balcony*" (which had been performed at the November entertainment). The society also heard shorter papers that evening on "Cleon" by Mrs. Turnbull and "The Case of Louscha" by John James Britton (d. 1936), a minor poet and novelist. The latter, a defense of Louscha's behavior in the poem "Ivàn Ivànovitch," provoked so juridical a discussion that the chairman, Augustine Birrell (1850–1933), "reminded the Browning Society that they were not the Old Bailey." [9] The lighthearted remark was typical of the author of that amusing collection of essays, *Obiter Dicta* (1884), which Browning himself enjoyed reading, though he did complain about one joke at the expense of the Browning Society.[10] Flippancy toward the society was not normally tolerated by its members, even in 1885, and so it is surprising to discover that Birrell was asked to preside over another meeting in January of the following year. But his skepticism about the society's usefulness did not diminish. Browning "took all life for his province," Birrell wrote in 1890. "This was the secret of that ever-growing popularity of his, which has so puzzled some people that they have actually attributed it to monthly meetings of the Browning Society in Gower Street." [11]

A paper on "Mr. Sludge, 'the Medium' " by Edwin Johnson attracted an unusual audience for the meeting in March. Frank Podmore (1855–1910), of the Institute for Psychic Research, delivered a long and expert speech on the character of the medium, concluding that he was a spineless creature capable of assuming two separate personalities. Shaw, who by now had acquired the role of privileged lunatic within the society, merely drew titters when he announced that "Mr. Sludge" was his favorite Browning poem. "Members seemed to consider that statement facetious," he hastily went on; "but he had no doubt he should find, in a full meeting of the Society, no lack of sympathisers in his preference." [12] Shaw's interest in supernatural manifestations went far beyond "Mr. Sludge"; on the following October 29, for instance, he spent the night in an allegedly haunted house on St. Anne's Hill, Wandsworth, with Frank Podmore. An entry in his diary for the next day reads: "Walked in from Wandsworth to Charing Cross with Goodman, very tired from want of sleep and fatigue. Made a speech at the Browning Institute in the evening." [13] The difficulty with being court jester, as Shaw was already discovering, is that one's words are never taken seriously, even when they are so intended.

For the following meeting (April 24, 1883), Jonathan Hutchinson (1828–1913), an eminent surgeon who had long been a faithful reader of Browning's poems,[14] was scheduled to take the chair, but he was unable at the last minute to do so. Had he been present, Hutchinson would have heard a paper by a new member, Dr. Berdoe, on "Browning as a Scientific Poet." It was, as we have seen, a thesis which Berdoe pursued relentlessly at the meetings and in his subsequent books, but this, the first major explication of Berdoe's views on Browning and science, called forth a decidedly negative response: "The Chairman [William Revell] considered that Dr. Berdoe had not proved his point; that he had only shown that Browning possessed a certain amount of scientific knowledge. The whole attitude of Browning's mind was opposed to the assumptions and hypotheses of modern science." [15] A briefer paper by John J. Rossiter, honorary secretary of the Reading Browning Society, raised once more the issue of Browning's plays and the degree to which they were capable of succeeding on the stage. Taking a more cautious position than some Browning enthusiasts, Rossiter maintained that *A Blot in the 'Scutcheon* was the best of the plays, but that all of them were marred by Browning's ignorance of stagecraft. Other Browningites, in contrast, were willing to argue that the fault lay with the contemporary stage, not with Browning; and here again Furnivall was guilty of heresy. When Arthur Symons said that *King Victor and King Charles* was an acting play, Furnivall scolded him by replying, "You might as well act a *Times* leader!" [16]

On May 22, 1885, the society listened to papers written by two men, both named Gibson. Edward Dowden had sent Furnivall a short manuscript, "On Browning as a Teacher," by James Gibson, of Trinity College, Dublin; and Dr. Berdoe read the proof sheets of an introduction by Dr. John Monro Gibson to a forthcoming American selection of Browning's poems for the Chautauqua Society. But something of the order of priorities at the meeting is indicated by the fact that both papers are merely abstracted in the transactions, whereas the introductory address by the chairman, Frederick Wedmore (1844–1921), is recorded in full, apparently by a shorthand reporter. Wedmore, who led a varied career as art and music critic, journalist, and novelist, had made Browning's acquaintance in 1865 when he sent to the poet an inquiry about Abt Vogler, whose career he was tracing in a biographical sketch.[17] Subsequently Wedmore dined occasionally with Browning, dedicated a novel to him in 1868, succeeded in persuading Smith, Elder to publish another novel (*A Snapt Gold Ring*, 1871) solely because of Browning's personal recommendation,[18] and wrote reviews of Browning's poetry for the *Academy*.[19] His address to the Browning Society (to which he did not belong, incidentally) emphasized the "freshness" and "massiveness" of Browning's work; these qualities, he said, were the only justification for the existence of a society designed "to study and elucidate a living poet." The Browning Society could further be defended, Wedmore thought, on the ground "that Browning is—at least I feel him to be—among the half dozen writers, after the writers of the Bible and after Shakspere, who may hope to form character, to enlarge or confirm a talent, to substantially influence life." [20]

The 1884–85 session ended on June 26 with an annual report that was as buoyant as ever and with a paper by Cyril Leslie Johnson on "Browning as an Artist, Considered in Relation to the Life of His Time." Unfortunately, it is difficult to reconstruct what took place at that meeting, since no notes were made of the discussion and Johnson was prevented by illness from preparing an abstract of his paper. On the basis of the title and the sketchy summary in the *Papers*, however, one can guess that Johnson advanced an argument familiar to Browningites: that Browning was a "representative" poet thoroughly in harmony with the spirit of the age. In a profound sense, as Robert Langbaum has shown recently, this is true, for Browning's adoption of the dramatic monologue, with its partial, distorted viewpoint, reflects the modern abandonment of intellectual and moral absolutes. The great verities of the past have disappeared; instead, in Browning's poetry, we catch glimpses not of the pure light of truth, but of that light refracted through the imperfect prism of a human mind.[21] But of course this is not at all what the members of the Browning Society had in mind when they described their poet as being "representative." They were drawn to him for the very opposite reason; they thought he had *not* relinquished the old certitudes. A statement in Miss Lewis' paper provides an excellent index of their thinking on the subject: "The best wish we can offer to the remaining years of the 19th century is, that future historians may be able to say that whereas Clough, Matthew Arnold, and Carlyle represented the philosophical and religious thought of its central period, Browning became the representative man of its close." [22] These Browningites, in other words, looked forward to a renaissance of traditional religious faith in England, brought about in part by Browning's influence, and he would then become "representative" of the *Zeitgeist* because he had remade the age in his own image.

By the autumn of 1885 the Browning Society was settling into some comfortable ruts, as can be seen by tabulating the number of persons who either read papers or sat in the chair for the first time during this and earlier sessions. (They are indicated by the word "new" in the following list; "repeat" means persons who performed in these respective capacities previously.)

| | Chairmen | | Lecturers | |
Sessions	New	Repeat	New	Repeat
1881–82	8	1	10	1
1882–83	8	1	9	3
1883–84	5	2	9	3
1884–85	3	4	9	2
1885–86	0	8	4	5

This session, in short, introduced few new faces, for the majority of both chairmen and writers of papers were appearing for the second or third time. In the recorded discussions, too, one detects a flagging of the energies which had originally set the society in motion and had thus far carried it forward in its attempts to popularize and explicate Browning's verse. At the October 30, 1885, meeting, for example, Nettleship's innocuous paper, "On the Development of Browning's Genius in His Capacity as Poet or Maker," called forth such wildly improbable responses as Berdoe's assertion that Browning was born "a Buddha on the highest peak of the Himalayas of thought," [23] and Shaw's counter-assertion that Nettleship was ignorant of Shakespeare. As the initial impulses behind the founding of the Browning Society faded, its members more and more displayed a mood of querulousness and dissension.

Even the topics of papers were becoming repetitious. On November 27, J. J. Britton delivered a paper on "Browning's Women," a subject which had been treated more thoroughly and analytically by W. G. Martley three years before. Unlike Martley, Britton made no attempt to classify or group Browning's heroines; rather, he merely listed the ones who interested him most and provided a short commentary on each. The chairman, Rossetti, found it a disappointing piece of work and even briefly considered revising it before the meeting. On November 24 he had written to Dykes Campbell: "Yesterday I read Mr. Britton's lecture, & feel with you that it is not firstrate, tho several things are well enough put in it. I c[oul]d not see any way to making excisions—*that* w[oul]d have demanded a second reading." [24] Though some members, including of course Furnivall and Gonner, expressed dissatisfaction with the paper's loose structure after it had been read, Rossetti, bland as ever, merely praised Britton's own poetry and discussed Browning's other heroines. On this evening, in fact, Rossetti was more than normally afflicted with stage fright, for until November 19, when he received a postcard from Campbell, he had entirely forgotten about his promise to take the chair at the November meeting. Worse yet, as he confessed to Campbell, he had "been a truant (unwillingly) to Browning's poetry from Fifine onward. I suppose I shall blunder into the affair somehow," he added.[25] Rossetti had a gift for getting himself into such comic predicaments: after agreeing to assume the chairmanship on April 29, 1887, he again put the matter out of his mind until Furnivall's postcard of reminder in March came upon him "like a thunder-clap." [26]

The chief paper for the evening of January 29, 1886, was an erudite study of *Aristophanes' Apology* by J. B. Bury, who in the following decade was to turn his attention fully to the history of Greece and Rome. The Browningites were clearly eager to debate the relative merits of Aristophanes and Euripides but were forestalled by the amused objectivity of the chairman, Augustine Birrell:

I notice Mr. Swinburne, in his list of the best books, includes Aristophanes, but excludes Euripides. On the other hand the Lord Chief

Justice includes Euripides but excludes Aristophanes. Acting with
the impartiality that always characterises an Englishman in the
chair, I give my vote for both.[27]

The evening concluded with a terse paper by Leonard Outram, whose
quarrel with Dr. Furnivall the following autumn was to have such
drastic consequences, already described, for the founder of the
Browning Society.

Frederick Wedmore once again held forth from the chair at the
next meeting (February 26, 1886), introducing with elaborate cour-
tesy a paper on "Andrea del Sarto" by Albert Fleming (d. 1923), a
disciple of John Ruskin's who had started a Ruskinian handicrafts
school near Ambleside.[28] Fleming's thesis was that the best commentary upon the poem was a self-portrait of Andrea in the National Gallery, which he described at some length. Furnivall, in the discussion,
called Andrea "one of those weak failing types which interest us most
when treated by poets of insight," a remark which provoked two notable rebuttals. Shaw complained that the artist's weakness has been
unduly stressed, for he had painted "many very fine pictures." However, he added, this was "a protest against pharisaism, and not a criticism on the paper." Miss Whitehead, on the other hand, denied that
"people were the more interesting for being weak" and disclaimed any
interest in Andrea beyond the boundaries of Browning's poem.[29]

For the March meeting William Revell presented another of his
studies of Browning's moral system as seen from a theistic rather
than a Christian viewpoint; but on April 30, 1886, the society's attention was again turned to art, this time because of a paper by Howard
S. Pearson (1838–1923) on "Browning as a Landscape Painter."
Pearson, who was Lecturer in English Language and Literature at the
Midland Institute in Birmingham until shortly before World War I,[30]
asserted that Browning's landscapes, though brilliantly executed, are
"rapid, reticent and reserved" [31] because he does not wish to compete
with nature and because the real center of his interest is man. Pearson's paper was one of the best of the session, but, as so often happened in the Browning Society, its merits were obscured by a muddled
response from the audience. The chairman, J. T. Nettleship, indignantly rejected Pearson's approach and threatened to write an answer
to the paper (this display of ill temper led him a few days later to
apologize to Campbell for the "bad Chairmanship" [32]); and Furnivall
seized the occasion to make an irrelevant excursion into politics:

As a strong Radical, Dr. Furnivall felt very glad that it was from
manufacturing Birmingham—the home of the Caucus so dreaded

by the flabby conservatism of London clubdom—that Mr. Pearson
had come to tell metropolitan Browningites what their poet's treatment of landscape was. . . . What he (Dr. Furnivall) had so
often had to say in politics, he could now repeat in art, "Well done,
Birmingham! you've led us." [33]

For one evening at least—on May 28, 1886—it appeared that the
society might free itself from the morass of clichés which surrounded
that dreary topic, Browning's "harshness," since a most interesting
paper on "The Reasonable Rhythm of Some of Browning's Poems," by
the Reverend H. J. Bulkeley, persuasively argued, through an examination of individual poems, that Browning's metrical irregularities actually constitute a suiting of the sound to the sense. "My subject is
inexhaustible," concluded Bulkeley. "May I venture to hope that my
imperfect treatment of it may induce some other members of this Society to look more at the artistic side of Browning's work, not to be led
away by the excellence of his matter to neglect the marvellous work-
manship of the caskets which so appropriately contain it?" [34] But, as
the discussion which followed plainly shows, the Browningites were
unwilling to abandon or examine their prejudices on the subject. Furnivall and Gonner declared that the metrical quality of Browning's
verse was wretched, Slater and Kingsland thought the poetry uniformly melodious, and neither side took up Bulkeley's challenge.

Still another example of the manner in which carefully reasoned
arguments were inevitably levelled down to the faulty comprehension
of the members can be seen at the following meeting, on June 25.
Charles H. Herford (1853–1931), a bright young literary critic who
later became Professor of English Literature at the University of Manchester,[35] contributed a paper on the sophistries present in *Prince Hohenstiel-Schwangau*; but afterwards Furnivall, whose attitudes toward poetry were rarely characterized by subtlety, reduced the critical
problem to its most inelegant terms: "It seemed to him [Furnivall]
that Browning delights to take one of these scamps, and then sit down
to work with the remark, 'Now let us see what excuses we can make
for him.'" [36] At the same meeting the annual report was distributed,
announcing, among other things, that Walter Slater had accepted the
honorary secretaryship of the society. What the report did not reveal
was the startling fact that the office had first been offered to Edward
Gonner (1862–1922), the avowed enemy of all Browningite shibboleths. The temptation to speculate what would have happened to the
Browning Society had Gonner accepted is almost irresistible; at the

very least it is safe to assert that the society's course would have been quite different from what it was under Slater's timid, vacillating leadership. Gonner was not nearly so quarrelsome at this time as he was two years later, and perhaps his incisive mind, which subsequently made him a dazzling teacher of economics at Liverpool University,[37] could have brought fresh vigor to the society. He declined the secretaryship, however, and Campbell next turned to George Todd (1844–1913), an examiner and later First Assistant Secretary in the Scottish Education Office.[38] When he also turned down the offer, Campbell then wrote again to Gonner, who this time gave two reasons for his refusal:

> (1.) My health which is I am sorry to say anything but satisfactory. For instance I was quite laid up twice last year and have been confined to the house for the last three weeks or so. Indeed I am only just getting about in terms of my work.
> (2.) My engagements. I have a good deal of uncertain work and of course I want some of a settled character. But for example these two terms I am lecturing at the Bristol University Coll. Even this would have been altogether impossible with the secretaryship.[39]

After Gonner introduced his infamous amendment in 1888, one of the accusations made by Berdoe, Slater, and others was that Gonner was complaining without having done anything himself for the Browning Society. To this Gonner replied that he had brought about the establishment of a Browning Society in Australia, but a better answer, one which indicates Gonner's unique contribution to the society, was provided by Furnivall, who "held that Mr. Gonner had conferred a great benefit on them by his very stringent criticisms, if only because every one felt that if he brought forward a fallacy, Gonner would be down on him. No doubt a great many soap-bubbles had been blown there, and had very promptly been pricked."[40] Instead of this destroyer of illusions, however, the new honorary secretary of the Browning Society in 1888 was a man who found Gonner "nothing if not sarcastic"[41] and looked forward with simple delight to religious discussions under a literary guise. The choice was symptomatic of the direction the Browning Society was taking.

For the 1886–87 session, the first speaker was Archdeacon Farrar, who had just returned from a lecturing tour in the United States.[42] One of the lectures which had been most cordially received there was on Browning, and Furnivall was eager to have it delivered to the Browning Society; but Farrar was reluctant to accept the invitation:

If I thought my lecture worthy the notice of the B.S. I w[oul]d come. But it was of a proselytising & propagandistic character, & many of its best views w[oul]d already be extremely familiar to the Soc. from its own papers. Hence I feel the greatest hesitation.[43]

At Furnivall's urging, however, Farrar did deliver the lecture to the society on October 29, 1886. It was, as he said, a commonplace survey of Browning's "characteristics," but it was received by the members with "repeated acclamations," [44] since Farrar's endorsement of their cause seemed incontrovertible proof of Browning's "growing popularity among the educated classes"—to quote a phrase used by Campbell on another occasion.[45]

A paper of similar generalizations was offered at the next meeting (November 26, 1886) by Roden Noel, who cited "Saul" as "the finest poem Browning ever wrote, and it has the note of immortality." [46] Actually, Noel's paper had been published in slightly different form several years before,[47] as this meeting was hastily scheduled when the *Strafford* performance was postponed because of the Furnivall-Outram quarrel. Edwin Johnson, the chairman, perhaps described the situation as delicately as possible when he declared, "The paper of Mr. Noel, if it has offered nothing particularly novel on the subject of Browning, presents at least many just observations, often expressed with grace and felicity." [48]

At the January 28, 1887, meeting the Browning Society listened to Dr. Todhunter's analysis of the December production of *Strafford* as well as to Furnivall's reading of an American essay on Browning's views on personal immortality; but, true to pattern, the discussion was infinitely more lively, though less enlightening, than the papers. Shaw, who was in the chair, objected to the portrayal of the Younger Vane in *Strafford* as being too excitable for a revolutionist: "Mr. Shaw said he had had considerable experience of Socialist and other meetings of a similar nature, and very rarely did any of the speakers *rant*." Todhunter, in defending the Younger Vane's characterization, replied with heavy sarcasm that "he had not the chairman's experience in attending 'seditious' meetings, and if they behaved in the way described he was glad he hadn't." The members were also treated that evening to one of Furnivall's remarkable monologues. Furnivall did not merely disagree with critics of the Browning Society; he crushed them with invective:

Now some of the people who had criticised *Strafford* had appeared to imagine that Irving himself was there, and that it had been put on the stage with all the accessories *he* would have used. All Dr. F. could say was, they were asses to do so. Knowing the circumstances of the Society, he could not understand how the critics could make such fools of themselves as to write in the strain they did.

Furnivall, passionate democrat that he was, thought the play's real weakness was its theme: "the noble man sacrificing himself for the royal sham whom he knew to be sham." [49]

At the February meeting Furnivall offered his grammatical dissection of "O Lyric Love," a paper which seems to have fallen upon its audience's ears with a resounding thud; at least it provoked no discussion. Furnivall's curious contribution was preceded, however, by a useful paper on "A Death in the Desert" by Mrs. Ethel Glazebrook (d. 1926), wife of a Harrow master and diligent organizer of small literary study groups.[50] "The tendency of the [poem's] argument," Mrs. Glazebrook declared, "is to diminish the importance of the original events—historical or traditional—on which the Christian religion is based." Offended by what he regarded as Strauss's crude attack upon Christianity, Browning attempted to represent his faith as entirely spiritual, "independent of external, material agencies." [51] Yet, as one might expect, this sensitive, informed study provoked merely another clash between the Christians and the unbelievers in the society. William Revell observed with embarrassing candor that "it was long since he had read the poem. It was, however, full of theology—and he had had enough of *that*." When Gonner also complained about "the difficulty of keeping out personal theology in the discussion," Miss Whitehead, that formidable writer of tracts for the Moral Reform Union, replied that "the poem most emphatically summed up Mr. Browning's belief in Christ, and she considered the poem most helpful to our faith." But Furnivall managed to put in the last word: "the talk concerning Christ in the poem," he said, "was simply dramatic." [52]

The discussion during the meeting of March 25, 1887, was equally desultory, in this instance because no one was quite certain what James Lecky (1856–90), an active young member of the Philological Society and other learned organizations,[53] meant when he spoke of "Browning's Realism." (The paper itself was never prepared for publication, since Lecky was already suffering from a fatal disease.) Dr. Berdoe, the chairman, revealed solemnly that he had consulted both a dictionary and an encyclopedia in a vain attempt to learn the meaning of "realism." The other members were not much better informed on the subject, though Shaw said he thought the paper "a remarkably intelligent one, which made it more difficult to discuss." [54]

By the spring of 1887 the Browning Society was clearly losing momentum; one sign of this, aside from the aimless discussions, is the increasing skimpiness of the minutes and records of papers in the published transactions. For the remainder of this session, in fact, the *Papers* fell into considerable confusion, probably as a result of Walter Slater's pronounced sloppiness as an administrator. At the April meeting, for example, following Arthur Symons' "Some Notes on Mr. Browning's Latest Volume," Furnivall delivered one of his long speeches on the rhymes and meters of *Parleyings*. "His notes were handed to the Hon. Sec.," according to the *Papers*, "but have unluckily been mislaid." [55] (Significantly, on at least one other occasion before his retirement Slater managed to lose some important documents.[56]) For the next meeting, in April, at which Miss Helen Ormerod (d. 1926), honorary secretary of the Torquay Browning Society, read a paper demonstrating Browning's technical knowledge of music, no record at all of the discussion appears in the transactions.

Likewise, the June 24 meeting is not mentioned in the transactions, nor is Ernest Radford's paper printed there; but the notes which Furnivall took that evening are still among the Furnivall papers at King's College, London, and so it is possible to piece together what Radford (1857–1919), the barrister and poet who had founded the Scarborough Browning Society,[57] said. Attempting to predict the future estimate of Browning, his paper took a most un-Browningite view of the poet's style, and it would be edifying to know what response it evoked from the other members. The very existence of the Browning Society, Radford began, was a "crushing criticism" on the poet. Describing Browning as "sadly deficient as an artist," he objected to his obscurity, to the "frightful difficulty in his range of illustration," and to his "stickjaw parentheses." "By the Fireside" he called a "hard chestnut," and—in the unkindest cut of all—Tennyson's "Ulysses" he characterized as a "Browning work with all [of] B.'s faults left out." "I shall hope at least to provoke some discussion," Radford had written to Furnivall the previous January. His wish was fulfilled. According to the *Pall Mall Gazette*, "The address was both warmly attacked and warmly defended by different parts of the audience." [58] But that his unpopular viewpoint was never published in the Browning Society's *Papers* may be due to deliberate design rather than carelessness by the honorary secretary.

The 1887–88 session, which was to be marked by a widening rift between the Christian and agnostic elements in the society, began on a sufficiently peaceful note, for the first meeting, on October 28, illustrates once more that these opposing factions were actually in remarkable accord in their attitudes toward Browning's moral pronouncements. On that evening, Revell, an unbeliever, and Berdoe, a Christian (of sorts), delivered papers with nearly identical titles, and though Revell tried to make Browning out to be a theist, in broad terms the papers were in perfect agreement, Revell emphasizing his valuable optimistic philosophy and Berdoe lauding his "clear, definite gospel for the age." The only sharp dissent came, as usual, from Furnivall: "As regarded Dr. Berdoe's paper, he [Furnivall] might accept his views the more readily if he knew Browning was a worker at the East-end of London." [59] Religious issues continued to occupy the society's attention in November, when Percy A. Barnett (1858-1941), Professor of English at Firth University College, Sheffield,[60] offered a comparison of Browning's Jews with Shakespeare's Shylock.

In an effort to avoid theological questions, Furnivall invited Helen Ormerod at the next meeting (January 27, 1888) to present a strictly factual account of Abt Vogler's career. He and Gonner were pleased with the paper, but the more religious Browningites rose up in wrath. Miss Whitehead said that it was "rather disappointing that the essential idea of the poem was not brought out, namely, that seeming failure is truly success, and that we are allowed to fail here that we may succeed hereafter." Echoing this sentiment, Miss Stoddart read quotations from Heine and Pater "to illustrate the point of failures that bear their fruit hereafter, and the immortality of earnest effort, however unsuccessful." [61]

The society's believers, now on the offensive, were grimly determined to find a religious message in every poem by Browning, and Mrs. Jane Simpson, at the February meeting, climaxed her paper on *Fifine at the Fair* with this unlikely question: "What is the moral aspect of *Fifine* to me?" The answer (lest it not be immediately obvious) was that "it showed that even Don Juan had joined in the revolt against state-regulated or any other vice, and the Pharisaism of men who were themselves to blame for the social evils." [62]

In March, Kineton Parkes (1865-1938), an art critic and journalist[63] who was in charge of the Birmingham branches of both the Shelley and Browning societies, innocently ignited the fuse by surveying the ideas of *Ferishtah's Fancies*. Furnivall, with language even more caustic than usual, leaped to the attack:

> Browning had been getting away from men and women and into opinions and morals; and into teaching didactics rather than realities. These late poems he thought would not hold men and women in the same way that the earlier ones did, which dealt with men and

women. This poem got farther from life and more like sermons. How many people could find any part of *Ferishtah's Fancies* to which they went back again and found fresh help and strength as they did in earlier works? (Mr. Todd. I do—to the lyrics.) Well, there was one lyric on page 76 (quoting). Now, if anyone could honestly call that a lyric he would like to know who he was, and of what stuff he was made.

In addition, Furnivall was offended by Browning's theory that suffering was essential in order to call forth love. "The idea," he said, "was that you could not cultivate your sympathies unless you had a number of poor victims ground down to the earth by misery to promote *your* spiritual welfare. He thought that the poem failed in that as Browning's philosophy failed." Miss Whitehead naturally took strong exception to this view, but Revell came to his defense, agreeing that "in the later poems of Browning we were being a little over-done with theology and philosophy." After a rebuttal by Dr. Berdoe, Edward Gonner moved his heavy artillery into position. He, too, found fault with Browning's notion of the necessity of pain:

If Mr. Browning comes to that position and quietly sweeps away all logic, . . . we could scarcely be grateful to him for having evaded the question rather than solved it. To the plain common-sense mind of Dr. Furnivall, and he might add to his own mind, this did not commend itself. . . . That was the reason why he (the speaker) disliked Browning's discussions of theology and metaphysics, because when they were getting near to the solution, they suddenly found themselves entangled in a veil of words, and then they emerged on one clear sentence that all things that are, are right. Perhaps they are, but then we were no nearer solving the question. He emphatically dissented from the treating of a literary question from a moral point of view. . . . He thought *Ferishtah's Fancies* a very bad book indeed. It was an unintelligible book, and there was not in *Ferishtah's Fancies* one single poem which he would put against almost any of Wordsworth's best works. With regard to the paper, he would simply add that, having belonged to the Society for a long time, and having heard a very long series of very bad papers, and a short series of very good ones, he remembered none that more certainly belonged to the former category.[64]

Thereafter, as we have already seen, the situation deteriorated rapidly. It was a singular piece of bad luck that the papers for the April and May meetings were scheduled to be given by Catherine Whitehead (d. 1917) and Anna Stoddart, for in this tense atmosphere their militant piety merely brought the crisis to a head. Miss Stoddart (1840–1911) was in particular a most uncompromising Browningite: a member of the Browning Society committee and from 1887 to 1890 the editor of the Notes and Queries in the transactions, she also regularly attended the meetings, where she championed the cause of Christianity with more zeal than wisdom. Miss Stoddart was a writer and teacher, and her last work before she died was to correct the final proof sheets of a biography of Paracelsus which was inspired by Browning's poem.[65] After she announced in April, 1888, that she wished to make "an especial stab at Mr. Shaw," [66] Gonner's comrade in arms, it was obviously time for the Browning Society to reach a decision: were the Gonners or the Stoddarts to prevail? At the June business meeting the agnostics were driven from the field, but not without much bloodletting on both sides, and it is surely no coincidence that the membership of the society began to decline almost immediately. The annual report of 1888 indicated a net gain of five members; a year later, however, the annual report displayed in plain view the consequences of internecine strife:

> The Committee regret to be unable this year to present so satisfactory a Report as hitherto. The membership of the Society has decreased considerably; the decrease had probably taken place when the last list was issued [October, 1888], although the fact was only discovered recently, by the failure of the Hon. Secretary to receive due response to an urgent request for payment of overdue subscriptions.[67]

The Browning Society had now passed the peak of its popularity and power. Ironically, the annual report which had been distributed at the meeting of June 29, 1888, glibly predicted that Browning's influence would cause the narrowly orthodox to adopt a broader creed, and that "many a Freethinker and Agnostic who rejects the poet's theology and view of the scheme of the world may be led to acknowledge the power and helpfulness of Browning's works." [68] But by the middle of that evening the agnostic faction in the Browning Society had been put to rout, and the members could settle back to listen to a paper by the president of the New York Browning Society on "Browning's Presentation of the Other Side," secure in the knowledge that the "other side" would hereafter be heard much less distinctly in their own circle.

It is appropriate that the first paper of the new session, on October 26, 1888, was by Dr. Berdoe, one of the triumphant survivors of the previous session's civil war. Berdoe spoke on the historical Paracelsus, attempting to clear his name and restore his reputation, but Furnivall and Shaw, the latter of whom was to remain in the society for a few more months (though Gonner had dropped out immediately), were not persuaded. Furnivall said that he

> could not pretend to judge of the character of Paracelsus until his works had been printed in English. It seemed to him however that there must be some fire to give rise to all the smoke that was raised about him. . . .
> If Paracelsus had not been somewhat of an impostor, Browning would have cared nothing for him.

Shaw added that "Paracelsus was not what would now be called a respectable member of society, not the kind of man who becomes a churchwarden and—one of your good British virtues—never sets himself against established usages." [69] The chairman of the meeting was Mark Wilks (d. 1894), a Congregationalist minister who was one of the founders and leaders of the School Board System in London.[70] Wilks was evidently asked to take the chair that particular evening because he had lectured on *Paracelsus* the previous March, though he had declined to present the same lecture, which he called a "popular performance," to "a critical assembly like the Browning Soc[iet]y." [71] Wilks reported that Furnivall had told him to prepare to criticize Berdoe's paper with the "language of slaughter," [72] but of course that was unnecessary so long as Furnivall himself and Shaw were present.

The next meeting was a disappointment to many members, for since the previous year Furnivall had been attempting to arrange a lecture by William Boyd Carpenter (1841–1918), Bishop of Ripon, whose skill as an orator was well-known.[73] At last it was agreed that he would speak on November 30, 1888, and that the Reverend John Llewelyn Davies would serve as chairman, though Davies took a bemused view of his own role, as he explained to Furnivall:

> I shall be very happy to take the Chair when the Bishop of Ripon praises Browning with his charming eloquence. But he will not like my Chairmanship the better because we are both clerics. It is as if you thought that a lady would rather have a lady on each side of her at dinner.[74]

However, again arrangements broke down, and in the end Carpenter never spoke to the society.[75] In his stead the society heard a paper on "Andrea del Sarto and Abt Vogler" by Helen Ormerod, in which she commented that after her last paper she had been asked "to explain what 'C major' meant!" [76] During the discussion period Dr. Berdoe confessed that he was the one who had thus betrayed his ignorance of music; but, he went on, he *did* wish that Miss Ormerod had chosen a fresher subject. Furnivall rose to this challenge:

> He would first deal with his friend Dr. Berdoe, who at their last meeting read a paper on *Paracelsus*—a poem that was written long before *Andrea del Sarto;* and then—if Dr. Berdoe would not be offended at his saying so—had the audacity to wish that people would write about something later than *Andrea.* Dr. Furnivall thought that was cool.[77]

Berdoe, by now the most powerful figure in the society except for Furnivall, also occupied the chair on January 25, 1889, at which meeting the Reverend W. Robertson of Scotland read a paper on "La Saisiaz." This naturally produced a discussion centering around Browning's belief in a future life. Furnivall, apparently filling the vacuum left by Gonner's absence, flatly disagreed with the paper's premises: "For himself," he said, "he could only say that having once believed most strongly in eternal life, and not believing in it now, he could not find one scrap of difference in his happiness." [78] William Kingsland, on the other hand, declared that Browning's belief in immortality was a source of encouragement to those of lesser intellect like himself.

The society received a momentary jolt at the February meeting when James Bertram Oldham (1861–1937), a Stockport solicitor who headed the local Browning Society there,[79] contributed an analysis of the "Difficulties and Obscurities Encountered in a Study of Browning's Poems." Oldham recognized that what he had to say would be unacceptable to many members; nevertheless, he offered his paper as an antidote to the cultist tendencies of the society which were leading Browningites into a "blind, indiscriminate, and unreasonable idol-worship" of Browning. Hitherto, Oldham asserted, "the greater portion of our energies have . . . been directed towards unravelling those abstruse, ethical, intellectual, metaphysical, and psychological problems which the poet appears to have invented for the special mystification of that class among his readers who seem to be pleased with such puzzling playthings," whereas in fact the society ought to be clearing up his obscurities so that Browning's special message for this generation could be heard clearly by all the world.[80]

This was actually very close to orthodox Browningite dogma: James Russell Lowell in 1884 had also decried excessive partisanship and had confessed that Browning was "occasionally whirled away by the very sweep and torrent of his abundance," and the transactions record that this particular sentence was greeted with enthusiastic approval.[81] But that had been Lowell speaking, and it had taken place in 1884, when the society's temper was sweeter and a zeal for exposing heresies had not yet become the distinguishing mark of the Browningite faith. In 1889 Oldham's paper was received with cold hostility. Dr. Berdoe declared that "he did not see the use of such a paper." Falling back on a favorite metaphor of the society, he inquired rhetorically why they should not accept Browning's gold without grumbling about his quartz. Shaw also delivered his valedictory speech to the society that night, concluding that "he was sorry if his remarks had been almost uniformly abusive, and could only say that the writer of the paper richly deserved it." [82] Dr. Furnivall of course defended the paper, insisting that it was precisely the sort of treatment that Browning's poetry needed, but the meeting ended in an atmosphere of unrelieved gloom.

At Furnivall's suggestion, Joseph King, Jr., honorary secretary of the Bradford Browning Society, offered a detailed explication of *Prince Hohenstiel-Schwangau* in March; such papers, Furnivall explained, were superior to those which treated "some more popular topic." [83] Similarly, at the April meeting Mrs. Annie Ireland (1843–1893), whom Arthur Symons described as "a very clever woman, & an intense Browningite," [84] delivered an analysis of "A Toccata of Galuppi's." Mrs. Ireland had recently taken to lecturing and writing, especially on Browning, in order to pay the debts incurred by her husband through the sale of the Manchester *Examiner*, which he had edited.[85] Though her appearance was forbiddingly masculine, Mrs. Ireland's paper was written with such delicate grace that it prompted Symons to make his only visit to one of the society's meetings.

The 1888–89 session ended dismally. In May Mrs. Glazebrook's paper on "Numpholeptos" was all but discarded when Browning disagreed with it; and at the June meeting the Reverend James J. G. Graham, the editor of two volumes of selections from Milton, read a lackluster paper on "The Wife-Love and Friend-Love of Robert Browning." The new session also opened with a pronounced limp the following November. Furnivall read an excerpt from a new American book on Browning by Professor William J. Alexander; afterwards William Michael Rossetti offered an unspeakably dull treatise on some "Historical Details Illustrative of 'Sordello' "—". . . a very small affair," Rossetti recalled later with becoming modesty; "but I took pleasure in writing it." [86]

Then, on December 12, the unthinkable happened: Browning died in Venice, a shattering event which profoundly affected the morale of the Browning Society.

Furnivall, who had been in touch with the family during the last illness, went into a frenzy of activity when the news reached England, writing articles for the *Pall Mall Gazette* about his memories of Browning and attempting to arrange a burial in Westminster Abbey.[87] For a moment it appeared that the Browning Society itself, already faltering, would also succumb, but a few days later Furnivall was writing to a friend, "Aren't you pleasd we left the Soc[iet]y going? I am, very." [88] Still, the society's future was very much in doubt. "After the Society has run 10 years we shall have to consider how much longer it is to be carried on," Furnivall confessed in February to E. H. Blakeney, who he hoped would be Slater's successor. "The point'll turn on you of the young generation." [89]

On the gray, foggy last day of the year, amidst pomp and ceremony that expressed the nation's tardy recognition of his stature, Browning's body was interred in Westminster Abbey. The Browning Society was out in force for the funeral,[90] and a month later, at the January meeting, its members were still in mourning. Furnivall decided to turn the evening into a testimonial service in which each member present was invited to bear witness to Browning's impact on his own life. The results were predictable:

> [Furnivall:] For himself he thought that if they had to characterize Browning's service to the world, most people, and especially the women readers, would say as Miss Beale did, that it was the constant preaching of buoyant hope, the never giving way under any stress of circumstance, that was his greatest service to them.
>
>   *   *   *
>
> Miss Wilson thought Browning's greatest service was as a tonic in imparting strength and hope.
>
>   *   *   *
>
> [Miss Stoddart:] Personally, he had certainly been to her an expression of certainty, and hope and faith in real things, and this had helped to make her happy and complete and contented . . . [Browning] ought to drag this generation and future generations forward into a new orbit of faith, and hope, and work.
>
>   *   *   *
>
> Dr. Berdoe did not know that Browning had done him any good by making him optimistic, because that was his nature. The greatest good that Browning had done had been to instill the gospel of love.[91]

Not content with this tribute, Berdoe launched into a tedious account of Browning's views on vivisection, until at length another member said that he was "a little disappointed with the tone of the discussion" and angrily complained about the introduction of such an irrelevant topic on this solemn occasion. Even over a "scarcely-closed grave," Dr. Berdoe could not abandon his hobby horse.[92]

From this juncture the Browning Society's decline was rapid and inexorable: three times between January and April the scheduled papers were not ready, throwing the meetings into greater confusion than ever. In February, William Revell was not able to deliver his paper, and so Furnivall intoned some excerpts from the wills of Browning's ancestors; then, according to the *Papers*, he "asked for some suggestion as to the remainder of the evening." [93] At the March meeting the society was given a paper (originally intended for January) on "The Beautiful Commonplaces of Browning" by Mrs. Bertha Jane de Courcy Laffan (d. 1912), a popular novelist, who was married to the Rector of St. Stephen, Walbrook.[94] Since she had been unwilling to come to London during the influenza season, Mrs. Laffan was not present to defend herself against Dr. Berdoe's charge that the paper should have been called "The Beautiful Commonplaces of Mrs. Laffan." [95] Mrs. Ireland and Benjamin Sagar, the honorary secretary of the Manchester Browning Society, also contributed shorter papers, though Sagar's, a technical study of the line-numbering in *The Ring and the Book*, was distributed rather than read.

On April 25 Furnivall, compelled to announce "they were again without a paper," filled up the time by reading an article on Browning from the *Jewish Quarterly Review*. Following this, Edwin Johnson, the chairman, remarked lamely that he really had nothing to say on the topic of the article but that "he presumed they were at liberty to launch out into anything that occurred to them." With this advice in mind, Furnivall cheerfully began to attack Christianity, so that at last Miss Stoddart protested that he "had gone off on a side issue merely for the purpose of rousing opposition." "This is of course a misunderstanding of my motive," Furnivall replied in a footnote to the minutes of the meeting.[96]

Revell's postponed paper was introduced in May by the Reverend Mr. Hawker, who declared that "Browning had been his deliverer in a time of stress." [97] Nearly two years before Slater had suggested his name to Furnivall as a possible chairman, and at the time Furnivall was pointedly unenthusiastic ("Hawker'll do, no doubt, tho' no one has ever heard of him in Literature");[98] but in its present state the society could no longer afford to be choosy. Finally, in June, with still another paper cancelled, Dr. Furnivall provided some impromptu remarks on "In a Balcony," and, mercifully, the session ended.

Beyond this point it is neither desirable nor possible to trace the society's activities in much detail. For another year the papers, though not the discussions, were printed, but for the last session (1891–92) all is silence. The final parts of the *Papers* were never published, despite the occasional efforts of E. E. Davies and Thomas Wise to raise funds for that purpose. (For a list of the papers of the last two sessions, however, see Appendix A.) The ugly truth was that the society had simply run out of money. In the summer of 1889 the ailing Slater had written to a new member, Miss Florence Mary Wilson, inviting her to take over the honorary secretaryship. When he described the society's financial condition, Miss Wilson spurned the offer with horror:

> You did of course tell me the Browning Society had had difficulty in paying its way and as you remember staggered me very much by saying you had on one occasion advanced £100. However I had no idea its present debts are what they are, its balance in hand—with any view to future effectiveness—so infinitesimally small as about £25 only. How could any one contemplate a play, the cost of which w[oul]d be £60, for this coming year? . . . You understand business and have money you can lend—I fail, in both respects.[99]

In particular the American membership, which had always been large, was falling off at an alarming rate. "Our case is really pressing," Furnivall wrote to Jenkin Lloyd Jones in Chicago on May 30, 1891. "If our American subscribers pay up their back & their current subscriptions, our Soc[iet]y can pull through. If not, it is bankrupt, & must wind up after next year."[100] In August, E. E. Davies sent Jones a report of the response: of the American members, twenty had paid up their subscriptions, thirteen had not yet paid for the 1891–92 session, and sixty-nine (including Jones) had paid for neither 1890–91 nor 1891–92.[101] Davies begged Jones to raise some money from these tardy members, but by February of 1892 he still had received no reply from Chicago.[102] There was no longer any alternative to bankruptcy.

Even in this period of decline, however, the Browning Society heard several interesting papers and continued to attract talented new members. Owen Seaman (1861–1936), later editor of *Punch*, promoted the Browningite cause at Durham College of Science, Newcastle-upon-Tyne;[103] Richard Greene Moulton (1849–1924), a literary critic of some note, delivered two papers; and Professor William Hall Griffin, a teacher of literature at Queen's College, London, already be-

ginning to do research for his impressive biography of Browning, became active in the society's affairs. But after the end of the 1891–92
session the Browning Society held no public meetings. For a time the
members gathered in drawing rooms to hear papers, to recite poems to
each other, and, no doubt, to lament the society's days of glory that
were no more. At one of these "at homes," according to a newspaper
clipping among Furnivall's personal papers, Moncure Conway
"chatted most pleasantly for some 40 minutes about his personal
intercourse with Browning." [104] The anecdotes were familiar: they
were the same ones he had told at the first meeting of the society
eleven years before. The Browning Society had come full circle, and
despite the interludes of brilliance and wit, it ended as it had begun,
on a keynote of genteel triviality.

CHAPTER VIII

THE SOCIETY AND THE PUBLIC

=◈=

> This Society is founded to gather together some, at least, of
> the many admirers of Robert Browning, for the study and
> discussion of his works, and the publication of Papers on
> them, and extracts from works illustrating them. The Society
> will also encourage the formation of Browning Reading-Clubs,
> the acting of Browning's dramas by amateur companies, the
> writing of a Browning Primer, the compilation of a Brown-
> ing Concordance or Lexicon, and generally the extension of
> the study and influence of the poet.
> —Browning Society Prospectus (1881)[1]

WHETHER THE Browning Society made Browning's poetry more widely
read and appreciated, as Furnivall frequently claimed, is at least open
to question; but there can be no doubt that the society called a great
deal of attention to itself, if not to Browning, by its proselytizing activities. Unlike Furnivall's other societies, which were for the most part
pioneering ventures in scholarly publishing, the Browning Society was
conceived as a missionary society, which would persuade a presumably indifferent public of Browning's merits. To achieve this end, Furnivall envisioned that the society would produce his plays, publish
books, sponsor lectures, and organize branch societies and study
groups—all this in addition to regular monthly meetings. It was an
ambitious program, and since many of these activities made heavy
demands upon the society's financial resources, not to mention its
time and energy, the general mood of exhaustion which prevailed in
the Browning Society near the end of the decade is quite understandable. The solution to the society's ills, many Browningites came to feel
at that time, was to abandon the large public meetings with the techniques of noisy evangelism, and to create instead small, informal

Browning reading clubs with modest aims and expenditures.[2] But such counsel was symptomatic of the society's flagging spirits; in the early years the Browning Society had possessed a grandiose vision of compelling the allegiance of the entire English-speaking world to the poetry of Robert Browning.

Though Browning's plays were mentioned in the 1881 prospectus, the society did not attempt to stage one of them until 1884, for prior to this its annual entertainments—held at first in June, later usually in November—were comprised of recitations and music. At the first of these, for example, the large audience in the Botanic Theatre of University College heard readings of Browning's verse by Eleanor Marx, Augustine Birrell, Ernest Radford, and Miss Hickey, among others, and musical settings of "Cavalier Tunes" by Dr. Charles Villiers Stanford (1852–1924), whom the *Dictionary of National Biography* describes as "the most versatile British composer of the latter half of the nineteenth century." [3] Another important musical contributor to these early entertainments was Miss Ethel Harraden, who was invited by Furnivall in the spring of 1884 to compose melodies for any of Browning's poems that might interest her. When she ruefully admitted that she had never read Browning, Furnivall was prepared for even this emergency: he had with him fifteen volumes, which Miss Harraden carried off to her room and read at a furious pace while Furnivall chatted pleasantly with her father elsewhere in the house.[4] Before the evening was over, she had settled on "James Lee's Wife," and she also wrote to Browning asking for a poem especially written with musical values in mind. Browning's reply was somewhat indignant, as the note which Furnivall appended to his letter shows:

> Ethel Harraden's request for some words more suited to music, as B.'s written so few.
> B. doesn't like it, evidently.[5]

Despite the amateurishness of the entertainments, they were so successful that by June of 1884, 150 persons had to be turned away.[6] On at least one of these occasions the faithful gained admittance by wearing brown, a piece of whimsy which is probably the source of the most famous of all the Browning Society jokes which were circulating in England and America at the time. Furnivall wrote to Slater on November 11, 1884:

> Here is your bit of cinnamon brown ribbon, to tie in the top buttonhole of your coat on the 28th.
> The Miss Harradens [Ethel and her sister Beatrice] declare that

we must all turn up in brown velveteen shooting coats. So I've invested in a readymade one at 25/6 & look fine. Go then and do likewise.[7]

On November 16 Furnivall sent Slater further instructions on the back of an advertisement for a men's clothing shop:

> Go to this place, & try on a brown velveteen coat. See how well you look in it, & you'll buy it at once—make 'em put brown buttons on.
> You'll look better in brown velveteen than you've ever done in anything else. Don't be modest. Berdoe & I don't count ourselves good-looking; but we shall appear as the young ladies order us to. You can't do better than obey them.[8]

Four years later the editor of *Harper's* told a story—perhaps based on this episode—of a small Browning club in the American West which was unwilling to announce its name to the public. Visitors, however, noticed that everything was brown: the tablecloth, the sugar, the bread, the curtains, even the clothing. At length one guest said, "Well, I declare I really believe you are a Browning club." [9] The scores of periodicals that repeated the anecdote might have done so with even more gusto had they realized how close to the truth it was.

By the spring of 1884 several members of the Browning Society were wondering whether it would be possible to produce some of Browning's plays, which had met with so little success in their initial performances a half century earlier. At the May meeting Furnivall speculated aloud that "some of Browning's plays,—specially *In a Balcony*—might . . . be acted without scenery," [10] and the following November "In a Balcony" was indeed performed at Princes' Hall, Piccadilly, under the sponsorship of the Browning Society, with Miss Alma Murray taking the role of Constance. Though Alfred Domett, who was present, described the evening as "a great success" in a letter to Browning,[11] other observers were less charitable. Miss Nora Gerstenberg was clearly not satisfactory as the Queen; but, more fundamentally, the performance raised the essential question of whether "In a Balcony" could be done successfully on the stage under even the best of circumstances. The *Saturday Review*, in a particularly devastating critique of the society's efforts, pointed out that "In a Balcony" "surely could never have been intended for performance. It is a poem —a very beautiful and an exceedingly powerful poem—and not a play." [12]

By extension, the same criticism could be made of Browning's other plays, five of which, unlike "In a Balcony," were explicitly written for the stage.[13] The failure of Browning as a playwright must, in fact, be seen in the context of the failure of poetic drama generally in nineteenth-century England. Like nearly every major poet of the century, he produced merely closet drama. "The primary cause of his failure," according to H. B. Charlton, "was his conviction that man's relation to God is infinitely more important than his relation to his fellow-men," a conviction which must spell defeat in an art form that is primarily a social activity.[14] More specifically, Browning's plays suffered from minor defects of construction and motivation: at the end of "In a Balcony," for instance, the "measured heavy tread" of the palace guard obviously portends some climactic act—but precisely what? In "My Last Duchess" a line like "I gave commands;/Then all smiles stopped together" adds to the mystery of the sinister Duke of Ferrara; on the stage, however, such ambiguity, particularly in the important final lines of a play, merely puzzles. Except on rare occasions, Browning's subtle, labyrinthine mind was incapable of producing the straightforward exposition which the stage demands.

Undeterred by any of these considerations, Furnivall, at the close of the "In a Balcony" performance, "expressed his opinion that the performance proved the great poet in whose honour the audience had assembled to be a great dramatist as well." [15] Shortly thereafter Charles Fry, the professional stage manager of the Irving Dramatic Club, received the following letter from Furnivall:

> I must try hard to persuade you to take up one of Browning's Plays, *Strafford,* or the *Return of the Druses,* say. We Browningites are all very anxious to see a play of his on the boards again. A performance of one would draw every dramatic critic in London. . . . Will you kindly read Browning's plays if you don't know them, and tell me under what conditions your company would play one next autumn or spring, and then I'll see whether they can be met. I should immensely like, and so would Browning and all his readers, I am sure, to see a play of his in your company's hands. Pray do think the matter over and help us if it is possible.[16]

On April 30 and May 2, 1885, *A Blot in the 'Scutcheon* and *A Comedy of Errors* were performed by the Irving Dramatic Club under the auspices of the Browning Society and the New Shakspere Society. The Browning Society sponsored three more quasi-amateur productions— *Colombe's Birthday* (November 19, 1885), *Strafford* (December 21, 1886), and *A Blot in the 'Scutcheon* again (March 15, 1888), this time with Alma Murray as Mildred Tresham—but after 1888, with its funds severely depleted, the society had to be satisfied with occasional dramatic readings of the plays.

Probably the most that can be said for the Browning Society's efforts in this direction is that they revived a modest but nevertheless real interest in Browning's plays for a time. In the United States, the actor Lawrence Barrett produced *A Blot in the 'Scutcheon* with moderate success in several large cities, and at Oxford the son of Henry Irving appeared in the title role of *Strafford.* The underlying assumption of all these productions was that Browning's plays could somehow triumph if only they were presented properly on the stage, and this, as Oscar Wilde later observed in a letter to the *Daily Telegraph,* was not true:

> In the production of Browning's plays, . . . in London and at Oxford, what was being tested was obviously the capacity of the modern stage to represent, in any adequate measure or degree, works of introspective method and strange or sterile psychology. But the artistic value of *Strafford,* or *In a Balcony,* was settled when Robert Browning wrote their last lines.[17]

In short, not even the enthusiasm of Furnivall and his Browningites could redeem the flaws of Browning's plays.

Closely related to these dramatic performances were the Browning readings and lectures which members of the society gave throughout England, as well as the small Browning study groups which they directed. Some, like Furnivall and Miss Hickey, had carried on such activities for years, but the society as a whole did not become conscious of the proselytizing possibilities of readings and lectures until about 1885, when, at the annual June meeting, Furnivall suggested from the chair that members deliver in their own localities "popular lectures on Browning's works." Miss Whitehead, Dr. Berdoe, and Kingsland promised at once to do so, and the following November Berdoe and Edward Gonner (an unlikely pair, incidentally) were appointed as a subcommittee to co-ordinate and organize local Browning readings and lectures, "either independently or in connection with local Literary Societies."[18] Soon offers of assistance were pouring in from the members. Dr. Berdoe, the most earnest of all the devout Browningites, set a good example by forming a Browning study class at Hackney, and he reported later that "the pleasure and help he had obtained from that mutual study had been of no ordinary character."[19] One gathers, in fact, that Berdoe was the society's most indefatigable lecturer. "I was requested last night to lecture on Browning at

South Place [Chapel] today as the Professor announced was ill," he wrote Slater in 1888. "It was a difficult time but I wrote an entirely new lecture of an hour's reciting—on 'the Religion of Browning.' *An appreciative & large audience.*" [20]

Not always were the listeners so receptive, however. Mrs. Ireland has left an edifying account of her lecture on "The Spiritual Teachings of Robert Browning" to an audience of laborers at Toynbee Hall, where she was warned by a young man that "Whitechapel is not quite Belgravia; and these men are men who don't go to church, and in fact," he added, nervously clearing his throat, "if they are not interested in your lecture, I fear that they will put on their caps, and just walk out, and rather noisily too." Nevertheless, Mrs. Ireland spoke on her topic for an hour and a quarter, at the end of which time a man with grimy face and dress arose to ask: "Me and my friends has liked all you've been a-saying of, mum; it's been prime; though we was afeared at first as it was a sort of Sunday school dodge as don't run in our line. But I want to ask you, mum, one straight question. Why was the name of Robert Browning lugged in at all?" It was an intelligent question, one that might have been asked at many a Browning Society meeting. Mrs. Ireland answered it as well as she could, and then turned to face her next questioner, who disclosed that he and his wife had tried to read one of Browning's books (*Pacchiarotto*) but without any success. To him she gave a few words of encouragement and the assurance that *she* could not understand that volume either. Finally a third man, somewhat better-dressed, probably a tailor or shopkeeper, announced that he disliked Browning even though he enjoyed other poets. "I put it to you fairly," he said, "do you consider Browning to be a poet? Do you find him melodious and graceful? Does he come straight to your heart like Byron does?" Mrs. Ireland replied that Browning was "a great teacher" but recommended that the questioner continue to "rest" his mind by reading Byron, Leigh Hunt, and Longfellow. There were no more questions. And the next time she appeared at Toynbee Hall, Mrs. Ireland records, she lectured on a different subject.[21]

When a lecture was more successful, a new Browning club would often be established in the locality, perhaps with formal ties to the London Browning Society. As soon, in fact, as Miss Hickey and Furnivall had set up the parent organization in the summer of 1881, offspring began to appear all over England and America. Browning clubs flourished especially in the United States, where the "Browning craze" manifested itself in its most compelling form. Hiram Corson, Levi Thaxter, and Jenkin Lloyd Jones travelled about the countryside there as itinerant Browningite preachers, producing such enthusiasm for Browning that by 1890 one writer announced that "the Shakespeare clubs have been gradually elbowed to the wall." [22] In St. Louis a score of ladies founded a Sordello Club in order to examine that poem in detail, after each laborious session refreshing themselves with a cup of tea;[23] in Chicago booksellers could not keep Browning's books in stock, and a dozen Browning clubs were said to exist there;[24] and in Philadelphia the public library announced that Browning was the most widely read of all the modern English poets.[25] The Browningite movement attracted such disparate enthusiasts as the Philadelphia clergyman who, after his first reading of "Rabbi Ben Ezra," laid down the poem "with tears of thankfulness that such words of comfort and strength, spoken in such a way, had come to him," [26] and—quite surprisingly—Mark Twain, who claimed that he had read every other line of Browning's poetry to a study group without anyone's noticing the omissions.[27]

Matthew Arnold, finding himself in a small, remote New England village while lecturing in America, remarked to a companion that it reminded him in some ways of a solitary hamlet in the Tyrol. "And what do the good people do for amusement?" Arnold is said to have asked. "Well," replied the other, "they had a lecture on Browning last week." At this Arnold threw up his hands in amazement and responded, "I am evidently not in the Tyrol." [28] Nearly every village in America, it seemed, had its ardent Browningites, and observers tried in vain to offer a full explanation for this phenomenon. Most, however, agreed that it was symptomatic of the American thirst for a cultural life now that the frontier, with the harsh environment it represented, had disappeared. The literary critic E. C. Stedman, who was roundly abused by Browningites for his views on the subject, further suggested that the Browning clubs typified an American "rage for elucidation," the like of which "has not been witnessed since the days of the neo-Platonists and grammarians." [29] F. M. Padelford, who taught a highly successful course in Browning at the University of Washington, also theorized that Browning, with his vigor and optimism, held a special attraction for Westerners, who shared these traits.[30]

The fact remains, however, that the Browning clubs sprang up chiefly on the eastern coast of the United States. Hiram Corson, the prime mover of the cause in America, had founded the first Browning club anywhere in 1877 at Cornell, and by 1883 he and Levi Thaxter of Boston had established similar organizations in Philadelphia, Syracuse, and Baltimore.[31] In 1885 the Boston Browning Society held its first meeting, and soon jokes were being told about Boston's adoption of Browning as her own. Browning himself was greatly amused by a cartoon which depicted an Englishman approaching Boston on a train and asking the conductor, "What is the strange sound I hear?" The conductor replied, "Oh, that is the Bostonians reading Browning." [32] Of all the American Browning clubs, Boston's was easily the most distinguished, and to this day it meets regularly, sometimes hearing papers by eminent literary scholars.

In Chicago the Browningite cause was led by Jenkin Lloyd Jones (1843–1918), an activist Unitarian preacher,[33] who founded the first Browning club there in the autumn of 1882. F. W. Farrar's Browning lecture in November of 1885, which was attended by an enormous audience that included most of Chicago's leading citizens, touched off a "Browning fever" without precedent.[34] By the following March the chief bookseller in the city revealed that he was selling more copies of Browning than of any other poet, living or dead, and another bookseller, though his Browning stock was depleted, lectured to a customer on "Saul" and "declared it was the grandest poem of modern times, and proved to him that the timid hope of *In Memoriam* was nothing to the buoyant and confident faith of the robuster writer of *Prospice, La Saisiaz*, &c." [35] Browning took an interest in all this, telling several American visitors that his poetry was more fully appreciated and understood in Chicago than anywhere else.[36] When this piece of intelligence reached America, it prompted a writer for the New York *Sun* to observe that it was encouraging news for Chicago but depressing news for Philadelphia, Boston, London, East Orange, Bristol, Chestnut Hills, Huddersfield, and many other towns on both sides of the wide Atlantic. "Hereafter," the *Sun* columnist suggested, "no rendering of Browning, no new interpretation of his probable meaning, will be worth two cents until it has been tested and approved by the thoughtful and intelligent Browning critics of Chicago." [37]

In England the chief centers of Browning study outside London were Cambridge and Oxford. A preliminary meeting, attended by sixty, was held at Cambridge on November 11, 1881, in order to draft rules, which stipulated that the Cambridge Browning Society would meet in general gatherings twice a term and also conduct special weekly meetings every Friday.[38] The first regular session began the following autumn, but within a year the Cambridge Browning Society collapsed, only to be revived in 1890 through the joint efforts of E. H. Blakeney, then a Trinity student, and Furnivall.[39] The Oxford Browning society also organized in the autumn of 1881, though it decided to limit its membership to forty ("the number of the French Academy as well as the Forty Thieves," Furnivall observed): fifteen graduates, fifteen undergraduates, and ten ladies, as well as eight honorary members.[40] Representing, as Edward Gonner said, "the whim of the fashionable literary society of Oxford," it was defunct within a few years, although one or more smaller Browning clubs at Oxford survived into the next decade.[41]

One of the hardiest, perhaps because the least pretentious, of the English Browning clubs was the one formed on the northern edge of London by William G. Kingsland and the Reverend J. S. Jones in 1890. As early as 1883 Kingsland had been recommending the creation of such an organization in the *Islington News*,[42] and when the Clerkenwell and Islington Browning Union was at last founded he served as its honorary secretary. The club heard papers by such Browningite regulars as Miss Hickey, Miss Drewry, and Dr. Berdoe, but whatever success it achieved, as Kingsland recognized, resulted from its modest rules of operation: it required only a nominal subscription for membership, issued no transactions, and made "little public profession of faith." [43]

Assessing the importance of the hundreds of Browning societies and clubs which appeared in America and England at the end of the century is not an easy task, for many of them seem to have differed little from bridge or garden clubs. Mary Gladstone, the daughter of the Prime Minister, recorded in her diary in 1885 that she and some friends had enjoyed "a Browning Society afternoon" [44]—an interesting phrase which conjures up a picture of an informal gathering where genteel ladies entertain themselves by going through the motions of studying Browning. This view of the smaller Browning clubs is also advanced in a witty story by Arthur Conan Doyle entitled *A Duet*. A group of three matrons, reading in the *Lady's Journal* that an intellectual life preserves a woman's youth (the title of the article is "Shakespeare as a Cosmetic"), decide to form a literary society, but they are compelled to reject Shakespeare (even in Bowdler's version), Shelley, and Byron as possible objects of study because of either their indecency or untidy lives. That of course leaves only Browning, and so, like the ladies of the Sordello Club, they resolve to begin with his most difficult poem, which in their judgment is "Caliban." However, its twisted syntax leaves them confused, they react squeamishly to Caliban's earthy vocabulary, and finally Mrs. Beecher cries out, "What is the use? Two lines have positively made my head ache, and there are two volumes." "And so," concludes Doyle, "after one hour of precarious life, Mrs. Hunt Mortimer's Mutual Improvement Society for the elucidation of Browning came to an untimely end." [45]

And for the most part the other Browning clubs, which were once scattered around the world in such remote locales as South Africa, Australia, and Austria, shared this fate, although it should be pointed out that Browning study groups are still functioning in many American cities. A list of such clubs compiled a few years ago by the Armstrong Browning Library of Baylor University cites thirty-five of them, including six in Dallas, Texas, alone. Browning clubs today, however, carry a slightly musty odor about them, as if they do not quite belong to the twentieth century. As an elderly member of the now-defunct Seattle Browning Society explained to a newspaper reporter recently, "The members kept getting older and the fine print in the books became impossible for them to read and younger women had other things to do; so there were no new members." [46]

Yet if the dilettante quality of the local Browning societies and clubs made their contribution to our understanding of Browning negligible, the same cannot be said of the publications of the London Browning Society, for here if anywhere one must seek an explanation for the society's powerful influence upon our century's view of Browning. Indeed, that influence was more far-reaching than has been realized in the past, since a careful examination of the Browning Society's transactions and other related documents will demonstrate that the society had some connection with nearly every book about Browning published between 1881 and the end of the century. To cite only a few obvious examples, the two major ninetenth-century Browning handbooks (by Orr and Berdoe), the first three full-length biographies of Browning (by Sharp, Orr, and Griffin), and the first two important bibliographies (by Furnivall and Wise) were all written by members of the Browning Society. Obviously some of these books might have been written had the society never existed, but the Browning Society in every case lent encouragement by commissioning the book, publishing it, or, at the very least, buying several hundred copies of it for members. The society's dominance in this area had a twofold effect. On the one hand, Browning's poetry has received the kind of detailed study and explication that has been accorded few other writers of the Victorian period. This has made possible, among other things, such first-rate examples of Browning scholarship in our century as the DeVane *Handbook* and the Broughton, Northup, and Pearsall *Bibliography*. But, on the other hand, the sheer weight of the society's writings has given the illusory impression that nothing new can be said about Browning. By smothering his poetry with a fog of commentary, most of it naively moralistic, the Victorian Browningites have made his work largely inaccessible for many modern readers, and consequently Browning's reputation, which plummeted so badly after World War I when anti-Victorianism became fashionable, has not yet fully undergone the kind of rehabilitation that would put his poetic achievement in true perspective. It is as if that first band of Browningites, still haunting the environs of Bloomsbury, had gripped Browning's ghostly coatsleeve so tightly that he was not permitted to enter the twentieth century.

Clearly it is beyond the scope of this chapter to discuss individually the scores of books which emanated from the Browning Society; nonetheless it may be instructive to trace the writing and subsequent fortunes of two of the most important, both by Alexandra Orr (1828–1903). Mrs. Orr, whom Browning called "the dearest woman friend I can boast of in the world," [47] was born in St. Petersburg, where her father was court physician. Named after the Empress of Russia, her godmother, she travelled and studied extensively on the Continent, briefly in the winter of 1855–56 meeting Browning, with whom her brother, the painter Frederic Leighton, was already intimate. After a short marriage to an army officer, Sutherland Orr, who died as a result of privations suffered during the Indian Mutiny, Mrs. Orr settled in London in 1869, there quickly developing a close relationship with Browning. Since her eyesight was poor, for years Browning visited her home twice a week in order to read to her; he also encouraged her to write occasional articles for the *Contemporary Review* on women's suffrage (which she opposed) and on his own poetry. In 1873, for example, Browning was instrumental in getting her review of his *Red Cotton Night-Cap Country* published, and the following year her more general survey of Browning's poetry, which may be seen as a precursor of her *Handbook*, also appeared in the *Contemporary*.[48]

Though Mrs. Orr held no office in the Browning Society, she was from the beginning regarded as an unofficial court of appeal on all matters relating to Browning. Seldom appearing in person at the meetings, she was nevertheless invited on occasion to write a rebuttal to or critique of the paper which had been read. It was also understood from the first that Mrs. Orr would produce the most important of the society's *desiderata*, a "Primer," or elementary introduction to Browning's poetry. What she finally published under the sponsorship of the society was much more ambitious than that; it was a comprehensive, authoritative handbook to the poetry, based to a large though undetermined extent upon the personal assistance of Browning, who contributed many notes and read the book in proof. Mary Gladstone quoted Browning as saying that the *Handbook* was "an astonishing interpretation of him," [49] a thoroughly ambiguous statement, but his letters make it clear that he meant it as a compliment. To a correspondent in 1889 Browning wrote: "I should say that Mrs. Orr's Handbook is anything but a hindrance, rather the best of helps to anyone in need of such when reading—or about to read—my works. It is done far better than I could hope to do it myself." [50] Unlike T. S. Eliot, Browning felt no inclination to annotate his own work, and so he was rather relieved to be able to refer troubled readers to the *Handbook*. Something of this mood comes through in an indignant reply to a question by one "Ball-goer" (probably Wise himself) forwarded to him by Wise:

> Since I wrote the hasty answer to the inquiry in your letter, this morning, I had the curiosity to refer to the "Handbook" of Mrs. Orr in order to see whether the information I had just given was not to be found there. All and every particular to the minutest are given with the greatest care and preciseness: and I think the author's pains have been altogether thrown away if every idle "ball-goer" requires instruction which is already abundantly in reach.[51]

The press also treated the *Handbook* with generosity, describing it with such terms as "indispensable" and "the best," though many reviewers complained about Mrs. Orr's elaborate system of classifying the poems. The book went through six editions, some of them incorporating additional corrections and notes by Browning, and numerous reprintings.

Oddly enough, Furnivall was the one person who apparently disliked the *Handbook*. In the autumn of 1885, shortly after its publication, he was writing a short biographical sketch of Browning and his wife, which he sent to Browning for corrections. On reading it, Browning was disturbed to discover a disparaging remark about the *Handbook*, which was, as he reminded Furnivall, a book "begun—I have always understood—at your own suggestion, and toiled at with abundance of difficulty for some four years, unhelped by anybody: I simply answered every now [and] then a question, without the least notion of its exact bearing or purpose. The book at all events had the sanction of the Society of which you are the head." [52] A few days later Browning wrote again, still pleading for a reconciliation between Furnivall and Mrs. Orr.[53] Evidently it did not come, since she never thereafter participated in the Browning Society's activities.

But of course her relationship with Browning remained as warm as ever, and when his family realized that he was dying in 1889, they sent for her immediately; she arrived in Venice in time to help with the funeral arrangements.[54] Sarianna and Pen Browning, seizing upon a characteristically Victorian expedient, asked Mrs. Orr to write an authorized biography in an effort to forestall any "unofficial lives." Sarianna explained their decision to Katharine Bradley in 1890:

> I never read notices, or lives, or articles, and sometimes am tempted to wish that I might never see his name again. Yet in self-defense,— so many inaccurate statements being afloat, and so many *"friends"* (Heaven save us!) turning a penny by article-mongering [probably an allusion to Furnivall],—we have authorized Mrs. Orr to draw up a true memoir of his uneventful life, and I am looking through old letters to verify the same—you may imagine with what pain! [55]

Relying heavily upon Sarianna's memories and documents, Mrs. Orr pieced together a biography of Browning that was brisk, restrained, and a trifle dull. William Wentmore Story, who had contributed a few Browning letters, found it "rather colourless . . . & as for incidents and descriptions of persons & life it is very meagre." [56] William Kingsland, reviewing it in *Poet-Lore,* dismissed it as unenthusiastic and incomplete; the *Dial* lamented the lack of any literary or historical context; and reviewers in general found it excessively discreet and decorous.[57]

As is so often the case, the authorized biography also failed to satisfy the family which had commissioned it. Michael Field, visiting Pen and Sarianna at Asolo in 1895, learned that "Pen hates Mrs. Orr's *Life* as we do—the puling invalidism attributed to a man who never stayed in bed till he died in Venice." [58] In 1904 Pen Browning was still burning with resentment, "Oh, that is a very bad book!" he told William Lyon Phelps. "None of the family liked it." Mrs. Orr, he explained, had shown her manuscript to no one, and when the family attempted to make many revisions in the proofs, she had replied, "I cannot change the proofs." [59] The book is in fact replete with errors, though the Browning family was probably more concerned about questions of tact rather than of accuracy. Part of this may be attributed to the circumstance that Mrs. Orr was an imperfect Boswell who saw only one side of Browning's nature. Whenever he was with her he seems to have been grave and given to serious discourses on ethical questions, whereas in Furnivall's presence, for example, Browning assumed a bluff, hearty, masculine manner. Mrs. Orr doubtless often misunderstood the intent of Browning's observations to her simply because of her own excessive sobriety. "Mrs. Orr said, B if askt, w[oul]d confess that he had 'no sense of humour,' " Furnivall wrote. To Furnivall, this was "a tremendous joke." [60] (She had in actuality misinterpreted a chance remark on the subject.) In failing to discern Browning's essential gaiety of spirit, she revealed her chief shortcoming as a biographer.

However, what distressed many readers was her portrayal of Browning as a theist. The *London Quarterly Review*, for instance, accused her of reading "not a little of her own Agnosticism into the poet's utterances," [61] and several evangelical journals joined the attack. Attempting to defend herself in the *Contemporary Review*, Mrs. Orr asserted that her theistic interpretation of Browning's poems, especially "La Saisiaz" (which Browning had dedicated to her), was based directly on conversations with the poet.[62] This controversy, needless to say, was merely an extension of the fundamental quarrel that had shattered the Browning Society, and at this distance it seems impossible to pronounce final judgment. What is most striking, however, is Browning's elusiveness in all personal matters, his ability to assume the protective coloring he needed in order to be agreeable to everyone he met. How Browning privately regarded the central dogma of Christianity—the divinity of Christ—is a piece of information that seems to be beyond recovery. It is significant, nevertheless, that Mrs. Orr, his most intimate friend, could not fully penetrate his reserve. The other figures in the Browning Society, standing not nearly so close to him, understood him even less. Browning and his poetry might be "promoted" by the society, but there was a firmly drawn line of privacy beyond which they could not go.

* * *

Confronted with this program of aggressive propaganda, the public reacted to the Browning Society with indignation, amusement, hostility, and, in a few rare instances, with sympathy. Furnivall, experienced controversialist that he was, expected the worst from the press. "No doubt we shall have flippant article-writers affecting omniscience," he remarked at the society's first meeting, "and suggesting that there's no need for a Browning Society, because they know all about the poet—and everybody and everything else.—But old birds are not to be caught with chaff. Some of us have had to sift these all-knowing ready writers pretty often, and it is odd how little grain has come through the sieve." [63]

Indeed, the onslaught of adverse criticism had begun even before the October meeting. A week earlier the *Critic* had announced (though mistakenly) that "we understand that Mr. Browning was not consulted in the foundation of the Society in London which bears his name, and that it does not in any way meet with his approval." [64] Following the delivery of Kirkman's inaugural address, the *Nation* suggested that the Browning cult had reached the stage at which "the doors ought to be closed and locked, and the mysteries conducted in dead secrecy." [65] In the *Cambridge Review*, a few days later, a letter signed "B.H.H." decried the introduction of "the congregational spirit into the realms of art and poetry." [66] A number of periodicals accused the Browning Society of damaging rather than enhancing Browning's poetic reputation—a charge which has frequently been repeated in our century. Another claim which was often made in the press, with less justice, was that the society members were silly aesthetes of the Bunthorne-Wilde variety, whereas in actuality the sober evangelicals were probably the dominant faction in the organization. Many of the published comments on the Browning Society, too, were simply in bad taste, as when Furnivall was accused of being a "hanger-on" of Browning and a "journalistic ghoul." [67]

Furnivall, temperamentally incapable of remaining silent in the face of such criticisms, sent off some angry letters to periodicals in the society's first few months of existence. On October 29, 1881, for example, the *Echo*, assessing Kirkman's address, concluded that the Browningites could do Browning greater honor "by interpretation than by eulogy." Furnivall replied by praising Browning as "the greatest Christian philosophic poet now living," and he added, in a remarkable assertion, that "as to the interpretations of difficult poems, our Society will soon be able to make all clear." [68] In a year's-end survey of the literary world published on December 31, 1881, the London *Daily News* remarked that both Tennyson and Browning had written little of late; "indeed, the Browning Society may be said to have authoritatively announced to the latter that he is a classic, and as such must not write any more books." To the contrary, declared Furnivall in a letter on January 2: "the Browning Society earnestly hopes to see many a volume proceed from the pen of the poet in whose honour and to study whom it is founded." [69]

Of all these early attacks on the society, the one that seems to have annoyed Furnivall most appeared in the *Pall Mall Gazette* on December 22, 1881, possibly because of that newspaper's influential position in literary circles. In a long editorial on the Browning Society, the *Pall Mall* insisted that the function of all such societies was to publish essays rejected by periodicals, since "any critic worth attention would prefer to speak in open court and to the general public, not to a little clique, and in a place where any frankness of blame would have the air of impertinence." Indignantly Furnivall repudiated this viewpoint in a letter published January 2, 1882. "I have never known a literary society of repute publish a rejected essay," he wrote. He then went on to throw down a challenge to the writer of the editorial:

> Next, as to the probability of the Browning Society's papers being weaker than the public reviews. Let us come to the point. I challenge you, Sir, to produce from your own journal—or from any other review, living or dead—a paper on Browning's "Dramatic Idyls," Series II., or on any other single volume of Browning equal to that by Mr. Sharp[e]. . . . We invite [the *Pall Mall* writer] to offer himself for an examination in Browning—barring cram questions—and we undertake to reduce his estimate of his Browning knowledge 50 per cent before he leaves our "schools." [70]

Furnivall's fury subsided after 1882, and rarely did he again tilt with the critics of the Browning Society in print, though he did in 1889 write a complaint to the *Athenaeum* about its accusation that the Browning Society stressed unduly Browning's intellectual subtlety.[71]

The *Saturday Review,* witnessing these exchanges with some amusement, informed its readers that two newspapers (the *Pall Mall Gazette* and the *Daily News*) had dared "to touch the ark" the previous week, and provided a most unflattering summary of Furnivall's letters. Condolences were in order for Browning, the *Saturday Review* felt, since Furnivall's belligerent defenses of the society could only embarrass him.[72] Furnivall, however, had anticipated attack from that quarter. In a footnote to his remarks about the press at the opening meeting of the society, he had warned that the *Saturday Review* would be the worst offender: "But any one who has known a *Saturday* small-type man anxiously hunting for a subject, will feel no ill-will at a poor fellow making his £3 15s.—if that is still the pay—out of the Society, whatever he says against it. Fault-finding is his trade." [73] The *Saturday Review* retaliated with unfailing hostility toward every phase of the Browning Society's activities. In a highly unfavorable review of the fourth annual entertainment it remarked, apropos of nothing, "The most appreciative admirers of Mr. Browning are not likely to be found in a Browning Society." [74] The society's publications it loudly condemned, saying that "God has made Mr. Browning a very great poet, but the Browning Society persons of the type of Mr. Symons have sought out many inventions about him." [75] In 1891, when Mrs. Orr's biography appeared, the *Saturday Review*'s wrath had still not abated. Though the reviewer praised the book, he found a pretext for a lengthy digression condemning Browning's decision to tolerate the society.[76]

Private opinions of the Browning Society ranged from enthusiastic endorsement to outright damnation, though the most common reaction was one of tolerant amusement. The *Academy* published a letter from the poet R. H. Horne, once a collaborator with Mrs. Browning, which revealed that the Browning Society had his "deepest and warmest sympathy." [77] Alfred Domett, who had joined the society with some reluctance, sent Browning this lighthearted view of its activities:

> Indeed it [*Ferishtah's Fancies*] reminds me of what Carlyle somewhere gives as the battle-cry of the ancient Saxons, "Out with your gullies, ye Saxons!" So *Ferishtah's Fancies*, even more than any other works of yours, seems a sort of shout of defiance, "Out with your *nut-crackers*, you Browning Societies!" And I am confident the kernels will prove as sound and savory as any you ever gave them to "chew upon." [78]

Lady Eastlake was invited to join the society but pleaded "too great stupidity" and so, she said, was excused. "Dryden, Milton, and Pope are, I understand, quite commonplace in comparison," she wrote ironically to Sir Henry Layard; "that I am inclined to believe. But I like Browning himself." [79] Ellen Terry, the actress, thought that the Browning Society had "terrorized the ordinary reader into leaving Browning alone," and Benjamin Jowett, Master of Balliol College, Oxford, informed Furnivall that he would be "very unwilling" to join the society and that he doubted whether its formation would be agreeable to Browning himself.[80] Perhaps the most unexpected response came from Oscar Wilde, who solemnly admonished Browning to ignore the adulation of the Browning Society and to rise instead to the true task of the poet: "to stir the pulses of [a] man or woman, or create a desire to lead a higher, a holier, and a more useful life in the breast of the indifferent average citizen." [81]

The almost universal impulse, however, was to laugh at the Browning Society, which proved such an easy target for wits that during its eleven-year history it must have been the most satirized institution in England. The obvious excesses of Browning's admirers provided an admirable subject for parodies, anecdotes, and cartoons; even today, any mention of the society calls forth the obligatory jokes, though most of them sounded much funnier in the eighties than they do now. The body of folklore which the Browning Society engendered is, in fact, of such proportions that one can only dip into it here and there for some samples of Victorian humor. One story which Browning himself delighted to tell concerned the occasion of his receiving the honorary degree of D.C.L. at Oxford in 1882. During the ceremony a group of undergraduates lowered from the gallery a huge cartoon showing Browning surrounded by members of the Browning Society, who implored him with outstretched hands to explain his poems to them, "while Browning waved them off in despair as of one who has no explanation to give." [82] Satirical poems abounded. One, which appeared in the *Cambridge Meteor*, began: "There's a Me Society down at Cambridge. . . ." [83] *Punch* provided an elaborate account of a recent meeting of the "Whitey-Browning Society," where, it said, the following topics were proposed for discussion:

1. Whitey-Browning as a substitute for cheap Champagne.
2. His Narcotic Teaching.
3. Ready-made Clothing and its Psychological Disadvantages, as gathered from the Philosophy of Whitey-Browning.
4. His Estimate of Concrete Clog-Dancing.
5. The Inductive value of his after-dinner Adjectives.
6. Whitey-Browning regarded as an Omnibus Conductor. . . .[84]

Probably the most clever of all the stories told during the decade was "A Browning Courtship" in the *Atlantic*, which described a young man and a young woman feigning a love for Browning's poetry because each mistakenly thought the other was a Browning enthusiast.[85] The cream of this joke was that Browning, on hearing of it, claimed that he had known a *real* Browning courtship in which a Browningite woman spurned her suitor until he had been coached, possibly by Furnivall, in Browning's poetry. When he at last understood "A Death in the Desert," she said "yes," and Browning accepted an invitation to the wedding.[86]

It was, however, the demise of a branch of the parent organization, the Girton Browning Society, which provoked the greatest mirth among the Victorian reading public. A Browning Society was begun in the spring of 1882 at Girton, Cambridge University's newly established women's college. This was scarcely surprising, for Browning was especially popular with female readers, and Girton College drew its student body largely from the two preparatory schools run by those zealous Browningites, Miss Buss and Miss Beale.[87] The leader of the Girton Browning Society was Miss Alice Zimmern—later to become a distinguished teacher and writer—whose sister Helen, incidentally, knew Browning personally.[88]

The laughter started when the *Academy*, on March 20, 1886, published this whimsical note:

A correspondent [Furnivall] writes: "The Girton girls have proved faithless to Mr. Browning. They have formally dissolved their Browning Society, and not only voted that the balance of funds in hand should be spent on chocolates, but have actually bought the chocolates and eaten them." [89]

Two weeks later the *Academy* apologetically explained that the Girton Browning Society "was mainly formed for the purchase of Browning's works for the college library" and that it was disbanded because that goal had been achieved.[90] But the second announcement was ignored, and the comic possibilities of the first were exploited fully by English periodicals during the spring of 1886. Doubtless it proved irresistible to so many satirists because the *Academy* note had managed to link two widely ridiculed subjects: the Browning societies and higher education for women.

St. *James's Gazette* was the first, on March 23, to make somewhat clumsy humor out of the episode. It concluded that the Girton girls, even if they became ill from eating the chocolates, had probably made a wise decision. Indigestion would merely produce a dislike of chocolates, "whereas if they took too much Browning Society they might grow disgusted with the works of a great poet, and, indeed, of poets in general." [91] The physiological effects of the girls' action were also scrutinized by *Punch* in a lengthy poem entitled "A Story of Girton (By R-b-rt Br-wn-ng)." According to this version of what had happened at Girton, the president of the Browning Society became suddenly and mysteriously ill. Though Girton's principal diagnosed the illness as mental fatigue from wrestling with Browning's obscurities, the physician remarked that the symptoms were those of indigestion. Then both noticed that the hand of the student, who was now asleep in her room, was resting upon a half-open desk drawer:

> "Why does she clutch it so?" asked the leech;
> The Lady Principal supposed
>   That to have her dear Bard within reach
> Consoled her as she dozed.
>   "Let's look inside!" And at once—oh, dreams
> Of "Female Culture," and the rest!
>   They found—no masterly mystic themes,
> No *Pippa*, no *Duchess*, but—who would have guessed?—
>   A box of Chocolate Creams! [92]

On the other hand, some periodicals professed to sympathize with Browning, who was presumed to be brokenhearted at the news of this betrayal. *Funny Folks* published a cartoon showing three studious-appearing young ladies munching upon chocolates as they filed out of a sweetshop, while a distraught Browning stood at one side and wept into his handkerchief.[93] Lamenting the degradation of the Girton Browningites to "mere chocolate-worship," a parody of "The Lost Leader" which appeared in *Fun*, entitled "The (Choco)late-est News," began in this fashion:

> They just for a handful of chocolates left us—
> Just for some sweetmeats to put in their throats. . . . [94]

A similar parody of Browning's "A Grammarian's Funeral," called "A Girtonian Funeral," was printed in the *Journal of Education*, of which the following is an excerpt:

> Let us begin and portion out these sweets,
> Sitting together.
> Leave we our deep debates, our sage conceits,
> Wherefore? and whether?
> Thus with a fine that fits the work begun,
> Our labours crowning,
> For we, in sooth, our duty well have done
> By Robert Browning.
> Have we not wrought at essay and critique,
> Scorning supine ease?
> Wrestled with clauses crabbed as Bito's Greek,
> Baffling as Chinese?
>
> .   .   .
>
> Oh, the dull meetings! Someone yawns an *aye*.
> One gapes again a *yea*.
> We girls determined not to yawn, but buy
> Chocolate Menier.[95]

Judy observed that the Girton Girls had

> . . . ceased to study Browning's poems of late,
> And on his meaning to deliberate;
> But owning that *that* taste is out of date,
> They cultivate
> An appetite instead for chocolate.[96]

Perhaps the most ingenious detail, however, was supplied by the *Echo*. It reported that in retaliation for the *Academy*'s jesting announcement of their decision, "the youthful and wrathful damsels called a college meeting, and resolved that the *Academy* should no longer be taken in for their library." [97]

On a more serious level, of the many published evaluations of the London Browning Society, the one which most effectively combined insight and wit was an essay entitled "Esoteric Browningism" by Andrew Lang, who instanced "Childe Roland" as a simple poem that had been made obscure by the Browningites:

> By the boundless ingenuity of dullness, the abomination of desolation of pedantry standing where it ought not, the enchanted castle of Mr. Browning's verse has become nearly as inaccessible as the dark tower whither Childe Roland came. The land about is haunted by scarecrow scholiasts, disheveled essayists, male and female. . . . Their engines of torture, their examination papers, their pamphlets, their proceedings, are thick on the ground as the gins and snares of Giant Pope or Giant Despair.[98]

The remedy, Lang suggested, was for the "young adventurer" to go directly to the lucid poetry of Browning's middle years and to ignore the garrulous commentators of the Browning Society.

As even these few examples will show, the society has had a bad press, and though some of the criticisms were unjust (and some of Furnivall's replies very cogent), the society's own zeal and unsmiling pedantry must bear the major share of the blame for its unenviable reputation. The Browningites were of course conscious of their ludicrous image in the world's eyes. "The most hardened Philistine now hurries past the paragraph in which his eye catches the words 'Browning Society,' well knowing how inevitably the obvious old jokes will have to be waded through before he can arrive at such point as there may be," lamented a contributor to the transactions in 1886.[99] But there would have been fewer jokes, and correspondingly the Browningite campaign would have had greater effect, had more of the members been able to adopt the good-humored view of Miss Hickey, who thought the Browning Society could congratulate itself upon having provided amusement for so many Englishmen.[100] Most Browningites, unfortunately, preferred to endure their martyrdom with an expression of stern sobriety.

CHAPTER IX

THE POET AND THE SOCIETY

"Do you object to all this adulation?" his hostess asked
[Browning] once, when the crowds in some semi-public place
were too pressing and too audible. "Object to it? No, I like it!"
he answered her. . . . "I have waited forty years for it, and
now—I like it!"

— Rosaline Masson[1]

IN 1902 Furnivall sent a typically indignant letter to the *Academy*
about Edmund Gosse's biographical article on Browning in the *Dictionary of National Biography*, charging that Gosse had ignored Furnivall's findings on Browning's ancestry and his authorship of the
"prose *Strafford*," as well as misrepresenting the relationship between
Browning and the Browning Society. "It will interest Browning students to know that the poet's relation to the Browning Society was
closer than is stated by Mr. Gosse," declared Furnivall. "Its Papers
contain several passages from his pen, though not with his name,
explaining difficulties and allusions which members or correspondents sent or put to me, and to which Browning wrote me answers,
with leave to print them, but not to mention him."[2] Professor Hall
Griffin was interested in this controversy, particularly as it related to
the Strafford biography, and thought that Furnivall's views were probably correct, but to make certain he wrote to Gosse for further information. Gosse's reply was a savage, unrelenting attack upon Furnivall:

Of course, I never dreamed for a moment that what the reckless
old bandit wrote in the "Academy" was written with your warrant.
But I am glad of an opportunity to explain to you a few points. My

article in the Dictionary of Nat. Biogr. was composed with the greatest care, and I had throughout the help, and the minute revision at last, of Miss Browning (the poet's sister), of his son, and of Mr. George Smith, his published and life-long friend. Everything was therefore done to give exactitude to the biography, which is in some respects the fullest yet published.

It was my wish to be scrupulously just and even indulgent to Dr. Furnivall. But I cannot conceal from you that he presented a great difficulty. He is perfectly loathed by the family of Mr. Browning, and they were desirous that I should repudiate his statements with warmth. This I did not wish to do. But I must tell you that his pretention to speak for Browning and represent his ideas is preposterous. Browning's attitude to him was curious. He disliked him and feared him a little, and yet he found him too useful to be dismissed. He said once to me, "F. is certainly cracked." This I think is the kindest way in which to regard his aberrations. As to his pretended "discoveries" about Browning, they are all of them moonshine. The only serious one—the invention (for I can call it nothing else) that Browning wrote the "Life of Strafford"—has given acute pain to the Forster and the Browning family alike. It is utter fable, unqualified falsehood,—and no one ought to palter [?] with it for a moment.

F. used to go to Warwick Crescent,—as Miss Browning has explained to me,—and shout and gesticulate and chatter till B. would admit anything and assent to anything for the sake of getting the terrible fellow out of the house. But, alas! the Browning Society was useful to him, and he did not like to offend F. and break off the acquaintance.[3]

Several decades later Gosse summarized this indictment by telling F. G. R. Duckworth that "Furnivall did not hate Browning, but he loved him with a *deadly* love." [4]

If what Gosse said in this letter were true, it would be a very damaging portrait not only of Furnivall but also of Browning, who is described here as a sycophant willing to exploit Furnivall even though he feared and hated him. Yet aside from Gosse's reputation for unreliability as a witness, there are several substantial reasons to doubt the assertions he makes. First, it should be recalled that he and Furnivall were cordial enemies of long standing; Gosse had been distinctly a member of the Swinburne camp during the latter's quarrel with Furnivall, and Furnivall had made known his view of Gosse's poetic aspirations in a slighting allusion at the opening meeting of the Shelley Society.[5] Second, Sarianna Browning's hostility toward Furnivall is attested by other contemporaries, and so her testimony is scarcely trustworthy. And third, Browning's scores of letters to Furnivall simply do not bear out the impression that he thought him "cracked." Furnivall was no doubt often a nuisance, as in his persistent efforts to secure a Shilling Selection, but Browning, with his keen relish for human eccentricities, seems rather to have delighted in Furnivall's brash, iconoclastic personality. That the poet *was* annoyed by Furnivall's indiscretions is beyond question; where Gosse went astray was in not recognizing Browning's long-suffering, warm regard for his friend. Gosse was, of course, very near the truth: anyone but Browning would have lost patience. But the point is that Browning did not and that until his death he treated Furnivall with amused affection.

Repeatedly Furnivall displayed a provoking stubbornness which must have tested the generosity of even Browning. One of the earliest clashes between the poet and the founder of the Browning Society came in December, 1882, when he learned that Furnivall intended to print in the society's *Papers* a short poem which he had inscribed in a young lady's album. Twice Browning pleaded with Furnivall not to publish it; but despite these urgent appeals the poem appeared in the *Papers*.[6] Furnivall usually had his way in these matters, if only because of his unyielding persistence once he had made up his mind. In the same year he also raised subscriptions in order to purchase for Browning a carved oak bookcase filled with a complete set of his own works, a gift which pleased Browning enormously;[7] a year later, however, Browning was distressed to learn that Furnivall was now collecting funds for a matching case containing his wife's works. At this point Browning intervened. It was wrong, he wrote Furnivall, "to solicit subscriptions from people who certainly *may* refuse (as who may *not?*) but thereby lay themselves under the imputation of indifference, or ill-will, or merely stinginess." He also pointed out that whereas he had not previously owned his own books, his wife's were already in his library. Once again his letters fell on deaf ears: the money was raised and the gift delivered, though presented to Pen Browning instead.[8]

Furnivall was the source of other minor embarrassments as well. Browning was annoyed that the activities of himself and his son, whose career as an artist he was directing with such care, were reported in vivid detail in the *Academy* by Furnivall;[9] and there was also a misunderstanding about a proposal to reproduce the "Old Yellow Book." Browning had given his tentative authorization for its publication, and Furnivall had already begun soliciting funds from Corson and others for the project, but then Browning drew back, claiming he had never approved it in the first place and expressing horror at the

Emily Hickey

A level-headed Irish poetess, Miss Hickey provided a temperamental con-trast to the more impulsive Furnivall. She was co-founder of the society and its first Honorary Secretary, 1881–84.

Browning wrote of the co-founder and president of the Browning Society: "His peculiarities and defects are obvious—and some of his proceedings by no means to my taste: but there can be no doubt of his exceeding desire to be of use to my poetry, and I must attribute a very great part indeed of the increase of care about it to his energetic trumpet-blowing."

Frederick J. Furnivall

James Dykes Campbell

Honorary Secretary, 1884–86. Bernard Shaw found him "a very likeable gentleman," and Browning gave him a rare first edition of *Pauline*.

(*Illustrated London News*, June 8, 1895)

Honorary Secretary, 1886–90. A bibliophile and friend of T. J. Wise, Slater was an inept officer who left the society's financial records in hopeless confusion.

(*Bibliophile*, July 1909)

Walter B. Slater

J. T. Nettleship

Author of the first book on Browning in 1868, Nettleship later became a silent, balding painter of melodramatic lions and an unhappy member of the Browning Society.

(Thomas Wright, *The Life of John Payne* [London, 1919], p. 22)

"The oldest Browning Club in [America], so far as I know, is the Cornell Club, which I started six years ago," wrote Professor Corson in 1883. It was in fact the first Browning club founded in either the United States or England.

(Collection of Regional History and University Archives, Cornell University)

Hiram Corson

OH, THOSE GIRTON GIRLS!

A correspondent writes to the *Academy* : "The Girton girls have proved faithless to Mr. Browning. They have formally dissolved their Browning Society, and not only voted that the balance of funds in hand should be spent in chocolates, but have actually bought the chocolates and eaten them."

The disbanding of the Girton Browning Society provoked many satirical poems and cartoons, such as the one above from *Funny Folks*, March 27, 1886. Browning is shown weeping as the Girton College girls troop out of a sweetshop.

thought of exposing the "roots" of *The Ring and the Book* to the public gaze.[10] This time Furnivall acquiesced.

Browning had ample reason to be wary of Furnivall, even though, as he once told him, "I know you have my concerns at heart." [11] In the summer of 1881, when the Browning Society was being organized, the memory of what had happened in the New Shakspere Society was still fresh in everyone's mind. Furnivall's public quarrel with Swinburne and Halliwell-Phillipps had caused most of the eminent vice-presidents to resign (one report, probably false, said that Browning remained a vice-president only because the Browning Society was being formed at the same time[12]), and surely Browning must have pondered the possibility that Furnivall's newest society would stumble into the same kind of scandal, this time to the discredit of the poet whom it ostensibly honored. Even assuming that Furnivall could keep his temper, the Browning Society—as Browning perceived at once—might, with its inflated rhetoric and pretentious aims, make the poet look very silly indeed. D. S. Curtis, an American painter, was visiting Warwick Crescent when the first prospectus of the Browning Society arrived in the mail, and he records that Browning inspected it, then murmured to him in French, "It seems to me that that sort of thing borders on the ridiculous." [13] From the start Browning saw with apprehension that there was "a grotesque side to the thing." [14]

Browning nevertheless condoned the society, according to Gosse, because it brought him financial rewards; and here again if Gosse, in his malice, is not quite correct, he is at least telling a very persuasive half-truth. Browning, as well as the members of the Browning Society, did believe that the sales of his poetry had been increased by the society's efforts, and although exact figures are not available, it is true that his books found a larger audience in this decade than they had previously. Despite the increasing acceptance of Browning's verse by English and American readers following the publication of his collected works in 1863, as late as 1886 he was still receiving more income annually from the sale of his wife's works than from his own.[15] After the founding of the society, Furnivall said he had been amazed to learn that Browning's poetry brought him a yearly income of less than £100, in contrast to Tennyson's £5000.[16] Clearly, then, Browning had reason to be grateful for any improvement of his lot, and he chose to believe that his new popularity could be attributed to the Browning Society. "This little 'Jocoseria' . . . has had the usual luck of the little-deserving,—got itself sold (as Carlyle would say) at the rate of 2000 very early, and is now reprinting," he told J. D. Williams in 1883. "It all comes of the Browning Societies." [17] To Furnivall he

182 /   INTERROGATING THE ORACLE

wrote that the new royalties should properly go to him, and that whatever success his poems had achieved was a mystery to himself—
"though nothing is plainer than that your helping has pushed them
faster than, of their own force, they would have got forward." [18]

This effect of the society's activities had obviously presented itself
to Browning as a possibility when Miss Hickey and Furnivall proposed
to found a Browning Society. He received their request with noncom-
mittal laughter, according to Miss Hickey, and then told his guests an
anecdote about an old gentleman who had said to a bookseller, "I have
the greatest respect for Richard Monckton Milnes, Esquire, but I'll be
d——d if I give two pounds fifteen shillings and tenpence for his
poems!" [19] It was Browning's predicament exactly. A poll conducted by
the *Journal of Education* among its readers in 1883 ranked Browning
fourth among the ten greatest living English writers (after Tennyson,
Ruskin, and Arnold);[20] but not until this final decade of his life did his
books also sell in large numbers. Viewing the bustling activity of the
Browning Society, he decided without hesitation that in its fervent
espousing of his poetry must lie the explanation for his increased income.[21]

What Gosse chose to ignore, however, was that Browning's gratitude was prompted not primarily by a financial motive but rather by
the pleasant realization that his poetry was at last finding an appreciative audience. Being a poetic celebrity, of course, had its shortcomings. An American journalist wrote that one day he saw a party of
"Yankee schoolmarms" pursuing Browning around and around the Albert Memorial; fearing for Browning's safety, he was amazed when he
next saw the poet, for "he bobbed up just as bright as ever, so perhaps
it is a common experience." [22] At parties Browning would be cornered
by disciples who cross-examined him about the identity of "The Lost
Leader," and every day the mail brought endless inquiries about
"Childe Roland" and "How They Brought the Good News from Ghent
to Aix." And here Mrs. Orr and the Browning Society leaders performed a useful function by acting as a buffer between Browning and
his more eccentric admirers. In 1885, for example, Miss Annie
Matheson (1853–1924), an imperious spinster who composed verse
and edited a series of biographies for children,[23] wrote to Dykes
Campbell demanding to know whether *Colombe's Birthday* was not in
fact based upon the theme of Mrs. Browning's *Lady Geraldine's Courtship*. Campbell passed on the letter to Mrs. Orr, who in turn asked
Browning about it. His curt reply betrays the impatience of a man
who had suffered much from this kind of critical ingenuity: "The lady
is a goose: Colombe was written *long* before E.B.B.'s poem." [24]

Despite these annoyances, Browning revelled in the attention that was now paid to him. E. F. Benson tells a story of Browning's having accepted an invitation to read some of his poems to the young ladies of the Newnham Browning Society at Cambridge, and there, after the tea and muffins, having a garland of roses placed on his head by a trembling admirer. "So there he sat," wrote Benson, "bland and ruddy, and slightly buttery from the muffins, with the crown of pink roses laid upon his white locks, and looking like a lamb decked for sacrifice." With the members sitting at his feet, Browning began to read "A Serenade at the Villa" when suddenly he caught a glimpse of himself in the mirror. "My dear young ladies," he said, breaking into laughter, "shall I not read the 'Patriot' instead? 'It was roses, roses all the way.' " [25]

Success was sweet for a man who had been known for much of his life as Mrs. Browning's husband. There were many who professed to laugh at the Browning Society, he told F. W. Farrar, "but for his part he was grateful for this and every other indication of a dawning recognition, considering the dreary time of neglect and ignorant insult which he had been doomed to undergo." [26] Besides, as he declared to Furnivall, he enjoyed the "evident annoyance" the society was "giving my dear old critics who have gone on gibing and gibbering at me time out of mind." [27] Though he might value even more the encouragement of earlier friends,[28] Browning regarded the Browning Society as an instrument which had helped him to triumph at last over the hostility of the press and the indifference of the reading public.

The real dilemma Browning faced was not whether he should approve of the Browning Society—that decision had been made from the moment he offered no objections to the plans of Furnivall and Miss Hickey—but to what extent he could openly condone it and support its activities. It was a very delicate situation: if he acted too coolly toward it, he would offend his most loyal readers, but if he became too thoroughly identified with the society, he would be open to the charge of vulgar self-promotion. Naturally he failed to please everybody. The *Saturday Review* repeatedly charged in strident language that Browning had displayed bad judgment in allowing the Browning Society to be formed, and the *Pall Mall Gazette* described Browning's sanction as an evidence of the weakness of the flesh.[29] Browning, in a letter to Furnivall, reacted to this latter imputation with sarcastic indignation:

You may have noticed an article in yesterday's "Pall Mall" in which the writer has his doubts whether the B. Society "is altogether without the consent, not to say approbation of Mr. B.; if it is so, an excuse must be found in the fact that poets' flesh is but frail flesh after all." I conceive that the proper course for Mr. B. would have been to write to the Society and ask whether there had really been committed such an outrage as a combined endeavour on the part of certain people not only to read his poems but induce others to do so: because, were such the case, Mr. B., who had for so many years been composing what he meant nobody should attend to, must entreat that such proceedings should forthwith stop: it being plainly the duty of an author to submit, for no matter how long, to no matter what abuse of his books—and to make an instantaneous protest against the first non-editorial "we", who, in the shape of a society, might prefer to approve rather than condemn. Probably the next step would be that Mr. B. stations a detective at Smith & Elder's shopdoor to collar the first man who has the look of a B-buyer in his face.[30]

Exposed to attacks like these, Browning tried to take special precautions to disassociate himself from the society. When Furnivall in 1881 asked for names of friends who might wish to join the Browning Society, Browning declined to provide any, and encouraged his sister to write the following letter of advice to Furnivall:

> You are very kind and generous in your efforts to increase the acquaintance with my brother's writings, and you cannot suppose that we are, either of us, insensible or indifferent. I thank you most thoroughly for your warmhearted appreciation and disinterested endeavour to widen the circle of his readers. Yet you must feel that he cannot himself take any part in the matter. He has all his life felt that his duty was to work to the best of his power, and there leave it.[31]

To a woman who wrote in 1882 inquiring about some photographs which were being distributed by the society, Browning replied: "The photographs, of which you have heard, are intended for the members of a particular society, with which I have no concern whatever." [32] And to another correspondent he revealed that he had no tickets for an entertainment "given by what is called the 'Browning Society,' for the amusement of its members only—of whom I am not one, nor shall I be present." [33]

One of the most illuminating exchanges on the subject was between Browning and Edmund Yates, the editor of the London *World*, for it demonstrates perfectly Browning's calculated ambivalence toward the society. In November, 1881, Yates sent Browning a note which referred unfavorably to Furnivall and the Browning Society, explaining that he did not wish to print it without Browning's approval. Browning offered no objections, but it is significant that he did attempt a cautious defense of the society:

> The Browning Society, I need not say, as well as Browning himself, are fair game for criticism. I had no more to do with the founding it than the babe unborn; and, as Wilkes was no Wilkeite, I am quite other than a Browningite. But I cannot wish harm to a society of, with a few exceptions, names unknown to me, who are busied about my books so disinterestedly.[34]

Browning's correspondence during this decade contains numerous references to the Browning Society and to the men and women who delivered papers before it, and since his attitude toward it did not significantly change (except, perhaps, that his polite distrust was gradually dispelled by its successes), it would be pointless and repetitious to cite all the letters. One of the most important of them, however, deserves to be mentioned, for like those quoted above, it is one of his major evaluations of the society. Writing to Miss Elizabeth West in 1881, Browning emphasized to her, as he had to Yates, that aside from the leaders, most of the members of the Browning Society were strangers to him, and this he interpreted as an advantage: the society could not be described as "a clique—the man's personal following!" As for Furnivall, Browning was astonished at his friend's belated discovery of his poetry, but he knew at least that he was "most warmhearted, whatever may be the mistakes about me of which his head is guilty." And if the Browning Society verged on the idolatrous in its praise, that too was understandable, since "they react against a good deal." [35]

At a discreet distance, then, Browning observed the workings of the society which bore his name. He received all the society's publications, taking particular interest in Furnivall's bibliography, "this extraordinary halo of rainbow-hues with which your wonder-working hand has suddenly surrounded my dark orb." [36] (This same publication, though, made him feel the pangs of mortality: reading it, he wrote to Mrs. FitzGerald, gave him the uncomfortable sense of being "dead and *begun* with, after half a century." [37]) For the bibliography Browning read proofs, occasionally offering corrections and additions, but when proofs of the transactions continued to be sent him, he grew uneasy lest his acceptance of them be construed as official approval of their contents. In March, 1884, he asked that no more proofs be directed to him, and Dykes Campbell at once complied.[38] Once the

Browning Society's publications were in print, on the other hand, he was pleased to receive them. As a bibliophile he was amused by the *Pauline* facsimile,[39] and he saw too the unexpected usefulness of the transactions: when someone wrote to him asking for information on his poems, Browning directed him to Mrs. Orr's *Handbook* and *The Browning Society's Papers*.[40]

Browning also took much pleasure in the society's performances of his plays, though he refused to attend some of them in person, relying instead upon the reports of his sister, Furnivall, and other friends. It was clearly helpful to his ego to be reassured that his plays were actable after all and that the critics had been mistaken about them all these years. "The acting of my four plays by professionals, *unpaid*, for the Browning Society, is surely one of the greatest and most wonderful honours ever paid to a dramatic writer," he told William Allingham. What made it more remarkable, Browning thought, was that the plays were performed uncut and out of sheer love for his poetry.[41]

A journalist who sat near him at the performance of *Colombe's Birthday* in 1885 observed that Browning took such unaffected delight in it that he seemed to forget that he himself had any connection with it.[42] Though Browning hoped to see a dress rehearsal of *Strafford* in 1886, he was unable to do so because of illness;[43] but the previous year he had, at the urging of Charles Fry, attended incognito the Browning Society performance of *A Blot in the 'Scutcheon*. His concealment in a private box had been so carefully planned that not even Furnivall was aware of his presence, and afterwards, when the latter went backstage to congratulate the actors and to promise that he would tell Browning of their success, they replied in unison, "Oh, but we've just seen him!" Furnivall was for once speechless.[44] Browning also made an appearance at the second *Blot* production (March 15, 1888), chiefly in order to see the acting of Miss Alma Murray, whose successful portrayal of Beatrice Cenci he had witnessed as a guest of the Shelley Society two years before.[45] Miss Murray's talents seem to have captivated Browning's imagination, for he later corresponded with her on a number of occasions and even received gravely her plea that he write a new play.[46]

Occasionally attending a dramatic performance, reading with interest the publications, and welcoming into his home individual members, usually brought there by Furnivall—this was the extent of Browning's cooperation with the society, and beyond this point he would not go. He refused to preface his poems with short "arguments," as Furnivall and others often asked him to do (perhaps because it seemed a tacit admission that the poems themselves were unintelligible); he rejected Furnivall's more ambitious schemes to "hawk his wares";[47] and, by declining to read proofs or correct any errors in print, he would not be held responsible for the society's opinions. Stripped of its ambiguities, Browning's odd relationship with the Browning Society was based on his gratitude for its services and its evident good will, coupled with a lingering suspicion that the society, with the reckless Furnivall at the helm, might be shipwrecked at any moment. And Browning did not wish to go down with the ship.

Despite his distaste for jokes about the society, Browning, like his fellow citizens, was moved at last to laughter, thus helping to restore sanity to the slightly mad world of the Browningites. Told by a female visitor from Boston that she belonged to *two* Browning clubs, he received the news with barely suppressed amusement.[48] In December of 1881, upon the arrival home of his son, Browning informed Furnivall that "the Browning Society (Limited)" had just been augmented in size.[49] Five years later Browning's mirth at "the grotesque aspect" of the society had still not subsided. After explaining to a visitor his intention in writing "James Lee's Wife," he added with a smile: "But if you want to know any more, you had better ask the Browning Society, —you have heard of it perhaps?" [50] Had he possessed a greater sense of humor, or less, in the opinion of Andrew Lang,[51] Browning could not have tolerated the society; but, unlike most observers, he was able to laugh at it and love it simultaneously.

CONCLUSION

≈≋≈

> The existence of the Society brought the poet not only praise
> but "cheques," as he often acknowledged; it both increast his
> reputation and his power of influencing his generation. His
> death and the consequent outburst of laudation from all sides
> carried his name and fame over the whole world, and left no
> more work of popularisation for the Society to do. . . . Those
> members of the Society who have felt call'd to speak on the
> poet and his writings, have done so, either in print or out of
> it; and the Committee now feel that the Society may well
> draw to a close.
>
> —The Browning Society's Annual
> Report (1891)[1]

THE BROWNING SOCIETY ended with a whimper, but that should not
obscure the fact that in its heyday it was a remarkably influential
institution. Its meetings in the classrooms and lecture halls of University College were attended by many of the famous figures of the age—
writers, scholars, musicians, actors, and poets—and beyond Bloomsbury its impact could be felt in the books, articles, and lectures produced by its members and in the general wave of enthusiasm for
Browning which resulted from their activities. For one decade England and America were "Browning mad," and at the center of all this
strange enthusiasm, fostering it and at the same time deriving momentum from it, was the London Browning Society, which in its popular appeal and notoriety was unlike any other literary society of the
nineteenth century. Yet it was not a permanent phenomenon, and its
ultimate ignominy in the eyes of the next century was perhaps as
spectacular as its immediate success. The Browning Society, even before it had expired, became a late Victorian period piece, a pleasant

curiosity, which, like Oscar Wilde's lilies and velvet coats, provided subject matter for an entire generation of cartoonists and parodists.

Whether one regards the Browning Society as a real success or failure depends entirely upon one's interpretation of its aims. From Browning's point of view, the society was simply an expression of good will by his most faithful readers, and in that light it can be seen as highly successful, for clearly its existence brought mutual pleasure to the poet and all Browningites. However, Browning also believed, as did most of the members, that the Browning Society had made his poetry more widely read and purchased, and on this point the evidence is more elusive. Although the sales of Browning's books steadily increased during the eighties, it is difficult to link this phenomenon with absolute certainty to the efforts of the society. The Browning Society's program of proselytizing undoubtedly put his name on more lips during that decade, but whether it fostered an intelligent appreciation of his poetry is doubtful. Indeed, the comic reputation of the society in the public press was scarcely calculated to draw casual readers to a poet who inspired such excessive adulation. Shaw remarked at a meeting in 1888 that he could not "endorse what the Chairman [Furnivall] had said in regard to the advance in Browning's reputation being due to this Society. The question was now whether they were not rather a hindrance than a help." [2] If Shaw's evaluation was not wholly just then, he was at least a worthy prophet, for in our own century Browning's readers have, almost without exception, regarded the Browning Society as a dead albatross hung around his neck. This view, as I have attempted to show, fails to take into account the society's genuine contributions; but it is nevertheless the view that has prevailed. And Furnivall himself, in 1901, wrote these self-incriminating words to Sidney Lee about a newly-formed British Empire Shakespeare Society (which he thought "all piffle"): "Can't we trust Shakspere to popularise himself without a Soc[iet]y?" [3]

Yet presumably it was not the ordinary, well-educated reader whom the Browning Society wished to convert, but rather the working man who needed moral instruction. Until 1881 Dr. Furnivall had operated in two quite different spheres: as a scholar, he established learned societies which published literary texts and essays; and as a socialist, he labored on behalf of the poor, particularly in his role as teacher at the Working Men's College. In the Browning Society, Furnivall's two grand passions were united, for he saw Browning as not only a poet of distinction but also a great moral force whose broad religion could uplift the masses. Hence his concern for "simplifying"

Browning by providing a "Primer" and "arguments" to accompany the poems, and his equally intense desire to secure a cheap edition of the poetry. Many of the other members of the society, it must be said, shared this viewpoint and considered Browning's verse as perhaps the most effective means of transforming the brutalized lower class of England. It is surely not accidental that so many Browningites, though conservative in a religious sense, held "advanced" views on social and humanitarian questions. Miss Hickey, for example, had long worked in the slums of London. Dr. Berdoe maintained his practice in Hackney, even though many of his patients came from more fashionable areas of London. William Kingsland, as he told Furnivall in 1886, spent much of his spare time "lecturing to Societies composed largely of the working people." [4] Edward Gonner had not, therefore, been indulging in hyperbole when he described the Browning Society "as a kind of auxiliary missionary society for spreading abroad the gospel of Browning," nor was Dr. Berdoe employing irony when he defended it as a " 'first-rate' missionary society." [5] It was as a sort of religious tract society that many Browningites wished their organization to be judged, and in their opinion, at least, "spreading abroad the gospel of Browning" had done much to introduce moral ideas to the inhabitants of London's East End.

Still another measure of the society's achievement—and one which Furnivall frequently emphasized—was its annotation and explication of Browning's poems. To Furnivall, the problem was elementary: Browning wrote worthwhile but obscure poetry; let us, therefore, jointly remove those obscurities, and we can then enjoy his poems without having to puzzle over them. Furnivall did, in fact, offer this very justification for the society's existence at its first meeting:

> As a ducal correspondent of mine put it, "My dear Mr. Furnivall, I think it is 300 years too early for a Browning Society." To all such folk, I can only say: "You've never founded a Chaucer or Shakspere Society, and had to worry and bother over this word and that, this allusion and the other; the man Shakspere's Sonnets were written to, the lady of Chaucer's early love, and all the thousand and one puzzles these poets' works prezent [*sic*]. If you had, you'd never have thought it superfluous, for a set of contemporaries of each poet to have cleard up all your bothers for you. You'd have blest them every day of your life." That posterity will thank us for our work at Browning is certain. [6]

Posterity has, in fact, judged Furnivall and his followers rather harshly, but even the society's severest critics are compelled to admit that it did clear up at least some of Browning's "bothers." And if one accepts the premise that a poet's observations on his own poetry possess some value, then perhaps the Browning Society's most impressive achievement was that fascinating torrent of letters from Browning to Furnivall during the eighties.

The usual criterion for evaluating a literary society, however, is the quality of its papers, and here even the most sympathetic observer must find the Browning Society wanting. It was not that the society never heard good papers. Arthur Symons' "Is Browning Dramatic?", James Russell Lowell's speech, Elizabeth Dickinson West's "One Aspect of Browning's Villains," Howard Pearson's "Browning as a Landscape Painter"—to name only a few—all rank among the finest and most intelligent essays written on Browning in the nineteenth century. But the excellence of these was more than offset by the grimly evangelical sermons, disguised as literary essays, which were delivered by the devout. Members like Miss Beale and Miss Stoddart, not Symons or Lowell, set the intellectual tone of the Browning Society.

As a body of literary criticism, the society's papers were unsuccessful chiefly because of this predilection for moralizing and reducing Browning's poetry to the level of a religious tract. It is significant that some of Browning's best poems from his "middle period"—"A Grammarian's Funeral," "Love Among the Ruins," "A Serenade at the Villa," "The Statue and the Bust," "Two in the Campagna"—were almost entirely neglected by the Browningites, who were too busy identifying the allusions of *Sordello* or agonizing over the casuistry of *Fifine*. Even *The Ring and the Book*, with its puzzling moral relativism, was treated in detail in only one paper; "Saul" was much more reassuring.

To put it briefly, the Browning Society suffered from a failure of the moral imagination. Had the Browningites read "The Statue and the Bust" more carefully, they would have realized that Browning's respectable, bourgeois appearance concealed from the public gaze a poet who had once acknowledged Shelley as his master, who had flouted all conventions to marry Elizabeth Barrett, and who still in his poetry exalted passionate love above all other human values. But most of his admirers in the Browning Society saw only the cheerful, polite, neatly attired gentleman who, as Tennyson sardonically commented, would probably die in evening dress.

To understand the full implications of this misunderstanding of Browning's character, one must turn to an illuminating episode in the Shelley Society, which was in many respects the twin of the Browning Society, since it shared much of the same membership and leadership. In 1886 Edward Aveling, a brilliant but disagreeable socialist, was not allowed to join the Shelley Society, chiefly because, although already married to another woman, he was living with the daughter of Karl Marx without benefit of clergy. The irony of a Shelley Society adopting such a moral stance was not lost upon William Rossetti, who resigned in indignation from the society's committee because of this decision. "I then openly said that I didn't see how we c[oul]d think of resisting his claim to subscribe," Rossetti explained later to Furnivall, "& that on the same grounds the Shelley Soc[iet]y w[oul]d have turned out Shelley himself." [7]

Perhaps the hugest joke of all about the Browning Society, which has always been considered a very funny subject, is that Browning himself, with his profound contempt for merely conventional moral standards, might not have been admitted to membership.

APPENDIX A

BROWNING SOCIETY
MEETINGS AND PAPERS

It is unfortunate that the Browning Society's transactions, which are of considerable interest to literary historians, are rendered almost useless by their sloppy organization, their inconsistencies, and their lack of an index or an adequate table of contents. The information in *BSP* is indeed "scattered," as William C. DeVane once observed.[1] To make matters worse, individual sets of the papers differ considerably from each other. In 1903, for example, E. C. Williams, a librarian at Western Reserve University, sent to the *Library Journal* what he regarded as a full and accurate collation of *BSP*; yet, as subsequent letters to the *Library Journal* demonstrated, there were numerous variations in the pagination and arrangement of copies owned by other libraries. One correspondent concluded with this anguished observation: "I can only express my sympathy for the next man that tries to make up a set of the Browning Society Papers." [2]

Before I provide an analysis of the contents of *BSP*, therefore, it will be necessary to trace its publishing history and to account for its many irregularities. The thirteen parts of *BSP* (Part VI was never published, as will be explained below) were issued in light blue paper covers at the rate of approximately one per year; they were paged so that they could be bound into three volumes. Each volume was made up of three sections: the first, in Arabic numerals, contained the texts of papers delivered to the society; the second, in Arabic numerals followed by asterisks, contained the minutes of discussions at the meetings; and the third, in Roman numerals, contained the annual reports presented at the last meeting of every session.[3]

This apparently logical pattern broke down for the following reasons:

(1) Many of the individual papers and annual reports were issued in "proof" form before the meetings so that members could come prepared to discuss them. Naturally these "proofs" were paged separately, and some of them were later bound into sets of *BSP*. For instance, one copy of *BSP* owned by the Armstrong Browning Library, Baylor University, is made up almost entirely of these "proofs," and consequently this set has little continuous pagination. It is these maverick "proofs," bound into otherwise

normal sets of *BSP*, which produced such evident confusion among the contributors to the *Library Journal.*

(2) In every copy of *BSP* that I have seen, there is, in volume II, a substitution such as I have just described. The annual report for 1885–86, which ought to be numbered pp. ix–xv, is instead pp. 1–7. In this instance, too many "proofs" of the report must have been printed, and so they were simply bound into Part VII when it was distributed to members a few months later.

(3) Much confusion resulted from poor editorial supervision of *BSP*. Walter Slater, the society's third honorary secretary, was an outrageously bad editor: he habitually lost important documents, and his frequent illnesses forced others to issue the parts of *BSP* under difficult circumstances. The papers were printed out of sequence, some meetings were not even mentioned, and the numbers assigned to meetings and papers were highly inconsistent. Miss Anna Stoddart, who assisted Slater for a while, once confessed to him that she was baffled by two papers by Edward Berdoe and William Revell: "They have given their papers no title, & what on earth is the no. of the paper? I have put 45, and Mrs. [Ethel] Glazebrook's is 40—& I reckoned from that. I do not know either the no. of the last meeting." [4] *BSP* during these years reflects much of this sort of guesswork.

(4) By 1890 Slater's successor, E. E. Davies, faced even more serious problems. Benjamin Sagar, who was now responsible for preparing abstracts of some of the papers, became so ill that Part XIII (covering the 1890–91 session) was issued without the minutes of the meetings. A note inserted in *BSP* explained that "the Abstracts, &c., thus omitted will be included in Part XIV." [5] But the Browning Society's financial crisis prevented Part XIV from being printed, and as a result *BSP* contains no records of the society's activities during its last session (1891–92).

(5) Part VI was supposed to have been an index and table of contents to the whole of *BSP*, but it too never appeared. In a circular [6] dated May 1, 1895, Thomas J. Wise appealed to former members of the now-defunct society to send in subscriptions so that Part VI and other unfinished projects might be completed. However, what little money Wise was able to raise in this way he used to publish the first of his "privately printed" editions of Browning's letters rather than Part VI of *BSP*. Although Wise claimed that he had already prepared Part VI in manuscript, it was not found among his papers after his death. Probably it never existed.

What follows, therefore, may be regarded as an imperfect substitute for Part VI. In this list of meetings and papers I have adhered to a strictly chronological sequence, even when *BSP* itself does not do so. I have made no attempt to itemize the rich miscellaneous matter of *BSP*; only the actual meetings and papers are described here. For each meeting I have provided:

(1) The number of the meeting, usually as indicated in *BSP*. When I have supplied the number, it is placed in brackets.

(2) The date.

(3) The chairman.

(4) The page numbers in *BSP* for the record of what transpired at the meeting. After June, 1890, there are no such minutes.

(5) The reports in the *Academy* of the meetings. These are full and

accurate, sometimes written by the Browning Society officers, and on occasion supply details not found in *BSP*. For one meeting (June 24, 1887) a report in the *Pall Mall Gazette* is cited instead, as it is, to my knowledge, the only published account of that particular meeting. (6) The author and title of each paper. In only two instances have I been unable to learn an author's full name. (Brackets indicate that the title has been supplied.) Occasionally long speeches by chairmen are listed as papers. Following this are:

(a) The reference for the full paper if it has been published in *BSP* or elsewhere.

(b) Any reprinting of the paper. Many of the papers were reprinted in Edward Berdoe, ed., *Browning Studies* (London: Allen, 1895), which was printed from the *BSP* plates. Since reprints of the papers in pamphlet form were extremely common, I have not listed most of these.

(c) Any abstract or summary of the paper in *BSP*. (It should be kept in mind that the *Academy* reports usually also provide abstracts.)

The full name of a chairman or lecturer is given only on first reference. I am indebted to the Broughton *Bibliography* in the preparation of this list, though I have checked each item independently and have extensively corrected and supplemented the bibliography. The schedule of papers for the last session, 1891–92, is based primarily upon information given by William G. Kingsland in *Poet-Lore*, III (December, 1891), 650. Whenever I have been able to verify Kingsland's schedule by announcements in the *Academy*, I have cited them.

1. Oct. 28, 1881: Frederick J. Furnivall.
   BSP, I, 1*–6*.
   Acad., XX (Nov. 5, 1881), 351.
   (A) Joshua Kirkman, "Introductory Address."
       BSP, I, 171–90.
       Repr. in *Browning Studies*, pp. 1–20.
2. Nov. 25, 1881: John T. Nettleship.
   BSP, I, 7*–10*.
   (A) George B. Smith, "Robert Browning, His Genius and Works."
       Abstr. in *BSP*, I, 7*–9*.
   (B) John Sharpe, "On 'Pietro of Abano' and the Leading Ideas of *Dramatic Idyls*, Second Series 1880."
       BSP, I, 191–97.
       Repr. in *Browning Studies*, pp. 21–27.
3. Jan. 27, 1882: Frederick W. Farrar.
   BSP, I, 11*–16*.
   Acad., XXI (Feb. 4, 1882), 88.
   (A) Mary A. Lewis, "Some Thoughts on Browning."
       Macmillan's Magazine, XLVI (July, 1882), 205–14.
       Abstr. in *BSP*, I, 11*–14*.
   (B) James Thomson, "Notes on the Genius of Robert Browning."
       BSP, I, 239–50.

Repr. in Thomson, *Biographical and Critical Studies*
(London: Reeves and Turner, and B. Dobell, 1896),
pp. 437–57.
4. Feb. 24, 1882: Peter Bayne.
BSP, I, 17*–20*.
Acad., XXI (Mar. 4, 1882), 161.
(A) Nettleship, "On Browning's *Fifine at the Fair.*"
BSP, I, 199–230.
Repr. in Nettleship, *Robert Browning: Essays and
Thoughts* (London: John Lane, 1890), pp. 221–67.
5. Mar. 24, 1882: Roden Noel.
BSP, I, 21*–26*.
Acad., XXI (Apr. 1, 1882), 236.
(A) Kirkman, "Childe Roland to the Dark Tower Came."
Abstr. in *BSP*, I, 21*–25*.
6. Apr. 28, 1882: James Cotter Morison.
BSP, I, 28*–32*.
Acad., XXI (May 6, 1882), 325.
(A) John B. Bury, "Browning's Philosophy."
BSP, I, 259–77.
Repr. in *Browning Studies*, pp. 28–46.
7. May 26, 1882: Hugh R. Haweis.
BSP, I, 33*–40*.
Acad., XXI (June 3, 1882), 400.
(A) Edwin Johnson, "On 'Bishop Blougram's Apology.'"
BSP, I, 279–92.
(B) William Sharp, "Browning and the Arts."
Abstr. in *BSP*, I, 34*–40*.
8. June 23, 1882: Furnivall.
BSP, I, 41*.
Acad., XXII (July 1, 1882), 15.
(A) Hiram Corson, "The Idea of Personality, as Embodied in
Robert Browning's Poetry."
BSP, I, 293–321.
Repr. in Corson, *An Introduction to the Study of Robert
Browning's Poetry* (Boston: Heath, 1886), pp. 32–
71.
Repr. in *Browning Studies*, pp. 47–75.
[8a.] June 30, 1882: ENTERTAINMENT.
Program, *BSP*, I, 35*–37*.
Acad., XXII (July 8, 1882), 2.
9. July 7, 1882: E. Johnson.
BSP, I, 42*–43*.
Acad., XXII (July 15, 1882), 53.
(A) Annual report.
BSP, I, i–viii.
10. Oct. 27, 1882: Francis Storr.
BSP, I, 45*–47*.
Acad., XXII (Nov. 4, 1882), 334.
(A) Dorthea Beale, "The Religious Teaching of Browning."
BSP, I, 323–38.

Repr. in Beale, *Studies of Poems, New and Old* (London: George Bell, 1902), pp. 83–107.
Repr. in *Browning Studies*, pp. 76–91.
(B) E. Johnson, "Conscience and Art in Browning."
BSP, I, 345–80.

11. Nov. 24, 1882: John Llewelyn Davies.
BSP, I, 49*–54*.
Acad., XXII (Dec. 2, 1882), 401–02.
(A) Mrs. Frances M. Owen, "What Is 'The Flight of the Duchess'?"
Owen, *Essays and Poems* (London: John Bumpus, 1887), pp. 61–77.
Abstr. in BSP, I, 49*–53*.
(B) Sharpe, "The Songs in *Pippa Passes*."
Abstr. in *Acad.* (See above.)

12. Jan. 26, 1883: William C. Coupland.
BSP, I, 57*–63*.
Acad., XXIII (Feb. 3, 1883), 84.
(A) William G. Martley, "The Part Played by Women in Browning's Poems."
Modern Thought, IV (April, 1883), 151–59.
Abstr. in BSP, I, 57*–62*.

13. Feb. 23, 1883: William Holman Hunt.
BSP, I, 64*–65*.
Acad., XXIII (Mar. 3, 1883), 155.
(A) Hunt, [Address by chairman].
Abstr. in BSP, I, 64*.
(B) Nettleship, "Browning's Intuition, Specially in Regard of Music and the Plastic Arts."
BSP, I, 381–96.
Repr. in Nettleship, *Robert Browning: Essays and Thoughts*, pp. 268–89.

14. Mar. 30, 1883: Morison.
BSP, I, 67*–68*.
Acad., XXIII (Apr. 7, 1883), 244–45.
(A) William F. Revell, "Browning's Poems on God and Immortality as Bearing on Life Here."
BSP, I, 435–54.
[The ideas in this and Revell's subsequent papers appear in his *Browning's Criticism of Life* (London: Sonnenschein, 1892), but the papers are not actually reprinted in it.]

15. Apr. 27, 1883: Henry J. Bulkeley.
BSP, I, 69*–72*.
Acad., XXIII (May 5, 1883), 314–15.
(A) Elizabeth D. West, "One Aspect of Browning's Villains."
BSP, I, 411–34.
Repr. in *Browning Studies*, pp. 106–29.

16. May 25, 1883: Mark Pattison.
BSP, I, 74*–76*.
Acad., XXIII (June 2, 1883), 388.

(A) Bulkeley, "James Lee's Wife."
> *BSP*, I, 455–67.
> Repr. in *Browning Studies*, pp. 130–42.

17. June 22, 1883: Revell.
BSP, I, 77*–79*.
Acad., XXIII (June 30, 1883), 461.
>   (A) J. D. Williams, "*A Blot in the 'Scutcheon*: Guendolen as Compared with Shakspere's Beatrice."
> *BSP*, I, 77*–78*.
>   (B) Mrs. Francese H. Turnbull, "Abt Vogler."
> *BSP*, I, 469–76.
> Repr. in *Browning Studies*, pp. 143–50.

[17a.] June 29, 1883: ENTERTAINMENT.
Program, *BSP*, I, 139*–42*.
Acad., XXIV (July 7, 1883), 10.

18. July 6, 1883: John S. Jones.
BSP, I, 80*–83*.
Acad., XXIV (July 14, 1883), 32.
>   (A) Annual report.
> *BSP*, I, ix–xvi.
>   (B) Henry C. Beeching. "Saul."
> Abstr. in *BSP*, I, 80*–82*.

19. Oct. 26, 1883: Davies.
BSP, I, 85*–92*.
Acad., XXIV (Nov. 3, 1883), 303.
>   (A) John Todhunter, "*The Ring and the Book.*"
> Abstr. in *BSP*, I, 85*–90*.

20. Nov. 23, 1883: Richard Garnett.
BSP, I, 93*–97*.
Acad., XXIV (Dec. 1, 1883), 369.
>   (A) Sharpe, "Jocoseria."
> *BSP*, I, 93*–95*.
>   (B) James Dykes Campbell, [English trans. of rev. of *Jocoseria* by M. Léo Quesnel in *Revue Politique et Littéraire*, Aug. 4, 1883, pp. 152–56].
> Abstr. in *BSP*, I, 95*.

21. Jan. 25, 1884: Louisa Drewry.
BSP, I, 101*–05*.
Acad., XXV (Feb. 16, 1884), 119.
>   (A) Miss Arthur, "*Paracelsus.*"
> Abstr. in *BSP*, I, 101*–03*.

22. Feb. 22, 1884: Edward Berdoe.
BSP, I, 107*–08*.
Acad., XXV (Mar. 15, 1884), 188–89.
>   (A) Arthur C. Benson, "Waring."
> Abstr. in *BSP*, I, 107*.
>   (B) Walter A. Raleigh, "On Some Prominent Points of Browning's Teaching."
> *BSP*, I, 477–88.

23. Mar. 28, 1884: Nettleship.
BSP, I, 109*–11*.

Acad., XXV (Apr. 12, 1884), 264.
   (A) Jones, "Browning's Ecclesiastics."
      Abstr. in *BSP*, I, 109*–10*.
24. Apr. 25, 1884: James Russell Lowell.
  BSP, I, 112*–24*.
  Acad., XXV (May 3, 1884), 318–19.
   (A) Lowell, [Address by chairman].
      BSP, I, 112*–15*.
   (B) Morison, " 'Caliban upon Setebos,' with Some Notes on Browning's Subtlety and Humor."
      BSP, I, 489–98.
25. May 23, 1884: Moncure Conway.
  BSP, I, 125*–28*.
  Acad., XXV (May 31, 1884), 389–90.
   (A) Drewry, "*Luria.*"
      Abstr. in *BSP*, I, 125*–26*.
[25a.] June 27, 1884: ENTERTAINMENT.
  Program, *BSP*, I, 143*–53*.
  Acad., XXVI (July 12, 1884), 27–28.
26. July 4, 1884: Furnivall.
  BSP, I, 129*–31*.
   (A) Annual report.
      BSP, I, xvii–xxiii.
   (B) Turnbull, "In a Balcony."
      BSP, I, 499–502.
27. Oct. 31, 1884: William M. Rossetti.
  BSP, II, 1*–4*.
  Acad., XXVI (Nov. 8, 1884), 309–10.
   (A) Conway, "*Sordello.*"
      Abstr. in *BSP*, II, 1*–2*.
28. Nov. 28, 1884: ENTERTAINMENT. Concert and perf. of "In a Balcony."
  Program, *BSP*, II, Appendix, 1–15.
  See also *BSP*, II, 5*–7*, 33*.
29. Jan. 30, 1885: Furnivall.
  BSP, II, 13*–16*.
  Acad., XXVII (Feb. 14, 1885), 120–21.
   (A) Arthur Symons, "Is Browning Dramatic?"
      BSP, II, 1–12.
30. Feb. 27, 1885: Augustine Birrell.
  BSP, II, 29*–36*.
  Acad., XXVII (Mar. 3, 1885), 191–92.
   (A) John J. Britton, "The Case of Louscha."
      Abstr. in *BSP*, II, 29*–31*.
   (B) Benjamin L. Mosely, "On Miss Alma Murray's Creation of Constance, in 'In a Balcony.' "
      The Theatre [London], V (May 1, 1885), 225–30.
      Abstr. in *BSP*, II, 33*.
   (C) Turnbull, "Cleon."
      Abstr. in *BSP*, II, 34*–36*.
31. Mar. 27, 1885: Morison.
  BSP, II, 45*–48*.

Acad., XXVII (Apr. 11, 1885), 263–64.
   (A) E. Johnson, "On 'Mr. Sludge, the Medium.' "
       BSP, II, 13–32.
32. Apr. 24, 1885: Revell.
BSP, II, 49*–52*.
Acad., XXVII (June 6, 1885), 406.
   (A) Berdoe, "Browning as a Scientific Poet."
       BSP, II, 33–54.
       Repr. in Berdoe, *Browning's Message to His Time*
          (London: Sonnenschein, 1890), pp. 71–115.
   (B) John J. Rossiter, "Browning as a Dramatic Poet, with an
   Analysis of *A Blot in the 'Scutcheon.*"
       Abstr. in *BSP*, II, 50*–52*.
[32a.] April 30, May 2, 1885: ENTERTAINMENT. Perf. of *A Blot in the 'Scutcheon.*
BSP, II, ii.
33. May 22, 1885: Frederick Wedmore.
BSP, II, 53*–59*.
Acad., XXVII (June 6, 1885), 406.
   (A) Wedmore, [Address by chairman].
       BSP, II, 53*–56*.
   (B) James Gibson, "On Browning as a Teacher."
       Abstr. in *BSP*, II, 56*–57*.
   (C) John Gibson, [The characteristics of Browning's poetry].
       Gibson, "Introduction," *Pomegranates from an English
         Garden: A Selection from the Poems of Robert
         Browning* (New York: Chautauqua Press, 1885),
         pp. i–viii.
       Abstr. in *BSP*, II, 57*–58*.
34. June 26, 1885: Furnivall.
BSP, II, 73*–74*. [No report of discussion. See *Acad.*]
Acad., XXVIII (July 4, 1885), 15.
   (A) Annual report.
       BSP, II, i–vi.
   (B) Cyril Leslie Johnson, "Browning as an Artist, Considered in
   Relation to the Life of His Time."
       Abstr. in *BSP*, II, 73*–74*.
35. Oct. 30, 1885: Garnett.
BSP, II, 89*–92*.
Acad., XXVIII (Nov. 4, 1885), 328.
   (A) Nettleship, "On the Development of Browning's Genius in
   His Capacity as Poet or Maker."
       BSP, II, 55–77.
36. Nov. 19, 1885: ENTERTAINMENT. Perf. of *Colombe's Birthday.*
BSP, II, 93*–97*.
37. Nov. 27, 1885: Rossetti.
BSP, II, 105*–13*.
Acad., XXVIII (Dec. 12, 1885), 397.
   (A) Britton, "Browning's Women."
       Abstr. in *BSP*, II, 105*–09*.
38. Jan. 29, 1886: Birrell.

BSP, II, 117*–20*.
Acad., XXIX (Feb. 20, 1886), 136.
   (A) Bury, "On *Aristophanes' Apology.*"
      BSP, II, 79–86.
   (B) Leonard S. Outram, "Love's Value: On the Avowal of Valence
   [in *Colombe's Birthday*]."
      BSP, II, 87–94.
39. Feb. 26, 1886: Wedmore.
BSP, II, 125*–27*.
Acad., XXIX (Apr. 17, 1886), 277.
   (A) Wedmore, [Address by chairman].
      BSP, II, 125*–26*.
   (B) Albert Fleming, "Andrea del Sarto."
      BSP, II, 95–102.
40. Mar. 26, 1886: Davies.
BSP, II, 128*–30*.
Acad., XXIX (Apr. 17, 1886), 277.
   (A) Revell, "Some Aspects of Workers and Their Work in Brown-
   ing's Poems."
      Abstr. in *BSP*, II, 128*–29*.
41. Apr. 30, 1886: Nettleship.
BSP, II, 140*–46*.
Acad., XXIX (May 15, 1886), 349–50.
   (A) Howard S. Pearson, "Browning as a Landscape Painter."
      BSP, II, 103–18.
42. May 28, 1886: E. Johnson.
BSP, II, 148*–52*.
Acad., XXIX (June 19, 1886), 437–38.
   (A) Bulkeley, "The Reasonable Rhythm of Some of Browning's
   Poems."
      BSP, II, 119–31.
43. June 25, 1886: Furnivall.
BSP, II, 160*–61*.
   (A) Annual report.
      BSP, II, [ix–xiii]. [*BSP* is erroneously paged in Arabic
      numerals here.]
   (B) Charles H. Herford, "*Prince Hohenstiel-Schwangau.*"
      BSP, II, 133–45.
44. Oct. 29, 1886: Furnivall.
BSP, II, 165*–67*.
   (A) Farrar, "On Browning."
      Abstr. in *BSP*, II, 165*–66*.
45. Nov. 26, 1886: E. Johnson.
BSP, II, 168*–72*.
   (A) Noel, [Browning as a seer].
      Noel, *Essays on Poetry and Poets* (London: Kegan Paul,
      Trench, 1886), pp. 256–82.
      Abstr. in *BSP*, II, 168*–69*.
46. Dec. 21, 1886: ENTERTAINMENT. Perf. of *Strafford*.
BSP, II, 181*.
See also *BSP*, II, 147–52.

47. Jan. 28, 1887: George Bernard Shaw.
   BSP, II, 182*–84*.
   (A) Todhunter, "*Strafford* at the Strand Theatre."
      BSP, II, 147–52.
   (B) Heloise E. Hersey, "The Theory of Robert Browning Concerning Personal Immortality" [introductory essay], in Browning, *Christmas-Eve and Easter-Day and Other Poems* (Boston: D. Lothrop, 1886), pp. 7–24.
48. Feb. 25, 1887: Davies.
   BSP, II, 185*–86*.
   (A) Mrs. Ethel Glazebrook, "A Death in the Desert."
      BSP, II, 153–64.
      Repr. in *Browning Studies*, pp. 225–36.
   (B) Furnivall, "A Grammatical Analysis of 'O Lyric Love' [in *The Ring and the Book*]."
      BSP, II, 165–68.
49. Mar. 25, 1887: Berdoe.
   BSP, II, 209*–10*.
   (A) James Lecky, "Browning's Realism."
      [Not printed.]
50. Apr. 29, 1887: Rossetti.
   BSP, II, 211*–12*.
   (A) Symons, "Some Notes on Mr. Browning's Latest Volume [*Parleyings with Certain People of Importance*]."
      BSP, II, 169–79.
51. May 27, 1887: Furnivall.
   [No record of discussion.]
   (A) Helen J. Ormerod, "Some Notes on Browning's Poems Referring to Music."
      BSP, II, 180–95.
      Repr. in *Browning Studies.* pp. 237–52.
52. June 24, 1887: Furnivall.
   [No record of discussion.]
   Pall Mall Gazette, XLV (June 25, 1887), 13–14.
   (A) Annual report.
      BSP, II, xvii–xxi.
   (B) Ernest Radford, "The Browningite of the Future."
      [Not printed.]
53. Oct. 28, 1887: Furnivall.
   BSP, II, 213*–16*.
   Acad., XXXII (Nov. 5, 1887), 307.
   (A) Revell, "Browning's Views of Life."
      Abstr. in *BSP*, II, 213*–14* [Same in *BSP*, II, 197–99.]
   (B) Berdoe, "Browning's Estimate of Life."
      BSP, II, 200–06.
      Abstr. in *BSP*, II, 214*–15*.
54. Nov. 25, 1887: E. Johnson.
   BSP, II, 218*–23*.
   Acad., XXXII (Dec. 10, 1887), 395–96.
   (A) Percy A. Barnett, "Browning's Jews and Shakespeare's Jew."
      BSP, II, 207–20.

Repr. in *Browning Studies*, pp. 253–67.
Abstr. in *BSP*, II, 218*–19*.
55. Jan. 27, 1888: William A. Harrison.
BSP, II ,229*–34*.
Acad., XXXIII (Feb. 4, 1888), 84.
    (A) Ormerod, "Abt Vogler, the Man."
        BSP, II, 221–36.
        Repr. in *Browning Studies*, pp. 267–82.
        Abstr. in *BSP*, II, 229*–30*.
56. Feb. 24, 1888: E. Johnson.
BSP, II, 240*–43*.
    (A) Mrs. Jane H. Simpson, *"Fifine at the Fair."*
        Abstr. in *BSP*, II, 240*.
[56a.] Mar. 15, 1888: ENTERTAINMENT. Perf. of *A Blot in the 'Scutcheon.*
BSP, II, 250*–55*.
57. Mar. 23, 1888: Garnett.
BSP, II, 245*–50*.
Acad., XXXIII (Mar. 31, 1888), 226–27.
    (A) W. Kineton Parkes, *"Ferishtah's Fancies."*
        Abstr. in *BSP*, II, 245*–47*.
58. Apr. 27, 1888: Berdoe.
BSP, II, 257*–60*.
Acad., XXXIII (May 12, 1888), 328–29.
    (A) Catherine M. Whitehead, "Browning as a Teacher of the Nine-
    teenth Century."
        BSP, II, 237–63.
        Repr. in *Browning Studies*, pp. 283–309.
59. May 25, 1888: Furnivall.
BSP, II, 264*–68*.
Acad., XXXIII (June 2, 1888), 383.
    (A) Anna M. Stoddart, "Saul."
        BSP, II, 264–74.
        Repr. in *Browning Studies*, pp. 310–20.
60. June 29, 1888: Furnivall.
BSP, II, 274*–85*.
    (A) Annual report.
        BSP, II, xxv–xxx.
    (B) Harold G. Henderson, "Browning's Presentation of the Other
    Side."
        [Not printed.]
61. Oct. 26, 1888: Mark Wilks.
BSP, II, 287*–90*.
Acad., XXXIV (Nov. 3, 1888), 293–94.
    (A) Berdoe, "Paracelsus: The Reformer of Medicine."
        BSP, II, 275–96.
        Repr. in Berdoe, *Browning's Message to His Time* (Lon-
        don: Sonnenschein, 1890), pp. 145–92.
62. Nov. 30, 1888: Mosely.
BSP, II, 298*–303*.
Acad., XXXIV (Dec. 15, 1888), 391.
    (A) Ormerod, "Andrea del Sarto and Abt Vogler."

BSP, II, 297–311.
Repr. in *Browning Studies*, pp. 151–65.
63. Jan. 25, 1889: Berdoe.
BSP, II, 312*–16*.
Acad., XXXV (Feb. 9, 1889), 98–99.
(A) W. Robertson, "La Saisiaz."
BSP, II, 312–32.
Repr. in *Browning Studies*, pp. 166–86.
64. Feb. 22, 1889: Furnivall.
BSP, II, 321*–27*.
Acad., XXXV (Mar. 9, 1889), 171–72.
(A) James B. Oldham, "On the Difficulties and Obscurities En-
countered in a Study of Browning's Poems."
BSP, II, 333–48.
65. Mar. 29, 1889: Furnivall.
BSP, II, 331*–33*.
Acad., XXXV (Apr. 13, 1889), 259.
(A) Joseph King, Jr., "On *Prince Hohenstiel-Schwangau.*"
BSP, II, 349–62.
66. Apr. 26, 1889: Furnivall.
BSP, II, 334*–36*.
Acad., XXXV (May 11, 1889), 327.
(A) Mrs. Annie E. Ireland, "On 'A Toccata of Galuppi's.' "
BSP, II, 363–70.
Repr. in *Browning Studies*, pp. 187–94.
67. May 31, 1889: Furnivall.
BSP, II, 338*.
(A) Glazebrook, " 'Numpholeptos' and Browning's Women."
BSP, II, 371–79.
Repr. in *Browning Studies*, pp. 195–203.
(B) Berdoe, [Same subject].
[Not printed.]
68. June 28, 1889: Furnivall.
BSP, II, 339*–40*.
(A) Annual report.
BSP, II, xxxiii–xxxvii.
(B) James J. G. Graham, "The Wife-Love and Friend-Love of
Robert Browning."
BSP, II, 380–400.
Repr. in *Browning Studies*, pp. 204–24.
69. Oct. 25, 1889: ENTERTAINMENT. Reading of *Luria*.
BSP, III, 1*.
70. Nov. 29, 1889: Rossetti and Furnivall.
BSP, III, 1*–7*.
Acad., XXXVI (Dec. 7, 1889), 376–77.
(A) William J. Alexander, "An Analysis of *Sordello.*"
Alexander, *An Introduction to the Poetry of Robert
Browning* (Boston: Ginn, 1889), pp. 144–77.
BSP, III, 1–25.
(B) Rossetti, "Taurello Salinguerra: Historical Details Illustrative
of *Sordello*. Muratori and Browning Compared."

BSP, III, 82–97.
71. Jan. 31, 1890: Furnivall.
BSP, III, 32*–36*.
[The first meeting held after Browning's death. No papers read.]
72. Feb. 28, 1890: Furnivall.
BSP, III, 55*–56*.
(A) Furnivall, "Robert Browning's Ancestors."
BSP, III, 26–36. [Additional documents on the subject, pp. 37–45.]
73. Mar. 28, 1890: Frederic D. Matthew.
BSP, III, 57*–58*.
Acad., XXXVII (Apr. 12, 1890), 256–57.
(A) Mrs. Bertha J. de Courcy Laffan, "The Beautiful Commonplaces of Browning."
Printed as pamphlet (London, 1890). [So listed in Broughton, Bibliography. No copy located.]
(B) Ireland, "Some Remarks on Browning's Treatment of Parenthood."
BSP, III, 46–52.
(C) Benjamin Sagar, "On the Line-Numbering, Fresh Lines, &c. in The Ring and the Book."
BSP, III, 53–63. [This paper was distributed but not actually read at the meeting.]
74. Apr. 25, 1890: E. Johnson.
BSP, III, 80*–84*.
Acad., XXXVII (May 3, 1890), 306.
(A) Joseph Jacobs, "Browning's Theology."
Jewish Quarterly Review, II (April, 1890), 249–56.
Abstr. in BSP, III, 80*–82*.
75. May 30, 1890: Rev. Mr. Hawker.
BSP, III, 98*–102*.
(A) Revell, "The Value of Browning's Work—Part I."
BSP, III, 64–81.
76. June 27, 1890: Furnivall.
BSP, III, 118*–22*. [Hereafter there are no records of discussions in BSP.]
(A) Annual report.
BSP, III, i–v.
(B) Furnivall, [The character of Constance in "In a Balcony"].
Abstr. in BSP, III, 118*–20*.
[77.] Oct. 31, 1890: ENTERTAINMENT.
Program, BSP, III, 127*–29*.
[78.] Nov. 27, 1890: ENTERTAINMENT. Reading of Colombe's Birthday.
Program, BSP, III, 131*–33*.
79. Jan. 30, 1891.
(A) Henry Jones, "Browning's Proof of Optimism."
[Not printed.]
80. Feb. 27, 1891.
(A) Ireland, "On Browning's Poem 'Cristina and Monaldeschi.' "
BSP, III, 103–14.
Repr. in Browning Studies, pp. 321–31.

81. Mar. 20, 1891.
    (A) Jón Stefánsson, "How Browning Strikes a Scandinavian."
        BSP, III, 115–23.
82. Apr. 24, 1891.
    (A) Revell, "The Value of Browning's Work—Part II."
        BSP, III, 124–38.
83. May 29, 1881.
    (A) Oldham, "Browning's Dramatic Method in Narrative."
        BSP, III, 139–47.
84. June 26, 1891.
    (A) Annual report.
        BSP, III, ix-xii.
    (B) Richard G. Moulton, "*Balaustion's Adventure* as a Beautiful
        Misrepresentation of the Original."
        BSP, III, 148–67.
[85.] Oct. 29, 1891.
    (A) W. Hall Griffin, [Lantern slides of Italy illustrating Browning's
        poems].
        Announcement in *Acad.*, XL (Oct. 24, 1891), 358.
[86.] Nov. 26, 1891: ENTERTAINMENT. Reading of *The Return of the Druses*.
    Announcement in *Acad.*, XL (Nov. 21, 1891), 454.
[87.] Dec. 25, 1891.
    (A) Whitehead, "A Note on Browning."
        [Not printed.]
[88.] Jan. 29, 1892.
    (A) Ormerod, "Compensation."
        [Not printed.]
[89.] Feb. 26, 1892.
    (A) Graham, "The Glove."
        [Not printed.]
[90.] Mar. 25, 1892.
    (A) Radford, "Andrea del Sarto in Poetry and in Fact."
        [Not printed.]
        Announcement in *Acad.*, XLI (Mar. 19, 1892), 276.
[91.] Apr. 29, 1892.
    (A) A. H. Singleton, "A Grammarian's Funeral."
        [Not printed.]
[92.] May 27, 1892: Harry Buxton Forman.
    Acad., XLI (June 11, 1892).
    (A) Oscar L. Triggs, "Robert Browning as the Poet of Democracy,"
        Poet-Lore, IV (1892), 481–90.
        Expanded as *Browning and Whitman: A Study in Democ-
        racy* (London: Sonnenschein, 1893).
[93.] June 24, 1892.
    (A) Annual report [?].
        [Not printed.]
    (B) Moulton, "Caliban upon Setebos."
        [Not printed.]

APPENDIX B

SOME ADDITIONAL LETTERS

Although I have drawn heavily in this study upon the unpublished correspondence of Dr. Furnivall and other figures in the Browning Society, a few of the letters that I have seen strike me as so interesting or significant that they deserve to be quoted at greater length. Some brief observations of my own, in most instances, are appended.

1. *Furnivall to Henry W. Longfellow, Oct. 11, 1881*
(*Harvard*)

Mr. Moncure Conway told me today in the British Museum of the performance of Browning's *Colombe's Birthday* at the Harvard Athenaeum in Boston about in 1853 or −'54, at which you were present, & in which you took a great interest, as you, & specially Mrs. Longfellow, were Browning lovers. This encourages me to write to you, & ask you if you will honour our Browning Society by becoming one of its Vice Presidents. You would gratify us all very much by doing so; & at the present time when England has been drawn so near to your country by the suffering & death of your noble President & the devotion of his loving wife, your mark of goodwill would be doubly acceptable. I thrust then that you may feel free to give it us; & with wishes that you may still be spared many years to receive the tribute of loving hearts & lips from all quarters of the globe, I am, dear Sir, . . .

[This letter is interesting in two respects: it is the only letter by Furnivall which I have found that displays a high degree of tact, and it shows that Conway's Browning anecdotes were already being circulated before the Browning Society's first meeting was held (Oct. 28).]

2. *Longfellow to Furnivall, Oct. 29, 1881*
(*Huntington FU 13*)

I have had the pleasure of receiving your letter, & regret very much that I cannot see my way to grant your request.

If I were living in London, & could take part in the proceedings of your society, I should not hesitate to take this method of showing my admiration for the genius of Browning, but I am reluctant to join any society whose meetings I cannot attend.

3. *Sidney Colvin to Furnivall, Oct. 17, 1881*
(*Brit. Mus. Add. MSS. 49525*)

. . . But with reference to this Browning Society matter, my mind is made up, and I should, if we met, only be able to repeat what I have already written.—

I do not feel with you that the study of a living poet has anything to gain by the establishment of a Society of this kind. Browning, so far as my experience goes, *is* read and studied, as it is, by every one who cares for literature at all. By taking part in a Browning Society, I do not feel that I could do anything to further the study of his works, which I cannot do as well, or better, independently, in the incidental course of literary talk or discussion as it arises, or else in published criticisms which every one may read who chooses.—

[Colvin (1845–1927), an art and literary critic, was at this time Slade Professor of Fine Arts at Cambridge and director of the Fitzwilliam Museum. His attitude toward the society was shared by Frederic Leighton and Edward Dowden, among others.]

4. *James Russell Lowell to Furnivall, Jan. 15, 1882*
(*Huntington FU 13*)

. . . I wrote an article on B. in 1848, I think it was, & I dare say it was very bad, but (though written under hampering restrictions of editorial doubts & curtailings) it will at least show my hearty admiration for the poet. I thought then as I think still that in certain primary & essential qualities he was far above all other his contemporaries; & my faith in him has grown deeper with years & experience. I do not think he always does justice to his thought, nor that all his thoughts are of equal value, but I know of no greater pleasure than reading him where he is best. My reason for not joining the Society was not that I was behind the fondest in admiration & gratitude.

. . .

I hope I shall be allowed to subscribe to your publications even if I don't become a member. I found much to interest me in the one you were good enough to send me.

[Another passage from this letter was quoted in Chapter VI. The article by Lowell was "Browning's Plays and Poems," *North American Review*, LXVI (April, 1848), 357–400.]

5. *Editor of* Temple Bar *to Furnivall, Feb. 25, 1882*
(Bodleian MS. Don. d. 109, fol. 360)

[He declines to publish James Thomson's Browning Society paper because] the critical treatment of Mr. Browning's works has been abundantly supplied, & I hesitate to add yet one more paper to the copious literature under which the Poems themselves seem destined to get buried.

[This sort of response infuriated Furnivall, who, after reading Browning's reviewers in the preparation of his bibliography, decided that Browning had been grossly misunderstood and underestimated by the press.]

6. *James Dykes Campbell to Browning, Mar. 16, 1884*
(Brit. Mus. Add. MSS. 49526)

I have received your kind letter of yesterday and learn with extreme regret that anything should have been done to cause you inconvenience.

I was not aware that the Printers had been accustomed to send proofs to you, and have at once instructed them to discontinue the practice because I feel sure that the Committee would disapprove of the least delay in giving effect to the least wish of yours.

[The proofs were of the society's *Papers.* Browning's letter, which explains why he did not wish to receive them, is printed in *LRB*, p. 227.]

7. *Campbell to Hiram Corson, Jan. 17, 1885*
(Cornell)

It is most cheering to learn what you tell me of the growing popularity of Browning among your educated classes. Here the cult makes much progress—one sees it not merely in the accretions to the list of members of our Society (10 since this list was printed in our prospectus last month) but in the frequency with which Browning is quoted in fugitive articles— quoted like Tennyson & Shakespeare & Horace. It is no longer the "fashion" to deprecate our friend.

8. *Anna Stoddart to Walter Slater, Nov. 20, [1887]*
(Baylor)

I have read steadily 200 pages of Mr. Fotheringham's book on Browning's Poetry,—the rest I have not time to read just now. My opinion of what I have read is very high. It seems to me to show a deep & fine understanding of the poet, almost feminine in its persuasiveness, together with a vigorous expression of it, masculine this time in its intellectuality & sobriety. Of course I especially like his courage in making frankly articulate the growing sense amongst thoughtful people that the spiritual life is too real to be more than temporarily suspended in the consciousness of those who may have been staggered by the able blows of the Scientists & sophisms of the Positivists. The book will form a valuable addition to the Browning shelf in our libraries.

[The book was James Fotheringham's *Studies in the Poetry of Robert Browning* (London, 1887). "Dr. Furnivall (at the meeting of Nov. 25, 1887) referred to an advertisement which had appeared of *Studies in Browning's Poetry,* by Mr. Fotheringham, who had some time since lectured on the subject. He (Dr. Furnivall) had asked to see the proof-sheets of the book, and found that without being very brilliant, it was likely to be of use, the introductory chapters being extremely good. He then forwarded the sheets to Mr. Revell, who was pleased with them, as was Mr. Slater. The result was that 250 copies of the book at 2s. 6d. had been ordered, and one of these would be sent round to each of the members" (*BSP*, II, 218*).]

9. *Browning to J. D. Williams, Sept. 24, 1886*
(Texas)

I want to say a word about those "Transactions" you have been reading. I never see them before publication, having expressly begged the Secretary to let me have only the numbers when past correction: every now and then some question has been put to me through Mr Furnivall, which I made no difficulty to answer. His peculiarities and defects are obvious—and some of his proceedings by no means to my taste: but there can be no doubt of his exceeding desire to be of use to my poetry, and I must attribute a very great part indeed of the increase of care about it to his energetic trumpet-blowing. There is about to appear also a "Primer" by my friend and staunch ally Mrs Sutherland Orr: I have no conception of its plan, even: though, of course, I have given her whatever explanations she chose to consider necessary. I was hardly aware, till I became so—startlingly—during the course of the publishing these Transactions—how extraordinary is the "ordinary" way of considering a poet's method of work. I write, airily, "Quoth Tom to Jack, one New Year's day,"—and one "student" wants to know who Jack was,—another sees no difficulty there, but much in Tom's entity,—while a third, getting easily over both stumbling-blocks, says— "But—*which* New Year's Day?" Since all this must be done for me by somebody, I congratulate myself on having somebody so energetic as Mr Furnivall to do it. Even now, I cannot make out what it is he sees—or first saw—in my books to interest him: what leaps! From Chaucer to Shakespeare, down plump to—— (Observe it is heart-breaking to him that anyone should spell the great name as I persist in doing—yet he bears with me!)

[Unfortunately I did not see this letter until it was too late to make use of it in my text, and so I include it here. Browning refers in the last sentence to Furnivall's tenaciously held view that the original spelling of both the name and plays of "Shakspere" must be retained.]

NOTES*

INTRODUCTION

1. *Acad.*, XXIII (Mar. 31, 1883), 214.
2. Domett, *Diary*, p. 77.
3. *BSP*, II, 182*.
4. *BSP*, I, 186.
5. *BSP*, III, 36*.
6. *BSP*, I, 323–24.
7. *BSP*, II, 91*.
8. Actually, Ruskin societies had been established in Sheffield and Birkenhead during the seventies, but they attracted little attention, and neither Furnivall nor Miss Hickey seems to have been aware of their existence when they created the Browning Society.
9. Anne I. Thackeray, *Records of Tennyson, Ruskin, Browning* (New York, 1892), p. 187.
10. *BSP*, I, 19.
11. *BSP*, I, 1*.
12. For a general history of such societies, see Harrison Ross Steeves, *Learned Societies and English Literary Scholarship in Great Britain and the United States* (New York, 1913), esp. pp. 152–203.

CHAPTER I

1. *Fragments of Old Letters, E.D. to E.D.W.*, 2nd Ser. (1914), p. 157.
2. MS letter (Huntington HM 4995). (See bibliography for key to abbreviations of manuscript locations.)
3. This account of the society's founding is based on the following sources: *BSP*, I, 1*–2* (which was published separately by Furnivall in 1884 as a pamphlet entitled *How the Browning Society Came into Being*); Furnivall, "Recollections of Robert Browning," *PMG*, Dec. 14, 1889, p. 2; Enid Maud Dinnis, *Emily Hickey: Poet, Essayist—Pilgrim*.

* Unless otherwise indicated, the place of publication for all books is London.

A Memoir (1927), p. 28; Dinnis, "Emily Hickey—In Memoriam," *Catholic World,* CXX (March, 1925), 733. I have departed from these sources in only one detail. In Miss Dinnis' article she says the decision was made while crossing Kensington Gardens; in her book she writes that it was Hyde Park. Neither, I think, is correct, since it was Regent's Park that lay between the homes of Miss Hickey and Furnivall and that of Browning.

4. Caroline F. E. Spurgeon, in Munro, *Furnivall,* p. 184.

5. *Acad.,* XX (July 9, 1881), 28.

6. Corson, "A Few Reminiscences of Robert Browning," *Cornell Era,* XL (April, 1908), 295–96.

7. *BSP,* I, 1*.

8. *BSP,* I, 19.

9. *Literary World,* XIII (Mar. 11, 1882), 77.

10. *BSP,* II, 1.

11. Domett, *Diary,* p. 116.

12. *DNB;* Mary L. Bruce, *Anna Swanwick: A Memoir and Recollections, 1813–1899* (1903), p. 130. A MS letter from Miss Swanwick to RB, Feb. 11, 1873 (Baylor), accompanying a presentation copy of her Aeschylus translation, suggests that she did not know him at this time; probably the letter and book served as her introduction.

13. *Diary,* p. 116.

14. Michael Field [pseud. of Katharine Bradley and Edith Cooper], *Works and Days,* ed. T. and D. C. Sturge Moore (1933), p. 113.

15. Bruce, p. 134.

16. MS letter to unidentified correspondent [Slater?], Nov. 29, n.y. (Baylor).

17. MS letter, June 5, 1888 (Baylor).

18. *The Letters of John Stuart Blackie to His Wife,* ed. A. S. Walker (Edinburgh and London, 1910), p. 305.

19. *DNB;* James Milne, *The Memoirs of a Bookman* (1934), p. 15.

20. Haweis, "Robert Browning," *Independent,* XLIV (Dec. 15, 1892), 1776–77. See also *LRB,* p. 190.

21. Domett, *Diary,* p. 243.

22. The fullest accounts of Campbell's career may be found in the *DNB;* Leslie Stephen's memoir in Campbell, *Samuel Taylor Coleridge: A Narrative of the Events of His Life,* 2nd ed. (1896); and A. Taylor Innes, "James Dykes Campbell," *Bookman* (London), VIII (July, 1895), 107–08.

23. MS memoir of RB by Mrs. Campbell (Brit. Mus. Add. MSS. 49526).

24. Wise, "Introduction," *A Browning Library: A Catalogue of Printed Books, Manuscripts and Autograph Letters of Robert Browning and Elizabeth Browning* (1929), pp. xxvi–xxvii.

25. Quoted in Stephen memoir, pp. xxii–xxiii. The corrected set of Browning's works is now in the British Museum.

26. This concise work first appeared as a "biographical introduction" to an edition of Coleridge's works in 1893; in 1894 it was published separately.

27. Quoted in Partington, *Wise,* p. 316.

28. Walter Besant, "Mr. Dykes Campbell," *Athenaeum,* June 8, 1895, p. 739.

29. MS letters, Edward C. K. Gonner to FJF, Apr. 18, 1886; Gonner to Dykes Campbell, Apr. 23, 1886 (Baylor).
30. William Roberts, *The Book-Hunter in London* (1895), pp. 316–17; Harold F. B. Wheeler, "The Library of Mr. W. B. Slater," *Bibliophile*, III (July, 1909), 229–37. MS letter, Harry Buxton Forman to Slater, Dec. 22, 1902 (Pariser): "I noticed last night that you had all sorts of miscellaneous Browning stuff about."

John Carter has described Slater as "perhaps Wise's oldest and closest friend" (Carter, "Foreword," *Wise after the Event: A Catalogue,* ed. G. E. Haslam [Manchester, 1964], p. vii). Mr. Carter tells me that he bases this assertion in part upon some inscriptions by Wise in presentation copies of books. In George Barrow's *Marsk Stig* (1913) Wise wrote: "Walter B. Slater, From his ever affectionate Friend Thos. J. Wise" (Haslam, p. 26). In an extremely rare copy of Wise's own *Verses* (1882) is this inscription: "Walter B. Slater, with his friend's love. Xmas 1882. T.J.W." (Scribner Book Store, Rare Book Department, Catalogue No. 131, *Nineteenth Century Pamphlets, with an Appendix of Wiseana* [1945], p. 29). This latter catalogue, incidentally, indicates that Slater owned an almost complete set of the Wise forgeries.

For additional evidence of Slater's intimacy with Wise, see the Sotheby catalogue of the sale of the Pariser collection, Dec. 4–5, 1967. Perhaps the most damaging revelation of Slater's possible complicity in the forgeries is a letter from him to John Carter (p. 82) in 1933 or 1934 in which he claims to have disposed of his copy of the most notorious of the forgeries, the "Reading *Sonnets.*" A copy was in fact in his library, which was sold after his death by Hodgson's.

Wise was also named as one of the three executors of Slater's will (1931), but Wise died first. According to an unpublished account of Wise's funeral by J. A. Symington (Pariser), one of the few mourners present was Slater, "T. J. Wise's life-long friend and confidant."
31. Private information from Mr. Mark K. Whitlock, Slater's brother-in-law.
32. *BSP*, II, 130*.
33. *BSP*, I, 43*.
34. *BSP*, II, 216*.
35. *BSP*, II, 250*; II, 335*. Slater once contributed a note to the *Papers* which concluded with a quotation from Andrew Lang: "It is not the essence of poetry to be cryptic. Poetry lacks merit just in proportion to its need of commentators." Furnivall added this sarcastic comment: "This accounts, no doubt, for the lack of merit in the much commented-on poetry of Isaiah, Homer, Dante, Shakspere, etc." (*BSP*, II, 330*).
36. *BSP*, II, 151*.
37. *BSP*, II, 315*; II, 277*.
38. MS letter (Texas).
39. MS letter, Oct. 8, 1886 (King's).
40. MS letter, Sept. 3, 1888 (Baylor).
41. *BSP*, III, 55*.
42. *Ibid.*; MS letter, FJF to Blakeney, Feb. 25, 1890 (Cambridge Add. MSS. 7509, fol. 164). Blakeney (1869–1955) later enjoyed a successful career as a poet, author of textbooks, and headmaster of several schools (*Times*, Aug. 2, 1955, p. 9b).
43. Davis was a clerk of the Lower (or Second) Division, 1884–1905;

clerk of the Second Division, higher grade, 1905–1910; and minor staff clerk, 1910–1912 (D. Robinson, *et al.*, comp., *The War Office List* [1884–1912]).

His will mentions neither wife nor children. That he had strong artistic interests is demonstrated by his will, which mentions a contribution of £50 to the National Art Collections Fund, and by the following letter from Davies to Hall Griffin, Oct. 30, 1891 (Brit. Mus. Add. MSS. 45563, fol. 13–14): "Some years ago I was struck by a Della Robbia medallion in S. Kensington Museum, which corresponds exactly with the description of the lady's portrait in 'The Statue & the Bust.' With an audacity which now amazes me I made the accompanying rough sketch & sent it to Mr. Browning, asking if it could be by any chance the one he had in his mind in writing the poem. The enclosed is his reply." (Browning's letter is not in the Griffin papers.)

44. MS letter, Aug. 21, 1891 (Chicago: Jenkin Lloyd Jones papers).
45. Kingsland, "London Literaria," *Poet-Lore*, IV (October, 1892), 526.
46. MS postcard, FJF, July 11, 1883; MS letter, Hickey, July 16, 1883 (Browning scrapbook of Jenkin Lloyd Jones [Baylor]).
47. MS letter (Texas).
48. Dinnis, *Emily Hickey*, p. 25.
49. *BSP*, I, 43*.
50. Hickey, "Glorious Robert Browning," *Nineteenth Century*, LXX (October, 1911), 755.
51. Katherine Tynan, "Emily Hickey: A Catholic Poet," *Catholic World*, XCIII (June, 1911), 331.
52. This phrase is quoted from a brief autobiographical narrative by Miss Hickey in the Tynan article, pp. 332–35. I cannot find the source of this passage and therefore have concluded that it is from a private letter. Much of my own summary of her life is based on it.
53. *Ibid.*, p. 333.
54. *BSP*, I, 454, x. See also *NL*, p. 281.
55. MS letter, RB to Hickey, Aug. 3, 1883 (Baylor); *NL*, pp. 284, 291, 294.
56. MS letter, Hickey to Hiram Corson, May 26, 1884 (Cornell). When Miss Hickey sent Browning ten guineas early in 1883, apparently earned by some sort of trial printing of *Strafford* for the students at the Collegiate School for Girls, he returned them and asked that the money be given to the Browning Society (letter, RB to Hickey, Jan. 18, 1883, in W. Arthur Strain, "Rare and Unpublished Letters of Robert Browning" [University of Colorado master's thesis, 1925], p. 53). In the annual report of the society for 1882–83 is recorded "a Donation of Ten Guineas made through Miss E. H. Hickey" (*BSP*, I, xii).
57. *BSP*, I, 40*.
58. *BSP*, II, 104*; MS letters, Hickey to Campbell, Dec. 13, 1885 (Baylor); Hickey to Campbell, Dec. 30, 1885 (Baylor); Hickey to Slater, Sept. 20, 1886 (Texas). In 1882 she arranged a private performance of Browning's *Colombe's Birthday* in which she played the title role (undated clipping from London *Literary World*, enclosed in MS letter, Hickey to Corson, Feb. 3, 1882 [Cornell]).
59. *Times*, Sept. 11, 1924, p. 15e.
60. *Nineteenth Century*, LXX (October, 1911), 753–70.

61. "A Study of Browning's Saul," *Catholic World*, XCIV (December, 1911), 320.
62. "A 'Glorious Fourth' Indeed!" *Fellowship, Monthly Journal of the Robert Browning Settlement*, July 15, 1921, p. 67.
63. Noel, "The Browning Society" (letter), *PMG*, Dec. 17, 1889, p. 3.
64. *BSP*, II, 149*.
65. *BSP*, I, 25*; II, 172*.
66. *BSP*, II, 45*, 166*; III, 120*.
67. *BSP*, II, 302*.
68. *BSP*, II, 289*.
69. Shaw, *Sixteen Self Sketches* (New York, 1949), p. 95. See also Partington, *Wise*, p. 315.
70. The book is now in the library of King's College, London.
71. *BSP*, I, 24*. See also *BSP*, I, 128*: "Mr. F. thought this voluntary evaporation of heroes [in the plays] due to Browning's youth: it was in curious contrast to the strength of his own frame and character."
72. J. Schick, in Munro, *Furnivall*, p. 172. Furnivall also had a high regard for "Rabbi Ben Ezra," a poem which perfectly describes the kind of old age he himself enjoyed.
73. *BSP*, II, 165*.
74. *BSP*, II, 259*.
75. William E. A. Axon, "F.J.F.," *Bookman* (London), XLI (October, 1911), 42.
76. *BSP*, I, 65*. See also *BSP*, II, 129*-30*.
77. *BSP*, II, 265*.
78. Except where I have indicated other sources, my sketch of Furnivall's career is based upon Munro's biographical introduction to *Frederick James Furnivall*; the *DNB*; and the obituary in the *Times*, July 4, 1910, p. 12c.
79. Furnivall, rev. of *Memoir of Daniel Macmillan* by Thomas Hughes, *Acad.*, XXII (Aug. 12, 1882), 112.
80. Quoted in Munro, *Furnivall*, pp. xix–xx.
81. See John Llewelyn Davies, ed., *The Working Men's College, 1854–1904* (1904), passim.
82. Ker, "Frederick James Furnivall," *Proceedings of the British Academy*, IV (1909–10), 375.
83. Quoted in Munro, *Furnivall*, p. xlvii.
84. MS letter, Gladstone to FJF, Jan. 20, 1884 (Huntington FU 14).
85. MS letter, Jan. 22, 1884 (Brit. Mus. Add. MSS. 38904, fol. 40).
86. *Times*, July 4, 1910, p. 12c. At his death his estate was valued at £7961 19s 2d gross (*Times*, July 19, 1910, p. 15d). Since Furnivall had little cash at any given time, this figure must reflect investments and his large library.
87. MS letter, FJF to unidentified correspondent, Feb. 16, 1893 (owned by author).
88. MS letter, May 17, 1895 (King's).
89. *Notebook of the Shelley Society* (1888), p. 7.
90. *BSP*, II, 339*.
91. R. C., "Making a Dictionary: A Chat with Dr. F. J. Furnivall," *Great Thoughts from Master Minds*, LIII (April-September, 1910), 90.

92. *Letters from John Ruskin to Frederick J. Furnivall and Other Correspondents*, ed. T. J. Wise (1897), pp. 55–57. See also *BSP*, II, 339*; Furnivall, "Recollections of Robert Browning," p. 1.
93. "Recollections of Robert Browning," p. 1; "Making a Dictionary," p. 90. Earlier, in 1872, Furnivall had secured Browning's permission (presumably by mail) to reprint Mrs. Browning's published observations on Chaucer in the Chaucer Society's transactions (*BSP*, I, 111).
94. Quoted in T. J. Wise, *The Ashley Library* (1930), X, 31.
95. *LRB*, p. 267.
96. Furnivall [pseud. "Phi"], "Mr. Robert Browning's 'Inn Album'," *N&Q*, N.S. V (Mar. 25, 1876), 244–45. Part of this is repr. in *BSP*, I, 67n.
97. *Acad.*, XX (Oct. 1, 1881), 260; Oct. 15, p. 296; Oct. 29, p. 331; Nov. 19, pp. 385–86; Nov. 26, p. 403; Dec. 10, p. 437; Dec. 31, pp. 492–93.
98. *BSP*, I, 1*–2*.
99. *BSP*, I, 28.
100. *BSP*, I, 101n.
101. *BSP*, I, 25n; *LRB*, pp. 194, 197, 199, 201, 205.
102. *BSP*, I, 150, 168; II, 26*.
103. *LRB*, p. 303.
104. *BSP*, II, 168n.
105. Furnivall's intense interest in the subject is demonstrated by the profuse annotations and corrections in his own copy of the paper (in the library of King's College, London) and by his extensive correspondence with other members of the Browning family about their ancestry.
106. *BSP*, III, 36.
107. Furnivall, "Browning's Footman Ancestor" (letter), *Acad.*, LXII (Apr. 12, 1902), 394.
108. MS letter, May 20, 1895 (Texas).
109. "The Ancestry of Robert Browning, the Poet," *Genealogists' Magazine*, VIII (1938), 1–6.
    Though I have been unable to determine the accuracy of Furnivall's research, I am certain that his anti-aristocratic bias was no greater hindrance to objectivity than was Baddeley's unreasoning hatred of Furnivall. (Baddeley, moreover, was defending his own ancestry.) He describes Furnivall as having "a large following among the more second-rate intellectuals of his time" (p. 3) and seems to base his own case largely upon an unsupported statement by T. J. Wise in 1931 that Furnivall later retracted his views on the Browning genealogy; but of course Wise, in the latter part of his life, was conducting his own personal vendetta against Furnivall. In 1948, following the publication of Partington's biography of Wise, Baddeley raised the issue again in the columns of *TLS*. Partington, in reply, pointed out the obvious: that Wise, a proved liar and forger, was scarcely a reliable authority for the retraction story. (*TLS*, Feb. 21, 1948, p. 107; Apr. 10, p. 205; Apr. 17, p. 219.)
110. Repr. in *BSP*, III, 70*–71*. Later Furnivall sounded less self-assured on the subject: "I fear that we shall never get certainty about the S[trafford] *Life*. It's my fault for not taking my copy to Br. & going thru it with him" (MS postcard to Hall Griffin, June 11, 1902 [Brit. Mus. Add. MSS. 45563, fol. 154]).

111. Quoted in William G. Kingsland, "London Literaria," *Poet-Lore*, VII (November, 1895), 582. (For Pen Browning's full letter, see Ashley A. 2541.) Though most Browning scholars (e.g., William C. DeVane, *A Browning Handbook*, 2nd ed. [New York, 1955], pp. 62–63) have rejected Furnivall's theory, some interesting corroborative evidence is supplied by Emily Hickey in "Browning Biography," *Nineteenth Century*, LXVIII (December, 1910), 1067. Cf. *NL*, pp. 353–54.

    I treat this question at greater length in the autumn, 1969, issue of the *Browning Newsletter*.

112. *Athenaeum*, July 9, 1892, p. 66.

113. *BSP*, III, 34*. At the next meeting (Feb. 28, 1890) Furnivall announced that Browning's son "had also refused permission for the Society to reproduce the photograph of his dead father, so that in these matters they were, to put it broadly, snubbed; and although their work was hindered by this refusal—which he [Furnivall] characterized somewhat strongly—they must go on as well as they could . . ." (*BSP*, III, 55*).

114. *Times*, Dec. 13, 1890, p. 10a.

115. MS letter to Katharine Bradley, [December?], 1890 (Brit. Mus. Add. MSS. 45856, fol. 56).

116. MS letter, Gosse to Hall Griffin, May 8, 1902 (Brit. Mus. Add. MSS. 45563, fol. 147–50).

CHAPTER II

1. Quoted in Partington, *Wise*, pp. 316–17.

2. For Tennyson's refusal, see Frederick M. Padelford, in Munro, *Furnivall*, p. 141. Clement K. Shorter, in the introduction to his *The Browning Society* (1917), a collection of letters from Browning to Dykes Campbell, claims that Tennyson "promised to take this office, but apparently withdrew this promise" (p. 6). I doubt that this is true, because Furnivall would have announced his coup to the world without a moment's hesitation; moreover, Shorter's introduction contains a sufficient number of errors to shake one's faith in his reliability.

    Edward Robert Lytton Bulwer-Lytton declined in a letter to Furnivall dated Mar. 6, 1882 (Huntington FU 13).

    Furnivall's election is recorded, without comment, in *BSP*, II, xx.

3. Quoted in Munro, *Furnivall*, p. lxix. Munro says that the suggestion that Furnivall fill the office came from Browning, but his assertion is based on a misunderstanding of Browning's letter. The letter is not a "proposal"—though that word is used in it—but a congratulation. The letter is dated June 27, and the election had taken place on June 24.

4. The only meeting at which he did *not* speak was that of Oct. 27, 1882.

5. *BSP*, I, 3.

6. MS postcard, Apr. 8, 1902 (Chicago: Rickert papers).

7. *BSP*, I, 96*. After Browning's death, Furnivall wrote that whenever he thought of the poet, he saw him "on his green velvet sofa in Warwick Crescent, reading, proof in hand, with the pale eager face of my dead young friend by his side. This is the first image that always rises to

my mind" (Furnivall, "A Few More Words on Robert Browning," *PMG*, Dec. 18, 1889, p. 3). See also *LRB*, p. 217.

8. She had, however, promised to write a paper "On Shakspere and Browning" (*BSP*, I, xviii).

9. *LRB*, p. 222. The *Memoir* was published early in 1884 and reprinted in the *Cheltenham Ladies' College Magazine*, IX (February, 1884), 170–80. For evidence of Furnivall's authorship of it, see *BSP*, I, 132*.

10. *Diary*, p. 291.

11. See James O. Halliwell-Phillipps, *Copy of Correspondence* [between J. O. H.-P. and Robert Browning, concerning expressions respecting Halliwell-Phillipps, used by F. J. Furnivall in the preface to a facsimile of the second edition of *Hamlet*, published in 1881] (Brighton [?], 1881).

12. Munro, *Furnivall*, p. lix.

13. See Oscar E. Maurer, "Swinburne vs. Furnivall," *University of Texas Studies in English*, XXXI (1952), 86–96.

14. MS letter, Jan. 23, 1876 (Huntington FU 12). See also Lachlan Phil Kelley, "Robert Browning and George Smith: Selections from an Unpublished Correspondence," *Quarterly Review*, CCXCIX (July, 1961), 330.

15. Kelley, p. 330.

16. MS letter, RB to FJF, Mar. 11, 1881 (Baylor).

17. Kelley, pp. 330–31.

18. *BSP*, I, 77n.

19. *LRB*, p. 198.

20. Furnivall, "The Late Mr. George Smith," *Athenaeum*, May 4, 1901, p. 568.

21. *BSP*, I, ii.

22. *BSP*, I, 42*.

23. MS letter, Aug. 15, 1882 (Huntington FU 13).

24. MS letter, Aug. 22, 1882 (Huntington FU 13).

25. MS letter, Aug. 29, 1882 (Huntington FU 13).

26. *Academy*, XXIV (Dec. 22, 1883), 414; repr. in *BSP*, I, 100*.

27. Kelley, pp. 331–32.

28. Kelley, pp. 332–33.

29. *BSP*, I, 498.

30. *BSP*, I, xvii.

31. *LRB*, p. 236.

32. MS letter, Jan. 2, 1886 (Huntington FU 15).

33. See Kingsland, *Robert Browning: Chief Poet of the Age*, 2nd ed. (1890), p. 34. When Kingsland discovered what Furnivall had done, he wrote an apology at once to Browning, who replied: "I wish, with all my heart, I could give you the honey,—or what your good nature accepts as such,—freely and without price; but so long as there is an intermediary to account with, I am bound to consult his advantage—in business matters—as well as my own" (p. 36).

34. MS letter to FJF, Jan. 5, 1886 (Huntington FU 15).

35. *LRB*, p. 378n; *BSP*, II, xxxiv.

36. *BSP*, II, 340*–45*; III, 1–25.

37. *LRB*, p. 313.

38. Repr. in *BSP*, III, 47*–48*.

39. *BSP*, III, 33*.
40. MS letter (Cambridge Add. MSS. 7509, fol. 164).
41. *BSP*, III, 55*.
42. Repr. in *BSP*, III, 54*.
43. Furnivall, "Introduction," in Esther P. Defries, *A Browning Primer* (1898), p. v.
44. MS letter, Outram to FJF, Nov. 20, 1885 (Baylor).
45. MS letter, Outram to unidentified correspondent [probably FJF], Nov. 23, 1885 (Baylor).
46. MS letter (Baylor).
47. Outram was also on the platform at the inaugural meeting of the Shelley Society, Mar. 10, 1886 (*Notebook of the Shelley Society* [1888], p. 1). On May 7, 1886, he acted the part of Orsino in the society's private performance of *The Cenci* at the Grand Theatre, Islington.
48. This letter, along with ten others sent among the principal figures in the case of *Outram v. Furnivall*, was published (p. i) in a pamphlet issued by either Furnivall or his friends. The copy owned by the Stark Library, University of Texas, contains some annotation in the hand of Furnivall and has no title page; the last letter printed in it, however, is dated Oct. 22, 1886, and it is reasonable to assume that the pamphlet was printed and distributed within the next week or two, while the quarrel was most lively. (This particular copy evidently belonged to Walter Slater.) It will be referred to as Furnivall Pamphlet hereafter.
49. Furnivall Pamphlet, p. iii.
50. MS postcard (King's).
51. Furnivall's subsequent statements about the interview were not consistent. In his "Warning" circular (described below in text), written Oct. 23, 1886, he admitted he had promised Outram £60 for his services. A year later, at the libel trial, he claimed "there was no mention of £50 or £60 being paid to plaintiff" ("Outram v. Furnivall," *Times*, Feb. 3, 1888, p. 13d).
52. MS postcards, Outram to FJF, Oct. 11 and 13, 1886 (King's).
53. MS letter, Alma Murray to FJF, Oct. 24, 1886 (Texas).
54. Furnivall Pamphlet, p. iv. Dr. Clarke (1852–1931) was a widely respected homeopath who practiced in Mayfair and wrote medical books (*Times*, Nov. 26, 1931, p. 16d).
55. "Outram v. Furnivall," *Times*.
56. Furnivall Pamphlet, p. iv.
57. Furnivall wrote in his "Warning": "I never saw the Circular till Dr. Clarke sent me his copy on my telling him that I did not know what he alluded to."
58. On Oct. 4 Outram had written to Slater requesting a list of the Browning Society members (MS postcard [King's]). Slater, who had just taken office, supplied the list without asking any questions about its intended use.
59. I have not seen a copy of this circular; I am quoting from a facsimile (copy at Texas) printed by R. Clay and Sons, probably for the Browning Society.
60. Furnivall Pamphlet, p. ix.
61. *PMG*, Oct. 20, 1886, p. 6.
62. *PMG*, Oct. 25, 1886, p. 6.

63. Furnivall Pamphlet, p. xi. Alma Murray commented upon the letter thus: "I am very glad to see Mr. Campbell's letter as it now proves that Mr. Outram had not the *slightest* excuse for doing what he has done & to my mind proves he *knew* he was wrong by not sending the circular either to Mr. Campbell, you or me. I have heard nothing further from him" (MS letter to FJF, Oct. 24, 1886 [Texas]).

64. *PMG,* Oct. 26, 1886, p. 3.

65. Copy at Baylor.

66. MS letter, G. Gardner Leader to FJF, Oct. 30, 1886 (King's).

67. MS postcard, Dec. 10, 1886 (Cornell).

68. A series of seven MS letters from Foss to Slater, dated Nov. 12 through Dec. 13, chronicles these problems (Texas).

69. MS letter (Symington F724x). This is evidently the letter that Furnivall sent on to Browning, who read it "with great regret" (*LRB,* p. 259). Browning did not, in the end, attend the play.

70. *LRB,* p. 259. "Do you not think this is a very proper occasion for postponing the representation?" Browning asked. In the margin of the MS letter (Ashley A. 2531) is Furnivall's answer: "NO!"

71. Furnivall habitually scrawled hasty notes to his friends on postcards, a medium perfectly suited to his terse, no-nonsense style of writing; but at this time postcards were still considered only marginally respectable as a means of communication.

72. "Outram v. Furnivall," *Times.*

73. MS letter, Feb. 3, 1888 (Baylor).

74. MS letter, Campbell to FJF, Feb. 6, 1888 (King's). Furnivall read and approved the circular before it was distributed.

75. Copy at Texas.

76. *PMG,* Feb. 3, 1888, p. 4. MS note, FJF to unidentified correspondent [Slater or Campbell?] at bottom of letter, Paul L. Harluck [?] to Furnivall, Feb. 3, 1888 (King's): "Can you look in on me Sunday evening or afternoon? I shall be in after 4. Proprietor of *Pall Mall* [George Smith, Browning's publisher] says he'll come about other business between 6 and 6:30."

77. "The Hard Case of Dr. Furnivall," *PMG,* Feb. 8, 1888, p. 5.

78. *DNB.*

79. *PMG,* Feb. 13, 1888, p. 4.

80. MS letter to Slater, Feb. 14, 1888 (King's).

81. MS letter, Symons to Campbell, Feb. 15, 1888 (Brit. Mus. Add. MSS. 49522).

82. MS letter to FJF, Friday [ca. Feb. 3, 1888] (King's).

83. MS letter to Campbell, Feb. 23, 1888 (Brit. Mus. Add. MSS. 49526).

84. MS letter to editor of *PMG,* Feb. 11, 1888 (King's).

85. MS letter, Murray to Slater, Feb. 6, 1888 (King's); MS letter, Wedmore to Slater, Feb. 11, 1888 (King's); MS letter, Gonner to Slater, n.d. [ca. February, 1888] (Baylor); MS letter, Campbell to Slater, Mar. 2, 1888 (King's).

86. MS letter, Mar. 2, 1888 (Brit. Mus. Add. MSS. 49525). Campbell's reply to Lowell, dated Mar. 22, 1888 (MS letter, Harvard), may be quoted in part, since it provides an interesting summary of the case: "The case of 'Outram versus Furnivall' arose out of the unworthy conduct of the plaintiff in connection with the Browning Society's performance

of Strafford last winter. Furnivall spoke his mind in his usual impulsive way, and was undoubtedly libellous, and as he practically repeated the libel in Court, there was no fault to be found with the verdict, especially as Fitzjames Stephen who was in the bench summed up dead against Furnivall. You can readily imagine Stephen's view. Stress was properly laid by F's counsel on his client's disinterestedness throughout his career. Stephen laughed this to scorn, and declared roundly that he would not believe any man on his oath who professed to be disinterested. There was no such quality—& so forth."

87. MS post card (Brit. Mus. Add. MSS. 49525).
88. MS letter to FJF (King's). In Browning's personal account book (Ashley 5717), under the date of Feb. 14, 1888, is listed a check of £10 to "Campbell." Probably this represents his donation to the Furnivall Fund.
89. *LRB*, p. 287. On Feb. 17 Browning, again in a letter to Furnivall, commented: "As for the 'Trial,' everybody I have seen takes the right view of the subject" (*LRB*, p. 287).
90. *NL,* p. 356.
91. MS letter (Balliol).
92. MS letter (Balliol).
93. A receipt from his sister, Mary S. Davenport, dated Feb. 26, is among the Furnivall papers at King's.
94. MS letter to Campbell, Feb. 11, 1888 (Brit. Mus. Add. MSS. 49525).
95. MS letter, Feb. 14, 1888 (King's). There is an amusing sequel to this quarrel. Though the Browning Society had "got quit" of Outram, he did not lose his interest in Browning. By the end of the century he had written eight plays (Allardyce Nicoll, *A History of English Drama, 1660–1900* [Cambridge, England, 1952], V, 509), one of which was *A Mighty Error*, performed at the Avenue Theatre on July 14, 1891. The play was an elaborate reworking of Browning's "In a Balcony" and was indeed "a mighty error." Its unwieldy plot caused the *Athenaeum* (July 18, 1891, p. 107) to call the attempt "gallant rather than successful." Outram also remained penniless. When he died in the United States on May 6, 1901, he left an estate valued at £30.
96. MS letter, Seeley to FJF, Mar. 14, [1881] (Huntington FU 13).

CHAPTER III

1. Stedman, *Victorian Poets*, rev. ed. (Cambridge, Mass., 1887), II, 431.
2. "The Browning Society," *Saturday Review*, LVIII (Dec. 6, 1884), 722; F. G. R. Duckworth, *Browning: Background and Conflict* (New York, 1932), p. 134*n*.
3. MS letter, RB to FJF, Nov. 12, 1881 (Huntington FU 13).
4. Leonard Bacon, "Fifty Years After," *Saturday Review of Literature*, XXI (Dec. 9, 1939), 3.
5. "Browning Dead," *The Hawk*, Dec. 17, 1889, p. 669.
6. Shaw, *Sixteen Self Sketches* (New York, 1949), p. 96.
7. Quoted in Partington, *Wise*, p. 316.
8. Bodleian MS. Don. f. 24.
9. *BSP*, I, 174.

10. *LRB*, p. 202.

11. Dowden, in Munro, *Furnivall*, p. 36.

12. MS letter, Farrar to FJF, November, 1881 (Brit. Mus. Add. MSS. 49525).

13. MS letter, FJF to Longfellow, Oct. 11, 1881 (Harvard); MS letter, Longfellow to FJF, Oct. 29, 1881 (Huntington FU 13). (See Appendix B.)

14. MS letter, Leighton to FJF, Nov. 11, 1881 (Huntington FU 13).

15. Dobell, *The Laureate of Pessimism: A Sketch of the Life and Character of James Thomson ("B.V.")* (1910). William D. Schaefer, in his *James Thomson (B.V.): Beyond "The City"*, Univ. of California Perspectives in Criticism, No. 17 (Berkeley, 1965), has argued persuasively that the legend of Thomson's melancholy outlook is just that— a legend. Schaefer is undoubtedly correct in denying that Matilda Weller was "the peg on which he hung [his sorrow]" (p. 16), and he also provides solid evidence of Thomson's cheerful demeanor. I hope, therefore, that I have not fallen prey to the temptation to exaggerate Thomson's pessimism for rhetorical purposes in this chapter; however, I cannot dismiss that pessimistic philosophy as readily as Schaefer does, for it seems to me the key to an understanding of Thomson's grudging, even wistful, admiration for Browning, his temperamental opposite.

16. Harris, *Contemporary Portraits*, 2nd ser. (New York, 1919), p. 163.

17. Letter to Agnes Gray, May 14, 1859, *Poems and Some Letters of James Thomson*, ed. Anne Ridler (Carbondale, Ill., 1963), p. 239. Thomson also wrote a review of *Men and Women* for the *Jersey Independent* in 1862, repr. in *The Speedy Extinction of Evil and Misery: Selected Prose of James Thomson (B.V.)*, ed. William D. Schaefer (Berkeley, 1967), pp. 208–13.

18. James E. Meeker, *The Life and Poetry of James Thomson (B.V.)* (New Haven, 1917), pp. 56, 61–62, 64; Arthur Symons, *Studies in Two Literatures* (1897), p. 234; Henry S. Salt, *The Life of James Thomson ("B.V.") with a Selection from His Letters and a Study of His Writings* (1889), pp. 223, 233, 240; Imogene B. Walker, *James Thomson (B.V.): A Critical Study* (Ithaca, N. Y., 1950), p. 84; Schaefer, p. 75.

19. "Per Contra: The Poet, High Art, Genius," repr. in Thomson, *Essays and Phantasies* (1881), p. 126.

20. "A Note on Meredith," repr. in *Essays and Phantasies*, p. 289.

21. For a discussion of Browning's reception during the sixties, see Charlotte C. Watkins, "Browning's 'Fame within These Four Years,'" *MLR*, LIII (October, 1958), 492–500.

22. Salt, p. 169.

23. MS letter (Bodleian MS. Don. d. 109, fol. 287).

24. Unpublished diary of Thomson for 1881 (Bodleian MS. Don. f. 24), entry under Sept. 3. I have made extensive use of the diary in writing this account of Thomson's encounter with the Browning Society; but, in order to avoid cumbersome documentation, I do not hereafter cite it in footnotes.

25. *Gentleman's Magazine*, N.S. XXVII (December, 1881), 682–95; repr. in Thomson, *Biographical and Critical Studies* (1896), pp. 458–77. See also William S. Peterson, "A Hitherto Unpublished Essay on Robert Browning by James Thomson (B.V.)," *BNYPL*, LXXII (December, 1968), 637–40.

26. Quoted in Salt, p. 169.
27. *BSP*, I, 2*.
28. *BSP*, I, 248.
29. *BSP*, I, 250.
30. *BSP*, I, 26n.
31. MS letter, Jan. 26, 1882 (Bodleian MS. Don. d. 109, fol. 349–50).
32. MS letter, Jan. 31, 1882 (Bodleian MS. Don. d. 109, fol. 351).
33. MS letter (Cornell).
34. MS letter (Bodleian MS. Don. d. 109, fol. 546). Schaefer (p. 130) quotes a friend as saying that Thomson was recovering from a "sad sad spree."
35. MS letter, Jan. 31, 1882 (Bodleian MS. Don. d. 109, fol. 351).
36. *Ibid.;* editor of *Temple Bar* to FJF, Feb. 25, 1882 (Bodleian MS. Don. d. 109, fol. 360); editor of *Fraser's Magazine* to FJF, Mar. 1, 1882 (Bodleian MS. Don. d. 109, fol. 363). (For one editor's response, see Appendix B.)
37. MS letter (Bodleian MS. Don. d. 109, fol. 372).
38. MS letter (Bodleian MS. Don. d. 109, fol. 362).
39. *BSP*, I, vi.
40. "The Browning Society," *PMG*, June 25, 1887, pp. 13–14.
41. Raymond Blathwayt, "Browning and His Teaching: A Talk with Dr. Edward Berdoe," *Great Thoughts from Master Minds*, XLI (March-September, 1904), 312.
42. *Times*, Mar. 9, 1916, p. 12c. Berdoe was a Catholic at the time of his death.
43. Berdoe, *Browning and the Christian Faith: The Evidences of Christianity from Browning's Point of View* (1896), pp. viii–ix.
44. *BSP*, I, 68*.
45. Berdoe, *The Browning Cyclopaedia: A Guide to the Study of the Works of Robert Browning* (1892), pp. viii–ix.
46. *BSP*, I, 104*.
47. *BSP*, I, 107*.
48. I have taken the liberty of quoting this final phrase from some later remarks Berdoe made on the same subject. See *BSP*, II, 58*.
49. *BSP*, II, 50*.
50. A facsimile of the letter is printed in Berdoe, *Browning's Message to His Time* (1890), facing p. 126.
51. *BSP*, II, 233*.
52. *BSP*, II, 266*.
53. *BSP*, II, 275*–80*.
54. Blathwayt, p. 312.
55. *BSP*, II, 16*; *BSP*, II, 242*; *BSP*, II, 249*.
56. *BSP*, I, 75*.
57. *BSP*, II, 31*–32*.
58. *BSP*, II, 332*.
59. *BSP*, III, 121*.
60. *BSP*, II, 300*–01*.
61. Blathwayt, p. 312.
62. MS letter to Walter Slater, n.d. [1887 ?] (Baylor).
63. MS letter, n.d. [1905 ?] (Cambridge Add. MSS. 7509, fol. 42).
64. Here and elsewhere, when I refer to the contemporary reception of

books on Browning, the reader can find a list of the reviews I have consulted in Broughton, *Bibliography.*

65. "Chats on Coming Books: Dr. Edward Berdoe's 'Browning Cyclopaedia,'" *PMG*, Dec. 9, 1891, p. 1. Characteristically, Berdoe's boast ignores the existence of Mrs. Sutherland Orr's *Handbook to the Works of Robert Browning* (1885).

66. It is amusing to see that Dr. Furnivall's personal copy of the *Cyclopaedia* (King's) is still in mint condition. Since Furnivall's other Browning books are profusely marked and annotated, this may suggest that even the founder of the Browning Society found Berdoe's book dull reading.

67. *Acad.*, XLI (Feb. 6, 1892), 136.

68. [Clarke], "Browning as Others See Him: Berdoe, Jones and Nettleship," *Poet-Lore*, VIII (May, 1896), 266.

69. Dowden, *Fragments of Old Letters, E.D. to E.D.W.*, 2nd Ser. (1914), pp. 9–10.

70. Duckworth, *Browning: Background and Conflict* (New York, 1932), p. 71.

71. *DNB*; Julian O. Field [pseud. "Sigma"], *Personalia: Political, Social, and Various* (Edinburgh, 1903), pp. 215–16.

72. W. B. Yeats, *Autobiographies: Reveries Over Childhood and Youth, and the Trembling of the Veil* (New York, 1927), pp. 192–95.

73. Thomas Wright, *The Life of John Payne* (1919), p. 22.

74. *BSP*, I, 25*.

75. *London Quarterly Review*, XXXI (October, 1868), 133.

76. *BSP*, I, 28. Several years later Nettleship commented: "But in most cases I counted wrong, and got small credit for what seemed to me quite herculean efforts" (*BSP*, II, 66).

77. *BSP*, I, 231–34. Nettleship insisted, however, that his own classification was designed only to show the faulty logic of all such attempts to classify Browning's poetry.

78. *BSP*, I, 2*.

79. *BSP*, I, 17*–20*.

80. *BSP*, I, 64*–65*.

81. *BSP*, II, 89*–92*.

82. *BSP*, I, 53*–54*.

83. The promise was originally made at the meeting of Apr. 30, 1886 (*BSP*, II, 141*). On Jan. 28, 1887, it was announced that "owing to his unfortunate illness, Mr. J. T. Nettleship was unable to prepare his paper" (*BSP*, II, 182*).

84. MS letter (Texas). Nettleship had sent substantially the same message earlier to Slater (MS letter, Apr. 26, 1887 [Texas]).

85. *LRB*, p. 303.

86. *LRB*, p. 124.

87. Alfred Domett recorded in his diary (p. 124) on May 6, 1874, that Browning "said he owed nothing to literary men, editors, critics and the like; and that the most appreciative estimate ever made of him or his books was by an amateur. Probably he alluded to Nettleship." See also *LRB*, p. 304.

88. Furnivall, *Robert Browning's 70th Birthday* [circular] (Apr. 7, 1882). (Copy at Texas.)

89. Duckworth (p. 74) tells a story that might confirm this conjecture: "A surviving member of the Browning Society has told the writer that he well remembers visiting the poet one Sunday morning and bringing for his perusal the copy of the *Browning Society Papers* which contained Nettleship's essay [on 'Childe Roland']. Browning, after reading the paper, laughed heartily and remarked that he supposed it was there in the poem, though he hadn't known it when he wrote it!" Though Nettleship's paper on "Childe Roland" was never published in the *Papers,* this may be a slip of the pen, and possibly Duckworth's source meant the *Fifine* paper instead.
90. *LRB,* pp. 305–06.

CHAPTER IV

1. "Browningismus," *Saturday Review,* LXIII (Apr. 23, 1887), 595.
2. MS letter to Campbell, Aug. 6, 1887 (Brit. Mus. Add. MSS. 49522). Hereafter any Symons letter cited only as "Brit. Mus." will be Add. MSS. 49522 (unfoliated at the time of this writing).
3. Letter to Churchill Osborne, quoted in Roger Lhombreaud, *Arthur Symons: A Critical Biography* (Philadelphia, 1964), p. 44.
4. Lhombreaud, p. 55.
5. MS letter to Campbell, Feb. 15, 1888 (Brit. Mus.).
6. Add. MSS. 49522–23.
7. Lhombreaud, p. 22.
8. *Ibid.,* p. 24.
9. N.S. VI (December, 1882), 943–47.
10. Lhombreaud, p. 32.
11. *BSP,* II, 13*–17*.
12. *BSP,* II, 17*.
13. *BSP,* II, 80*–82*.
14. MS letter to Campbell, July 10, 1885 (Brit. Mus.).
15. MS letter (Brit. Mus.). Though the letter is among the Campbell papers, I assume that it was addressed to Furnivall, since "don't return" is written in the latter's hand at the top of the first page.
16. MS letter to Campbell, Mar. 18, 1885 (Brit. Mus.).
17. MS letter, June 22, 1885 (Brit. Mus.).
18. MS letters to Campbell, July 10 and 17, 1885 (Brit. Mus.).
19. *BSP,* II, 128*.
20. Symons, "Some Browning Reminiscences," *North American Review,* CCIV (October, 1916), 602.
21. MS letter, Sept. 20, 1886 (Brit. Mus.).
22. MS postcard to Campbell, Sept. 26, 1886 (Brit. Mus.). "Are you not the godfather of my infant book?" Symons wrote Campbell on Oct. 9 (MS letter, Brit. Mus.).
23. MS letter, Symons to FJF, July 16, 1887 (Baylor).
24. MS letter, Lowell to Campbell, Apr. 10, 1887 (Brit. Mus. Add. MSS. 49525). Campbell had sent him the book with the explanation that "the writer, Arthur Symons, whom I have never seen, is very young, but there is nothing in the book but what is good" (MS letter, Feb. 26, 1887 [Harvard]).

25. "Some Browning Reminiscences," p. 603.
26. Walter Pater, *Essays from "The Guardian"* (1901), pp. 41–42, repr. from the *Guardian*, Nov. 9, 1887.
27. MS letter, Jan. 2, 1888 (Brit. Mus.).
28. MS postcard to FJF, Jan. 31, 1887 (Texas).
29. *Ibid.*; MS letter, Symons to Campbell, Jan. 31, 1887 (Brit. Mus.).
30. MS letter, Mar. 28, 1887 (Brit. Mus.).
31. *BSP*, II, 211*–12*.
32. MS letter (Texas).
33. *BSP*, II, 334*–35*.
34. MS letter, Jan. 16, 1895 (Brit. Mus. Add. MSS. 49523).
35. Browning's letter to Furnivall, Nov. 5, 1882, is printed in both Lhombreaud, p. 23, and *NL*, pp. 280–81. When the poem in question was again attributed to Browning shortly after his death, Symons wrote a letter which appeared in the *PMG*, May 7, 1890 (repr. in *BSP*, III, 97*), citing Browning's denial of its authorship.
36. Letter to Churchill Osborne, Nov. 17, 1882, quoted in Lhombreaud, p. 23.
37. Browning wrote to Furnivall on Oct. 5, 1886: "I make haste to say by the early Post that Messrs. Cassell are in no danger of finding such a churl in me as they seem to think might possibly be the case: I receive by this same Post a set of Proofs of Mr Symons' 'Introduction' —which I will open and inspect presently,—and a letter from the Publishers to the same effect as yours. Will you kindly give them, on my part, the full authorization they require?" On Oct. 7 Browning wrote again to Furnivall: "By this Post, I return the 'Proofs' to Messrs. Cassell,—having read them carefully and set right the very little that was wrong in the printing. I enclosed in the parcel, a letter of acknowledgement to Mr Symons. I tell him truly that I hardly know how to praise his book without praising myself—but I try to convey some sense of the great gratification he has given me—however my poetry may come short of what his generosity endeavours to find there" (MS letters, Huntington FU 15).
38. "Some Browning Reminiscences," p. 603. It appears that Symons also corresponded with Browning earlier, before he completed his *Introduction*. A Hodgson's sale catalogue (Nov. 11, 1915) provides the following description of a letter from Browning to Symons, Apr. 13, 1886: ". . . declining to reply to certain questions respecting his Poems, and suggesting that the 'Handbook' by his 'intimate friend,' Mrs. Orr, rendered any 'further performance of a similar nature unnecessary.' "
39. "Some Browning Reminiscences," p. 605.
40. MS letter (Brit. Mus.).
41. MS letter May 29, 1889 (Texas).
42. MS letter to Campbell, Saturday (n.d.) (Brit. Mus. Add. MSS. 49523).
43. "Some Browning Reminiscences," p. 605.
44. *Ibid.*, pp. 606–08.
45. *Acad.*, XXXVII (Jan. 11, 1890), 19.
46. *Athenaeum*, Dec. 21, 1889, p. 860; repr. in *BSP*, III, 26*–27*.
47. *BSP*, III, 33*.
48. *Acad.*, XXVI (Dec. 13, 1884), 393.

49. *NL*, p. 314. The editors of *NL*, who describe it as "to an unidentified correspondent," evidently did not see the envelope—addressed to Symons—which accompanies the letter at the Huntington Library.

50. John Carter and Graham Pollard, *An Enquiry into the Nature of Certain Nineteenth Century Pamphlets* (1934); *Between the Lines: Letters and Memoranda Interchanged by H. Buxton Forman and Thomas J. Wise*, with a foreword by Carl H. Pforzheimer and an introductory essay and notes by Fannie E. Ratchford (Austin, Tex., 1945); Carter and Pollard, *The Firm of Charles Ottley, Landon & Co.: Footnote to an Enquiry* (1948); Partington, *Wise*; William B. Todd, ed., *Thomas J. Wise: Centenary Studies* (Austin, Tex., 1959); *Letters of Thomas J. Wise to John Henry Wrenn: A Further Inquiry into the Guilt of Certain Nineteenth-Century Forgers*, ed. Ratchford (New York, 1944). This list does not include several published catalogues of exhibits of Wise forgeries and correspondence. Messrs. Carter and Pollard have also of late begun to issue "working papers" in the course of preparing a second edition of their *Enquiry*.

51. P. H. Muir, who knew Wise in later years, has described him as "really unpleasant" and "crafty, greedy, pompous," with an "ugly, cockney voice" (Muir, "Elkin Matthews—Part VIII: Sherry and Shibboleths," *Book Collector*, III [Spring, 1954], 13, 27).

52. *BSP*, II, 192*; *LRB*, p. 261.

53. *BSP*, I, 43*.

54. *BSP*, I, ii.

55. *BSP*, I, xii.

56. For Wise's own account of this incident, see the "Introduction" to his *A Browning Library: A Catalogue of Printed Books, Manuscripts and Autograph Letters of Robert Browning and Elizabeth Browning* (1929), pp. xxvi–xxvii. Thurman Hood (in *LRB*, p. xii) quotes an article about Wise in the *Strand Magazine* which states that Wise first met Browning in 1884, but this is probably an error.

57. *LRB*, pp. 246–47. Browning's letter casts some doubt on Wise's story of the scene at Campbell's apartment. Browning wrote to Wise on Mar. 10, ". . . I have given away one of the copies already to a friend of mine." If, as Wise claimed, he was present when Browning made the offer to Dykes Campbell, it seems odd that Browning would have phrased this in such a vague manner.

58. Campbell, who received earlier the copy Wise had wanted, wrote to Wise on Sept. 18, 1887 (MS letter, Pariser): "I am glad you have got a copy of *Pauline*. You did rightly to take it when you could get it."

59. Partington (*Wise*, pp. 79–80), on the basis of a diary entry by one of Wise's contemporaries, believes that he began his career as a forger no later than 1887 and probably in 1886.

60. Quoted in Partington, pp. 46–47.

61. See, for example, *Letters of Thomas J. Wise to John Henry Wrenn*, p. 8. It is interesting that in Browning's last letter to Wise, Jan. 16, 1889 (MS letter, Pariser), he addresses him as "dear sir."

62. *LRB*, p. 251.

63. *LRB*, pp. 253, 256.

64. John Carter ("Thomas J. Wise in Perspective," *Centenary Studies*, p. 7) has remarked that Wise's type-facsimiles for the Browning and

Shelley societies "ultimately bankrupted both Societies." It is true that the Shelley Society quickly went through its funds because of ambitious publishing schemes, but the causes of the Browning Society's ultimate bankruptcy were quite different. Besides, Wise never succeeded in dominating the Browning Society to the extent that he did the Shelley Society.

65. *LRB*, pp. 260, 298–99.
66. MS postcard, postmarked July 22, 1887 (Ashley A.2530).
67. *LRB*, p. 286.
68. *BSP*, II, xix.
69. "Browningismus," pp. 595–96.
70. Copy at Baylor.
71. *The Ashley Library*, I, 136.
72. Partington, *Wise*, p. 132n.
73. The section on Browning in *Literary Anecdotes* (I, 359–627) was repr. separately as *A Complete Bibliography of the Writings in Prose and Verse of Robert Browning* (1897).
74. Broughton, *Bibliography*, p. 195, comments that "the Browning Society of London, named as beneficiary on the cover, was of course defunct." It has not been generally recognized that the former Browning Society members did in fact finance this volume.
75. MS letter (Ashley B.434).
76. Wise also privately printed a number of individual Browning letters. For details, see Broughton, *Bibliography*.
77. MS letter, May 20, 1895 (Texas).
78. MS letter, Campbell to Wise, May 2, 1895 (Ashley B.2567).
79. They are *Cleon* (1855), *The Statue and the Bust* (1855), and *Gold Hair* (1864); and Mrs. Browning's *Sonnets from the Portuguese* (1847) and *The Runaway Slave* (1849).
80. *The Ashley Library*, I, 137.
81. *BSP*, I, 28.
82. In this same copy of the bibliography (Pariser) are two letters from Wise to Furnivall, dated July 9 and Oct. 23, 1883, in which he speaks of "your" bibliography.
83. MS letter (Brit. Mus. Add. MSS. 49526).
84. Partington, *Wise*, pp. 62–63.
85. MS letter (King's).
86. "A Friend of Mr. Robert Browning. Death of Mr. William G. Kingsland: An Appreciation," *Islington Gazette*, Jan. 31, 1933, p. 2e.
87. *BSP*, II, 17*. For the meeting of Apr. 25, 1884, at which James Russell Lowell spoke, the society paid a shorthand reporter £5 7s 8d. During the sessions of 1887–88, 1888–89, and 1889–90, the society spent an average of approximately £4 each session for reporting the meetings. Since this amount would not have been sufficient to hire a reporter for every meeting, I assume that only occasional meetings were transcribed in shorthand.
88. Shaw, *Collected Letters, 1874–1897*, ed. Dan H. Lawrence (New York, 1965), pp. 87–88.
89. I have seen corrected proofs of the minutes of these two meetings: Oct. 31, 1884 (Brit. Mus. Add. MSS. 49526), and Feb. 23, 1883 (Har-

vard). Kingsland's MS notes for the meeting of Oct. 28, 1881, are at the Huntington (FU 13).

90. *BSP*, I, 104*.
91. *BSP*, II, 113*, 130*, 171*.
92. *BSP*, II, 59*.
93. *BSP*, II, 216*.
94. *BSP*, II, 250*.
95. *BSP*, II, 301*–02*.
96. "A Friend of Robert Browning."
97. *BSP*, I, 68*.
98. *BSP*, II, 130*.
99. *BSP*, I, 79*.
100. H. G. Groser, "The Late Mr. William G. Kingsland," *New Chronicle of Christian Education*, LXIV (Feb. 2, 1933), 79; private information from Mr. Peter W. Kingsland, his great-grandson.
101. "Offord-Road Young Men's Christian Debating Society," *Islington Gazette*, Nov. 9, 1877, p. 2e.
102. The first of these, beginning "O thou large-hearted poet of our time!" and dated Jan. 1, 1881, appeared in the *Islington Gazette* on that date; Kingsland enclosed it in a letter sent to Browning five days earlier (*Intimate Glimpses*, pp. 87–88). A second sonnet, dedicated to Browning on his seventieth birthday, was published in the *Islington Gazette* on May 8, 1882. For other sonnets by Kingsland, see *BSP*, II, 399–400, and the dedication of his *Robert Browning: Chief Poet of the Age*. His series of articles about Browning, entitled "Half Hours with Robert Browning," was printed in the *Islington Gazette* between Oct. 3 and 18, 1883.
103. See "Notes and News," *Poet-Lore*, II (March, 1890), 168.
104. Kingsland, "Browning Rarities," *Poet-Lore*, VI (May, 1894), 264–68.
105. "Notes and News," *Poet-Lore*, VI (September, 1894), 471–72.
106. *LRB*, pp. 128–29. Kingsland later gave the letter to the British Museum. Mr. Peter Kingsland tells me, incidentally, that several of his great-grandfather's letters from Browning were lent to Wise, who never bothered to return them.
107. Furnivall wrote: "Fêted as [Browning] was by the highest in the land, he had a working-man [Kingsland] and his wife to dinner with him, and treated them just like his grandest friends: and after our Shelley-Society performance of *The Cenci*, it was to this printer's-reader's house that he took his son and sister to tea" (Furnivall, "A Few More Words on Robert Browning," *PMG*, Dec. 18, 1889, p. 3).
108. *Robert Browning: Chief Poet of the Age*; "Browning as I Knew Him," in W. A. Knight, ed., *The Robert Browning Centenary Celebration at Westminster Abbey, May 7th, 1912* (Boston, 1912), pp. 45–54; "Browning: Some Personal Reminiscences," *Baylor Bulletin* (Baylor Univ. Browning Interests, 2nd Ser.), XXXIV (July, 1931), 28–40; "Some Browning Memories," *Contemporary Review*, CII (August, 1912), 202–10. Scattered throughout Kingsland's columns in *Poet-Lore* are further recollections of his association with Browning.
109. In about 1926 Kingsland discovered this note among his papers and immediately sent a copy of it to Dr. A. J. Armstrong, suggesting that

he might wish to publish it in the *Baylor Bulletin*. Dr. Armstrong did not use it, and so the note was simply filed among his correspondence and has never been published.

110. *DAB*; Morris Bishop, *A History of Cornell* (Ithaca, N.Y., 1962), pp. 115–17.

111. However, Moncure Conway, writing in 1864, claimed that "in America . . . I have even heard of a Browning Club" (Conway, "Robert Browning," *Victoria Magazine*, II [February, 1864], 298).

112. Corson, "Browning Clubs in the United States" (letter), *Literary World* (Boston), XIV (Apr. 21, 1883), 127.

113. Ella B. Hallock, "An Interpreter of Browning," *Methodist Review*, XCII (July, 1910), 614.

114. *Moses Coit Tyler, 1835–1900: Selections from His Letters and Diaries*, ed. Jessica Tyler Austen (Garden City, N.Y., 1911), p. 133.

115. Corson, "A Few Reminiscences of Robert Browning," *Cornell Era*, XL (April, 1908) 295–96. Corson was already a member of Furnivall's Chaucer Society, for which he had prepared a concordance in 1879.

116. MS postcard, FJF to Corson, May 7, 1882 (Cornell).

117. *BSP*, I, 293–321.

118. *BSP*, I, 41*.

119. MS note, postmarked Aug. 8, 1882 (Cornell). See also *FitzGerald*, pp. 144, 148. Miss Caroline Chase, an American girl, visited Browning's home in July, 1883, and reported that he "inquired especially for Professor Corson. 'He has been very kind; so have all the Americans' " (William Lyon Phelps, "A Conversation with Browning," *ELH*, XI [June, 1944], 155).

120. MS letter (Cornell). Cf. Furnivall's public statement in *BSP*, I, 63*.

121. The *Academy* (in a note probably written by Furnivall) described Corson's *Introduction* as "the most important" of the "many Selections from Browning now circulating in the States" (*Acad.*, XXX [July 24, 1886], 56).

122. MS letters, Campbell to Corson, July 11 and 13, 1886 (Cornell).

123. "Browningismus," p. 596.

124. MS letter to Campbell, Jan. 26, 1887 (Brit. Mus. Add. MSS. 49522).

125. MS postcard, Dec. 18, 1886 (Cornell).

126. On Jan. 16, 1887, Campbell wrote to Corson: "I saw Mr Browning this afternoon & he told me how good it [the *Introduction*] is—for he has read it already" (MS letter, Cornell).

127. MS postcard, FJF to Corson, Dec. 10, 1886 (Cornell); MS postcard, Corson to FJF, postmarked Dec. 26, 1886 (Huntington FU 15).

128. Corson, "Recollections of Robert Browning," *Nation*, L (Jan. 9, 1890), 28–29.

129. William V. Moody, *Letters to Harriet*, ed. Percy MacKaye (Boston, 1935), p. 285.

130. In a letter to Lilian Whiting, Apr. 3, 1911, Corson reported that the Macmillan Company had "strongly declined" his manuscript (MS letter, Boston). It is not unlikely that the manuscript was rejected because it recorded Corson's conversations with Browning in the spirit as well as in the flesh. In any event, Corson published what must have been the most important chapter in the *Cornell Era*. The

manuscript is not among the Corson papers at Cornell, and I have been unable to locate it elsewhere.

131. MS letter to Eugene R. Corson, Feb. 16, 1906 (Cornell).
132. MS letter, Corson to Lilian Whiting, Nov. 14, 1905 (Boston).
133. Chesterton, *Robert Browning*, English Men of Letters (1903), p. 192.

CHAPTER V

1. Lounsbury, *The Early Literary Career of Robert Browning* (New York, 1911), p. 196.
2. Mrs. Emilia Pattison (Lady Dilke), *The Book of the Spiritual Life*, with a memoir by the Rt. Hon. Sir Charles W. Dilke (New York, 1905), pp. 83–84. For my conjectural identifications, see *BSP*, I, xiii.
3. Letter, June 18, 1863, *From a Victorian Post-Bag: Being Letters Addressed to the Rev. J. Llewelyn Davies by Thomas Carlyle and Others*, ed. Charles L. Davies (1926), p. 75.
4. "The Whitey-Browning Society," *Punch*, LXXXIV (Apr. 21, 1883), 192.
5. "The Browning Clubs in Boston, U.S.," *Athenaeum*, Aug. 21, 1886, p. 252.
6. Eliza O. White, "A Browning Courtship," *Atlantic Monthly*, LXII (July, 1888), 99–112.
7. "On the Alleged Obscurity of Mr. Browning's Poetry" (1884), *The Collected Essays and Addresses of Augustine Birrell* (1922), II, 109.
8. For discussions of the Lady Ashburton affair, see *LRB*, Appendix, pp. 325–38; William O. Raymond, "Browning's Dark Mood: A Study of 'Fifine at the Fair,'" in *The Infinite Moment and Other Essays in Robert Browning*, 2nd ed. (Toronto, 1965), pp. 105–28.
9. MS letter, RB to FJF, Nov. 12, 1881 (Huntington FU 13).
10. *BSP*, II, 167*.
11. *BSP*, II, 3*.
12. *BSP*, I, 174–75.
13. *BSP*, I, 86*.
14. *BSP*, II, 333.
15. *BSP*, II, 368.
16. *BSP*, II, 250*.
17. *BSP*, I, 491.
18. *BSP*, II, 321*–22*.
19. *BSP*, I, 12*.
20. *BSP*, I, 241.
21. *BSP*, I, 11*.
22. *BSP*, II, 336.
23. *BSP*, II, 240*.
24. *BSP*, II, 170*. See also II, 324*.
25. *BSP*, II, 323*.
26. *BSP*, I, 74*; III, 100*.
27. *BSP*, II, 120.
28. *BSP*, I, 242.
29. *BSP*, I, 42*, 90*.
30. *BSP*, I, 176.

31. *BSP*, I, 33*, 5*.
32. *BSP*, II, 4*.
33. *BSP*, II, 119–31, 150*.
34. *BSP*, I, 375, 86*; II, 113, 80*–82*, 111*.
35. *BSP*, I, 96*.
36. *BSP*, II, 258*.
37. *BSP*, I, 182.
38. *BSP*, I, 19.
39. *BSP*, I, 108.
40. Furnivall, "Recollections of Robert Browning," *PMG*, Dec. 14, 1889, p. 2. In Furnivall's Browning bibliography (*BSP*, I, 27) is a disparaging reference to "Jingle"—i.e., Swinburne (so identified in Furnivall's personal copy of the bibliography [Pariser]).
41. *BSP*, II, 1–12; III, 142.
42. *BSP*, II, 14*.
43. *BSP*, I, 77*–78*; II, 207–20; 222*, 109*; I, 79*.
44. *BSP*, I, 71*.
45. Morgan, "The Society and the 'Fad,'" *Science*, XV (May 9, 1890), 282–86, 288–90.
46. *BSP*, I, 122*.
47. *BSP*, II, 32.
48. *BSP*, I, 46*–47*.
49. *BSP*, II, 168*.
50. *BSP*, II, 362. See also II, 161*, 210*.
51. *BSP*, I, 492.
52. *BSP*, I, 414.
53. *BSP*, I, 69*–71*.
54. *BSP*, II, 331*–32*.
55. *BSP*, II, 160*, 339*–40*.
56. *BSP*, II, 242*.
57. *BSP*, I, 47*.
58. *BSP*, I, 53*.
59. *BSP*, II, 38*.
60. *BSP*, I, 25*–26*.
61. *BSP*, II, 338*.
62. *BSP*, I, 21*.
63. Santayana, "The Poetry of Barbarism," in *Interpretations of Poetry and Religion* (New York, 1900), p. 189.
64. Furnivall, "The Browning Society" (letter), *Echo*, Oct. 31, 1881, p. 1f.
65. *BSP*, I, 28*.
66. *Ibid.*
67. *BSP*, I, 32*.
68. *BSP*, I, 45*.
69. *BSP*, II, 279*.
70. *BSP*, I, 31*.
71. *BSP*, III, 99*.
72. Shaw, *Sixteen Self Sketches*, p. 96.
73. *BSP*, II, 143*.
74. *BSP*, II, 186*.
75. *BSP*, II, 265*–68*.

76. Smalley, "Mephistopheles at the Conventicle: G.B.S. Amid the Brown-ingites," *Saturday Review of Literature*, XXVII (July 22, 1944), 15.
77. *BSP*, II, 275*–80*.
78. "Notes and News," *Poet-Lore*, III (November, 1891), 590–91.
79. See Eliot's "Religion and Literature," *Essays Ancient and Modern* (1936), p. 93.

CHAPTER VI

1. Lang, "Esoteric Browningism," *Forum*, VI (November, 1888), 300.
2. *BSP*, II, 335*.
3. *BSP*, II, 280*.
4. *BSP*, II, 331*. See also I, 9*.
5. *BSP*, II, 229*–34*.
6. *Times*, July 4, 1904, p. 13f; *BSP*, I, 105n.
7. *BSP*, I, 1*.
8. Kirkman, "On Robert Browning's Poems," *The Hampstead Annual*, ed. Ernest Rhys (1897), pp. 133–34; *LRB*, p. 205; *FitzGerald*, p. 132.
9. "On Robert Browning's Poems," p. 136.
10. *BSP*, I, 174.
11. *BSP*, I, 3*.
12. *BSP*, I, 186.
13. "Passing Notes," *Echo*, Oct. 29, 1891, p. 1d.
14. See Furnivall, "Recollections of Robert Browning," *PMG*, Dec. 14, 1889, p. 2.
15. *BSP*, II, 124*, 320*.
16. *BSP*, I, 172.
17. *Ibid.*
18. *FitzGerald*, p. 132.
19. Conway, "Recollections of Robert Browning," *Nation*, L (Jan. 9, 1890), 27–28; Conway, *Autobiography: Memories and Experiences* (Boston, 1904), II, 18–19, 21; Mary Elizabeth Burtis, *Moncure Conway, 1832–1907* (New Brunswick, N. J., 1952), p. 99; *NL*, pp. 157–58, 160–61, 184–85.
20. *Dearest Isa: Robert Browning's Letters to Isabella Blagden*, ed. Edward C. McAleer (Austin, 1951), p. 167.
21. Conway, *Autobiography*, I, 159.
22. MS letter, Lowell to FJF, Jan. 15, 1882 (Huntington FU 13).
23. *DNB; NL*, pp. 309–10.
24. *Times*, Dec. 10, 1895, p. 5f. Sharpe was a Fellow of Christ's College, Cambridge, and at this time held a living at Gissing, Norfolk.
25. *BSP*, I, 9*, 42*; Furnivall, "The Browning Society" (letter), *PMG*, Jan. 2, 1882, p. 12.
26. *DNB*; MS letter, Farrar to FJF, November, 1881 (Brit. Mus. Add. MSS. 49525); Reginald Farrar, *The Life of Frederic William Farrar* (New York, 1904), pp. 177, 287–88.
27. *DNB*. For her relationship with Browning, see *LRB*, pp. 207–08. Miss Lewis and her sister Elinor (afterwards Lady Hammick) were both members of the original (July, 1881) Browning Society committee.

236 / NOTES TO PAGES 119–123

In Furnivall's bibliography he quotes Miss Lewis as saying, "Browning has been more to me for the last two years than all the Sermons" (*BSP*, I, 26. The quotation is attributed to her in the Pariser copy of the bibliography). Browning was appropriately grateful for this extraordinary praise (*LRB*, p. 197).

28. MS letter, FJF to James Thomson, Jan. 26, 1882 (Bodleian Don. d. 109, fol. 349–50).

29. *BSP*, I, 14*.

30. MS letter, FJF to Thomson, Jan. 26, 1882 (Bodleian Don. d. 109, fol. 349–50).

31. *DNB*; *Athenaeum*, Feb. 15, 1896, p. 220.

32. *BSP*, I, 18*.

33. Percy Addleshaw, "Preface," in Noel, *Selected Poems* (1897), pp. xv–xxix; Emily Hickey, "Roden Noel, Poet," *Nineteenth Century*, XCI (April, 1922), 624–33.

34. *DNB*.

35. MS letters, Bury to FJF, Nov. 30, 1881 (Pariser); RB to FJF, Oct. 2, 1881 (Huntington FU 13).

36. MS letter, RB to FJF, Apr. 25, 1882 (Baylor); Norman H. Baynes, *A Bibliography of the Works of J. B. Bury* (Cambridge, England, 1929), p. 47.

37. Frederic Harrison, *In Memoriam J. C. Morison . . . A Discourse to the Positivist Society* (1888).

38. *BSP*, I, 28*, 31*.

39. Edward A. Petherick, "Edwin Johnson and His Writings," in Johnson, *The Rise of English Culture* (1904), p. xx.

40. *DNB*. Shortly after Browning's death Sharp wrote the first book-length biography of him, two hundred copies of which were distributed to Browning Society members, though accompanied by three pages of "corrections" by Furnivall.

41. *DNB*; F. Cecily Steadman, *In the Days of Miss Beale* (1930), p. 122.

42. *BSP*, II, 215*.

43. Josephine Kamm, *How Different from Us: A Biography of Miss Buss and Miss Beale* (1958), p. 105.

44. "Notes and News," *Acad.*, XXII (Oct. 7, 1882), 258.

45. *BSP*, I, 326.

46. *Who Was Who*.

47. *BSP*, I, 47*.

48. *DNB*; letter, Davies to Canon D. J. Vaughan, 1864, *From a Victorian Post-Bag: Being Letters Addressed to the Rev. J. Llewelyn Davies by Thomas Carlyle and Others*, ed. Charles L. Davies (1926), p. 75.

49. *BSP*, I, xiii.

50. *BSP*, I, 49*.

51. *BSP*, I, 53*.

52. *Acad.*, XXII (Dec. 2, 1882), 401–02. Sharpe examined in particular the lines which Phene recites to Jules, and the last of Pippa's songs.

53. *Alumni Oxonienses*.

54. *BSP*, I, 63*.

55. *BSP*, I, 62*.

56. *Who Was Who*.

57. *BSP*, I, 63*.
58. *DNB*.
59. The corrected proof is at Harvard.
60. *BSP*, I, 64*.
61. *BSP*, II, 278*. Despite Revell's prominence in the Browning Society, I have been able to learn little about him. He lived in Notting Hill (London) and is described in his will as a "gentleman"; his wife Mary also belonged to the Browning Society; and he was the author of a collection of agnostic essays, *Ethical Forecasts: Essays* (1887), temperately and intelligently written, in which he occasionally quotes Browning.
62. *BSP*, II, 277*.
63. *BSP*, I, 439–40.
64. *BSP*, I, 67*–68*.
65. *BSP*, I, 66*, 69*. For an account of Bulkeley's subsequent career, see the *Malvern News*, May 6, 1922, p. 4e.
66. *DNB*.
67. MS letter, Elizabeth D. Dowden to A. J. Armstrong, Nov. 19, 1922 (Baylor).
68. *LRB*, pp. 148–49.
69. *Intimate Glimpses*, pp. 54–55; *LRB*, pp. 150–51. Excerpts from her essay were reprinted in Furnivall's Browning bibliography with this comment by Dowden: "Among the very best Articles written on 'Browning'" (*BSP*, I, 98n).
70. MS letter, Elizabeth D. Dowden to A. J. Armstrong, Oct. 9, 1922 (Baylor).
71. *Acad.*, XX (Dec. 17, 1881), 455.
72. *LRB*, pp. 202–03.
73. *BSP*, I, 71*.
74. MS letter, Elizabeth D. Dowden to A. J. Armstrong, Apr. 18, 1920 (Baylor).
75. See Kingsbury Badger, "Mark Pattison and the Victorian Scholar," *MLQ*, VI (December, 1945), 423–47; *DNB*.
76. *BSP*, I, xi, xviii. On Pattison and the Oxford Browning Society, see *BSP*, II, 103*.
77. *Times*, Dec. 1, 1904, p. 12c; *LRB*, pp. 189, 213, 218, 274; *NL*, p. 376; *Intimate Glimpses*, pp. 84–85. From 1855 to 1878 he was headmaster and divinity lecturer at Christ's College, Brecon, and the *Times* obituary also reports that he was an "accomplished versifier."
78. *BSP*, I, 474.
79. *Times*, Oct. 19, 1896, p. 6b; *BSP*, II, 70*, 97*, 104*.
80. *BSP*, I, 83*.
81. *DNB*; Sir Sidney Lee, "Henry Charles Beeching, Dean of Norwich, 1911–1919," *Norwich Public Library Readers' Guide*, VII (April, 1919), 80.
82. *Times*, Oct. 27, 1916, p. 5d.
83. *DNB*.
84. MS letter, Garnett to T. J. Wise, May 22, 1886 (Texas).
85. *BSP*, I, 104*.
86. *BSP*, I, 108*. The *Academy* records a few additional remarks by Shaw:

"Mr. Shaw thought Browning was essentially unscientific. The tendency to make him evolve good always was exasperating. He is sometimes even pessimist" (*Acad.*, XXV [Mar. 15, 1884], 189).

87. MS letter, FJF to Shaw, Feb. 17, 1884 (Brit. Mus. Add. MSS. 50510, fol. 189).

88. Shaw, *Collected Letters, 1874–1897*, ed. Dan H. Laurence (New York, 1965), p. 79.

89. MS letter, Jan. 18, 1887 (Brit. Mus. Add. MSS. 50511, fol. 263–64).

90. Partington, *Wise*, p. 315.

91. Quoted from private letter to Beatrice White, in White, "Frederick James Furnivall," *Essays and Studies*, N.S. V (1952), 73–74.

92. Shaw, *Pen Portraits and Reviews*, rev. ed. (1932), p. 180.

93. Partington, *Wise*, pp. 315–16.

94. *LRB*, p. 212.

95. *Alumni Cantabrigienses*.

96. *Times*, May 15, 1922, p. 18e.

97. *BSP*, I, 488.

98. *Times*, Oct. 19, 1896, p. 6b.

99. *BSP*, I, 110*–11*.

100. MS letters, Lowell to FJF, Jan. 23 and [Jan.] 28, 1884 (Huntington FU 14).

101. MS letter, Jan. 23, 1884 (Huntington FU 14).

102. *Browning to His American Friends: Letters between the Brownings, the Storys and James Russell Lowell 1841–1890*, ed. Gertrude Reese Hudson (New York, 1965), passim. For an eyewitness description of Browning and Lowell at the same dinner table, see M. A. D. Howe, "Victorian Poets: A Side Light," *Atlantic Monthly*, CLII (August, 1933), 225–27.

103. Transcript of letter, Lowell to Mrs. [G. W.] Smalley, Dec. 16, 1889 (Texas).

104. *LRB*, p. 245.

105. *BSP*, I, 112*.

106. "Browning's Plays and Poems," *North American Review*, LXVI (April, 1848), 357–400.

107. MS letter, Morison to Campbell, Mar. 17, 1884 (Brit. Mus. Add. MSS. 49525):

I have received your letter with much regret and even pain. I thought I had made it so plain to Miss Hickey that I should not be able to read a paper at the Browning Society this year that your note has taken me by surprise. I suppose that Miss Hickey's severe illness has prevented the real state of things being presented to you.

I have been nearly two months in the South of France with a view of getting rid of a painful bronchial irritation which causes nearly incessant coughing. Though partially successful, the return Northward even to the climate of Paris has caused a considerable return of my malady. I much fear that the air of London will be even less favourable.

Having been ill since November and half the time en voyage, I have not prepared a paper which you could read to the Society. The kind words you use in reference to this matter would be almost enough to induce me to make an effort at this eleventh hour. But the effort would be a vain one in my present condition.

However, Morison did make the effort "at this eleventh hour," and William C. DeVane, in his *Browning Handbook*, 2nd ed. (New York, 1955), p. 301, has described the paper as "perhaps the best critique in Browning's own day."
108. *BSP*, I, 122*.
109. *BSP*, I, xvii.
110. *BSP*, I, 129*.
111. MS letters, Meredith to FJF, Apr. 8, 1882 (Huntington FU 13); Meredith to Campbell, May 13 and July 16, 1884 (Brit. Mus. Add. MSS. 49525).
112. *BSP*, I, 129*.

CHAPTER VII

1. *BSP*, I, 173.
2. Quoted in F. G. R. Duckworth, *Browning: Background and Conflict* (New York, 1932), p. 67.
3. *BSP*, II, 312*.
4. Jerome Thale, "The Third Rossetti," *Western Humanities Review*, X (Summer, 1956), 277–84; *Germ*, No. 4 (May, 1850), pp. 187–92; Rossetti, "Portraits of Robert Browning," *Magazine of Art*, XIII (May, 1890), 182, 184.
5. MS letter to Campbell, June 19, 1884 (Brit. Mus. Add. MSS. 49526).
6. MS letter, Oct. 14, 1884 (Brit. Mus. Add. MSS. 49526).
7. Brit. Mus. Add. MSS. 49526. (Emphasis supplied.)
8. *Law Times*, CXLI (July 29, 1916), 244; Joseph Foster, *Men-at-the-Bar: A Biographical Handlist of the Members of the Various Inns of Court* (1885). Shortly before his death Mosely was Judge in the Native Tribunals, Cairo, Egypt. He was also the founder of the English branch of the Wagner Society.
9. *BSP*, II, 31*.
10. *FitzGerald*, p. 182. See also *Intimate Glimpses*, p. 99; Birrell, *Things Past Redress* (1937), p. 267.
11. [Birrell], "A Literary Causerie," *Speaker*, I (Jan. 4, 1890), 16.
12. *BSP*, II, 47*.
13. Quoted in St. John Ervine, *Bernard Shaw: His Life, Work and Friends* (1956), p. 150.
14. Herbert Hutchinson, *Jonathan Hutchinson: Life and Letters* (1946), passim.
15. *BSP*, II, 50*.
16. MS letter, Symons to Campbell, Nov. 11, 1886 (Brit. Mus. Add. MSS. 49522).
17. *Intimate Glimpses*, p. 33; Wedmore, *Memories* (1912), pp. 52–53.
18. *Intimate Glimpses*, p. 53; George Douglas, "Mr. Frederick Wedmore," *Bookman* (London), V (November, 1893), 44–45.
19. Rev. of *Fifine*, *Acad.*, III (July 1, 1872), 243–44; rev. of *Dramatic*

Idyls, Acad., XV (May 10, 1879), 403–04; rev. of performance of *A Blot in the 'Scutcheon, Acad.*, XXXII (Mar. 24, 1888), 212–13.

20. *BSP*, II, 54*.

21. See Robert Langbaum, *The Poetry of Experience: The Dramatic Monologue in Modern Literary Tradition* (New York, 1957); William O. Raymond, " 'The Jewelled Bow': A Study in Browning's Imagery and Humanism," in *The Infinite Moment and Other Essays in Robert Browning*, 2nd ed. (Toronto, 1965), pp. 193–213. I am unable to identify Johnson except to say that he was admitted to Jesus College, Cambridge, in 1882 (*Alumni Cantabrigienses*).

22. *BSP*, I, 14*.

23. *BSP*, II, 91*.

24. Brit. Mus. Add. MSS. 49526.

25. MS letter, Nov. 19, 1885 (Brit. Mus. Add. MSS. 49526).

26. MS letter, Rossetti to FJF, Mar. 1, 1887 (King's).

27. *BSP*, II, 118*.

28. Michael Field, *Works and Days*, ed. T. and D. C. Sturge Moore (1933), p. 169.

29. *BSP*, II, 126*–27*.

30. *Times*, Sept. 17, 1923, p. 18d.

31. *BSP*, II, 113.

32. MS letter, May 11, 1886 (Brit. Mus. Add. MSS. 49525).

33. *BSP*, II, 143*.

34. *BSP*, II, 131.

35. John G. Robertson, *Charles Harold Herford, 1853–1931* (1933).

36. *BSP*, II, 160*.

37. For a biographical sketch, see the *Liverpool Daily Post and Mercury*, Feb. 25, 1922, p. 9b.

38. *Times*, Jan. 3, 1913, p. 9c. At the bottom of Gonner's first letter of refusal to Furnivall, Apr. 18, 1886 (Baylor), is a note in the latter's handwriting, presumably to Dykes Campbell: "Will you ask Todd?"

39. MS letter, Apr. 23, 1886 (Baylor).

40. *BSP*, II, 279*.

41. *BSP*, II, 277*.

42. For some reports of this tour, see *BSP*, II, 114*–16*, 121*–22*; and for an estimate of its effect upon Browning's reputation in America, see Louise Greer, *Browning and America* (Chapel Hill, N.C., 1952), pp. 203–05.

43. MS postcard to FJF, May 29, [1886] (Baylor).

44. *BSP*, II, 166*.

45. MS letter to Hiram Corson, Jan. 17, 1885 (Cornell). (See Appendix B.)

46. *BSP*, II, 168*.

47. Noel, "Robert Browning," *Contemporary Review*, XLIV (November, 1883), 701–18.

48. *BSP*, II, 169*.

49. *BSP*, II, 182*–83*.

50. *Times*, May 21, 1926, p. 11e.

51. *BSP*, II, 163.

52. *BSP*, II, 186*.

53. *Times*, Apr. 4, 1890, p. 8c.

54. *BSP*, II, 210*.

55. *BSP*, II, 211*.
56. *BSP*, II, 326*n.
57. Joseph Foster, *Men-at-the-Bar* (1885). Michael Field recorded the following description of Radford in their diary on Apr. 8, 1891: "Her husband held me long in talk—he has a slow voice, aquiline features, & fixed eyes, curiously pied. He converses in the 'Middle Voice'—heaving himself all the time; but he says individual things, it is worth one's while to hear" (Brit. Mus. Add. MSS. 46779, fol. 55). Radford was secretary of the Rhymers' Club, to which W. B. Yeats belonged, and at one time delivered art lectures for the Cambridge Extension Scheme.
58. *PMG*, June 25, 1887, pp. 13–14. This article, which provides an extremely brief account of the paper and the meeting, has enabled me to identify Furnivall's notes. The notes are simply labelled "Radford" with no date given (on University College, London, letterhead stationery of 188-), but there can be no doubt that they are a record of this particular address. The *PMG* provides the following information: "A very interesting address was then given by Mr. Ernest Radford . . . on 'The Browningite of the Future,' or what poems of Browning will live fifty years hence." Furnivall's notes begin: "opinion on B. 50 years hence/ B.'ll survive in some respects."
    Radford's earlier remark is quoted from a MS postcard to FJF, Jan. 26, 1887 (Texas).
59. *BSP*, II, 214*–15*.
60. *Times*, Oct. 28, 1941, p. 7e.
61. *BSP*, II, 232*, 234*. The chairman of this meeting was the Reverend William A. Harrison (1828–92), for twenty-three years the Vicar of St. Anne's, South Lambeth (*Times*, Feb. 12, 1892, p. 5e).
62. *BSP*, II, 240*.
63. *Who Was Who*.
64. *BSP*, II, 248*–50*.
65. *Times*, Aug. 31, 1911, p. 7d; Stoddart, *The Life of Paracelsus, Theophrastus von Hohenheim, 1493–1541* (1911).
66. *BSP*, II, 268*.
67. *BSP*, II, xxxiii.
68. *BSP*, II, xxv.
69. *BSP*, II, 288*–89*.
70. *Times*, June 7, 1894, p. 10d.
71. *BSP*, II, 243*; MS letter to FJF, May 14, 1888 (Baylor).
72. *BSP*, II, 287*.
73. MS letter, Carpenter [to Slater], Oct. 15, 1887 (Baylor). Poor Miss Anna Swanwick, who was eager to have some friends hear the bishop's address, wrote in vain three times to Slater attempting to learn the correct date (MS letters, Nov. 22, [1888], Dec. 28, [1888], Jan. 7, [1889] [Baylor]).
74. MS letter, Nov. 2, 1888 (Baylor).
75. MS letters, Carpenter to Slater, Nov. 15, 1888; John Llewelyn Davies to FJF, Dec. 18, 1888 (Baylor).
76. *BSP*, II, 307.
77. *BSP*, II, 302*.
78. *BSP*, II, 313*–14*.

79. *Alumni Cantabrigienses.*
80. *BSP,* II, 334–35.
81. *BSP,* I, 114*.
82. *BSP,* II, 321*, 323*.
83. *BSP,* II, 331*.
84. MS letter to FJF, Sept. 14, 1887 (Texas).
85. MS letters, Symons to FJF, postmarked Sept. 26, 1888 (Baylor); Symons to Campbell, Feb. 8, 1889 (Brit. Mus. Add. MSS. 49523); Ethel Alleyne Ireland, "Introduction," in Mrs. Annie E. Ireland, *Longer Flights: Recollections and Studies* (1898), p. vii; *BSP,* II, 317*; III, 46*, 52*.
86. Rossetti, *Some Reminiscences* (1906), II, 481. Rossetti had been threatening for three decades to prepare some sort of exposition of *Sordello.* In 1858 he had mentioned the idea to Browning (Rossetti, *Ruskin: Rossetti: PreRaphaelitism: Papers, 1854–1862* [1899], pp. 218–19), and in 1885 it was still on his mind (MS letter to FJF, May 9, 1885 [Brit. Mus. Add. MSS. 49526]):

I am afraid my "promised transcription" of Sordello must be regarded as an *un*promised transcription. I never regarded myself as promising it any express way: but I perfectly remember that the subject was mooted & that I said it was a task the performance of wh[ich] I sh[oul]d regard with some predilection—& the matter has often recurred to my mind since then. But I have not buckled-to at the task, nor do I see any particular expectation of buckling-to: am clear that I c[oul]d not undertake to do anything producible by Octr. or Novr. next, for I have a good deal of other work already engaged for, & don't know when my hands w[oul]d be free for a new & volunteer job.

I don't know what Mrs. Orr has written about Sordello. 20 pages well employed might do a good deal for the general purport & substance of the poem. What I most thought of however was going thru the poem page by page, &, wherever a difficulty or uncertainty occurs to me, offering any observation for wh[ich] I might feel myself qualified—& this might perhaps make a book hardly shorter than Sordello itself.

But Professor Alexander's paper covered precisely this ground, and so the study which Rossetti finally offered in 1889 was merely an examination of one of the poem's sources.
87. *BSP,* III, 8*. MS letter, FJF to Mrs. Dykes Campbell, Dec. 16, 1889 (Brit. Mus. Add. MSS. 49525):

I've been very busy since Friday when the news of Browning's death reacht me by telegraph. The Dean of Westm[inste]r refused me to make an offer of an Abbey burial, but I suppose the Government has interfered. One could hardly believe that the author of *Asolando* would die so soon. I was up till 1.30 this morn[in]g writing a 2nd article on him, but it's [held] over till tomorrow.

His first article on Browning appeared in the *PMG* on Dec. 14, pp. 1–2; the second article appeared Dec. 18, p. 3.

88. MS note to unidentified correspondent [ca. Dec. 17, 1889], on the back of a letter from F. W. Farrar (King's).

89. MS letter, Feb. 25, 1890 (Cambridge Add. MSS. 7509, fol. 164).

90. For a list of those who attended, see *BSP*, III, 15*.

91. *BSP*, III, 34*.

92. Berdoe's speech was much longer than the transactions indicate. For a full transcript of the speech in its pristine glory, one must consult a pamphlet published by the Victoria Street and International Society for the Protection of Animals from Vivisection (of which Berdoe was member of the central executive committee), entitled *Anti-Vivisection at the Browning Society* (1890). Berdoe was exceptionally agitated about the subject at this time because Browning, just a few months before his death, had given his moral support to a proposed new antivivisection hospital. On Dec. 19, 1889, while other Browningites were mourning their poet's death, Berdoe wrote to Furnivall (MS letter, King's): "Did I tell you of the nice letter I had from . . . B. recently about Anti-V.? I will bring it up to the next [Browning Society] Committee." For a discussion of Browning's relationship with the antivivisectionist cause, see William C. DeVane, *A Browning Handbook*, 2nd ed. (New York, 1955), pp. 440–42, 539.

93. *BSP*, III, 55*–56*.

94. *Times*, Sept. 7, 1912, p. 9e.

95. MS letter, Mrs. Laffan to FJF, Jan. 16, 1890 (Baylor); *BSP*, III, 57*.

96. *BSP*, III, 80*, 82*, 84*n.

97. *BSP*, III, 98*.

98. MS letter, FJF to Slater, Sept. 25, 1888 (King's). Lacking his first name, I have been unable to identify the Reverend Mr. Hawker, as *Crockford's Clerical Directory* for 1890 lists five Hawkers. Of these, the two most likely ones seem to be Henry Ernest Hawker and John Hawker, especially the latter.

99. MS letter, July 25, [1889] (Baylor). I have so dated the letter for the following reasons: (1) in the summer of 1888 the society's financial crisis was not yet apparent, and (2) by the summer of 1890 Slater had been replaced by E. E. Davies.

100. MS letter (Chicago: Jenkin Lloyd Jones papers).

101. MS letter, Aug. 21, 1891 (Chicago: Jones papers).

102. MS letter, Davies to Jones, Feb. 4, 1892 (Chicago: Jones papers).

103. MS letters, Seaman [to Slater], June 4, 7, and 15, 1889 (Baylor); *Who Was Who*.

104. "Recollections of Browning," *Westminster Gazette*, Feb. 24, 1893, p. 2. The Shelley Society also seems to have expired very slowly. On Apr. 26, 1901, Harry Buxton Forman wrote to Slater (MS letter, Pariser) of "a promise I have made to Wise that I will meet the old Shelley Society Committee for business *when* & where the Chairman may appoint."

CHAPTER VIII

1. *BSP*, I, 19.
2. See, e.g., William G. Kingsland's views on this subject in *Poet-Lore*, V (January, 1893), 53.
3. For his personal relationship with Browning, see Stanford, *Pages from an Unwritten Diary* (1914), p. 234. After the entertainment Miss Marx wrote to her sister: "The place was crowded, & as all sorts of 'literary' & other 'swells' were there I felt ridiculously nervous—but [got] on capitally. Mrs. Sutherland Orr . . . wants to take me to see Browning & recite his own poems to him!" (Quoted in Chushichi Tsuzuki, *The Life of Eleanor Marx, 1855–1898* [Oxford, 1967], p. 68).
4. Munro, *Furnivall*, pp. 65–66.
5. MS letter, RB to FJF, Mar. 27, 1884 (Huntington FU 14).
6. *BSP*, I, xix. The first entertainment (June 30, 1882) was so hastily put together that Emily Hickey wrote a public letter of apology and explanation afterwards (*Acad.*, XXII [July 15, 1882], 50).
7. MS letter (King's).
8. MS letter (King's).
9. George W. Curtis, "Editor's Easy Chair," *Harper's New Monthly Magazine*, LXXVII (October, 1888), 798.
10. *BSP*, I, 128*.
11. Domett, *Diary*, p. 298.
12. "The Browning Society," *Saturday Review*, LVIII (Dec. 6, 1884), 721.
13. Of Browning's nine plays, *Strafford*, *King Victor and King Charles*, *The Return of the Druses*, and *A Blot in the 'Scutcheon* were written for W. C. Macready, and *Colombe's Birthday* for Charles Kean; but *Pippa Passes*, *Luria*, *A Soul's Tragedy*, and "In a Balcony" were intended to be closet dramas.
14. Charlton, "Browning as a Dramatist," *Bulletin of the John Rylands Library*, XXIII (April, 1939), 67.
15. *BSP*, II, 7*.
16. Quoted in Munro, *Furnivall*, p. 60.
17. *The Letters of Oscar Wilde*, ed. Rupert Hart-Davis (New York, 1962), p. 310.
18. *BSP*, II, 73*, 97*.
19. *BSP*, II, 167*.
20. MS letter, Oct. 28, 1888 (Baylor).
21. Ireland, "How It Strikes an Outsider," *Longer Flights: Recollections and Studies* (1898), pp. 131–35.
22. Heloise E. Hersey, "Browning in America," *New England Magazine*, N.S. I (January, 1890), 543.
23. Annie R. Wall, "The Sordello Club," *Poet-Lore*, I (September, 1889), 424.
24. *BSP*, II, 135*; "Notes and News," *Academy*, XXIX (Mar. 13, 1886), 182.
25. "Notes and News," *Acad.*, XXIX (Feb. 6, 1886), 92.
26. "American Jottings," *Acad.*, XXIII (Mar. 10, 1883), 169.
27. C. H. C., "Mark Twain and Browning" (letter), *Spectator*, CXXIII (July 26, 1919), 114.
28. Curtis, "Editor's Easy Chair," p. 798.

29. Stedman, *Victorian Poets*, rev. ed. (Cambridge, Mass., 1887), II, 430; Laura Stedman and George M. Gould, *Life and Letters of Edmund Clarence Stedman* (New York, 1910), II, 46–47.

30. Frederick M. Padelford, "Browning Out West," *Cornhill Magazine*, N.S. XXII (February, 1907), 253–62.

31. Corson, "Browning Clubs in the United States" (letter), *Literary World* (Boston), XIV (Apr. 21, 1883), 127.

32. Maria S. Porter, "Robert Browning at Home," unidentified newspaper clipping, dated Dec. 18, 1889, in Browning scrapbook of William Lyon Phelps (Baylor). For another version of the story, see the *Literary World* (Boston), XXIII (Apr. 23, 1892), 153.

33. *DAB.*

34. The details of this slightly hysterical occasion may be found in the Browning scrapbook of Jenkin Lloyd Jones (Baylor).

35. "Notes and News," *Acad.*, XXIX (Mar. 13, 1886), 182.

36. "Current Criticism," *Critic*, N.S. VI (Nov. 6, 1886), 228.

37. [R. G. Cooke, ed.], *Casual Essays of "The Sun"* (New York, 1905), pp. 150–51.
    I have not attempted to provide a full account of the Browning clubs in America, since that ground has been covered so admirably by Louise Greer in her *Browning and America* (Chapel Hill, N.C., 1952), pp. 163–86. Detailed reports of the activities of both the English and American clubs are to be found in *Poet-Lore, BSP*, and the *Academy*.

38. See the news columns of the *Academy* and the *Cambridge Review* during November, 1881, for details.

39. Blakeney, [Letter], *Cambridge Review*, XI (Feb. 6, 1890), 187.

40. *BSP*, I, 149n.

41. *BSP*, II, 280*; T. A. Haultain, *Goldwin Smith: His Life and Opinions* (1913), p. 46.

42. [Kingsland], "The Browning Society," *Islington News*, July 7, 1883, p. 4e.

43. *Poet-Lore*, V (January, 1893), 53.

44. *Mary Gladstone (Mrs. Drew): Her Diaries and Letters*, ed. Lucy Masterman, 2nd ed. (1930), p. 347.

45. Doyle, *A Duet, with an Occasional Chorus* (1899), pp. 218–35.

46. Dorothy Brant Brazier, "Days of Browning, Dickens Fade Away," Seattle *Times*, Feb. 28, 1966, p. 31a.

47. MS letter, RB to FJF, Nov. 19, 1885 (Huntington FU 14).

48. *NL*, pp. 216–17, 225; *DNB*; Orr, "Mr. Browning's Place in Literature," *Contemporary Review*, XXIII (May, 1874), 934–65.

49. Gladstone, *Diaries*, p. 454.

50. Letter to R. M. Leonard, Jan. 21, 1889, quoted in W. Hall Griffin and H. C. Minchin, *The Life of Robert Browning*, 3rd ed. (1938) p. 271n.

51. *LRB*, pp. 260–61.

52. MS letter, Nov. 19, 1885 (Huntington FU 14). On Sept. 7, 1885, Browning wrote to Furnivall: "Certainly nobody will ever treat my wife and myself more graciously and partially . . . than you; so, by all means biographize about both of us" (*LRB*, pp. 238–39). The planned biography seems to have been abandoned after Browning offered objections to Furnivall's treatment of Mrs. Orr.

53. MS letter, Nov. 28, 1885 (Huntington FU 14).
54. "The Diary of Miss Evelyn Barclay," *Baylor Bulletin* (Baylor Univ. Browning Interests, Ser. 5), XXXV (December, 1932), 9.
55. MS letter, May 16, [1890] (Brit. Mus. Add. MSS. 45856, fol. 44–47).
56. *Browning to His American Friends*, ed. Gertrude Reese Hudson (New York, 1965), p. 161n.
57. *Poet-Lore*, III (October, 1891), 522–28; Anna B. McMahan, *Dial*, XII (September, 1891), 140–43.
58. Field, *Works and Days*, ed. T. and D. C. Sturge Moore (1933), p. 216.
59. Phelps, *Autobiography with Letters* (New York, 1939), pp. 449–50.
60. MS note by FJF (Ashley A.2527), explaining RB's letter to FJF, Feb. 17, 1882 (*LRB*, p. 209).
61. *London Quarterly Review*, N.S. XVII (October, 1891), 18.
62. Orr, "The Religious Opinions of Robert Browning," *Contemporary Review*, LX (December, 1891), 876–91.
63. *BSP*, I, 2*.
64. "Literary Notes," *Critic*, I (Oct. 22, 1881), 294.
65. *Nation*, XXXIII (Nov. 24, 1881), 415.
66. *Cambridge Review*, III (Nov. 30, 1881), 103.
67. *Land and Water*, Dec. 31, 1889; *Truth*, Jan. 2, 1890, both clippings in Browning scrapbook of William Lyon Phelps (Baylor).
68. "Passing Notes," *Echo*, Oct. 29, 1891, p. 1d; Furnivall, "The Browning Society" (letter), *Echo*, Oct. 31, 1881, p. 1f.
69. The literature of the year, *Daily News* (London), Dec. 31, 1881, p. 5c; Furnivall, "The Browning Society" (letter), *Daily News*, Jan. 2, 1882, p. 2g.
70. "The Browning Society," *PMG*, Dec. 22, 1881, p. 11; Furnivall, "The Browning Society" (letter), *PMG*, Jan. 2, 1882, p. 12. Furnivall was not being entirely candid. In 1882 he printed James Thomson's paper in *BSP* after it had been rejected by several periodicals.
71. *Athenaeum*, Dec. 28, 1889, p. 897.
72. "The Browning Society," *Saturday Review*, LIII (Jan. 7, 1882), 12.
73. *BSP*, I, 2*n.
74. "The Browning Society," *Saturday Review*, LVIII (Dec. 6, 1884), 722.
75. "Browningismus," *Saturday Review*, LXIII (Apr. 23, 1887), 596.
76. *Saturday Review*, LXXI (May 30, 1891), 666.
77. *Acad.*, XXVII (Apr. 18, 1885), 277.
78. Domett, *Diary*, p. 298.
79. *Journals and Correspondence of Lady Eastlake* (Elizabeth Rigby), ed. C. E. Smith (1895), II, 274.
80. Terry, *The Story of My Life* (New York, 1908), p. 61; MS letter, Jowett to FJF, July 5, 1881 (Huntington FU 13).
81. Wilde, "The Poets and the People. By One of the Latter" (1887), in Stuart Mason [pseud. of Christopher Sclater Millard], *Bibliography of Oscar Wilde* (1914), p. 148.
82. William B. Carpenter, *Some Pages of My Life* (1911), p. 201.
83. James K. Stephen, *Lapsus Calami and Other Verses* (Cambridge, England, 1905), p. 25.
84. "The Whitey-Browning Society," *Punch*, LXXXIV (Apr. 21, 1883), 192.
85. Eliza O. White, "A Browning Courtship," *Atlantic Monthly*, LXII (July, 1888), 99–112.

86. "Notes and News," *Poet-Lore*, V (March, 1893), 166–67.
87. According to the *Times* obituary of Miss Buss (Dec. 25, 1894, p. 8b), sometimes one-third of the students at Girton were graduates of her school.
88. Alice Zimmern, *Times*, Mar. 23, 1939, p. 21d; Helen Zimmern, *Times*, Jan. 13, 1934, p. 12f.
89. *Acad.*, XXIX (Mar. 20, 1886), 200. In Furnivall's own copy of his Browning bibliography (Pariser) is this note: "Lily Revell, then at Girton, told me by letter about it."
90. *Acad.*, XXIX (Apr. 3, 1886), 263.
91. Quoted in *BSP*, II, 134*.
92. *Punch*, XC (Apr. 17, 1886), 186.
93. *Funny Folks*, XII (Mar. 27, 1886), 98.
94. *Fun*, N.S. XLIII (Mar. 31, 1886), 146.
95. *Journal of Education*, N.S. VIII (May 1, 1886), 207–08.
96. "Events of the Week," *Judy*, XXXVIII (Apr. 7, 1886), 157.
97. "Daily Gossip," *Echo*, Apr. 3, 1886, p. 2.
98. Lang, "Esoteric Browningism," *Forum*, VI (November, 1888), 303. The metaphor was not original: Dr. Berdoe introduced his paper of Oct. 28, 1887, by saying, "If all the hard things which have been said of Mr. Browning's works were in any sense true, we should have in his 'Childe Roland to the Dark Tower came' a very good allegory concerning him and his students" (*BSP*, II, 200–01).
99. *BSP*, II, 134*.
100. *BSP*, I, 43*.

CHAPTER IX

1. Masson, "Robert Browning: A Recollection," in *A Volunteer Haversack*, ed. Archibald S. Walker (Edinburgh, 1902), p. 109.
2. Furnivall, "Browning's Footman Ancestor" (letter), *Acad.*, LXII (Apr. 12, 1902), 394.
3. MS letter, May 8, 1902 (Brit. Mus. Add. MSS. 45563, fol. 147–50).
4. Duckworth, *Browning: Background and Conflict* (New York, 1932), p. 67.
5. *Notebook of the Shelley Society* (1888), p. 7.
6. MS letters, RB to FJF, Dec. 9 and 13, 1882 (Huntington FU 13); *BSP*, I, 48*.
7. Furnivall's two circulars on the subject, dated Apr. 7 and May 8, 1882, may be seen at Texas. For Browning's response to the gift, see Lilian Whiting, *The Brownings: Their Life and Art* (Boston, 1911), p. 244; *NL*, pp. 274–75.
8. MS letters, RB to FJF, June 24 and 25, 1883 (Huntington FU 13). A copy of Furnivall's circular, dated May 9, 1883, is at Texas. A description of the gift is found in the Sotheby, Wilkinson, and Hodge auction catalogue, *The Browning Collections* (April and May 1913), p. 76.
9. MS letter, RB to FJF, Dec. 24, 1883 (Huntington FU 13); *FitzGerald*, pp. 170, 174.
10. MS postcard, FJF to Corson, June 13, 1883 (Cornell); MS letter, RB to FJF, Jan. 29, 1884 (Huntington FU 14).

11. MS letter, RB to FJF, Aug. 16, 1885 (Baylor).
12. "Robert Browning," *Critic*, N.S. XIII (Jan. 4, 1890), 10.
13. Quoted from the MS notebook kept by Curtis of his conversations with Browning between 1879 and 1885 (Baylor).
14. *LRB*, p. 212.
15. Roma A. King, Jr., *Robert Browning's Finances from His Own Account Book*, Baylor Univ. Browning Interests, Ser. 15 (Waco, Tex., 1947), p. 18.
16. Furnivall, "The Late Mr. George Smith," *Athenaeum*, May 4, 1901, p. 568. For the last four years of his life, we have a record of Browning's income from the sale of his poetry (King, *Browning's Finances*, p. 19):

1886	£ 436 5s.
1887	£ 756 5s.
1888	£1,252 2s.
1889	£1,013 4s.

These figures do not include income from authorized American editions.
17. *LRB*, p. 218.
18. *NL*, p. 282; MS letter, RB to FJF, Aug. 22, 1882 (Huntington FU 13).
19. Hickey, "Glorious Robert Browning," *Nineteenth Century*, LXX (October, 1911), 753.
20. "Notes and News," *Acad.*, XXIV (Dec. 1, 1883), 364.
21. Since I am here chiefly concerned with the actual sales of Browning's books, I have deliberately skirted the issue of his critical reputation, which is of course another matter. For a judicious survey of the latter question, see William C. DeVane, "Robert Browning," in *The Victorian Poets: A Guide to Research*, ed. Frederic E. Faverty (Cambridge, Mass., 1956), pp. 66–67.
22. "Death of Robert Browning," *PMG*, Dec. 13, 1889, p. 6. The story sounds apocryphal, but Browning himself is said to have told it to friends (James Sully, *My Life and Friends: A Psychologist's Memories* [1918], p. 166).
23. *Times*, Mar. 17, 1924, p. 14b.
24. Transcript of letter, Matheson to Campbell, Feb. 27, 1885, with annotation by Mrs. Campbell (Brit. Mus. Add. MSS. 49526).
25. Benson, *As We Were: A Victorian Peep Show* (1930), pp. 123–24.
26. Farrar, *Men I Have Known* (New York, 1897), p. 63.
27. *LRB*, p. 207.
28. W. G. Kingsland, "Browning: Some Personal Reminiscences," *Baylor Bulletin* (Baylor Univ. Browning Interests, Ser. 2), XXXIV (July, 1931), 35.
29. "The Browning Society," *Saturday Review*, LIII (Jan. 7, 1882), 12; rev. of Mrs. Orr's *Life and Letters*, *Saturday Review*, LXXI (May 30, 1891), 666; "The Browning Society," *PMG*, Dec. 22, 1881, p. 11.
30. MS letter, Dec. 24, 1881 (Baylor).
31. MS letter, Friday evening, n.d. (Huntington FU 14). Though the letter is undated, probably it is the one to which Browning refers in a letter to Mrs. FitzGerald, Aug. 6, 1881: "The founder [Furnivall] applied to my Sister for 'names of friends who might wish to join'—but she reso-

lutely refused to give any information of the kind—saying that I had
kept free of all attempts to help myself to a reputation, except by writing books" (*FitzGerald*, p. 119).

32. MS letter to unidentified correspondent, June 26, 1882 (Baylor). The
Browning Society issued photographs of Browning (in three sizes), of
his home, and of some of the paintings which had figured in his poetry.
33. *NL*, p. 313.
34. *LRB*, p. 212, where the letter is misdated as 1882. For Yates's letter
to Browning, see *Intimate Glimpses*, p. 90. The note appeared in the
World, Nov. 9, 1881, p. 13.
35. *LRB*, p. 202.
36. *Ibid.*, p. 200.
37. *FitzGerald*, p. 125.
38. *LRB*, p. 227. A transcription of Campbell's reply, Mar. 16, 1884, is in
the British Museum (Add. MSS. 49526). (See Appendix B.)
39. *NL*, p. 360.
40. MS letter, RB to FJF, July 21, 1886 (Baylor).
41. Allingham, *A Diary*, ed. H. Allingham and D. Radford (1907), p. 373.
42. L. B. Walford, "London Letter," *Critic*, N.S. XIII (Jan. 4, 1890), 8.
43. MS letter, RB to FJF, Dec. 20, 1886 (Huntington FU 15).
44. Fry, in Munro, *Furnivall*, pp. 61–62; W. G. Kingsland, "Robert Browning—the Man. Some Further Reminiscences," *Poet-Lore*, V (May,
1893), 233. Kingsland does not mention Furnivall's name, but elsewhere he connects him with this episode, in an unpublished MS (Baylor) entitled "Robert Browning: A Personal Note to Professor A. J.
Armstrong."
45. *LRB*, p. 288.
46. Some of these letters have not been published; others appear in *LRB*
and a pamphlet printed by M. Buxton Forman, *Ten Letters of Robert
Browning Concerning Miss Alma Murray* (Edinburgh, 1929). In the
latter (p. 14) is Browning's refusal to write another tragedy.
47. The phrase is used in a MS letter, RB to FJF, Oct. 8, 1881 (Huntington
FU 13), but the same attitude is expressed in many other letters, both
published and unpublished.
48. Maria S. Porter, "Robert Browning at Home," unidentified newspaper
clipping, dated Dec. 18, 1889, in Browning scrapbook of William L.
Phelps (Baylor).
49. MS letter, Dec. 24, 1881 (Baylor).
50. Lilian Whiting, *The Brownings*, pp. 261–62.
51. Lang, rev. of *Life and Letters of Robert Browning* by Alexandra Orr,
Contemporary Review, LX (July, 1891), 79.

CONCLUSION

1. *BSP*, III, ix–x.
2. *BSP*, II, 278*.
3. MS letter, Sept. 2, 1901 (Bodleian MS. Eng. Misc. d. 177, fol. 129–30).
4. MS letter, Jan. 2, 1886 (Huntington FU 15).
5. *BSP*, II, 275*, 312*.
6. *BSP*, I, 2*.

7. MS letter, Mar. 8, 1887 (Ashley 1449, fol. 15-17). For further details of this case, see MS letters, Rossetti to FJF, Mar. 11 and 16, 1887 (Huntington FU 15); Rossetti to T. J. Wise, Mar. 11, 1889 (Ashley 1448, fol. 61-63). On Aveling and Eleanor Marx, see Felix Barker, "The Life and Strange Death of Eleanor Marx," *Cornhill Magazine*, CLXVIII (Autumn, 1955), 167-79; Lewis S. Feuer, "Marxian Tragedians: A Death in the Family," *Encounter*, XIX (November, 1962), 23-32; Chushichi Tsuzuki, *The Life of Eleanor Marx, 1855-1898* (Oxford, 1967).

APPENDIX A

1. DeVane, *A Browning Handbook*, 2nd ed. (New York, 1955), p. 584.
2. *Library Journal*, XXVIII (February, 1903), 52; March, p. 104.
3. Some sets of *BSP* also contain, bound in at the end of each volume, programs of Browning Society entertainments and other miscellaneous publications of the society.
4. MS letter, Nov. 20, [1887] (Baylor).
5. *BSP*, III, facing 102.
6. Copy at Baylor.

BIBLIOGRAPHY

I. Unpublished Sources

Ideally a study of the Browning Society would be based upon the papers of Dr. F. J. Furnivall and the four honorary secretaries—Miss Emily Hickey, James Dykes Campbell, Walter Slater, and E. E. Davies—but, needless to say, much of this material has disappeared from view. We are fortunate in the case of Dr. Furnivall, at least, since most of his correspondence was acquired some years ago by the Huntington Library; and a fairly sizeable collection of miscellaneous papers, as well as his personal library, may be found in the Library of King's College, London. Miss Hickey's papers, I regret to say, I have been unable to locate, though they were intact as late as 1927, when Enid Maud Dinnis, her literary executor, used her correspondence and diaries in writing a memoir. At the death of Miss Dinnis in 1942, her personal effects were bequeathed to her sister Aimee Dinnis; but beyond this point I found no clues, despite the kind assistance of Miss Dinnis' niece and nephew. As for Campbell, most of his papers were given to the British Museum by his wife. Walter Slater's papers and library were sold at public auction in 1945, and the two largest groups of correspondence are now at Baylor University and the University of Texas. However, two folders of correspondence from and dealing with Dr. Furnivall, which were sold at the same time, cannot be traced. E. E. Davies seems to have left no descendants, and I have consequently had no success in locating his papers.

The following list is arranged alphabetically by the abbreviations used in my notes. In each instance I have attempted to provide an extremely brief description of the materials in the collection which I have used.

Ashley   The Ashley Library (of Thomas J. Wise), British Museum. *Correspondence of Wise.*
Balliol   The Balliol College Library, Oxford. *Browning letters.*
Baylor   The Armstrong Browning Library, Baylor University. *Browning letters; correspondence of Walter Slater.*
Bodleian   The Bodleian Library, Oxford University. *Papers of James Thomson.*

252 / 5BIBLIOGRAPHY

Boston   The Boston Public Library. *Letters of Hiram Corson.*
Brit. Mus. The British Museum. *Correspondence of James Dykes Camp-*
            bell; Browning collections of Hall Griffin; miscellaneous corre-
            spondence.
Cambridge The Cambridge University Library. *Correspondence of E. H.*
            Blakeney.
Chicago   The University of Chicago Library. *Correspondence of Jenkin*
            Lloyd Jones and Edith Rickert.
Cornell   The Collection of Regional History and University Archives,
            John M. Olin Research Library, Cornell University. *Papers of*
            Hiram Corson.
Harvard   The Harvard College Library. *Miscellaneous correspondence.*
Huntington The Huntington Library and Art Gallery, San Marino, Califor-
            nia. *Correspondence of Furnivall.*
King's   The King's College (London) Library. *Furnivall's personal li-*
            brary and some of his correspondence.
Pariser   Private collection of Sir Maurice P. Pariser of Manchester,
            England. *Correspondence of T. J. Wise and Walter Slater; an-*
            notated copy of Furnivall's Browning bibliography. [This col-
            lection has since been dispersed in a sale at Sotheby's, Dec.
            4–5, 1967.]
Symington The Symington Collection, Rutgers University Library. *Miscel-*
            laneous correspondence.
Texas   The Miriam Lutcher Stark Library, University of Texas (Aus-
            tin). *Browning and Lowell letters; correspondence of Walter*
            Slater; materials relating to the Outram lawsuit.

II. *Wills (Somerset House, London)*

Davies, Edward Ernest Underwood:
    d. June 24, 1944.
Drewry, Louisa: d. July 16, 1916.
Fleming, Albert: d. Mar. 31, 1923.
Lewis, Mary A.: d. Mar. 26, 1905.
Martley, William G.:
    d. Feb. 17, 1920.
Ormerod, Helen J.:
    d. Feb. 11, 1926.
Outram, Leonard S.:
    d. May 6, 1901.
Radford, Ernest:
    d. Sept. 25, 1919.
Revell, William F.:
    d. Feb. 20, 1911.
Slater, Walter B.: d. July 4, 1944.

III. *Published Sources*

Academy. The "Notes and News" column regularly carried reports of Browning Society activities, often written by Furnivall.

Allingham, William. *A Diary*, ed. H. Allingham and D. Radford. London: Macmillan, 1907.

"American Jottings." *Academy*, XXIII (Mar. 10, 1883), 168–69.

Anti-Vivisection at the Browning Society. London: Victoria Street and International Society for the Protection of Animals from Vivisection, [1890].

Armstrong, A. J., ed. *Intimate Glimpses from Browning's Letter File*. Baylor Univ. Browning Interests, 8th Ser. Waco: Baylor University Press, 1934.

Axon, William E. A. "F.J.F." *Bookman* (London), XLI (October, 1911), 42–43.

Bacon, Leonard. "Fifty Years After." *Saturday Review of Literature*, XXI (Dec. 9, 1939), 3–4, 16.

Baddeley, Sir Vincent. "The Ancestry of Robert Browning, the Poet." *Genealogists' Magazine*, VIII (1938), 1–6.

——. "Browning's Footman Ancestor" (letter). *TLS*, Feb. 21, 1948, p. 107. Reply by Wilfred Partington, Apr. 10, p. 205. Rejoinder by Baddeley, Apr. 17, p. 219.

Badger, Kingsbury. "Mark Pattison and the Victorian Scholar." *MLQ*, VI (December, 1945), 423–47.

Barclay, Evelyn. "The Diary of Miss Evelyn Barclay." *Baylor Bulletin* (Baylor Univ. Browning Interests, Ser. 5), XXXV (December, 1932), 3–10.

Barker, Felix. "The Life and Strange Death of Eleanor Marx." *Cornhill Magazine*, CLXVIII (Autumn, 1955), 167–79.

Barnett, Percy A.: obituary. *Times*, Oct. 28, 1941, p. 7e.

Bayne, Peter: obituary. *Athenaeum*, Feb. 15, 1886, p. 220.

Baynes, Norman H. *A Bibliography of the Works of J. B. Bury*. With a Memoir. Cambridge: Cambridge University Press, 1929.

Benson, Edward F. *As We Were: A Victorian Peep Show*. London: Longmans, Green, 1930.

Berdoe, Edward. *Browning and the Christian Faith: The Evidences of Christianity from Browning's Point of View*. London: Allen, 1896.

——. *The Browning Cyclopaedia: A Guide to the Study of the Works of Robert Browning*. London: Sonnenschein, 1892.

——. *Browning's Message to His Time*. London: Sonnenschein, 1890.

——, ed. *Browning Studies*. London: Allen, 1895.

——. *A Primer of Browning*. London: Routledge, 1904.

—— [pseud. "AEsculapius Scalpel"]. *St. Bernard's: The Romance of a Medical Student*. London: Sonnenschein, 1887.

Berdoe, Edward: funeral. *Times*, Mar. 9, 1916, p. 12c.

Besant, Walter. "Mr. Dykes Campbell." *Athenaeum*, June 8, 1895, p. 739.

Birrell, Augustine. *The Collected Essays and Addresses of Augustine Birrell*. 3 vols. London: Dent, 1922.

B[irrell], A[ugustine]. "A Literary Causerie." *Speaker*, I (Jan. 4, 1890), 16–17.

————. *Things Past Redress*. London: Faber and Faber, 1937.

Bishop, Morris. *A History of Cornell*. Ithaca: Cornell University Press, 1962.

Blackie, John Stuart. *The Letters of John Stuart Blackie to His Wife*, ed. A. S. Walker. Edinburgh and London: Blackwood, 1910.

Blakeney, E. H. [Letter.] *Cambridge Review*, XI (Feb. 6, 1890), 187.

Blakeney, E. H.: obituary. *Times*, Aug. 2, 1955, p. 9b.

Blathwayt, Raymond. "Browning and His Teaching: A Talk with Dr. Edward Berdoe." *Great Thoughts from Master Minds*, XLI (March–September, 1904), 312–14.

The Boston Browning Society's Papers. New York: Macmillan, 1897.

Brazier, Dorothy Brant. "Days of Browning, Dickens Fade Away." Seattle *Times*, Feb. 28, 1966, p. 31a.

Broughton, Leslie N., Clark S. Northup, and Robert Pearsall, comp. *Robert Browning: A Bibliography, 1830–1950*. Ithaca: Cornell University Press, 1953.

Browning, Robert. *The Browning Society . . . Being Letters from Robert Browning to James Dykes Campbell*, ed. Clement Shorter. London: privately printed, 1917.

————. *Browning to His American Friends: Letters Between the Brownings, the Storys and James Russell Lowell 1841–1890*, ed. Gertrude Reese Hudson. New York: Barnes and Noble, 1965.

————. *Dearest Isa: Robert Browning's Letters to Isabella Blagden*, ed. Edward C. McAleer. Austin: University of Texas Press, 1951.

————. *Learned Lady: Letters from Robert Browning to Mrs. Thomas FitzGerald 1876–1889*, ed. Edward C. McAleer: Cambridge: Harvard University Press, 1966.

————. *Letters of Robert Browning*, ed. Thurman L. Hood. New Haven: Yale University Press, 1933.

———— [erroneous attribution]. *A Miniature*. With a Prefatory Note by F. J. Furnivall. [London], 1904.

————. *New Letters of Robert Browning*, ed. William C. DeVane and Kenneth L. Knickerbocker. New Haven: Yale University Press, 1950.

————. *Pauline: A Fragment of a Confession* [fac. of 1st ed.], ed. Thomas J. Wise. London: Clay and Taylor, 1886.

————. *Strafford*. With Notes and Pref. by Emily Hickey and Introd. by Samuel R. Gardiner. London: Bell, 1884.

————. *Ten Letters of Robert Browning Concerning Miss Alma Murray*, ed. M. Buxton Forman. Edinburgh: privately printed, 1929.

Browning, Robert Barrett. "A Complaint" (letter). *Athenaeum*, July 9, 1892, p. 66.

"The Browning Clubs in Boston, U.S." *Athenaeum*, Aug. 21, 1886, p. 252.

"Browning Dead." *Hawk*, Dec. 17, 1889, p. 669.

"The Browning Society." *Pall Mall Gazette*, Dec. 22, 1881, p. 11.

"The Browning Society." *Pall Mall Gazette*, June 25, 1887, pp. 13–14.

Browning Society Prospectus and Membership List: *You Are Invited to Join the Browning Society*. London: Trübner, August, 1881: January, 1882; November, 1882; etc.

"The Browning Society," *Saturday Review*, LIII (Jan. 7, 1882), 12–13.

"The Browning Society," *Saturday Review*, LVIII (Dec. 6, 1884), 721–22.

The Browning Society's Papers. 3 vols. London: Trübner, 1881–91.

"Browningismus." *Saturday Review,* LXIII (Apr. 23, 1887), 595–96.

Bruce, Mary L. *Anna Swanwick: A Memoir and Recollections, 1813–1899.* London: Unwin, 1903.

Bulkeley, Henry John: obituary. *Malvern News,* May 6, 1922, p. 4e.

Burtis, Mary Elizabeth, *Moncure Conway, 1832–1907.* New Brunswick, N.J.: Rutgers University Press, 1952.

Buss, Frances Mary: obituary. *Times,* Dec. 25, 1894, p. 8b.

C., C. H. "Mark Twain and Browning" (letter). *Spectator,* CXXIII (July 26, 1919), 114.

C., R. "Making a Dictionary: A Chat with Dr. F. J. Furnivall." *Great Thoughts from Master Minds,* LIII (April-September, 1910), 88–90.

Campbell, James Dykes. *Samuel Taylor Coleridge: A Narrative of the Events of His Life.* With a Memoir of the author by Leslie Stephen. 2nd ed. London: Macmillan, 1896.

Campbell, James Dykes, and Walter B. Slater. [Circular announcing the Furnivall Fund.] London, 1888.

Carpenter, William B. *Some Pages of My Life.* London: Williams and Norgate, 1911.

Carter, John, and Graham Pollard. *An Enquiry into the Nature of Certain Nineteenth Century Pamphlets.* London: Constable, 1934.

———. *The Firm of Charles Ottley, Landon & Co.: Footnote to an Enquiry.* London: Hart-Davis, 1948.

Chambers, E. K. "The Browning Cyclopaedia" (letter). *Academy,* XLI (Feb. 6, 1892), 135–36.

Charlton, H. B. "Browning as a Dramatist." *Bulletin of the John Rylands Library,* XXIII (April, 1939), 33–67.

"Chats on Coming Books: Dr. Edward Berdoe's 'Browning Cyclopaedia.'" *Pall Mall Gazette,* Dec. 9, 1891, pp. 1–2.

Chesterton, G. K. *Robert Browning.* English Men of Letters. London: Macmillan, 1903.

"The (Choco)late-est News." *Fun,* N.S. XLIII (Mar. 31, 1886), 146.

C[larke, Helen A.]. "Browning as Others See Him: Berdoe, Jones, and Nettleship." *Poet-Lore,* VIII (May, 1896), 265–70.

Clarke, Dr. John H.: obituary. *Times,* Nov. 26, 1931, p. 16d.

Conway, Moncure D. *Autobiography: Memories and Experiences.* 2 vols. Boston: Houghton Mifflin, 1904.

———. "Recollections of Robert Browning." *Nation,* L (Jan. 9, 1890), 27–28.

———. "Robert Browning." *Victoria Magazine,* II (February, 1864), 298–316.

[Cooke, R. G., ed.] *Casual Essays of "The Sun".* New York: R. G. Cooke, 1905.

Corson, Hiram. "Browning Clubs in the United States" (letter). *Literary World* (Boston), XIV (Apr. 21, 1883), 127.

Corson, Hiram. "A Few Reminiscences of Robert Browning," *Cornell Era,* XL (April, 1908), 295–303; (May, 1908), 358–65.

———. *An Introduction to the Study of Robert Browning's Poetry.* 2nd ed. Boston: Heath, 1889.

———. "Recollections of Robert Browning." *Nation,* L (Jan. 9, 1890), 28–29.

"Current Criticism," *Critic,* N.S. VI (Nov. 6, 1886), 228.

Curtis, George W. "Editor's Easy Chair." *Harper's New Monthly Magazine*, LXXVII (October, 1888), 795–99.

"Daily Gossip." *Echo*, Apr. 3, 1886, p. 2.

Davies, Charles L., ed. *From a Victorian Post-Bag: Being Letters Addressed to the Rev. J. Llewelyn Davies by Thomas Carlyle and Others*. London: Peter Davies, 1926.

Davies, John Llewelyn, ed. *The Working Men's College, 1854–1904*. London: Macmillan, 1904.

"Death of Robert Browning." *Pall Mall Gazette*, Dec. 13, 1889, p. 6.

Defries, Esther P. *A Browning Primer*. With an Introd. by F. J. Furnivall. London: Sonnenschein, 1898.

DeVane, William C. *A Browning Handbook*. 2nd ed. New York: Appleton-Century-Crofts, 1955.

Dinnis, Enid Maud. "Emily Hickey—In Memoriam." *Catholic World*, CXX (March, 1925), 732–36.

———. *Emily Hickey: Poet, Essayist—Pilgrim. A Memoir*. London: Harding and More, 1927.

Dobell, Bertram. *The Laureate of Pessimism: A Sketch of the Life and Character of James Thomson ("B.V.")*. London: privately printed, 1910.

Domett, Alfred. *The Diary of Alfred Domett, 1872–1885*, ed. E. A. Horsman. London: Oxford University Press, 1953.

Douglas, George. "Mr. Frederick Wedmore." *Bookman* (London), V (November, 1893), 44–46.

Dowden, Edward. *Fragments of Old Letters, E.D. to E.D.W.*, ed. Elizabeth Dickinson Dowden. 1st and 2nd Ser. London: Dent, 1914.

Doyle, Arthur Conan. *A Duet, with an Occasional Chorus*. London: G. Richards, 1899.

Duckworth, F. G. R. *Browning: Background and Conflict*. New York: Dutton, 1932.

Eliot, T. S. *Essays Ancient and Modern*. London: Faber and Faber, 1936.

Ervine, St. John. *Bernard Shaw: His Life, Work and Friends*. London: Constable, 1956.

"Events of the Week." *Judy*, XXXVIII (Apr. 7, 1886), 157.

Farrar, Frederick W. *Men I Have Known*. New York: Crowell, 1897.

Farrar, Reginald. *The Life of Frederic William Farrar*. New York: Crowell, 1904.

Faverty, Frederic E., ed. *The Victorian Poets: A Guide to Research*. Cambridge: Harvard University Press, 1956.

Feuer, Lewis S. "Marxian Tragedians: A Death in the Family." *Encounter*, XIX (November, 1962), 23–32.

Field, Julian O. [pseud. "Sigma"]. *Personalia: Political, Social, and Various*. Edinburgh: William Blackwood, 1903.

Field, Michael [pseud. of Katharine Bradley and Edith Cooper]. *Works and Days*, ed. T. and D. C. Sturge Moore. London: John Murray, 1933.

Forman, Alfred: obituary. *Times*, Dec. 23, 1925, p. 7b.

Foster, Joseph, ed. *Alumni Oxonienses: The Members of the University of Oxford, 1715–1886*. 4 vols. London: J. Foster, 1888.

———. *Men-at-the-Bar: A Biographical Handlist of the Members of the Various Inns of Court*. London: Reeves and Turner, 1885.

"A Friend of Mr. Robert Browning. Death of Mr. William G. Kingsland: An Appreciation." *Islington Gazette*, Jan. 31, 1933, p. 2e.

Furnivall, Frederick J. "The Browning Society" (letter). *Daily News* (London), Jan. 2, 1882, p. 2g.

——. "The Browning Society" (letter). *Echo*, Oct. 31, 1881, p. 1f.

——. "The Browning Society" (letter). *Literary World* (Boston), XIII (Mar. 11, 1882), 77–78.

——. "The Browning Society" (letter). *Pall Mall Gazette*, Jan. 2, 1882, p. 12.

——. "Browning's Footman Ancestor" (letter). *Academy*, LXII (Apr. 12, 1902), 394.

——. "An Earlier English Original of Mr. Browning's 'Pied Piper'" (letter). *Academy*, XX (Nov. 19, 1881), 385–86.

——. "The Early Writings of Mr. Robert Browning" (letter). *Academy*, XX (Dec. 10, 1881), 437.

——. "A Few More Words on Robert Browning." *Pall Mall Gazette*, Dec. 18, 1889, p. 3.

——. *How the Browning Society Came Into Being*. London: Trübner, 1884.

——. "The Late Mr. George Smith." *Athenaeum*, May 4, 1901, pp. 567–68.

——. [Letter.] *Athenaeum*, Dec. 28, 1889, p. 897.

——. "Maclise's Picture, 'The Serenade,' and Mr. Browning's Poem, 'In a Gondola'" (letter). *Academy*, XX (Oct. 15, 1881), 296.

——. "Mr. Browning's 'Andrea del Sarto'" (letter). *Academy*, XX (Nov. 26, 1881), 403.

——. "Mr. Browning's 'Karshook,' and J. S. Mill's Notes on 'Pauline'" (letter). *Academy*, XX (Oct. 1, 1881), 260.

——. "Mr. Browning's Thunderstorms" (letter). *Academy*, XX (Dec. 31, 1881), 492–93.

——. *Mr. L. S. Outram's Appeal . . . Warning from Dr. Furnivall* [circular]. London, 1886.

—— [pseud. "Phi"]. "Mr. Robert Browning's 'Inn Album'." *N&Q*, N.S. V (Mar. 25, 1876), 244–45.

——. "The Original of Robert Browning's 'Pied Piper'" (letter). *Academy*, XX (Oct. 29, 1881), 331.

——. "Recollections of Robert Browning." *Pall Mall Gazette*, Dec. 14, 1889, pp. 1–2.

——. Rev. of *Memoir of Daniel Macmillan* by Thomas Hughes. *Academy*, XXII (Aug. 12, 1882), 112.

——. *Robert Browning's 70th Birthday* [circular]. London, Apr. 7, 1882.

——. [Robert Browning's 70th birthday: circular.] London, May 8, 1882.

——. [Robert Browning's 71st birthday: circular.] London, May 9, 1883.

[——]. *Teena Rochfort-Smith: A Memoir*. [London], 1883.

——. "An Unwarrantable Liberty" (letter). *Pall Mall Gazette*, Oct. 20, 1886, p. 6.

Furnivall, Frederick J.: obituary. *Times*, July 4, 1910, p. 12c.

Furnivall, Frederick J.: will. *Times*, July 19, 1910, p. 15d.

Furnivall, Frederick J., and James Dykes Campbell. [Letters.] *Pall Mall Gazette*, Oct. 26, 1886, pp. 3–4.

[Girton girls buy chocolates: a cartoon.] *Funny Folks*, XII (Mar. 27, 1886), 98.

"A Girtonian Funeral." *Journal of Education*, N.S. VIII (May 1, 1886), 207–08.

Gladstone, Mary. *Mary Gladstone (Mrs. Drew): Her Diaries and Letters*, ed. Lucy Masterman. 2nd ed. London: Methuen, 1930.

Glazebrook, Ethel: obituary. *Times*, May 21, 1926, p. 11e.

"A 'Glorious Fourth,' Indeed!" *Fellowship, Monthly Journal of the Robert Browning Settlement*, July 15, 1921, pp. 67–69.

Gonner, Edward: obituary. *Liverpool Daily Post and Mercury*, Feb. 25, 1922, p. 9b.

Greer, Louise. *Browning and America*. Chapel Hill: University of North Carolina Press, 1952.

Griffin, W. Hall, and H. C. Minchin. *The Life of Robert Browning*. 3rd ed. London: Methuen, 1938.

Groser, H. G. "The Late Mr. William G. Kingsland." *New Chronicle of Christian Education*, LXIV (Feb. 2, 1933), 79.

H., B. H. "Cambridge Browning Society" (letter). *Cambridge Review*, III (Nov. 30, 1881), 103.

Halliwell-Phillipps, James O. *Copy of Correspondence* [between J. O. H.-P. and Robert Browning, concerning expressions respecting Halliwell-Phillipps, used by F. J. Furnivall in the preface to a facsimile of the second edition of *Hamlet*, published in 1881]. Brighton [?], 1881.

Hallock, Ella B. "An Interpreter of Browning." *Methodist Review*, XCII (July, 1910), 610–14.

"The Hard Case of Dr. Furnivall," *Pall Mall Gazette*, Feb. 8, 1888, p. 5.

Harris, Frank. *Contemporary Portraits*. 2nd Ser. New York: privately printed, 1919.

Harrison, Frederic. *In Memoriam J. C. Morison . . . A Discourse to the Positivist Society*. London: Chiswick Press, 1888.

Harrison, William A.: obituary. *Times*, Feb. 12, 1892, p. 5e.

Haslem, G. E., ed. *Wise after the Event: A Catalogue*. Manchester: Manchester Libraries Committee, 1964.

Haultain, T. A. *Goldwin Smith: His Life and Opinions*. London: T. Werner Laurie, 1913.

Haweis, Hugh R. "Robert Browning." *Independent*, XLIV (Dec. 15, 1892), 1776–77.

———. "Robert Browning's Voice" (letter). *Times*, Dec. 13, 1890, p. 10a.

Hersey, Heloise E. "Browning in America." *New England Magazine*, N.S. I (January, 1890), 542–45.

Hickey, Emily. "Browning Biography." *Nineteenth Century*, LXVIII (December, 1910), 1060–75.

———. "Glorious Robert Browning." *Nineteenth Century*, LXX (October, 1911), 753–70.

———. "Roden Noel, Poet." *Nineteenth Century*, XCI (April, 1922), 624–33.

———. "A Study of Browning's Saul." *Catholic World*, XCIV (December, 1911), 320–36.

Hickey, Emily: obituary. *Times*, Sept. 11, 1924, p. 15e.
Horne, Richard H. [Letter about the Browning Society, quoted by George Barnett Smith.] *Academy*, XXVII (Apr. 18, 1885), 276–77.
Howe, M. A. D. "Victorian Poets: A Side Light." *Atlantic Monthly*, CLII (August, 1933), 224–27.
Hutchinson, Herbert. *Jonathan Hutchinson: Life and Letters*. London: Heinemann, 1946.
Innes, A. Taylor. "James Dykes Campbell." *Bookman* (London), VIII (July, 1895), 107–08.
Ireland, Mrs. Annie E. *Longer Flights: Recollections and Studies*. With a Biographical Introd. by Ethel Alleyne Ireland. London: Digby, Long, 1898.
Johnson, Edwin. *The Rise of English Culture*. With an Account of the author and his writings by Edward A. Petherick. London: Williams and Norgate, 1904.
Jones, John Samuel: obituary. *Times*, Oct. 19, 1896, p. 6b.
Kamm, Josephine. *How Different from Us: A Biography of Miss Buss and Miss Beale*. London: J. Lane, 1958.
Kelley, Lachlan Phil. "Robert Browning and George Smith: Selections from an Unpublished Correspondence." *Quarterly Review*, CCXCIX (July, 1961), 323–35.
Ker, W. P. "Frederick James Furnivall." *Proceedings of the British Academy*, IV (1909–10), 375–78.
King, Roma A., Jr. *Robert Browning's Finances from His Own Account Book*. Baylor Univ. Browning Interests, Ser. 15, Waco, Tex.: Baylor University Press, 1947.
Kingsland, William G. "Browning Rarities." *Poet-Lore*, VI (May, 1894), 264–68.
K[ingsland], W[illiam] G. "The Browning Society." *Islington News*, July 7, 1883, p. 4e.
Kingsland, William G. "Browning: Some Personal Reminiscences." *Baylor Bulletin* (Baylor Univ. Browning Interests, 2nd Ser.), XXXIV (July, 1931), 28–40.
———. "Half Hours with Robert Browning: His Specially Religious Teaching." *Islington Gazette*, Oct. 3, 1883, p. 2; "Browning's View of Life," Oct. 9, p. 3; "Browning as a Poet," Oct. 18, p. 3.
K[ingsland], W[illiam] G. [The Islington and Clerkenwell Browning Union.] *Poet-Lore*, V (January, 1893), 53.
Kingsland, William G. "London Literaria." *Poet-Lore*, III (December, 1891), 649–53.
———. "London Literaria." *Poet-Lore*, IV (October, 1892), 524–27.
———. "London Literaria." *Poet-Lore*, VII (November, 1895), 581–84.
———. Rev. of *Life and Letters of Robert Browning* by Alexandra Orr. *Poet-Lore*, III (October, 1891), 522–28.
———. *Robert Browning: Chief Poet of the Age*. 2nd ed. London: Jarvis, 1890.
———. "Robert Browning—the Man. Some Further Reminiscences." *Poet-Lore*, V (May, 1893), 229–36.
———. "Some Browning Memories." *Contemporary Review*, CII (August, 1912), 202–10.
Kirkman, Joshua: obituary. *Times*, July 4, 1904, p. 13f.

[Kirkman's address: a comment.] *Nation,* XXXIII (Nov. 24, 1881), 415.

Knight, W. A., ed. *The Robert Browning Centenary Celebration at West-minster Abbey, May 7th, 1912.* Boston: Houghton, Mifflin, 1912.

Laffan, Mrs. Bertha Jane: obituary. *Times,* Sept. 7, 1912, p. 9e.

Lang, Andrew. "Esoteric Browningism." *Forum,* VI (November, 1888), 300–10.

———. Rev. of *Life and Letters of Robert Browning* by Alexandra Orr. *Contemporary Review,* LX (July, 1891), 70–81.

Langbaum, Robert W. *The Poetry of Experience: The Dramatic Mono-logue in Modern Literary Tradition.* New York: Random House, 1957.

Lecky, James: obituary. *Times,* Apr. 4, 1890, p. 8c.

Lee, Sir Sidney. "Henry Charles Beeching, Dean of Norwich, 1911–1919." *Norwich Public Library Readers' Guide,* VII (April, 1919), 79–90.

Lhombreaud, Roger. *Arthur Symons: A Critical Biography.* Philadelphia: Dufour Editions, 1964.

"Literary Notes." *Critic,* I (Oct. 22, 1881), 294–95.

[The literature of the year.] *Daily News* (London), Dec. 31, 1881, p. 5c.

Litzinger, Boyd. *Time's Revenges: Browning's Reputation as a Thinker, 1889–1962.* Knoxville: University of Tennessee Press, 1964.

Lounsbury, Thomas R. *The Early Literary Career of Robert Browning.* New York: Scribners, 1911.

[Lowell, James Russell]. "Browning's Plays and Poems." *North American Review,* LXVI (April, 1848), 357–400.

McMahan, Anna B. Rev. of *Life and Letters of Robert Browning* by Alex-andra Orr. *Dial,* XII (September, 1891), 140–43.

Mason, Stuart [pseud. of Christopher Sclater Millard]. *Bibliography of Oscar Wilde.* London: T. Werner Laurie, 1914.

Matheson, Annie: obituary. *Times,* Mar. 17, 1924, p. 14b.

Maurer, Oscar E. "Swinburne vs. Furnivall." *University of Texas Studies in English,* XXXI (1952), 86–96.

Meeker, James E. *The Life and Poetry of James Thomson (B.V.).* New Haven: Yale University Press, 1917.

Milne, James. *The Memoirs of a Bookman.* London: John Murray, 1934.

Moody, William V. *Letters to Harriet,* ed. Percy MacKaye. Boston: Hough-ton Mifflin, 1935.

Morgan, Appleton. "The Society and the 'Fad.'" *Science,* XV (May 9, 1890), 282–86, 288–90.

Mosely, Benjamin L.: notice of death. *Law Times,* CXLI (July 29, 1916), 244.

Muir, P. H. "Elkin Matthews—Part VIII: Sherry and Shibboleths." *Book Collector,* III (Spring, 1954), 11–27.

[Munro, John, ed.]. *Frederick James Furnivall: A Volume of Personal Record.* London: Frowde, 1911.

Nettleship, John T. *Essays on Robert Browning's Poetry.* London: Mac-millan, 1868.

———. *Robert Browning: Essays and Thoughts.* London: Elkin Mat-thews, 1890.

Nicoll, Allardyce. *A History of English Drama, 1660–1900.* 6 vols. Cam-bridge: Cambridge University Press, 1952–59.

Nicoll, William R., and Thomas J. Wise, eds. *Literary Anecdotes of the Nineteenth Century.* 2 vols. London: Hodder and Stoughton, 1895.

Noel, Roden. "The Browning Society" (letter). *Pall Mall Gazette,* Dec. 17, 1889, p. 3.

———. "Robert Browning." *Contemporary Review,* XLIV (November, 1883), 701–18.

———. *Selected Poems.* With a Biographical and Critical Essay by Percy Addleshaw. London: Elkin Matthews, 1897.

Notebook of the Shelley Society. London: Reeves and Turner, 1888.

"Notes and News." *Poet-Lore,* II (March, 1890), 159–68.

"Notes and News." *Poet-Lore,* III (November, 1891), 589–96.

"Notes and News." *Poet-Lore,* V (March, 1893), 166–67.

"Notes and News." *Poet-Lore,* VI (September, 1894), 469–72.

"Offord-Road Young Men's Christian Debating Society." *Islington Gazette,* Nov. 9, 1877, p. 2e.

Orr, Alexandra. *A Handbook to the Works of Robert Browning.* London: Bell, 1885.

———. *Life and Letters of Robert Browning.* 2 vols. London: Smith, Elder, 1891.

———. "Mr. Browning's Place in Literature." *Contemporary Review,* XXIII (May, 1874), 934–65.

———. "The Religious Opinions of Robert Browning." *Contemporary Review,* LX (December, 1891), 876–91.

———. Rev. of *Dramatic Idyls. Contemporary Review,* XXXV (May, 1879), 289–302.

———. Rev. of *Red Cotton Night-Cap Country. Contemporary Review,* XXII (June, 1873), 87–106.

[Outram case: a collection of correspondence among the principals.] London, 1886 [?].

[Outram case: Dr. Furnivall's adjectives.] *Pall Mall Gazette,* Feb. 3, 1888, p. 4.

[Outram case: the Furnivall Fund.] *Pall Mall Gazette,* Feb. 13, 1888, p. 4.

Outram, Leonard S. *The Browning Society's Dramatic Productions, 'Strafford'* [circular appealing for subscriptions]. London, 1886.

———. "An Unwarrantable Liberty" (letter). *Pall Mall Gazette,* Oct. 25, 1886, p. 6.

"Outram v. Furnivall." *Times,* Feb. 3, 1888, p. 13d.

Padelford, Frederick M. "Browning Out West." *Cornhill Magazine,* N.S. XXII (February, 1907), 253–62.

Partington, Wilfred. *Thomas J. Wise in the Original Cloth.* Rev. ed. London: Robert Hale, 1946.

"Passing Notes." *Echo,* Oct. 29, 1891, p. 1d.

Pater, Walter. *Essays from "The Guardian."* London: Macmillan, 1901.

Pattison, Emilia (Lady Dilke). *The Book of the Spiritual Life.* With a Memoir by the Rt. Hon. Sir Charles W. Dilke. New York: Dutton, 1905.

Pearson, Howard S.: obituary. *Times,* Sept. 17, 1923, p. 18d.

Peterson, William S. "A Hitherto Unpublished Essay on Robert Browning by James Thomson (B.V.)." *BNYPL,* LXXII (December, 1968), 637–40.

Phelps, William Lyon. *Autobiography with Letters*. New York: Oxford University Press, 1939.

————. "A Conversation with Browning." *ELH*, XI (June, 1944), 154–60.

Radford, Ernest W., ed. *Illustrations to Browning's Poems*. Parts 1 and 2. London: Trübner, 1882–83.

Raleigh, Walter A.: obituary. *Times*, May 15, 1922, p. 18e.

Ratchford, Fannie E., ed. *Between the Lines: Letters and Memoranda Interchanged by H. Buxton Forman and Thomas J. Wise*. With a Foreword by Carl H. Pforzheimer. Austin: University of Texas Press, 1945.

Raymond, William O. *The Infinite Moment and Other Essays in Robert Browning*. 2nd ed. Toronto: University of Toronto Press, 1965.

"Recollections of Browning." *Westminster Gazette*, Feb. 24, 1893, p. 2.

Rev. of *Essays on Robert Browning's Poetry* by J. T. Nettleship. *London Quarterly Review*, XXXI (October, 1868), 133–34.

Rev. of *Life and Letters of Robert Browning* by Alexandra Orr. *London Quarterly Review*, N.S. XVII (October, 1891), 1–26.

Rev. of *Life and Letters of Robert Browning* by Alexandra Orr. *Saturday Review*, LXXI (May 30, 1891), 666–67.

Rev. of *A Mighty Error* by Leonard Outram. *Athenaeum*, July 18, 1891, p. 107.

Revell, William F. *Browning's Criticism of Life*. London: Sonnenschein, 1892.

Rhys, Ernest, ed. *The Hampstead Annual*. London: Sydney C. Mayle, 1897.

Rigby, Elizabeth. *Journals and Correspondence of Lady Eastlake*, ed. C. E. Smith. 2 vols. London: John Murray, 1895.

"Robert Browning." *Critic*, N.S. XIII (Jan. 4, 1890), 10–11.

Roberts, William. *The Book-Hunter in London*. London: Elliot Stock, 1895.

Robertson, John G. *Charles Harold Herford, 1853–1931*. London: Humphrey Milford, 1933.

Robinson, D., *et al.*, comp. *The War Office List*. London: H. M. Stationers Office, 1884–1912.

Rossetti, William M. "Portraits of Robert Browning." *Magazine of Art*, XIII (May, 1890), 181–88; June, pp. 246–52; July, pp. 261–67.

[————.] Rev. of *Christmas-Eve and Easter-Day*. *Germ*, No. 4 (May, 1850), pp. 187–92.

————. *Ruskin: Rossetti: Pre-Raphaelitism: Papers, 1854 to 1862*. London: Allen, 1899.

————. *Some Reminiscences*. 2 vols. London: Brown, Langham, 1906.

Ruskin, John. *Letters from John Ruskin to Frederick J. Furnivall and Other Correspondents*, ed. T. J. Wise. London: privately printed, 1897.

Salt, Henry S. *The Life of James Thomson ("B.V.") with a Selection from His Letters and a Study of His Writings*. London: Reeves and Turner, 1889.

Santayana, George. *Interpretations of Poetry and Religion*. New York: Scribners, 1900.

Schaefer, William D. *James Thomson (B.V.): Beyond "The City"*. Univ. of

Calif. Perspectives in Criticism, No. 17. Berkeley: University of California Press, 1965.

Scribner Book Store, Rare Book Department. Catalogue No. 131. *Nineteenth Century Pamphlets, with an Appendix of Wiseana.* New York: Scribner Book Store, 1945.

Sharpe, John: obituary. *Times,* Dec. 10, 1895, p. 5f.

Shaw, George Bernard. *Collected Letters, 1874–1897,* ed. Dan H. Laurence. New York: Dodd, Mead, 1965.

————. *Pen Portraits and Reviews.* Rev. ed. London: Constable, 1932.

————. *Sixteen Self Sketches.* New York: Dodd, Mead, 1949.

Smalley, Donald. "Mephistopheles at the Conventicle: G.B.S. Amid the Browningites." *Saturday Review of Literature,* XXVII (July 22, 1944), 13–15.

Sotheby and Company catalogue. *The Celebrated Collection of Wiseiana formed by Sir Maurice Pariser . . .* London, Dec. 4–5, 1967.

Sotheby, Wilkinson, and Hodge catalogue. *The Browning Collections.* London, April and May, 1913.

Stanford, Sir Charles Villiers. *Pages from an Unwritten Diary.* London: E. Arnold, 1914.

Steadman, F. Cecily. *In the Days of Miss Beale.* London. E. J. Burrow, 1930.

Stedman, Edmund C. *Victorian Poets.* Rev. ed. 2 vols. Cambridge, Mass.: Riverside Press, 1887.

Stedman, Laura, and George M. Gould. *Life and Letters of Edmund Clarence Stedman.* 2 vols. New York: Moffat, Yard, 1910.

Steeves, Harrison Ross. *Learned Societies and English Literary Scholarship in Great Britain and the United States.* New York: Columbia University Press, 1913.

Stephen, James K. *Lapsus Calami and Other Verses.* Cambridge, England: Macmillan and Bowes, 1905.

Stoddart, Anna. *The Life of Paracelsus, Theophrastus von Hohenheim, 1493–1541.* London: John Murray, 1911.

Stoddart, Anna: obituary. *Times,* Aug. 31, 1911, p. 7d.

"A Story of Girton (By R-b-rt Br-wn-ng)" (poem). *Punch,* XC (Apr. 17, 1886), 186.

Strain, W. Arthur. "Rare and Unpublished Letters of Robert Browning." University of Colorado master's thesis, 1925.

Sully, James. *My Life and Friends: A Psychologist's Memories.* London: Unwin, 1918.

Symonds, John Addington. Rev. of *Jocoseria. Academy,* XXIII (Mar. 31, 1883), 213–14.

Symons, Arthur. "Dead in Venice" (poem). *Athenaeum,* Dec. 21, 1889, p. 860.

————. "A Fancy of Ferishtah" (poem). *Academy,* XXVI (Dec. 13, 1884), 393.

————. *An Introduction to the Study of Browning.* London: Cassell, 1886.

————. Rev. of *Asolando. Academy,* XXXVII (Jan. 11, 1890), 19–20.

————. "Robert Browning as a Religious Poet." *Wesleyan Methodist Magazine,* N.S. VI (December, 1882), 943–47.

————. "Some Browning Reminiscences." *North American Review,* CCIV (October, 1916), 602–09.

————. *Studies in Two Literatures*. London: Smithers, 1897.

Terry, Ellen. *The Story of My Life*. New York: McClure, 1908.

Thackeray, Anne I. *Records of Tennyson, Ruskin, Browning*. New York: Harper, 1892.

Thale, Jerome. "The Third Rossetti." *Western Humanities Review*, X (Summer, 1956), 277–84.

Thomson, James. *Biographical and Critical Studies*. London: Reeves and Turner, 1896.

————. *Essays and Phantasies*. London: Reeves and Turner, 1881.

————. *Poems and Some Letters of James Thomson*, ed. Anne Ridler, Carbondale: Southern Illinois University Press, 1963.

————. *The Speedy Extinction of Evil and Misery: Selected Prose of James Thomson (B.V.)*, ed. William D. Schaefer. Berkeley: University of California Press, 1967.

Todd, George: obituary. *Times*, Jan. 3, 1913, p. 9c.

Todd, William B., ed. *Thomas J. Wise: Centenary Studies*. Austin: University of Texas Press, 1959.

Todhunter, John: obituary. *Times*, Oct. 27, 1916, p. 5d.

Tsuzuki, Chushichi. *The Life of Eleanor Marx, 1855–1898*. Oxford: Clarendon Press, 1967.

Tyler, Moses Coit. *Moses Coit Tyler, 1835–1900: Selections from His Letters and Diaries*, ed. Jessica Tyler Austen. Garden City, N.Y.: Doubleday, Page, 1911.

Tynan, Katherine. "Emily Hickey: A Catholic Poet." *Catholic World*, XCIII (June, 1911) 328–40.

Venn, John, and J. A. Venn, comp. *Alumni Cantabrigienses: A Biographical List of All Known Students, Graduates and Holders of Office at the University of Cambridge, from the Earliest Times to 1900*. 10 vols. Cambridge: Cambridge University Press, 1922–1954.

Walford, L. B. "London Letter." *Critic*, N. S. XIII (Jan. 4, 1890), 8–9.

Walker, Archibald S., ed. *A Volunteer Haversack*. Edinburg: privately printed, 1902.

Walker, Imogene B. *James Thomson (B.V.): A Critical Study*. Ithaca: Cornell University Press, 1950.

Wall, Annie R. "The Sordello Club." *Poet-Lore*, I (September, 1889), 424–26.

Watkins, Charlotte C. "Browning's 'Fame within these Four Years.'" *MLR*, LIII (October, 1958), 492–500.

Wedmore, Frederick. *Memories*. London: Methuen, 1912.

Wedmore, Frederick. Rev. of *Dramatic Idyls*. *Academy*, XV (May 10, 1879), 403–04.

————. Rev. of *Fifine*. *Academy*, III (July 1, 1872), 243–44.

————. Rev. of performance of *A Blot in the 'Scutcheon*. *Academy*, XXXIII (Mar. 24, 1888), 212–13.

West, Elizabeth D. "To Robert Browning, on Re-reading Some Poems Long Unread" (poem). *Academy*, XX (Dec. 17, 1881), 455.

Wheeler, Harold F. B. "The Library of Mr. W. B. Slater." *Bibliophile*, III (July, 1909), 229–37.

White, Beatrice. "Frederick James Furnivall." *Essays and Studies*, N.S. V (1952), 64–76.

White, Eliza O. "A Browning Courtship." *Atlantic Monthly*, LXII (July, 1888), 99–112.

"The Whitey-Browning Society." *Punch*, LXXXIV (Apr. 21, 1883), 192.

Whiting, Lilian. *The Brownings: Their Life and Art*. Boston: Little, Brown, 1911.

Wilde, Oscar. *Letters of Oscar Wilde*, ed. Rupert Hart-Davis. New York: Harcourt, Brace, and World, 1962.

Wilks, Mark: obituary. *Times*, June 7, 1894, p. 10d.

Williams, E. C. "The Browning Society Papers" (letter). *Library Journal*, XXVIII (February, 1903), 52. Replies, March, p. 104.

Williams, J. D.: obituary. *Times*, Dec. 1, 1904, p. 12c.

Wise, Thomas J. *The Ashley Library: A Catalogue of Printed Books, Manuscripts and Autograph Letters Collected by Thomas J. Wise*. 11 vols. London: privately printed, 1922–36.

———. *A Browning Library: A Catalogue of Printed Books, Manuscripts and Autograph Letters of Robert Browning and Elizabeth Browning*. London: privately printed, 1929.

———. *A Complete Bibliography of the Writings in Prose and Verse of Robert Browning*. London: privately printed, 1897.

———. *Letters of Thomas J. Wise to John Henry Wrenn: A Further Inquiry into the Guilt of Certain Nineteenth-Century Forgers*, ed. Fannie E. Ratchford. New York: Knopf, 1944.

Wright, Thomas. *The Life of John Payne*. London: Unwin, 1919.

Yeats, William B. *Autobiographies: Reveries over Childhood and Youth, and The Trembling of the Veil*. New York: Macmillan, 1927.

Zimmern, Alice: obituary. *Times*, Mar. 23, 1939, p. 21d.

Zimmern, Helen: obituary. *Times*, Jan. 13, 1934, p. 12f.

INDEX

267